SAFE TRIP
TO EDEN

SAFE TRIP
TO EDEN

10 Steps to Save Planet Earth from
the Global Warming Meltdown

DAVID STEINMAN

Foreword by Wendy Gordon Rockefeller

THUNDER'S MOUTH PRESS • NEW YORK

SAFE TRIP TO EDEN:
10 Steps to Save Planet Earth
from the Global Warming Meltdown

Published by
Thunder's Mouth Press
An imprint of Avalon Publishing Group, Inc.
245 West 17th Street, 11th Floor
New York, NY 10011
Copyright © 2007 by David Steinman

AVALON
publishing group incorporated

Foreword copyright © 2007 by Wendy Gordon Rockefeller

First Printing, January 2007

Library of Congress Cataloging-in-Publication Data is available.

ISBN-10: 1-56025-806-3
ISBN-13: 978-1-56025-806-3

9 8 7 6 5 4 3

Book design by Bettina Wilhelm

Printed in Canada
Distributed by Publishers Group West

ENVIRONMENTAL BENEFITS STATEMENT

NEW LEAF PAPER™

Avalon Publishing Group saved the following resources by using New Leaf Paper, made with 100% recycled fiber and 40% post-consumer waste, processed chlorine free.

trees	water	energy	solid waste	greenhouse gases
51 fully grown	20,824 gallons	53 million Btu	4,519 pounds	13,591 pounds

Calculations based on research by Environmental Defense and other members of the Paper Task Force.

©2006 New Leaf Paper   www.newleafpaper.com

For our children.

Contents

Foreword

by Wendy Gordon Rockefeller

WHAT'S THE POINT of writing a book if not to evoke a strong response? It's certainly the reason David Steinman, the acclaimed environmental health and consumer advocate, wrote *Safe Trip to Eden: 10 Steps to Save Planet Earth from the Global Warming Meltdown*. Steinman, who jumped onto the national scene in 1990 with his groundbreaking book *Diet for a Poisoned Planet*, became an overnight hero among concerned consumers like myself. He courageously fought many in the food industry who labeled him a "food terrorist." Dave is familiar with being a reporter of some tough truths—but more importantly, he is a catalyst for real action.

Safe Trip resonated with me just as I know it will speak to you. Even those of us who have been working in environmental fields for our entire adult lives struggle daily to live more eco-conscious lives, to consider the consequences of our most quotidian decisions, and to make responsible choices. Dave takes us on a very personal journey of discovery—not always a safe one, I might add—of some of the worst and best of human and institutional behavior, including his own. As a consequence, *Safe Trip* is a spiritual quest for an awakening of the inner environmentalist in all of us. At the same time, it is a well-researched road map to the very real and practical solutions that we all can take to address the local and global eco-challenges we face, from toxins in our homes and communities to global deforestation and climate change.

A journalist by training, David Steinman is first and foremost a lover of research and a believer in the power of facts. He turns this encyclopedic eye on his subjects, which makes *Safe Trip* possibly the most comprehensive exploration of the linkages between environmental toxins, global warming, national security, the ways businesses do business, and our own day-to-day lives. He is seeking a better world for all of us—the parent, the child, the conservative, the liberal, the employee, the employer, the retiree, the faithful, the agnostic. You see, most experts writing on these weighty subjects typically leave the "you" and the "me" out of the equation, or relegate us to an appendix, but not Dave. To him, the real power lies in "we, the people"—in particular how we think, what we do, and the ways we do it. From the alarm clock or the coffee that wakes us in the morning, to the way we get to work, to the pillow we lay our head on, and the light we turn out when we go to bed, Dave sees how our day is filled with everyday things and decisions that connect us—for better or worse and thanks to our global economy—to the rainforests of South America, the fishermen in the Northwest, the migrant workers in California, the chemical factories in New Jersey, and yes, the much-coveted oil supplies in often politically volatile countries in the Arab peninsula, the Sudan, and Venezuela.

Dave's second book, *The Safe Shopper's Bible*, is on my desk right next to *Stedman's Medical Dictionary* and the Worldwatch Institute's *Vital Signs 2006–7*. I'm making room, though, for this new book, *Safe Trip*, which I'm nicknaming "the green patriot's handbook." Much has been made since 9/11 of the fact that our dependence on oil, lots of it foreign-owned by petro-authoritarian states, renders us less secure as a people but also makes us the largest contributor of global climate-change gases in the world. So what if we as a people made a pledge—a patriot's energy pledge—to change the way we live and how we make and power things? What if we vow to reduce our dependence on nonrenewal petroleum and maybe spare our sons and daughters from fighting resource wars in the future? It's a transformative concept, but as Dave explores in *Safe Trip*, one that should resonate with all Americans who might have never thought of themselves as environmentalists, but who fundamentally share the same values—love of family, community, and country—and are connected by many of the same dreams: to be healthy, happy, safe, and free.

Dave is a powerful, passionate writer, both a poetic storyteller and an "in your face" investigative reporter. He is also one of the best list-makers I know. For a world-class "who's who" of the people and businesses reshaping the American dream and a "if it's not here, it's not anywhere" shopping list for all the green patriots his journey will inspire, go on a *Safe Trip to Eden* with David Steinman.

But fasten your seat belts. *Safe Trip* packs its own shock and awe.

Wendy Gordon Rockefeller is president of The Green Guide Institute and publisher of The Green Guide. To learn more about The Green Guide, visit them at www.thegreenguide.com.

Preface

AS A BUSINESSMAN and father of three, I wanted to ignore global warming. I wanted to leave it up to God. I didn't want to have anything to do with it. I knew all about the doomsday prophecies of environmentalists. I didn't want to get into that hysteria anymore. I thought I'd done my job and I could focus on my family and on building my business.

I wanted to be just like any other God-fearing global warming skeptic and forget about the world's problems for awhile. I was tired of hysteria. The place where I lived was beautiful, even if the city wasn't. Trouble was, life intruded in big rolling fashion in the verdant California coastal mountains.

To many well-meaning patriotic Americans, the environmental movement died after 9/11. Americans' attention turned to the immediate concern of terrorism. We were boycotting French wine and gulping down freedom fries containing cancer-causing acrylamide. How could environmentalism have anything to do with winning the war against terrorists?

During this time, especially before the war began in earnest, many well-known mainstream environmental organizations carried their work over to the antiwar movement. Their participation in boisterous antiwar marches across the country appeared to be completely out of step with mainstream America—at least at that time; to call yourself an environmentalist was tantamount to saying that you not only opposed the war in Iraq but probably in Afghanistan, too. The perception was that tree huggers were basically all effete pacifists who didn't see a mortal enemy when he was there beaming in over al Jazeera and looking them in the whites of their eyes. In rallies against the Iraq war in Washington, D.C., and San Francisco, among the banners was one that read ENVIRONMENTALISTS AGAINST THE WAR. Of course, members of the Greens, America's leading environmental political party, were at anti-war rallies.[1] According to a January 19, 2003, report in the *Washington Post*, "Working Assets began two weeks ago organizing Environmentalists Against the War—which includes the Sierra Club and the Rainforest Action Network."[2]

Throughout 2003 and 2004 as well as early 2005, it looked as if environmentalists and the American people who supported the war were not only from different planets but also separate universes. How could someone who voted for George W. Bush be comfortable supporting the cause of a group that was so clearly different from them when it came to such weighty issues as war and peace? I mean, would anyone come out alive if liberal talker Randi Rhodes met conservative Sean Hannity face-to-face? April 2005 had been a bad month, and May was no better. Public enthusiasm for war diminished as asymmetrical insurgent attacks escalated. The Iraqi pre–government coalition the administration put together was weak and vacillating and couldn't control the nation. Nouri al-Maliki became prime minister in 2006 and emerged initially as a decisive strong man who was willing to use negotiation as well as force and outright illegal violence with the enemy for the so-called protection of the Iraqi people's rights. But even he needed American troop support—and where were the weapons of mass destruction we were promised? And how were we going to get out of this fix without compromising American security?

So what could green patriotism possibly have to offer to a nation's future? What could it do to address such weighty issues as national security and the war against terrorism? I think everything. I think it's the missing link.

Green patriotism is the missing element in winning the war against terrorism—but it's also a lot more. I think it's your mainline to God, Jesus, Allah, or in whomever you believe, as well as a way of living your life so that you are a true patriot who is making his or her nation strong and secure and your own life healthier and more fulfilling.

I'm not saying it's the only element. Sure, we must have the best law enforcement, intelligence, and military might, as well as international cooperation.

But let me put it to you this way: we won't win the war against terrorism without green patriotism.

It's time to take a journey and I'll show you what I mean. I'll show you green patriots in action and even the progress of wannabes like myself who are trying hard to make a difference and do something good for America, good for this planet, good for our religious lives, good for our ethics, good for our bodies.

I took a trip across America to find incredibly inspiring Americans who are anything but ordinary from all walks of life—from Fortune 500 companies to unsung heroes whose ecologically driven companies might be small but are having profoundly good vibrations for not only this nation's fate but for the fate of all nations. These people I call green patriots, and they're the reason why America has a chance at winning not only the war against terrorism but also reclaiming our very own most positive and inspiring ways of leading the world.

Think of the power when millions of people embrace being green patriots as a positive way of also fighting the war against terrorism here at home and giving back to America, a land that has been good to so many.

In ten really simple steps, I'll show you why I think being a green patriot is a way of fulfilling God's mandate for you on Earth, and why living green is as much a necessary part of our spiritual life as oxygen is to our physical life.

One of the strongest links we have today between peoples whose governments might otherwise be at war with one another is the undeniable shared reverence we all have for the mysteries of our universe as embodied in the stars, moon, and sky. We are all in awe of this mystery.

The environmental movement at its core is religious; yet, it predates societal belief in one God. (We humans were in awe of nature long before monotheism.)

If we're going to make connections between peoples of all major faiths, these will come, I bet, thanks to the environmental movement that most people thought died after 9/11—but, indeed, these are times when we should be waging peace.

Maybe underneath the threat of war between governments, human connections between sane people can be made on the basis of planetary survival. It's worth trying to bring as many people together as possible; I'll show you how green patriot environmentalism crosses seemingly insurmountable cultural and political barriers.

And we should be able to find some common ground between conservatives and liberals in America, too. Can we promote renewable energy as well as carbon sequestration and still call ourselves environmentalists? Or would everyone go home crying in their milk and cookies?

My hope is that this book will have the same impact as my previous book, *Diet for a Poisoned Planet*. People got all worked up with *Diet* because I dared to point out the impact of chemical toxins on our health. But I know that we need this information in order to be smart consumers and use our shopping dollars wisely.

After asking some of the big existential questions, life gets down to the smart little things, too, and dealing with them as best we can; so you might have a lot of little to-do questions and issues you also want to know about. Where do you go to find out about all of this practical daily stuff anyway? I'll show you. Dig in and enjoy. That's part of the trip, too.

ONE
Chemical Nation

THE SIKORSKY S-76 twin engine jet copter lifted off from the rolling green fields of Mercer County Airport at the West Trenton headquarters of the New Jersey State Police, and suddenly we were rising fast. The Delaware River flowed below, between deep green banks. But we left it behind quickly.

At first, looking down, I saw the beautiful green meadows of the Garden State, and the rippling river that at this point divides the states of New Jersey and Delaware. The two men with me joked that the Delaware River Valley was the last green thing I'd see for a while.

Quickly, the Sikorsky headed north-northeast, and meadows morphed from green to dull red and brown. Dirty-beige storage tanks dotted the landscape. They were modern industrial ponds, not made to hold water but custom manufactured to hold in reserve the blood of industrial America—1 to 2 million barrels at a pop. The air turned sulfurous yellow, and smokestacks rose and spewed burning black soot.

A chemical nightmare right next to Manhattan—I was flying over potentially the most dangerous array of petrochemical complexes in America. I saw Lincoln and Liberty parks and, farther away, the Statue of Liberty. I looked down at moored oil tankers pumping petroleum, at swamps, a horseracing track and football stadium in the Meadowlands, home upon home on Staten Island. We passed long concrete wharves lined with receiving facilities. There was no difference now between here and there. Manhattan's people might as well be there, since what happened there would hit them. Road after road with trucks and rails bisected sandy-brown, flat fields filled with beige tanks of industrial blood. With Newark to our backs, we were nearing Upper New York Bay and closing in on what we now know to be among the most vulnerable, dangerous petrochemical manufacturing and storage facilities in the world.

All varieties of manufacturing chemicals come from these raw materials—benzene, polyethylene, nonoxonyl, phenolics, acids, polymers that become our computers, serving ware, flooring, clothing, medical devices, foods, and even portions of our bodies. The facilities—sparse, industrial, not ornate—rise up out of the simple brown earth that is near the sea. But it is not green. This is where is the earth is paved black with asphalt, and the water is dark from pollution and environmental degradation. The flat spaces of tanks, distillers, vast pipes, and burners serviced by enormous ships alongside docks, trucks like tiny toys, steel fences, very few business offices—this is American might and industry. What did you expect? And it all unfolds before a child's eyes below. So vulnerable, so susceptible, rising to the sky. Here, where the Hackensack and Passaic waters meet north of Port Newark, men and women and their children drive, eat, breathe, and live with oil. Oil is life. It is a good thing. But this cluster of humanity within a cloud of these petrochemical complexes provides an unimaginably tempting target. A chain reaction from one plant to the next would create an inferno worse than any Hollywood movie could ever film.

This was the big one. Strapped in on my right was Captain

Stephen G. Serrao, Assistant Director for Operations at the State of New Jersey Office of Counter-Terrorism. The New Jersey native lost three close friends on 9/11. His dark hair was close-cropped. He wore a pale blue shirt, tie, and sunglasses. His ID card hung around his neck. He was compact, just under six feet, and used to ride a motorcycle for the New Jersey State Troopers. He knew well what was at stake, and he was looking out the window at the terrain below. With more than twenty years in the New Jersey State Police, starting out as a motorcycle cop and rising through the ranks to become a decorated officer, his specialty was homeland investigations, especially tracking down anyone who wanted to mess with these plants.

In another pale blue shirt, with a pen in his pocket, Gene Haplea (wearing sunglasses), Deputy Assistant Director of the Office of Counter-Terrorism, sat to my left. Haplea was military all the way, a 1976 U.S. Naval Academy graduate with more than twenty-five years of active and reserve duty, usually where conflict was imminent. He was at another hot spot on 9/11 when a terrorist-controlled jetliner crashed into the Pentagon. Haplea told me with evident pride that he was back at work by noon on the same day. The naval intelligence expert hadn't left active duty for long at all when Sidney J. Caspersen, New Jersey's brilliant director of the Office of Counter-Terrorism, offered him the assistant director's position. ("The kind of talented people we want here at homeland security," Caspersen tells me later when we're back at his office in West Trenton.) "We have to work with every aspect of the community," Haplea says. "We have to have strong relationships with every agrichemical supply house, truck rental, and self-storage business, not only in the state but throughout the country. If there are suspicious activities, for example, the purchase of large amounts of ammonium nitrate fertilizer, renting a truck, or paying six months in advance for storage facilities [where bomb-making materials could be stored], we need to know. We're the ears to the ground for the country. This job is all-encompassing; it is the most challenging any of us could ask for."

Talking into his headset is the pilot, Trooper I. R. A. Mitchell of the Aviation Bureau of the New Jersey State Police Homeland Security, Special Operation Section, and the copilot, Sergeant Clint Pryor. Guiding us through the intense commercial air traffic of Newark Airport and in constant communication with air traffic controllers, Trooper Mitchell takes us down in elevation over Bayonne. Not by accident is HOMELAND SECURITY emblazoned in big bold letters along the fuselage of this Sikorsky. Trooper Mitchell said that on the outside of the Sikorsky is a million-dollar camera that can send imagery back to command headquarters in real time, as well as at night with infrared nighttime vision equipment with 1 million candlepower. "This is called making your presence known," Serrao said.

From Port Elizabeth north to Port Newark (the third busiest port in the United States after the California ports of Los Angeles and Long Beach), this landscape stores only about one day's worth of petroleum and liquefied natural gas for the entire Northeast. An attack on the chlorine plant or one handling liquefied natural gas could cause a chain reaction that would kill tens of thousands locally, and the crippling of the Northeast would be a million times worse than inflicted by the hurricanes Katrina and Rita.

Mitchell took us over the Pulaski Skyway. It looked familiar, and Serrao told me it was in the opening credits for *The Sopranos*. The original span was constructed in 1932, but it had become a succession of interconnected bridges and roadways that soared over the Hackensack and Passaic rivers and the town of Kearny. It was a potential dropping-off point, literally, for dangerous activities, including improvised explosives.

Here, along with oil tankers, there were some 600 onshore holding tanks with a total capacity of 15.3 million barrels. In another area, not far away, a chemical plant processes chlorine gas. It was so close to Manhattan, the Empire State Building served as a backdrop. It was eerie.

"If you consider that right now refineries in America are operating at near capacity, imagine what would happen to our economy, including the price of oil on the world market, if one or two refineries in this area were attacked and rendered inoperable," Haplea said.

This maritime center handled the most cargo on the East Coast; additionally, New Jersey possessed numerous maritime facilities along the Delaware River that annually served more than three thousand vessels. In fact, according to an intelligence report I obtained from New Jersey state officials, the Delaware Bay and River area "has the second largest petroleum center in the country, and 20 percent of the nation's crude oil is delivered through this region."[1]

A sizeable attack on a New Jersey petroleum and petrochemical port "could quickly cascade into a national or international crisis, with the potential to ultimately bring international trade to a virtual standstill and inflict billions of dollars of damage on the world economy," the report stated.

International terrorist organizations such as al Qaeda have demonstrated a persistent interest in attacking American and other Western maritime targets, according to this report. Terrorists could attempt to launch a direct, land-based attack on a chemical plant or port in order to destroy chemical plant facilities. As seen in numerous raids on land facilities around the world, international terrorists could use a combination of operatives on foot and in vehicles to overpower perimeter security and force their way into a port's interior. After getting inside, terrorists could attack people, docked vessels, facilities, and chemical storage tanks. Terrorists could also sneak into a port through a gap in perimeter security, an adjacent building, or truck traffic and cargo containers coming into or out of a port. Haplea emphasized that the risks are probably not from within (a sort of industrial fifth column). Their primary concern is infiltration from cells in the area, from other states, or from around the world. Global reports indicate that terrorists are keenly interested in attacking petroleum and petrochemical plants.

A May 11, 2005, intelligence report from the Office of Counter-Terrorism spelled out the worldwide threat to petrochemical facilities.[2] According to the report:

- On October 30, 2001, the Liberation Tigers of Tamil Eelam (LTTE), known to operate a large maritime fleet and sea-based terrorist division, rammed at least five of their boats into the *MV Silk Pride*, a ship carrying 650 tons of diesel fuel and kerosene, while it was en route to the port of Jaffna in Sri Lanka. Three sailors died in the attack.
- On October 6, 2002, a suicide attack was launched against the French oil tanker *Limburg*, docked in the Gulf of Aden, Yemen. The blast rocked the ship, ripping a large hole in the ship's hull and killing one crew member.
- In 2003, Greek authorities seized the *Baltic Sky*. The ship, packed with 750 tons of industrial-grade ammonium nitrate-based explosives and 140,000 detonators, was flying a flag from the Comoros Islands, a small country in the Indian Ocean branding itself the "first Islamic flag of convenience" for maritime shipping.
- International terrorism analysts are also especially concerned about three mysterious hijackings of tankers in the Strait of Malacca in June 2003. In one incident, the

hijackers immobilized the crew of a chemical tanker registered in Indonesia and spent about an hour piloting the ship. Experts believe the temporary hijackings were training exercises for terrorist attacks.

- In the United States, in January 2004, a security guard was shot outside a BASF Corp. ammonia terminal in Freeport, Texas, after he questioned a man described as Middle Eastern taking photographs of a multistory ammonia tank. Authorities suspect that the guard may have stumbled upon a terrorist reconnaissance operation.

- Perhaps even more relevant is the terrorist attack on March 14, 2004, in which ten people were killed and sixteen were wounded in a double suicide bombing at Israel's highly secure Ashdod Port. The bombers, armed with assault rifles, official-looking uniforms, grenades, and explosives entered the port by hiding behind a false wall in a shipping container. Although the suicide bombings employed conventional explosives, Israeli officials feared the perpetrators of the attack intended to blow themselves up near the port's chemical storage tanks to cause mass casualties and damage to the port and surrounding area. Hamas and al-Fatah claimed responsibility for the attack.

- On April 24, 2004, Iraqi insurgents launched three boat attacks on the offshore oil terminal in Basra, Iraq. Two boats exploded alongside the terminal while another vessel exploded after it was intercepted by a coalition ship. The facility, which is vital to Iraq's oil exports, was shut down for two days, costing the nation almost 1 million barrels of oil exports the day of the stoppage.

- In September 2004, U.S. intelligence agencies passed warnings to several countries in East Asia that Jemaah Islamiyah, a terrorist group linked to al Qaeda, planned to turn a hijacked tanker into a floating bomb. The terrorists were purportedly discussing plans to seize a vessel using local pirates. The hijacked ship would then be wired with explosives and directed toward other vessels, a port, or a narrow and congested waterway around Indonesia.

- On December 20, 2004, Spanish media reported that North African terrorists associated with al Qaeda planned to conduct suicide boat attacks on supertankers bound for the Canary Islands.

- On January 12, 2005, a duffel bag filled with several pounds of explosives was found a few hundred meters from Europe's largest port in Rotterdam, Netherlands. The bag reportedly did not contain a detonation device. The perpetrators and the target of the explosives are currently unknown.

- On March 12, 2005, approximately thirty-five "pirates" armed with rocket launchers hijacked a tanker of Indonesian registry carrying methane gas through the Strait of Malacca. The ship was redirected to another destination, and its captain and engineer were kidnapped.

- In addition, analysts have surmised that al Qaeda may own a fleet of fifteen to three hundred phantom vessels of various sizes and capabilities whose credentials, registration, and names have been altered.

Terrorists could attempt to use aircraft to attack a port, docked ships, hazardous petrochemical facilities, or fuel supplies in a manner similar to the September 11 attacks. Many ports are located in close proximity to both large and local airports. There is every possibility terrorists may use explosive-laden small aircraft, helicopters, or unmanned aerial vehicles to attack a port. Since May 2002, the federal Department of Homeland Security and the FBI have repeatedly warned that scuba divers could be used to attack ports and chemical facilities.

• • •

Just beyond this two-mile strip of petrochemical manufacturing was one of the most densely populated regions in the country. Staten Island was one deadly southward moving chlorine cloud away. Nearby Bayonne, with its large Italian, Irish, and Polish populations; Jersey City, with a high percentage of African Americans; West Elizabeth (largely Hispanic); and Newark (more than half African American) were vulnerable.[3,4,5,6] In the next few years, massive stone, steel, and glass edifices will rise from the concrete ashes of the World Trade Center site, and at ground zero a new Freedom Tower, already under construction, will punctuate American financial might. This, too, is nearby.

"In this area, twenty of the United States' largest [shopping] malls exist," Haplea said. "All of this is *not* in the middle of nowhere."

In fact, terrorism experts who were quoted in the *New York Times* call this region from Port Elizabeth to Port Newark "the most dangerous two miles in America."[7] Security is lax, the paper said. "At the chlorine plant, trucks and cars drive by a scant 100 feet from storage tanks. A *Times* reporter and photographer found the plant only loosely guarded as they drove back and forth for five minutes snapping photos."

I asked Haplea when chemical plants in this area started to respond to terrorist threats. "September 12, 2001," he said, ruefully. "Since then, we've found industry to be very responsive."

But what are we missing now that we should be addressing? To Haplea and Serrao, one critical area to address is stopping any homegrown terror cells within the state of New Jersey.

"If you look at the history of terrorism in the United States, with the exception of the Oklahoma City bombing of the Murrah building, New Jersey is at the center of terrorist activity," Haplea said. "The first World Trade Center bombing in 1993 was planned in New Jersey. The bomb was made in

New Jersey. The vehicles used to carry the bomb as well as the materials were stored here. In the case of 9/11, eleven of the nineteen hijackers lived or spent time in New Jersey."

Captain Serrao and Trooper Mitchell scanned the area below, looking for suspicious activities—"congregations of trucks, cars, or people where they should not be," Serrao said.

"About a year ago, we received information on general threats to chemical plants," Captain Serrao told me. "So, the plants are moving to create buffer zones around their most vulnerable portions, putting in place security cameras, and state troopers are responding to every possible lead."

"Any breakdown could lead to devastating consequences," said Haplea. "The ripple effect on the entire nation would be devastating. In spite of the enormous size of the industrial complex, what's stored here is about a day's worth of petroleum for the region. The region has about two to three days' worth of food. If the port were rendered inoperable and petroleum or food supplies cut off, the effects would be devastating not just on New York and New Jersey, not just on the region, but on the entire nation."

The federal Environmental Protection Agency has identified 123 chemical plants in twenty-four states where a terrorist act or accident could threaten a million or more people.[8] The EPA's own records also show that the United States is home to 2,500 to 2,800 facilities that each put more than 10,000 people at risk of injury or death if there were a major chemical release.[9] In total, some 15,000 chemical plants and refineries are at risk of being turned into chemical time bombs by a terrorist attack.

Chalmette Refining is near New Orleans. A joint venture of ExxonMobil and PDVSA (Petróleos de Venezuela, S.A.), the site has on hand some six hundred thousand pounds of hydrofluoric acid. If it were attacked successfully from a nearby park, everybody in the city of New Orleans would be at risk of death or serious injury. Oh, that's right, no one is living in New Orleans anymore, as we lost the Big Easy to the alleged rising tide of global warming and global warming–inspired hurricanes.

The *Austin American-Statesman* reported in its August 5, 2005, edition that there are fifty sites, using toxic acids, including a dozen in Texas, that are "sitting ducks" for terrorism.[10]

According to a report in the *Chicago Tribune*, figures from a congressional research service ranked Illinois fourth in the nation in terms of risk to local populations of 100,000 to 999,000 from "worst-case scenario" chemical-facility terrorist attacks or accidents. (Ahead of Illinois, with as many as 25 such facilities, are 67 in Texas, 58 in California, and 50 in Louisiana.)

"The fact is, we have a very diversified economy and our enemies look at some of our economic assets as targets," former Homeland Security Director Tom Ridge told a congressional committee. "And clearly, the chemical facilities are one of them. We know that there have been reports validated about security deficiencies at dozens and dozens of those."[11] But can the chemical industry and Homeland Security stay ahead of the terrorists?

Now we passed over two storage tanks near the Meadowlands containing liquefied natural gas. Imagine that it is a Sunday afternoon, the nearby stadium and racetrack are filled with fans, and an explosion occurs. It would burn across the sky and kill thousands almost immediately. We passed facility after facility, and I snapped lots of pictures just like a terrorist would, and they didn't seem to mind me doing so, although they kidded me that if I should learn about things I am not supposed to know about, well, they might have to toss me out of the Sikorsky. I laughed, uneasily.

"One unintended consequence of the war in Iraq," said Director Caspersen when we return to the West Trenton headquarters of the Office of Counter-Terrorism on the sixteenth floor of 240 West State Street, "is that foreign terrorists are receiving battlefield experience." Caspersen himself served in the U.S. military as an explosives expert. "It's one thing to set a booby trap in a training exercise and quite another to do so in the heat of actual battle. Our enemies are receiving battle training and becoming more experienced and 'battle hardened,'" he said. "That makes our job that much more difficult."

Legislation that is seemingly perennially before Congress, sponsored by the governor, John Corzine (when he was the Democratic senator from New Jersey), would direct chemical companies to look at using the least-toxic substances to get the job done. Corzine's chemical plant security legislation required the federal Environmental Protection Agency to work with the Department of Homeland Security to establish minimum requirements for the improvement of security and the reduction of potential hazards at chemical plants and other industrial facilities that store large quantities of hazardous materials. Senator Corzine introduced the Chemical Security Act on October 31, 2001, and hearings were held on November 14, 2001. On July 14, 2005, the Senate finally and unanimously passed a near-meaningless, nonbinding resolution that called for federal standards to protect the country's chemical plants from terrorist attacks, the first time either body of Congress has done so.[12]

The immediate threat from terrorists deserves number one priority, and we have to do everything possible to secure the safety of our chemical plants. They are our greatness, but they are also a great vulnerability. America is dangerously dependent on foreign oil.

Also, increasingly scientific evidence is mounting that must be taken seriously: manufacturing and processing of petroleum and fossil fuels and petrochemicals is not only a great source of industrial might, they are also alleged to be linked with global warming. These selfsame chemicals are also clearly causing long-term, multigenerational damaging effects on our reproductive health—this unbridled dependency on fossil fuels almost exclusively places a great nation in a vulnerable position. Our addiction to oil from unfriendly governments has distorted our foreign policy, and the same chemicals are now thought to be feminizing the population with small nanodoses of estrogenlike chemicals. By greening our patriotism, we have the chance to do something that is great for our country and ourselves and our own capacity to effectively meet the challenges of the future.

Even though most of us will never face the same challenges as Captain Serrao, Deputy Assistant Director Haplea, or Director Caspersen, we all must have a mission in life that takes us beyond role-playing into a realm where our actions and deeds are in line with our values—and we're doing something important for our country.

I would never trade our advances for an earlier time. The Sikorsky I flew in; the laptop I am typing on; the R. L. Burnside I am grooving on through petrochemical headphones; my very ability to have been flying three thousand miles at timewarp speed to reach the East Coast; and then my long drive into West Trenton in my fossil-fuel rental car—these were all the result of our ingenious exploitation of oil, coal, and natural gas.

I love what we have, and I'd be stupid to want to go back in time. But I have to tell you something: I do want to get on with our future.

We have to be wise and progressive. That night, after flying all day with Homeland Security, when I arrived in Manhattan,

I stayed at the Sheraton New York Hotel & Towers at Seventh Avenue and 53rd Street. Why? Because it was the only hotel in the world that I knew of that was using nonpolluting hydrogen fuel cells instead of burning fossil fuel for power. We have one foot in the muddy waters of the past and one foot in the cool, clear waters of the future.

TWO
Be a Green Patriot

I THINK OF myself most of the time as a businessman who runs a publishing company called The Freedom Press in Los Angeles. I have to meet payrolls, deal with workers' compensation, taxation, payroll, pensions, hire, fire, insure, counsel, and along the way, the company has to turn a profit. We publish *The Doctors' Prescription for Healthy Living*, a consumer magazine that is sold on national newsstands as well as at health food stores, large natural-product supermarkets, and elsewhere; and books about health, medicine, food, lifestyles, and other topics. We have a lot of readers in "red" states, indeed, throughout what we commonly refer to as the Bible Belt or what Michael Moore refers to as Jesusland, and what I simply refer to as the heartland. Being a successful publisher, which I hope I am, requires listening to people carefully and seeing things as they are, or else your books and magazines will never connect with people. That's one thing I've learned—to listen—and in doing so, I've come to know that portion of America that sits quietly and powerfully between the two coasts—that sends its boys off to fight and upholds our traditions. We have readers, from whom we hear often, in Fort Worth, Shreveport, Pittsburgh, Cleveland, Milwaukee, Royal Oak,

Monroe (in North Carolina), Las Vegas, Topeka, and thousands of others.

From daily conversations, I know without doubt that people of our heartland truly care about the environment but that they are waiting for someone to speak to them who is not going to weigh down the environmental message with tons of political baggage with which they do not agree, or come off as some finger-pointing hypocrite or limousine liberal.

Here's the problem: the heartland sees the environmental movement as filled with stone-tossing hypocrites—and you know something? They're right. If the truth be told, environmentalists—the whole lot of us—are hypocrites. Why should anyone listen to us when most of us can't even get our own act together?

It's easy to talk about what everybody else should be doing. But you just know that the talkers we hear most often, sobbing the loudest over some environmental cause, fly private jets that produce more greenhouse emissions on one trip than most of us do in a year. If so, just 'fess up and be real with the folks. It's not a big deal, really. It just shows how far we have to go, both as a nation and individually.

All of us are guilty of falling short of our environmental goals. It's just that this lack of candor causes the message of environmentalists and other self-righteous crusaders to fall flat and sound hypocritical when it comes to speaking to the heartland. For this reason, I have harbored the suspicion that what passes for the mainstream environmental movement has been, for the most part, unfortunately, preaching to the left while the rest of America is wondering what planet these eco-hypocrites are from. Just be real.

I know the heartland. I like the heartland, always have. A friend shared with me an ancient Chinese proverb: "In an age of deceit, the truth is revolutionary."

• • •

I had to fly to Washington, D.C., on business. It was October 2005. The weather was still good, and when I got there I took the subway out to the Pentagon. None of us can ever forget the events of 9/11 or the nation's call to arms. Two things have become clear: Successfully fighting the war on terror is critical to winning what many public affairs experts now call the fourth world war (the Cold War being the third), and additional strategies are going to be required to win the peace and secure our future. In addition, we have to address global warming if for no other reason than that national security preparedness is, as I'll show, part of our critical response to this issue. These strategies have to go beyond weapons and politics. In other words, there is more to winning this war on terror and to ensuring a peaceful future founded on strength than what we see on cable news being beamed in from Iraq, Afghanistan, and Washington, D.C. We can address the war on terrorism and global warming at the same time. We have to.

As a publisher, I have learned that many different kinds of good people hunger to express their patriotism during these times and to do good things for their country. They really care and want to be leaders. But how do people become leaders when so much of the time they are feeling powerless? It's a question I've been asking and why I went on this trip. I needed to undergo a change in consciousness and live the change. I didn't want to be politically impotent in my personal life any longer.

I stepped out of the subway and I began the long walk to the perimeter. I walked around to the front of the massive building to the southwest corner and the 9/11 Memorial Gate.

"The plane came in so low it scraped the top of a taxi," said John Paige, a member of the Pentagon police force (part of the State Department but under control of the secretary of defense).[1] He pointed to where the plane came in. "I was there that day. Imagine you're just minding your own business and then you feel it scrape the roof of your car and see an airliner crashing into the Pentagon."

His pink tongue articulated and spilled out over his lip and beneath imperfect teeth in a perfect American smile. He had a trim salt-and-pepper beard and brown soulful eyes that went along with thirty-eight years of government service, including at the Central Intelligence Agency, "where when you do something wrong you don't hear about it the next day like here at Defense. You hear about it in thirty minutes or less." He laughed. "We didn't even know what had happened," he said.

> That's how big this building is. How some found out is you can see all the windows along the sides don't open and burning jet fuel was sucked up by the heating and ventilation system; it circulated throughout the building. Some people—when we were removing bodies—you would see them still at their desk reaching for a cup of coffee like skeletons with charred bodies and lost skin. Some officers—two, I think—died from heart attacks that day, and a lot of people took early retirement after that and never came back. I came back though. I have a hundred and twenty days though till I'm out of here. I'm going to go on the road and make some money as a mobile DJ. I make more money as a mobile DJ than I do here. I put my time in and I want to go have some fun. Some people, you know, they get out at seventy and they are gone at seventy-one.

I noticed that the wall where the Pentagon was hit was a different color from the rest of the older portions of the building.

I sat on a stone bench under the steps where we had just spoken. Engraved into massive stone was General George

Washington's wise counsel: "To be prepared for war is one of the most effectual means of preserving peace."

To be prepared for war has many meanings and contains many layers, all of critical importance to a society. To be prepared for war is to maintain vigilance and to head off crises. I came to the issue of global warming because I know it is critical to our nation. The science is serious and should be considered seriously. To dismiss it as just a tool of the left is to be closed off to the truth. If we affect climate by only 1 percent, could that still be dangerous?

I obtained a copy of a hitherto secret Pentagon report that had allegedly been suppressed by U.S. defense chiefs.[2,3,4] The report itself was commissioned by an influential Pentagon defense adviser, Andrew Marshall, age eighty-two, a Pentagon legend who heads a secretive think tank dedicated to weighing risks to national security called the Office of Net Assessment, says the *Guardian*.[5]

Net Assessment once reported directly to Henry Kissinger and to this day gives secret testimony to the highest levels of government and to the military. Since 1973, every president has reappointed Marshall to his position, and Net Assessment's accomplishments are legendary, according to *Wired* magazine. "For 40 years, the man Pentagon insiders call Yoda has foreseen the future of war—from battlefield bots rolling off radar-proof ships to GIs popping performance pills. And that was before the war on terror."[6]

Marshall, the national security futurist, is out searching for America's enemies, predicting scenarios that we must take seriously. Marshall's job is to deliver the news ahead of time. At that point, it's up to the branches of government to assess and prepare accordingly.

"Two very simple events triggered the report," said Peter Schwartz, a Central Intelligence Agency consultant and former head of planning at Royal Dutch/Shell Group, in a telephone interview with me.[7] He, along with Doug Randall of the California-based Global Business Network, coauthored the Pentagon report. He told me, "It was triggered by the National Academy of Sciences study on abrupt climate change. And the Office of Net Assessment is charged with looking at long-term issues. We have done a lot of work in the past for this office, and Andy Marshall knows that I have done a lot of work in climate change." But was the report suppressed? "I think what actually happened is there was a tendency once the *Guardian* article came out for the Pentagon to distance themselves from the report.

"The Pentagon report is an assessment of the earliest possible date where you might begin to see some effects from global warming," he said.

By 2010, it is increasingly probable these will show up and certainly more likely by 2050 the changes will begin to become manifest. The issue really becomes one of extreme climate change and rapid movement from where we are today. The magnitude and pace of change are the issues. I feel quite confident that some big part of the change we are seeing is the increasing carbon dioxide emissions from industry—this is a big factor. Whether it accounts for 10 or 90 percent, I do not really know. It is enough, though, to radically, extremely, and rapidly cause climate change. The consequences of not getting this right are so large and so great a challenge to our civilization and so profound that we cannot afford to take the chance that we are wrong.

• • •

Like a lot of you, I don't know how much of the alleged global warming we see now is the result of industrialization, or if the scenario presented to the Pentagon will come to pass. But no less a conservative journal than *Fortune* magazine opines that just like no one expected terrorists to commandeer jetliners and fly them into the World Trade Center, taking actions now to shape our safe trip to the future is critical, and we need to get away from partisan politics and do what is right.[8]

No one knows for sure what will happen. But given the damage inflicted by hurricanes Katrina and Rita, we have to wonder whether this is a first shot across the bow. The Pentagon report gave a model scenario that includes particularly severe storms, one of which would cause the ocean to break through levees in the Netherlands, making a few key coastal cities such as The Hague unlivable. Delta island levees in the Sacramento River region in the Central Valley of California would flood, creating an inland sea and disrupting the aqueduct system transporting water from northern to southern California because the saltwater could no longer be kept out of the area during the dry season. Of course, before us, we see the disappearance of New Orleans as a viable city and the encroaching ocean. The massive glacial ice fields of Greenland are already melting, says the report. How much worse can it get? Melting along the Himalayan glaciers would accelerate, disrupting water supplies for more than 40 percent of the Earth's population, causing billions of desperate refugees to seek drinking water. Mass migrations would heighten nuclear tensions. Floating ice in the northern polar seas, which had already lost 40 percent of its mass from 1970 to 2003, would be mostly gone during summer. As glacial ice melts, sea levels rise, and as wintertime sea extent decreases, ocean waves increase in intensity, damaging coastal cities. Additional hundreds of millions of people would be put at risk from flooding around the globe. It would make the December 26, 2003, Indian Ocean tsunami disaster and August 29, 2005, flooding of New Orleans appear inconsequential. Whole islands like Tuvalu in the South Pacific would succumb to the rising tide.

Nations seek nuclear power as a hedge against fossil fuels, and nuclear weapons proliferate. These skirmishes place increasing stress upon the world, with less-resilient developing nations reacting most acutely, since their economic systems haven't the capacity to absorb change.

Each of these local disasters could be handled, but the cumulative effect on the global community could plunge the United States into an environmental abyss fueled by declining resources, including oil. According to the Pentagon report, here's what to expect:

First Decade

- Severe cold and drought push Scandinavians south to Africa's shore. Disagreements with Canada and Mexico over water increases tension with the United States, driving wedges between nations, and increasing northward migration to America and Canada. Asia erupts into border skirmishes and conflict between Bangladesh, India, Pakistan, and China; there are mass migrations toward Burma of people seeking fresh water.

- Regional instability and skirmishes over the last of peak oil reserves in disputed oceanic and terrestrial regions leads Japan to develop force projection capability against China. (In 2005, China was drilling for oil in lands under dispute with Japan.) There is a flood of refugees from the Caribbean islands to the southeast United States and Mexico. European migration (mostly wealthy) will accelerate to the United States, which is building up its borders against global migration.

- Around 2020, conflict will emerge within Europe over food

and water supplies, leading to skirmishes and strained diplomatic relations.

- A strategic agreement between Japan and Russia is reached for Siberian and Sakhalin Island energy resources, depriving American oil companies of natural gas reserves. China is choked off for more fossil fuels.
- Russia joins the EU and provides energy resources as Siberian permafrost lifts and natural gas reserves are tapped. Late in the decade, China intervenes in Kazakhstan to protect pipelines regularly disrupted by rebels and criminals.

Second Decade

- Migration occurs from northern countries such as Holland and Germany toward Spain and Italy. Persistent conflict emerges in Southeast Asia among Burma, Laos, Vietnam, India, and China.
- Due to drought and inability to grow enough food to feed its people, internal conditions in China deteriorate dramatically, leading to civil war and border wars.
- Oil prices increase as the security of the supply is threatened by conflicts in the Persian Gulf and the Caspian Sea Region.
- In Europe, we see old-time skirmishes between France and Germany over commercial access to the Rhine.

Third Decade

- Nearly 10 percent of the European population has moved to a different country. Tension grows between China and Japan over Russian energy.
- The EU nears collapse. Increasing migration continues to Mediterranean countries such as Algeria, Morocco, Egypt, and Israel.
- Internal struggle in Saudi Arabia brings Chinese and U.S. naval forces to a face-off in the Persian Gulf.

• • •

The United States and Australia are likely to build defensive fortresses around their countries because they have the resources and reserves to achieve self-sufficiency. With diverse growing climates, wealth, technology, and abundant resources, the United States could likely survive shortened growing cycles and harsh weather conditions without catastrophic losses. Borders would need to be strengthened around the country to hold back unwanted, starving immigrants from the Caribbean islands (an especially severe problem), Mexico, and South America, they say. The energy supply will be shored up through expensive (economically, politically, and morally) alternatives such as nuclear, renewable, hydrogen, and Middle Eastern contracts. The intractable problem facing the nation will be calming the mounting military tension around the world and stopping the proliferation of nuclear materials used for bomb making.

According to the report,

As famine, disease, and weather-related disasters strike due to the abrupt climate change, many countries' needs will exceed their carrying capacity. This will create a sense of desperation, which is likely to lead to offensive aggression in order to reclaim balance. Imagine eastern European countries, struggling to feed their populations with a falling supply of food, water, and energy, eyeing [Russia], whose population is already in decline, for access to its grain, minerals, and energy supply. Or picture Japan, suffering from flooding along its coastal cities and contamination of its fresh water supply, eye[ing] Russia's Sakhalin Island oil and gas reserves as an energy source to power desalination plants and energy-intensive agricultural processes. Envision Pakistan, India, and

China—all armed with nuclear weapons, and other countries going nuclear so that anyone can rule the world—skirmishing at their borders over refugees, access to shared rivers, and arable land. . . . With over 200 river basins touching multiple nations, we can expect conflict over access to water for drinking, irrigation, and transportation. The Danube touches twelve nations, the Nile runs through nine, and the Amazon through seven.

Most ominously, "In this world of warring states, nuclear arms proliferation is inevitable. As cooling drives up demand, existing hydrocarbon supplies are stretched thin. With a scarcity of energy supply—and a growing need for access—nuclear energy will become a critical source of power, and this will accelerate nuclear proliferation as countries develop enrichment and reprocessing capabilities to ensure their national security. . . . When carrying capacity drops suddenly, civilization is faced with new challenges that today seem unimaginable."

New Orleans was just the tip of the melting icebergs. Toss in the loss of entire coastal regions of Florida, Texas, and Louisiana. We could end up losing much of the Gulf Coast.

Picture the fall 2005 hurricane season but ten times worse. Imagine massive regional wildfires in Arizona, Southern California, and New Mexico, with annual massive flooding in Utah and the Midwest, and landslides throughout coastal California—all regular events—ever more intense, the nation in a state of constant environmental crisis caused by natural disasters within and at war without, due to our excessive reliance on fossil fuels. Such North American–based disasters are bad enough. Couple with this our need to become petrochemical raiders and the accumulation of heavy debt through natural disasters as well as foreign policy entanglements; this, combined with the expensive and costly warring our fossil fuel addiction causes, bankrupts our treasury. Our nation experiences ever more stress by such massive refugee movements from Mexico and South America (as border security zealots have never imagined in their worst nightmare). Who knows if we might not be responsible for the civil wars of other nations? Think of what environmental destabilization will precipitate within the global context in terms of warring over oil resources, as well as proliferating nuclear arms fueled by increasing global use of nuclear power; it's easy to see why some preventive health measures now for our future national security should pay off handsomely. According to experts, reports the *Guardian*, the threat to global stability and our national security from the prospect of global warming is much greater than from terrorism, and, taking the long view, these experts might well be right

How Quickly Can the Weather Change?

Scientists never thought dramatic changes in the global climate could happen within as little as a few years or decades. Until a decade ago it was generally thought that all large-scale global and regional climate changes occurred gradually over many centuries or millennia, scarcely perceptible during a human lifetime, say Jonathan Adams, Mark Maslin, and Ellen Thomas in the journal *Progress in Physical Geography*.[9]

The tendency of climate to change relatively suddenly—within decades or even a few years—has been one of the most surprising outcomes of the study of earth history, specifically the last 150,000 years, said a 1993 article in *Nature*.[10]

"Once considered incredible, the notion that climate can change rapidly is becoming respectable," states "A Chilling Possibility," a report from the National Aeronautics and Space Administration (NASA).[11] In 2003, Robert Gagosian, president and director of the Woods Hole Oceanographic Institution (WHOI), warned of "rapidly advancing evidence [from, e.g., tree rings and ice cores] that Earth's climate has shifted abruptly and dramatically in the past."[12]

With respected scientists from NASA and WHOI talking about global warming, no wonder there is concern that industrial buildup of greenhouse gases is hastening radical climate change.

Scientists admit that it is possible that Earth's climate may suddenly cross the critical threshold needed to trigger abrupt climate change at any time, and that the extra "forcing" humans apply to the climate system by emitting large amounts of greenhouse gases into the atmosphere makes this possibility far more likely than it would be otherwise.

It's possible that as glaciers melt and more fresh water pours into the Atlantic, the great ocean conveyor, which strongly influences global climate, might temporarily slow down, potentially causing an ice age era like the "Little Ice Age," a time of hard winters, violent storms, and droughts between 1300 and 1850, say Randall and Schwartz. That period's weather extremes caused horrific famines, but it was relatively mild. However, a total shutdown of the ocean conveyor might lead to a big chill like the Younger Dryas, when icebergs appeared as far south as the coast of Portugal. Expect ice sheets over Spain and massive southward migration into Morocco—and even there it will be chilly.

According to the report in the *Guardian*, "a group of eminent UK scientists recently visited the White House to voice their fears over global warming, part of an intensifying drive to get the United States to treat the issue seriously. Among those scientists present at the White House talks were Professor John Schellnhuber, former chief environmental adviser to the German government and head of the UK's leading group of climate scientists at the Tyndall Centre for Climate Change Research. He said that the Pentagon's internal fears should prove the 'tipping point' in persuading the United States to accept climatic change." Also present was evangelical Christian and weather scientist Sir John Houghton, former chief executive of the Meteorological Office. According to the *Guardian* article, Houghton, "the first senior figure to liken the threat of climate change to that of terrorism—said, 'If the Pentagon is sending out that sort of message, then this is an important document indeed.'"

Global warming is happening. We don't know its consequences. Some of us think we know why. But we don't, really. Yet national security is reason enough to take this threat seriously. If we are part of the problem, we should not be unbridled in a gallop to the apocalypse.

Wall Street has no need to fear that shares of ExxonMobil, Kerr-McGee, Halliburton, Baker Hughes, or other oil and energy companies will go down in value. There's going to be plenty of room for fossil fuels in the world's future and probably always will be—but we need to be prepared for the global warming challenge because how we meet this challenge will determine our future.

> For the life of me, I can't figure out why President Bush isn't more proactive on the environment. . . . The truth is that only God knows if greenhouse gases and vehicle emissions are changing the climate, but everybody knows that the fewer emissions there are, the better it is for the planet. So why don't we stop all the nonsense and work toward that goal, instead of playing politics with the environment?

While this might sound like a routine attack from the left, in fact the author of this quote is none other than Bill O'Reilly of the Fox News Channel's *The O'Reilly Factor*.

Linking ecology with patriotism and winning the war on

terror should be of strong interest to Republicans and other conservatives and traditionalists, in addition to already environmentally sensitized liberals.

Indeed, I think it's very possible that a whole host of neo-conservatives will begin to look favorably upon environmentalism—as described in this book—as a means of winning the war on terror. Half the Republican Party is strongly proenvironment, and so are most Democrats, even if a lot of them are really only once-over light. Doing the simple math tells me that probably three-quarters of all voters want a president from either party who can energize the nation by articulating a coherent, practicable and visionary environmental policy that ties together our future sources of energy with an inspired response to the threat of global warming and our national security—what I call being a green patriot. For the growing number of Republicans who have long closeted their environmentalism or who desire to build for themselves a coherent *conservative* outlook that includes proenvironmental policies—the message in this book can help to clarify the links between environmentalism, conservatism, patriotism, and national security.

Our elected leaders also need to recognize finally, if belatedly, that environmentalism can help to win the war on terror. When it comes to international diplomacy, we need carrots and sticks. Sound environmental policy, aimed at addressing both global warming as well as dependence on foreign oil and nuclear proliferation, can become one of our most powerful sticks.

"Yes, there is an alternative to the Euro-wimps and the neocons, and it is the 'geo-greens,'" said Thomas L. Friedman in his January 30, 2005, *New York Times* column.[13]

> I am a geo-green. The geo-greens believe that, going forward, if we put all our focus on reducing the price of oil—by

conservation, by developing renewable and alternative energies and by expanding nuclear power—we will force more reform than by any other strategy. You give me $18-a-barrel oil and I will give you political and economic reform from Algeria to Iran. All these regimes have huge population bubbles and too few jobs. They make up the gap with oil revenues. Shrink the oil revenue and they will have to open up their economies and their schools and liberate their women so that their people can compete. It is that simple.

The current Bush policy might be better termed "No Mullah Left Behind," Friedman told interviewer Don Imus on his MSNBC cable show.[14]

The United States now imports some 12 million barrels a day, more than half the oil it consumes.[15] Production capacity is stretched so thin, demand is so high, and supply is so fraught with uncertainty that we're just a few riots or explosions away from another oil crisis. The lack of spare capacity is eerily similar to what it was in 1973, says Peter Schwartz. For those who do not know the history of oil embargoes, that year prices tripled within months. Our gas lines were evidence of extreme dependency on foreign oil, he said. Thanks to President Jimmy Carter's prescient leadership in the late seventies, however, America actually did a good job of reducing its oil dependency during his tenure and in the immediate years following. Unfortunately, we all became gluttons during the Reagan and Clinton eras.

Richard N. Haass, who was in charge of policy and planning at the U.S. State Department from 2001 to 2003 and is president of the Council on Foreign Relations, says that America and other industrialized nations are tremendously vulnerable because of our oil dependency. With current oil production scarcely able to keep up with demand, military action against Iran would cause such a dramatic spike in the price of oil that our economy would be crippled. He admonishes the United States: "Get your house in order. The United States will not remain a great power for long if the economic foundation of its power erodes. . . . America must also develop a serious and responsible energy policy. The only debate needed is over the right mix of mandated efficiency improvements, investment in alternative fuels and (get the children out of the room) new taxes."

This long view of the next century is part and parcel of national security and is totally related to environmental issues. All of us need to be activists and green patriots, and we need to pressure our political and business leaders to take actions consistent with our national values. There are some high stakes here, folks. No one wants the world's industrial powers to become entangled in more oil wars simply because we didn't take environmental issues seriously when we had the chance to do the right thing. What will it be like if we don't take steps now to win a long-standing peace when the warning signs are so clear? There is little down side and so much to gain by taking environmentalism and global warming seriously, especially where they intersect with clear-cut national security interests. All of the new energy technologies are being created out of the global warming debate. New innovations energize economies. Going carbon-neutral will improve your personal health and the health of the nation. Meanwhile, embarking on an era of carbon-neutral consciousness can take over the world and bring back good, high-paying manufacturing jobs to America and other nations and ease the growing gap we now see between the very rich and the very poor.

It would be great to have our president and Congress leading the way; they are the elected leaders of our nation and we need them, and the world needs an American president to articulate an environmental vision that responds thoughtfully to the national security implications of the global warming crisis. But we are a nation without such a leader.

We need green patriots. Even if you don't buy into the theory of global warming, the other benefits I've mentioned are not to be slighted by any country's leaders. Becoming carbon-neutral is the right thing to do in all walks of life: personal, political, business, public. Carbon neutrality is the future.

Philip R. Pryde, professor emeritus at San Diego State University, with a doctorate in geography from the University of Washington, is an expert on the link between the decline of great nations and environmental degradation. He is also a board member of REP America, a Republican environmental group, as has written, "Rome. China. The Mayans. The Anasazi. The USSR. A most eclectic group of peoples, but they all had two things in common. At one time, each was the most advanced culture in its part of the world. And after their period in the sun, all of these remarkable culture-states collapsed; in some cases, they disappeared. Today, the United States enjoys the dubious honor of being 'the world's only superpower.' But could we eventually suffer the fate of those other great powers? What should we be doing to avoid this?"

As we learned from the Pentagon report, when faced with a serious depletion of resource, nations either die or raid. Usually, they choose to raid. But it doesn't always work, and, admonished Pryde, even once-invincible civilizations lose their day in the sun.

If our actions are accelerating global climate change by only a single degree, this could well be significant, said Jeffrey D. Sachs, director of the Earth Institute at Columbia University and of the United Nations Millennium Project. "Our social and economic systems are . . . highly sensitive to climate perturbations," he wrote in the July 2006 issue of *Scientific American*. "Seemingly modest fluctuations in rainfall, temperature and other meteorological factors can create havoc in vulnerable societies."[16]

It is the way that America manages its resource base and strategically aids other nations to do so that will determine its longevity as a prosperous nation, and it is the way other nations manage theirs that can help to promote peace and stability throughout the world. This is why we have to hope green patriotism's residues permeate the issues and tissues of every place and person in the world.

What is it to be a patriot?

Certainly, even the most conservative leaders recognize green is one of the colors of patriotism.

If you don't buy any other argument, let's agree, at least, that it would certainly be tragic if, twenty years from now, we find ourselves in the midst of fighting another war for oil because we didn't do our fair share today.

I'm not writing this book to become the darling of the elite left or the far right.

If the truth be told, environmentalists need new recruits, people who have never realized that they even were environmentalists but who are ready to look at patriotism with new eyes, clean eyes—that is, independent, future-oriented people who love America.

Each of us can make a difference—and that's what is so exciting about being a green patriot, knowing we are part of something larger that is making the world a more peaceful, healthier, and safer place to live and that we have the power to create this future ourselves.

THREE
Put Good Food on Your Table

INTERSTATE 5 GETS interesting and good once you leave the San Fernando Valley. Till then it is all strings of cookie-cutter homes running up flattened, bulldozed shale-stone mountainsides, interlaced with periodic peaks of cars lined up at the Jack-in-the-Box, McDonald's, Wendy's, and Burger King fast-food stop-offs. There's a lot of jockeying in and out of traffic. I tried not to blow my top and maybe I felt a bit of wonder at how big this population in Southern California has become, as well as how utterly dependent we are here on our dinosaur-fueled cars. Fortunately for me, I am leaving the city, so the freeway traffic is relatively light. But I am also headed toward hell and about to see things about our fossil-fuel ways that will shake me to my very core, and that will never allow me to consume bad food in peace again.

Going south (in the other direction) into the Big Enchilada, the line of traffic is backing up heavily with the line of petro-beasts starting well north of Rinaldi, the last thoroughfare before the big sharp mountains start rising. As I leave the city, the car-spangled asphalt banner ripples downward with white-flight refugees from Simi Valley and Saugus in their beast machines, headed into a city that is becoming more and more a part of

Latin America, a brown-skinned land of immigrants who make their money at jobs they hate and love—and that some white people might even love or at least not hate so much if it weren't for the long line of creeping traffic that makes them insane (and they take it out on the brown-skinned people and blame them for all their problems). This line of cars is like a ribbon insanely wrapped around a gift box in every strangulating direction, overwrapped, bound up until this little gift could never be opened again. It wraps up all of the freeways in a triangular package that extends from Mission Hills in the north more than one hundred miles south into Orange County, moving eastward toward Riverside County (where the current housing boom outstrips L.A. in terms of sheer growth). No pockets for cruising to work exist anymore. You can't be cool in your car anymore in L.A. I used to go out to the desert with my dad. But, today, there is almost no desert left. Everywhere I look now, it's all malls and homes and fast-food places.

If you work in L.A. and get to work by car, you are in with a bunch of overcrowded, stressed-out rats, even if you are riding in a pretty cage, like the blonde in the Jaguar who passes me with a flash of her taillights.

You are not safe even if you are ensconced in steel and high-impact petroleum-based plastics. Before leaving, I read in the paper that another person in a car was shot, this time on the Costa Mesa Freeway in Tustin, and local authorities say there seemed to be no motivation, no road rage, no previous contact between victim and criminal, only a silver, late-model Toyota extended-cab pickup, not even a human ID, just knowing the suspect by the car. According to a newspaper report, at least four other men have been killed in similar incidents in the last six weeks, including one of those killed in the same locale as the most recent shooting.[1] The reports never seem to make the connection that this is the kind of behavior overcrowded caged rats would exhibit if they carried guns (only they'd shoot the scientists who caged them first). Are we no better than rats? Is this where our technology has brought us? Do we shoot the scientists? Politicians? Attorneys? Shoot them all; they're all bastards, I muttered and kept on driving.

The best thing in the world for local traffic is the rising price of oil. At this writing, we're nearing the sixty-dollar-a-barrel price ceiling, and it will prove, I fear, a false ceiling. We get happy when prices go down a few dollars on the market and a few cents at the pump, but the overall trend is for the price of oil to rise, mightily, perhaps into the hundred-dollar range, as one expert at Ford Motor Company told me.[2] More people are thinking of carpooling and other alternatives to the high price of gas, which is a household budget bleeder. Meantime, GM and Ford are also bleeding uncontrollably as sales of their cash-cow SUVs lag, and nobody wants to spend money on gas guzzlers. No wonder their stocks and bonds are rated junk status by Moody's.[3] The biggest joke is when I see some sap in his Hummer. Sales for the Hummer are going down in flames. California's Austrian-born governor Arnold Schwarzenegger first popularized the Hummer. I hope he has buyer's remorse. These days I can't stand seeing them on the road. All I can think about are our less than optimally equipped troops in Iraq who're being blown up in their Hummers. Let's get our men and women the tools they need to stay as safe as possible. After all, they're on the front lines of this massive war—and let's quit wasting oil over here.

The weirdest thing in L.A. is the disconnect all of us have experienced between the war and who really caused it. No one but a comparatively few brave, caring souls seems to care about the Earth anymore, and the fact that our spendthrift, wasteful ways were the distant but nonetheless root cause of the war in Iraq. Most of us are experiencing psychic pain, but we are so totally disconnected from the Earth as we roll around in our cagelike dino cars, we don't even notice that the disconnect has become more real than the connection. I'm just another angry L.A. driver. I'm pissed at everybody. Sometimes I don't even know why. I look at the long line of cars. I tell myself to be Buddha and not to get caught up in it. But, hey, I am smothered in oil.

Ironically, what most people in L.A. don't know is that we live so close to our oil. Much of the oil that cars in Los Angeles use comes from barely 150 miles from where we live. Thanks to Merle Haggard, Buck Owens, and Bakersfield, I sing my way into the Tehachapi range, which is beginning to show itself with grassy slopes and fields of orange California poppy, the milder alternative to the Afghanistan variety and sold in natural health stores for use as a sedative. I might pick some up on my way home.

First came shale peaks, angled like knife blades. These were the first of the oil fields, with ride lines that were sharp, harsh, pointed up and down, and bleak. I saw a few oil rigs along the highway, not many, though. This was north county Los Angeles. This area was prone to earthquakes. The site of the Simi Valley quake was land in geological motion, no smooth hills, everything angled dramatically, up and down, agitated, glittery, as sharp as glass shards. Jagged outcrops pointed like spears at the sky. This was harsh, terrible land. Not many folks lived there. You had to like sharp things to live there.

But, soon, the harsh, jagged peaks disappeared. The big grass mountains opened up, and I felt a little uptick in the happiness factor as the road powered up in multiple lanes into the Grapevine, part of the old Ridge Route, thoroughly bulging and pregnant with yellow-green grasses that lent the otherwise hard-stubble earth its soft contours.

• • •

There are these towns, you see. I pass by them nowadays on my hurried way to noplace. I've not really taken the time to see them or their people. I used to visit them when I was reporting and researching, for *The Arizona Republic*, a series of award-winning articles called "The Poison Within." But I don't know anything about them or the people anymore. Hell, I wanted to be a businessman and raise my family, take care of my wife and children. Wasn't that enough? For the last ten years or so, I'd tried to go about living blissfully, not really wanting to feel their pain anymore. But now everything had changed in my life and even with my children home with me I felt the pain of aloneness, and I had to find refuge. I had to join the environmental movement again. I needed my soul to touch somebody else's who shared a vision of what could be but who wasn't afraid or unwilling to see what is. So I had to feel pain again (maybe just to know that I was alive), and I was going to make sure you shared this hell with me, too, because all trips that end in Eden have to pass through hell first or we won't even know that we've arrived in Eden. It is just the way things are; you can argue it all you want but that won't change it.

You can drive from L.A. to the Bay Area on Interstate 5 and truly stay in the world of the Burger Kings and Jack-in-the Boxes while you are in your air-conditioned luxury automobile, your Mercedes, amidst the eighteen wheelers, always on the autobahnlike interstate. You can do that if you want, but you will end up gypping your soul. But if you choose a different path, the path John Steinbeck's men and women trekked in their weighted-down, open-bed Dodges, you are talking about something older, much more eternal; you are talking about the *Camino Real*, the road of the Indians and friars that everybody in this golden state once used that is now State Highway 99, which has its start south of the junkyard auto scrap trailer town of Mettler until it finally joins the 149 on the way to Chico. Highway 99 takes you into the little capillary towns that are the heart of the San Joaquin Valley: Mettler, Arvin, Fowler, Weedpatch, Alpaugh, McFarland, Buttonwillow, Earlimart, and Rosamond. This is where life begins in California.

I was down from the Grapevine and in Kern County now, which is a microcosm of America. There is so much to Kern County. This is the region in California that you go to if you want to see how the beasts are fed and their cars are fueled. It is the perfect marriage of oil extraction and petrochemical poisoning.

On the west side of the southern portion of this huge valley, far away still, are the oil fields where the oil was pumped from the ground and then transported, coursing up and down rocky jagged mountains via arterial pipelines, south to refineries in Los Angeles County to fuel our coaches. But also from this oil when distilled and chlorinated come highly prized yet toxic petrochemical pesticides that the enormous farms, also lining this valley, use to grow crops.

The land of Kern and Tulare counties comprises perhaps the most profitable, richest, and productive fruit and vegetable growing region in the United States, if not the world. That is, if you own the land and run the corporations. Caught at the bottom rung of the ladder of opportunity, however, are the farm workers, who share little of the wealth and receive more than their share of the poison.

So many goods things that have fueled modern living come from this valley. "It has been called 'the world's richest agricultural valley,' a technological miracle of productivity where dog-eat-dog competition is at its keenest," says UC Berkeley geographer James J. Parsons.[4]

In 2001, California's agricultural revenues were $27 billion, which means the growers can afford a powerful lobby in the state legislature. These large-scale farms and the transport industry associated with them were, as a whole, the state's largest polluters. In 1980, there were about 8,000 diesel trucks transporting goods on the roads of the San Joaquin Valley. Just twenty years later, in 2000, there were more than 55,000.[5] If California were a country, it would be the sixth largest agricultural exporter in the world. The San Joaquin Valley supplies one-quarter of the food America eats.[6] An estimated one-third of all pesticides sold in the United States are used in California.[7] Ninety percent of these, or more than 200 million pounds, are used in agriculture each year.[8]

Past Lebec, the road coasts down in a free fall into the valley, and soon the alluvial plains spread into what was once an inland sea not even ten thousand years ago, the blink of an eye in geologic time. However, when explorer Don Pedro Fages first viewed the Valley south over Tejon Pass, what he saw was "a barren desert waste with scattered saltbush [the plant genus Atriplex]. . . . Beyond he could see the tule marshes, fed by streams carrying Sierra snowmelt, that for several months each year became the wintering grounds for migrating waterfowl, including Canadian geese, pintails, cinnamon teal, and whistling swan. But it was and is dry country. Less than five inches of rain annually falls in southwestern Kern County, maybe ten inches at Fresno. Pan evaporation in a summer month on the west side pushes 20 inches."[9]

An oil pump rose far off in some field, bringing up the crude that eventually will be refined and distilled into gasoline and possibly the pesticides that are sold to the farmers and whose residues are absorbed into our children's tissues.

I pass by Route 58, which Dad and I took everywhere into the mountains when I was kid when we were going up to the Sierra Nevada to backpack and fish. I wanted to go back into the mountains with my sons, and I hope that they will be able to do so with theirs and that some family stories will be passed along. I like the sense of continuity, and I'm trying so damn hard to see that the continuum keeps on. One thing is clear to me now in my fifth decade: my dad kept me away from the reality of the valley floor. He'd take me up to the alpine lakes to camp, and all I knew of the floor of the valley was what I saw driving down Buck Owens Boulevard in Bakersfield to go have pancakes at one of the California Street breakfast places.

The snow pack was heavy this year in the Sierra, but Mount Pinos, in the west near the sea, appeared almost bare. Even though the rains were torrential this year, we had no snow at Christmas, and we were all disappointed when we drove up and there was nothing at all to show for all of that driving. The trip was a big bust. Nothing feels permanent anymore, not even the Tehachapi snows I once thought we could count on. The length of time until the valley is again an inland sea might not be too distant. A system of intricate, massive, and aging systems has tamed the flow of four major rivers that once filled the largest inland sea in western America. The farmers of the San Joaquin dammed and tamed the Kings, Kaweah, Tule, and Kern rivers that filled the Tulare Lake, and they now farmed the fertile bottom of one of the last of the great inland seas of the West. But the tide is rising, and, as futurists tell us, the Upper San Joaquin Valley might no longer be able to hold back the rising delta one day. That would be a hell of a sight, to see this valley as an inland sea again.

I am here because I was once here as a reporter, single, broke, probably just as depressed and disconcerted as I am today, and living on the edge. This is poverty. In spite of all that Americans can point proudly to, there is a sense of shame Americans would feel if they were aware of what is happening here in these small towns in the San Joaquin Valley. These are some of the most poisonous towns in America. Not long ago, clusters of cancer were discovered among many children throughout this area in the towns of McFarland, Fowler, Earlimart, and Rosamond.

More than 80 percent of the 9.5 million acres of San Joaquin Valley farmland is divided among only five thousand growers, averaging 1,520 acres each.[10] Some of these farmers also received huge amounts of public subsidies. The American King of Cotton, J. G. Boswell Co., for example, farmed 844 acres in the Henry Miller Water District, 16,988 in the Kern Delta, 146,877 in Tulare Lake Basin, and "only" 79 acres in Wheeler Ridge–Maricopa water districts for a total of 164,788 acres. The company farmed alfalfa, beans, corn, onions, and safflower, but the two big crops were alfalfa (with 23,833 acres, which grows in alkaline soils) and, by far, cotton with 76,838 acres. Between 1995 and 2003, the company received $17,290,870 in farm subsidies and Step 2 payments from the federal government.[11,12] The Buttonwillow Land & Cattle Co. farmed 3,286 acres in the Rosedale–Rio Bravo water district. Cotton, carrots, and potatoes were its major crops. It received slightly more than $8 million in subsidies between 1995 and 2003.[13]

"Sierra Gold" read the signs alongside the road. Walnut and almond trees, some fully mature and neatly coiffed and other saplings that were barely waist high and still under protective wrap, had sprung everywhere—and these were indeed golden. Times were good. Farmland was worth more than ever. Some land was going for $6,000 an acre, when only years earlier you could get an acre of prime farmland at $1,000 or $2,000.

"All We Ask Is One Pound a Week," proclaimed another sign from the Blue Diamond Walnut Growers cooperative on I-99. McFarland kept looming up ahead. I saw signs for Arvin, Taft, and Pumpkin Center.

And then I hit McFarland or, rather, it hit me. It proclaimed itself "The Heartbeat of Agriculture," according to a sadly peeling billboard.

I pulled off the 99 and turned onto Sherwood Road.

The Loop was the Big Drive, and it took about two minutes to drive and reach the road I came in on.

First Street bordered the 99 with its centers of hardy green bushes and chain link along its edge. Where you are not getting it from the farm fields, you are getting it from the highway. Everything hangs flat in McFarland today; it was spring but it was already hot as nails.

The town hardly existed but for the farm fields that extended for miles upon miles of flat land. Up close, along a fence, hung cotton bolls on brown shriveled plants, and then there were rows of grapevines, and, in other vast fields, were perfectly pruned walnut trees—these were cash crops for November 2004 and throughout 2005. The grapes on the vines were as tempting as a goddess or, maybe as a consolation prize, a glass of good wine. I would have loved to pluck a bunch. Every grapevine was staked on a cross with its vines outspread like Jesus. Because pesticide-related cancers make no distinctions between classes of people, by now, the meaning was clear to farm owner and farm worker alike. When you work in agriculture, you will take the chance of dying for our sins; you take the risk of an increased chance of cancer from the pesticides.

The road passed into infinity into the West, into the mountains, and past the mountains to the sea.

I stopped by some homes built on agriculture fields, surrounded by more fields, sometimes on three sides, sometimes two, and sometimes on all sides. The McFarland Community Health Center was next to the Women, Infants, and Children Center, and there were nearly as many WIC stores in Garland as *carnicerías*. Outside the community center was a sign that said, "If Your Child Has a Rash, Please Stay Outside and Ring for the Doctor." Like most towns in the Valley, McFarland was all about farming, with a large proportion of the population of nearly eight thousand made up of Hispanic families that earned their livelihood in the surrounding fields of cotton, grapes, citrus, and almond orchards. Almost everyone worked in the fields, and all breathed the chemicals that came from the petroleum extracted from the Earth that was then distilled, refined, and chlorinated to make them even more toxic when they were sprayed back on the soil and vegetation.

The town was filled with young women and their babies. Most people in McFarland were under age twenty-five, poor, and either working in agriculture or had family members who did. Most were undocumented and fearful of making trouble. There was a funeral home in McFarland that doubled as a flower shop. There were a few *carnicerías*. Don't walk into ABC Nutrition Market to get a soft drink because it only takes WIC coupons and offers infant foods. There was no health food store. The markets had no organic milk. A man and his family walked solemnly in single file into the one formal restaurant in town. I could see its tables with high-backed stiff chairs through the window. I went to get a haircut and the barbershop was closed in one part of town, and I punted when I got to the other after seeing the barber ensconced comfortably in the second chair of his two-chair shop reading a paper. It is good, this town, that it takes life to this level, I initially think, and then back off. I came here to see reality, not romanticize poverty. This town has lots of problems. It has lots of kids with lots of potential whom I see congregating outside the high school (which is in close proximity to the prison). But I worried about them as I eyed them driving their cars and walking on the sidewalk. The homes are on farm fields. Farm fields surrounded the schools. Everybody becomes surrounded by farm fields. A casual visitor might think the flames of hell are comforting in their warmth at first touch. But just stay for a while and feel the heat and toxic fumes. Everybody was surrounded by the pesticides. I worry these pesticides will affect the human potential in a profound manner, possibly even in the womb, dumbing down kids from conception. That's not to say that great kids won't come from this town, but I wonder how many more would be great if their parents didn't work so closely with the petrochemical pesticides that are part and parcel of work and life in this town—and that affect our children's potential even before conception. Nearby, at the ball field, high levels of cadmium, a toxic heavy metal, have been found in the soil, according to federal studies. I got back in my car. Elmo Highway took me across the 99, heading south.

I stopped at a market, went inside, and bought nothing. I walked out across the hot asphalt and looked at a town carved out of fields. It was barely making itself known. It was barely above the fields. It was really, really poor. I was just a visitor and I did not mean any harm.

The homes were small, with lawns behind white and black wrought iron fences mounted in pink cement blocks. Lots of bicycles were strewn on the sidewalk. Women were busily pushing strollers. In back of the homes were fence posts and then the grapevines and then the miles of vineyards and cotton, interspersed with bean fields or fields with carrots or watermelon.

Homes had small yards enclosed by wrought iron fences. Garages were attached to living rooms. Muscle trucks and cigarette boats on trailers lined the streets and were parked on driveways, carelessly facing out to the street. Lots of pickups, of course, were parked in driveways as well as blocking portions of the sidewalk, making walking down the sidewalk impossible. It was, after all, a poor farm town. Inexpensive, but with big trucks. Absolutely. Graffiti mucked the garage door of a boarded-up home beside the cotton fields. I suddenly felt lonely and fearful, and wondered what the hell I was doing there.

I understood why the town called itself the heartbeat of American agriculture. It was the bright side of a darkness. It was not good to take life or poverty to this level when it came to children. It would be difficult to leave this town without having been changed by it.

The town was growing and its population exceeded eight thousand, or would soon. The big deal right now was Vineyard Estates. It was a new subdivision of supercheap homes carved out of farm fields—and I would see more and more homes on farm fields as I went farther into the valley of hell. So much had gone on here. Transmission lines were slung across the valley. *Voice of America* once broadcast transmissions from this area into Central America during the height of the Contra-Sandinista battling in Nicaragua and El Salvador, and its huge electromagnetic fields could have played a role in the town's elevated cancer rates, although one report said that the levels were within normal range.[14] (Nonetheless, the *VOA* reduced its EMFs significantly.)

When I was working with *The Arizona Republic* to produce our series of stories, one of my assignments was to take this trip into the valley during the height of the cancer cluster. I met a lot of people then and learned a lot.

Connie Rosales's son played football for the high school team until he was stricken with lymphoma. In the town and nearby: Kiley Price got kidney cancer. Her father was the McFarland High volleyball coach. Fortunately, they had health insurance, which covered the operation to remove one of her kidneys. Esmerelda Sanchez got brain cancer. She died. Her father worked in the fields. She was the cousin of Carlos

Sanchez, who got lymphoma. His father and mother both worked in the fields. Sally and Borjas Gonzales's son, Franky, died of bone cancer. Adrian Esparza, five, son of Rosemary, was diagnosed with cancer. Angela Ramirez got adrenal cancer. Gonzalo Ramirez, a grape picker, told a reporter he was certain that exposure to pesticides gave his seven-year-old daughter, Natalie, near-fatal cancer of the kidney. The government, he told the reporter, "Don't want to go up against the farmers . . . we just don't count for much."[15] JoAnn Tarpley lost her son Greg to brain cancer. She was kept in the dark. She accused the state of a "cover-up . . . we're just left here wondering who's gonna get sick next."

Schoolchildren made fun of some of the sick kids. They did not come near them at the hospital when brought for a visit for fear of "catching" the disease.

During this time, in the late 1980s, two more cases developed in Fowler and six cases in Earlimart. There were also some in Rosamond, but there were fourteen in McFarland, and who knew about what was happening in towns the county supervisors had long given up on, that is, towns like Alpaugh in Tulare County and Buttonwillow near the railroad tracks? Or what about the towns that were ten or fifteen miles off the 99 or between the 99 and Interstate 5? It was a lot of cancer. But was it too many? A total of eleven children contracted nine different kinds of cancer between 1981 and 1984, a number four times the expected cancer rate, according to studies of the cancer data from the National Cancer Institute. The cancers continued to occur at abnormally high rates through the early 1990s.

What had happened to the towns? Had the towns recovered? Were things better or worse?

Even when the EPA came to town in 2005 to reassure

people that their cancers were not caused by pesticides, the people felt as though they had been taken advantage of. I read one of their reports. The language I reviewed was monstrous. It contained the language of bureaucrats and scientists and wore the mantle of the authority of science but demonstrated little understanding or common sense. The report was paradoxically educated, yet foolish, containing the kind of arrogant language writing you master in college and try to get rid of by the time you're thirty if you have any ambition at all about being a good or even great writer. "During 1987–1991 monitoring for pesticides in many agricultural areas, including McFarland, was conducted by the California Air Resources Board (ARB) and researchers from U.C. Davis. No unusual risks were identified for the pesticides detected in McFarland air."[16] The report then went on to say, "Environmental contamination that is 1) plausibly related to human exposures, 2) suggests an elevated cancer risk, or 3) is higher in McFarland than in other areas in California has not been found in McFarland. Because none of these criteria have been met, environmental contamination in McFarland has not been found to be associated with the cancer cluster." Later, of course, the authors admitted the data on which they built the case were "limited" and "inadequate."

The people I spoke with there said they loved America, yet they felt ripped off by the narrow-minded bureaucrats and scientists who couldn't see it plainly. All the authorities told them no link existed with the water or any other environmental influence—everything was by chance—and they actually expected people to believe them. But nowhere in this state-sponsored report did the authors mention the most toxic pesticide to which the children were exposed. I'll tell you the story that I uncovered.

You see, it's really pretty simple from what the folks tell me:

a very toxic petrochemical pesticide that was manufactured by Shell Oil Company and Dow Chemical, dibromochloropropane (DBCP), had been in the well water of the valley starting sometime in the late 1970s. Unfortunately, its presence was not discovered or widely known until after it had been contaminating the drinking water in the town for years.

I stopped my gas-guzzling 4-Runner in front of Well #5, located at the corner of Fernwood and Glenwood, where arsenic and DBCP were detected. The well wasn't deactivated until 1987, thus exposing almost all the families in the town.

According to the secretary in the McFarland Public Works office, Well #5 was abandoned several years ago because it "kept bringing up sand."[17] But how long had the exposure to DBCP had been going on? New research shows toxic effects on health can be inherited by children and grandchildren, even when there are no genetic mutations involved. These inherited changes are caused by subtle chemical influences, and this new field of scientific inquiry is called "epigenetics."[18] The cancers also occurred during this time. M. D. Whorton and D. E. Foliart wrote in the September 1983 *Mutation Research* that DBCP became widely used on citrus fruit, grapes, peaches, pineapple, soybeans, and tomatoes. In Central America and Israel, banana trees were treated with DBCP. By 1975, 25 million pounds were being produced in the United States per year. The majority of U.S. production was applied in the Pacific Coast states, particularly California's San Joaquin Valley and the Southern Atlantic Coast states.

Yet animal studies in the early 1960s revealed hepatic and renal damage and testicular atrophy in DBCP-treated rats. Indeed, atrophying of testicles was noted at the lowest exposure level tested. In 1973, DBCP was found to cause experimental stomach and breast cancer. A later study linked DBCP to nasal cavity tumors in rats. Subsequent studies of occupational exposures revealed high rates of sterility among men.

Because this petrochemical pesticide was so toxic, uses of DBCP for all but pineapples in Hawaii were banned by the EPA in 1979.

Experts who study clusters say that they can devastate towns. But that was a long time ago, ten years at least. So the towns should be recovering, right?

Again, the authorities will tell you that these small towns are much better off today than ever before. But this is not true. It is just one big lie coming from the hacks in Sacramento who are supposed to protect all the people of California.

The thing about toxic poisoning that I am learning and that most people don't know is that it morphs over time into many forms, with different health outcomes, depending on which chemicals, which combinations, who is exposed, and how they are exposed. Unlike laboratory rats, who are kept in a relatively controlled environment, people are not; as a result, the outcomes aren't always the same as what would show up in a laboratory rat. It's true that cancers were readily detected in the 1980s in McFarland and the neighboring towns, but since then other maladies have crept into the population and become health concerns.

In 2005, McFarland was one of the most dangerous places in the world for a baby to be born. McFarland is the ZIP code with the eighth highest rate of premature infant death in the state. Its rate is similar to that of Tonga or Fiji, according to an investigative report by the *San Francisco Chronicle*.[19] From 2001 to 2002, the number of reported pesticide poisonings in the state doubled, according to the California Department of Pesticide Regulations summary of pesticide illness information (released in February 2004).[20] Los Angeles may be the nation's smog capital, but the valley's towns aren't far behind.

According to the American Lung Association, the San Joaquin Valley towns of Visalia and Bakersfield, in Tulare and Kern counties, rank two and three, respectively. According to a *Los Angeles Times* report in 2002, residents breathed substandard air six out of every seven days.[21] On every one of those days, with every breath, 3.2 million men, women, and children living in the San Joaquin Valley inhaled emissions from livestock waste, poisons from diesel fuel, and pesticide residue. In 2004, the San Joaquin Valley led the nation in clean-air violations for the sixth consecutive year with 104 violations of the eight-hour smog standard.[22]

I drove across Kern County from Highway 33 through McKittrick down the hills of the 58 and across flat land, some in agriculture, some left wild. I passed through Darby Acres, population 386, into Shafter. I passed through Shafter and entered Wasco, the rose capital of the San Joaquin Valley.

This town was substantial, and, like many of the most prosperous valley towns, it had a state correctional facility. I parked in front of Wasco High School. I entered the centrally located administration building. Before I could ask for Thomas Frantz, a high school teacher and activist, he came out to greet me. I am pretty large myself and so was taken aback by his hulking size and broad farmer's shoulders, yet he is a gentle giant. He teaches algebra at Wasco High and grew up here. His mother and brother farm near Wasco.

"Show me what concerns you," I said. We got in his pickup.

The first place we visited was a dilapidated area of Wasco, Myreck's Corner, on a bad road where shacks leaned against each other for support. "There are no foundations and a septic tank is shared by everybody. They rent for four hundred a month. And people cram themselves into these places, ten, eleven, fourteen people in one shack," he said. They were clustered together, close to farm fields; children played in the yard.

A man in an undershirt stood outside his home and yawned when he saw us.

"I grew up here," Frantz told me. "We call this Myreck's Corner because the Myreck family had a store on the corner where I used to go buy nickel candy. You might not know this, but this is also the site of one of the farm labor camps Steinbeck wrote about in *The Grapes of Wrath*."

Down the road, in the town of Shafter, a mother lost her twin babies.

"Many people believe it is because of water contamination, possibly nitrates, combined with air pollution."

We end up in forlorn Alpaugh, which doesn't have many shops—just homes on the fields, poor, with shared septics, sloping roofs, high rickety gray porches, and lots of unkempt grass. Frantz says, "Alpaugh is the poorest town in Tulare County.

"Alpaugh is a town without a future. Even a county supervisor says it won't be funded by public funds 'because it has no future.' In many of these towns, they all share the same wells. They might be dug two or three hundred feet at most and owned by someone so they are not under state control. This water is too near the surface now to avoid contamination from livestock and pesticides. Their water has high nitrate levels.

"To escape poisoned water supplies, these small towns are trying to hook up to large cities' supplies, which are dug deeper to avoid nitrates and pesticides," Frantz said. "But there is a lot of red tape and bureaucracy in Sacramento that makes this difficult."

The problem is the air the people are breathing, according to Beate Ritz, MD, PhD, a researcher at the University of California at Los Angeles School of Public Health, whose findings show that particulate pollution at high levels, combined with carbon monoxide and ozone pollution, causes heart problems in babies and premature infant death. There were thirty days in 2001 when Shafter's ozone level exceeded safety standards.

"We do not know what level of particle pollution we have in Shafter, but we know that in Bakersfield, we have the number three local rate in the nation for particle pollution, ranking only behind the valley town of Visalia in Tulare County, and Los Angeles," Frantz said.

In towns like Buttonwillow, Shafter, and Alpaugh, the poor are the most vulnerable species. These little towns, I noticed, had no songbirds; they had all disappeared. It was totally silent. Not a bird was in sight.

America, once a land of wealth and opportunity, was leaving good people behind; it was a national tragedy.

I got back in my 4-Runner and was listening to KGET 970 on the AM dial with Rush Limbaugh when the news reporter broke in and issued a special report about a weekend barbecue in Shafter in which around thirty people were poisoned by a chemical being sprayed in a nearby farm field. Many of the people required emergency room treatment.[23] Sandrini Road ended in a field of grapevines. I reached Earlimart in neighboring Tulare County. I drove down West Armstrong, where there was a convenience store, gas station, and auto shop; the street was bordered by farm fields. I ended up at the last row of homes by some more farm fields. Way out in the distance was a silvery trailer that seemed to be in the middle of the farm fields. I turned right and arrived at 959 Lane Road, a thin gray strip that ran between the farm fields and home. Two yap-yaps and a lumbering, overweight golden retriever ran up to me. The small front yard had a waist-high chain-link fence. A young man selling ice cream pushed a cart past; bells tinkled.

Teresa DeAnda, whom I had come to meet, wore blue cotton jeans and a checked-print blouse. Her nose was flat and her eyes were brown. Her hair was short. She reminded me of the many caring Filipino women who have long worked as nurses and assistants in California's hospitals. To me, she was a healer for her community, today helping people to fight back against pesticide poisonings. She told me she had lived in this modest home with maybe five or six rooms and an addition for a long time. "My family lived here many years and certainly before there were farm fields here," she told me.

Do not call her a newcomer to the valley or America or anything that might smack of racism. Some people might think she was Mexican because, after all, she was a farm worker and it was Tulare County, California, and isn't it undocumented Mexicans—almost nonpeople—who pick our crops? Don't think this way.

Her father, Pancho Antheta, saved enough money from work on the sugar plantations in the Philippines to come to the states via Hawaii and San Francisco in 1926 when he was sixteen. He never talked about racist things to Teresa, but there was a lot of racism in America then. Filipinos were not allowed to marry and were not allowed to procreate "by law in the United States." His was one of the first generations to come. Quite a few Filipino families lived in Earlimart and Delano. Today, they are third generation and mixed up with Mexican and white blood.

Pancho did not know how to read or write; he traveled all over California doing migrant work, following the lettuce, grape, and sugar beet harvests. "He worked in just about everything, and in Delano he met a guy who was really taken with him," she said. The man sponsored Pancho to become a farm labor contractor and even put up the bond.

"Anybody who is in their fifties or sixties will tell you Pancho was a real good guy, not a ruthless guy, a good guy."

Her mother, who was from Mexico, met her father in the

town of Brawley, California, "and they got together. He was a lot older than her, about twenty-six years older. She was born in 1936."

He was very strong always. He had to be since he was much older than his new wife. She related how her mom and dad bought this house in the late 1950s. We walked out in the yard. Her husband handed me wonderful-tasting plums that he had picked from work that day. Soon, Teresa took me on a tour of the town and we started meeting the people, and a new world opened up to me that I had never seen before but that had been right there in front of me.

Earlimart had about five or six thousand people, mostly Hispanic, mostly living in poverty, almost all undocumented, most without real identities, and fearful. This town was so poor and transient the postal service won't deliver mail to the homes. The people have to go to the post office and pick up their mail. Nobody in the town ever thought of complaining. They know they are invisible in our society and act like it. Some of us might wish we were invisible. Let me tell you: It makes life worse for them.

People here were on the bottom of the earning scale. Half the town worked in the fields, Teresa said.

"Most make less than nine thousand a year," she added. "The total undocumented population is about eighty percent. We have no black people. We have maybe twenty white families living here, too. They and the Filipinos might still work in the fields but have higher corporate farm jobs. These are really good. They might work in the fields, too, but at least their work is steady for farming companies like Delano Farms, Simonovich, Paramount, or Caratan. The farmers are all corporate now, and they give people insurance when the people make enough money and they get health benefits too—if they work enough hours. The trick is that employees have to put in a certain number of hours—and that sort of thing is not easy to manage due to the oversupply of workers who all do not put in enough hours to qualify for health plans."

Both the documented and undocumented workers are employed by farm labor contractors, and they are afraid to organize for fear they will be deported. When the United Farm Workers union comes to town, they do not respond to what the organizers tell them because they are afraid and do not want to get into trouble and have the *migra* called. They have no insurance, nothing. The UFW is trying to unionize the undocumented, but a lot of people don't want to do that. DeAnda wishes they would. It would make so much difference, but the lack of documentation makes them fearful; they are also afraid that they won't get called back for a job. If they get sick at work from pesticides, they won't even complain because they won't be called back for work. That's how it goes. Not even the UFW can help these days.

DeAnda told me her family, like many families, had been poisoned. She told me that she could remember being little, and many times the chemical applicators would be spraying and the poisons would just end up everywhere in their house. (Her home on Lane Road was maybe twenty or fifty feet away from the fields.)

Another time she said, "My son was three years old then and he and I were in the front yard. The guy on the tractor was spraying and he was not turning off his sprayers when he came near the street and he went out one row and out onto the street to do the turnaround. He make his U-turn to go into the next row without turning off the sprayers."

Did he not see them? He had to have seen them. Did they just not exist?

"I saw the spray on my arm. I saw the spray on my son. I freaked out. I felt scared for my son. He wasn't going to tell me if he was sick or something. I got to call somebody, I told myself. I looked in the phone book and called the poison control center, which is in Fresno, and somebody came out three hours later and they took our clothes and told me to let them know if any of us felt sick. Three days later, my son was lethargic, but I did not even take him to the doctor or call them.

"They called me about two days later. They said they found a chemical on my clothes. I did not even know to ask them about the chemical. I told them about my son. They said to let them know if he got worse. They did not tell me if the chemical was illegal. They did not tell me where to go to get help. They did not tell me to take him to the doctor because of the pesticide."

A health official came out. "It might have been someone from the county Ag Commission who came out. I have no idea. I was so ignorant."

The next time was in 1999. It was a hot May that year. Teresa was with her kids. By this time, she had Anthony, Tina, Marissa, Nicholas, and Leticia. They were all sleeping. She was the only one up. Her home was getting foggy and smelly and foggier and smellier. So she looked out the window, and there was a guy on the tractor spraying. A powder was drifting over her home and into her living room, into her babies' lungs while they were sleeping. But she was up and had to do something herself (her husband, a farm laborer, was working in the fields)—but the man on the seat of the tractor, how could he not see them? "But he did not see the house or the home in his head or his mind. We were nothing. He was not turning off the sprayers mounted on the tractor when he turned around outside our home and what was coming out looked like the tule fog or worse. I was so scared for my kids. I called my husband. I asked him what to do. 'What do I do? Do I take the kids out of here? Do I turn the cooler on or off? What do I do?' I asked. He said, 'Call the sheriff.' So I called the sheriff at Pixley. The sheriff said, 'Unfortunately, we can't do anything about it. We can't tell the farmer to stop spraying.' 'What do you mean? I pay taxes. You're here to protect me, and I want to be protected from this. I don't know if my kids are going to live or die, if I should stay here or leave.'

"And so the sheriff said, 'We might go out there. Try calling the fire department.'"

So she called the fire department, and the fire department told her the same thing: the farmer had a right to farm. This was Tulare County, he said, and when she moved to where she lived, she certainly signed the paper that said she knew she was moving near agriculture and she knew and recognized and conceded that the farmers had a right to farm. But she never signed a paper saying anything like that, she told him. The house was here for a long time and they had been, if anyone noticed or cared, there since before the farm even existed. The fireman said to call the sheriff and he might go out there, and he hung up.

She kept looking at her sleeping little ones. Nicholas, born in February 1998, was not even one yet. He was very little. So she called the sheriff back, and they said they would take a cruise and see what was going on. She never saw them come by. The sheriff was white. But it was not a race thing, she said. It was just that the county is so pro-Ag, and Ag was king.

The next day, everything in the yard was green. The dog bowl was green. The wading pool was green. So she was just kind of thankful that the kids had survived. She didn't want to go out and get everyone scared. But when she turned on the air conditioning for another hot day, green powder drifted into her home and fell on her children, and they began inhaling it.

Two days later a man who sounded official called.

"Hello, I heard you had something going on with the farmer?"

"Who is this?"

"Leonard Craft, I am the agriculture commissioner in Tulare. I am the one you should call when these things happen."

"I want you to come and get my dog bowl and prove to you that I have this stuff he was spraying," she said.

"It's been too long now since the incident to analyze it. But next time it happens I will talk to the farmer."

"But I have this green stuff on my dog's bowl."

"No, it's been too long. Not this time."

She did not exist to him.

"That's just wrong." He told her he came from Oklahoma when his people were Okies, and it wasn't a compliment. "I feel for you guys and I really want to help," he said. She wasn't sure what to make of the agricultural commissioner.

She talked to neighbors after that. They told her they were scared, too.

Two weeks later the dog developed weird lesions on his tongue that looked like upside down mushrooms. He had three, and as big as dice. She took him to the veterinarian. The vet said she must have sulfur bags around the home.

"No, I don't," she said.

She paid the vet bill. She never contacted the farmer. But all of this was small stuff compared with what happened next.

On a Saturday evening, November 13, 1999, as Evander Holyfield squared off against Lennox Lewis in the world heavyweight boxing championship, everybody was ready to have one last barbecue of the year, and families were gathered together on Lane and Church and the other tiny streets of Earlimart to eat and watch the fight. One was a family of twenty-five. In the southeast, half a mile away, men working for the Shafter-based

Wilbur-Ellis Company were applying Sectagon 42, generically known as metam sodium, by sprinkler.[24] Metam sodium (also known as Vapam) turns into cyanide and is deadly. It is used to sterilize fields before planting, like the potato field across the street from Teresa's home.

Metam sodium, also used on rice, was the pesticide that killed off a large portion of the Dunsmuir River in Northern California after a railroad tanker car crashed along a dangerous curve—the Cantara Loop—in the mountains on July 14, 1991. The chemical toxin spilled into the river.[25] Every living thing in the river was killed. Many animals like deer and bear succumbed immediately. That accident caused many long-term maladies. People experienced chronic headaches, muscle aches, impotency, memory loss, and other signs of acute chemical exposure, as well as liver damage. Cynthia Watson, MD, on the *Doctors' Prescription for Healthy Living* medical board, helped to treat many of people hurt by the exposure, including one of the barge men who heroically stayed out on the water to try and hold back the toxic currents. She used medicinal herbs such as milk thistle and antioxidants like n-acetyl cysteine, and they helped, although, after all, none of the pharmaceutical drugs could prevent further liver damage. It is difficult—if not impossible—to recover from such an acute poisoning incident.

What happened in Earlimart was different. It was insane because all it was was a giant lawn sprinkler, really. Think of your own lawn sprinkler magnified one million times in a large field with neighbors' homes along the side and your sprinkler spewing not water but a fine mist of cyanide molecules. These deadly volatile gases rise and drift if the application is not properly sealed with additional water vapor that causes the poisonous molecules to fall to the ground. Unfortunately for DeAnda and the rest of the people living on Lane and Church and the other tiny streets by the fields being sprayed, the sealing procedures were not working.

The first people calling in lived 300 feet from the field in a little trailer down a country block away from Teresa. Their trailer was in the middle of the field, posted like a sentry, first in line to be affected by the moving vapor cloud. They called the fire department.

Fire department personnel arrived, and somebody talked to them and sniffed something resembling propane and then they did not smell anything.

Then they looked south of the trailer where the field being sprayed was located, and they saw the cloud moving away. Somebody went to look at the sign saying what chemical was being applied—and the rest of the fire department personnel quickly departed, leaving the trailer people to fend for themselves. They could get out if they were so inclined; they were all in danger. Certainly the fire department was not heroic. The people were left for two hours without any help. They were already pretty sick but they were not advised that there was a deadly poison in the air.

No one was there to take care of the field either. There was always supposed to be someone qualified to supervise the spraying of such a deadly poison; usually a farm worker would be assigned, but the field was unmanned.

The 911 operator received bunches of calls from desperate people in the dirt-poor town of Earlimart who were being poisoned and did not know what to do. Kids were vomiting, said the callers. Their eyes were burning.

DeAnda had gone out to get Chinese food with her family. When she returned around six-thirty, she smelled something in the air, and saw all the emergency crews. Her husband, who worked now as a labor organizer, was talking to a sheriff. He finished and turned back to his wife. "We've got to get out of here," he told her. "It's serious, honey."

They piled in their car, taking only the little dog, but they had to leave their big dogs, including their golden retriever, in the yard. She remembered that she was crying. But she kept her head because they had to get the kids out of there. Her husband had to load up their *compadre* Larry, who was eighty-four and blind, and Uncle Andrew, who was also eighty-four. She took the kids in the van, and her husband got in the truck and they drove south a few miles to Delano. But when they arrived at their friend Valerie's home, DeAnda was scared to come in. They had the smell of the Sectagon 42 on them. "I hope we do not make you guys sick and you do not die and we do not die," she told her friend.

"It's okay," Valerie said, putting her hand on DeAnda's shoulder and pulling her inside her home. "Come in. Let's help you get cleaned off."

Worried about who had been left behind in Earlimart, DeAnda used the phone and called her friend, an elderly Filipina, Edelmira Alcazar.

"You have to get out of here," Teresa said.

"I am going to stay," Edelmira said. "We have nowhere to go. And we don't want robbers to rob our house."

But, in truth, she owned no car. How could she leave?

"All of the town was being poisoned," she told me. "It wasn't just me." DeAnda led me to a tiny wood home on South Church Street. Consuelo and Estevan Agpalza lived there. It was spare and old with faded white paint, and the porch sat right out on the sodden walk. Both of the Agpalzas were sitting on the porch, enjoying the cool part of the afternoon. Estevan wore blue-jean overalls and a straw hat. Consuelo was in a big straw hat and a sundress with a scarf over her shoulders. She had crinkly eyes. She was diminutive. She came here in 1974 from the Philippines.

"The emergency crews knocked on my door on South

Church Road, and the moment they opened the door, I vomited on the man," she said. "He told me to go to the middle school if I felt sick."

Estevan, who was about sixty and had good work with Cal-Pacific Farms in Delano, told me, "We could see the fog coming closer like a big five-foot anvil." He began coughing in my presence; the cough hadn't gone completely away. When the poison hit him, though, his eyes began to burn like acid was on them, and he vomited. He lay on his bed with his grandson. Overnight, he became chronically dizzy. His vision was being affected; he was being poisoned. "'I need help,' I told the sheriff. 'I feel sick.' 'Well, go to your doctor,' a deputy told me."

Estevan said, "What the hell? It is Saturday night." Estevan did not get his name. He wished he had. The smart-aleck deputy deserved a dressing down. His grandson Jaco was six. Elvis and Eric were there, too. The deputy told them to go inside, then, if they were not going to see their doctor. The fog was there already. They trusted the sheriff, but the sheriff did not care. Maybe he thought they were just Mexicans. The sheriff's car outran the clouds of vapors coming in their home.

That was about seven-thirty. Down the street, in rentals and little second houses and trailers, the residents were not even told to get out. On Oak Street, half the people in the homes were not even told to get out.

A lot of people who were sick were afraid to go to the hospital because of the cost. But what was worse was the conspiracy to tell them nothing. The people who *had* to take the kids to the hospital did not know others were there, too, for the pesticide poisoning, and no one from the hospital told them others were there because of the pesticides. Two families who went to the middle school were told they were going to get medical treatment but never did. In total, more than twenty people went for medical treatment. But the hospital people wouldn't mention pesticides as the cause and wouldn't tell them that, well, so and so was there, too, and had come from Earlimart, too.

We traced our way back to Lane Road to meet another victim.

Edelmira Alcazar lived around the corner from Teresa. Her home had chickens in the front yard and sometimes Edelmira and Teresa's grandma had tiffs but they got over it, just like Edelmira's chickens fought with Teresa's grandma's chickens. It was a neighborhood with plenty of neighborly intrigue, spats, and truces. A birdcage with a cockatiel hung from the branch of a big tree. Edelmira sat just to the side of the cage in a small child's chair at a small table with her tightly knitted fists resting on the tabletop. She wore a red skirt and had gold hair and bronze skin and dark eyebrows and blue-white nail polish with sparkles. She was sitting in her yard with her family. All the men wanted to watch the fight later and they were celebrating something important like the last day of the Indian summer, and her eyes became watery and were burning and she had a bad stomachache. All of her family was having *carnitas*. They had just killed a pig; they loved fried pork, and at first they thought it was the salsa or garlic. They thought she had put too much garlic in the salsa.

Then they saw something that looked like a white fog. She thought it was a fire. She never before remembered being so badly affected by the chemicals, and she had been living here nine years when she found out it was pesticides. Somebody else had called the police already, and the *policía* were going home to home. When they came to her house, she thought they had come to arrest somebody. They told her and her family to leave, that a pesticide had spilled. The police had on medical dust masks but offered them none. They said nothing more and might not have known much. Her eyes watered and her nose was stuffy. She went to her sons. Everybody took baths. She was the last to go. She didn't want to go. But she got in the car and went, just like everybody else around her street and Lane Road. They were told to go into town. At about 9:45 P.M., the men and women were told to take their clothes off, men, women, and children, everybody. One woman didn't want to take off all her clothes in front of her children, but no privacy was provided, and everyone was ordered to "strip" if they wanted the pesticide to be hosed off. In one case, emergency crewmen, yanked the clothes off a fifty-year-old woman. The sickest people were vomiting. They couldn't breathe and their eyes were burning. Emergency crewmen hosed off the men, women, and children between between two tarps held up on each side by other young male volunteer firemen. A lady from Alpaugh who had been in Earlimart said the volunteer firemen were laughing. "It was so humiliating. It was so bad." Two fire department hoses were used to wash off the pesticide with cold water, at about ten P.M.

The baby from the trailer in the middle of the field that made the first call is six now and sickly. Even though the baby was hosed down, the hosing did only a little good because the insidious thing about Sectagon 42 is that it permeates the tissues and causes an almond body smell, which means you are poisoned and the terrain of your body is forever charred from oxygen deficit.

They hosed Edelmira down twice and promised there would be an ambulance to take her to the hospital.

But there was no ambulance. The people were waiting for the ambulance, but none came. When, finally, the ambulances arrived, the oxygen masks given to the children did not fit, and some of the tanks were empty and did not contain oxygen. It was a very bad emergency response. Overcapacity problems and the fact that there were so many people needing help caused them to be separated; the people from the middle school were taken to Delano Regional Medical Center, Porterville, and to Tulare—three different hospitals. At Delano, another lady from Church Road, who got very, very sick due to difficulty breathing ended up calling an ambulance. She and her daughers were met at Delano Emergency by someone who said, "Oh, you are just a Chavista [follower of César Chávez], trying to make propaganda." When others got to the hospital, the doctor called poison control. Poison control told them there was nothing wrong with the people. Subsequently the people were given enemas, and sent home. They should be okay, they were told. It was nothing. Hospital personnel did not even record their vitals but took their information for the billing.

Their contaminated clothes were returned. Some people had to put on the same poisoned clothing. Outside, though, hospital personnel were hosing down the ambulance.

Edelmira was afraid that somebody could take something from her home with everybody gone. A thief could break in and rob them blind. But she went to the school where she was told to go and she was terribly fearful when saw that the men were making the women strip and hosing them down. She saw the people and the raised curtains and the men hosing the women, and so she went through it and it was completely humiliating.

When Teresa DeAnda came back at around ten-thirty or eleven, it was because she was told it was okay to come back. She came back into her house, and it smelled worse. It smelled even worse now—like rotten eggs. They say it smelled like different things at different times. The rotten egg smell was definitely the methylisothiocyanate (MITC), and the people were being slowly and profoundly poisoned even as public officials told them it was okay to return. Some people smelled gas. Some people said it just smelled bad. The poison was floating in the air.

Agricultural Commissioner Kraft and his helpers came out. They were going around sniffing and deemed everything safe. No detection devices or monitoring devices were brought out.

The health officials probably figured the hosing down of the people completed their duty.

But hosing down does not get rid of metam sodium. It goes in your lungs, skin, eyes, and under your fingernails. It permeates the body like the body-ready gas it is, slipping into your lungs and blood. It won't just rinse off. In fact some said the hosing aggravated the poisoning.

The next day Teresa said she thought everything was going to be okay. So she invited all of the family over for her daughter Valerie's twenty-second birthday. She had all of her family there breathing as if it were okay. She has pictures of that day carrying on as if everything was okay. But nothing was normal. Sectagon 42, a deadly nerve toxin, vaporized Earlimart's people, especially the ones who lived on Lane and Church and the other roads near the fields.

The poison was in the air, and she knew it, and everybody was trying to be good about it and pretend the poison did not exist when it was entering every cell in each of them. For a few weeks they all tried to pretend that their town was the same. But it wasn't.

Everything in Earlimart was different. Everybody went downhill. The whole town seemed to age. Everybody aged *ten years* in one night.

Teresa's *tio* Larry, who was eighty-four, started complaining that his lungs hurt badly. The clinic kept telling him he had respiratory infections.

He just got worse and worse and died soon after that.

Before that he was out there cleaning up, watching after Teresa's kids and dogs. He was like a forty-year-old, cooking and doing everything. He died less than a year later, in August 2000. She really blames that accident for his death.

Her blind *compadre* had also had a lot of respiratory problems since then. Around that time her uncle made an observation. He said there were no birds. It was so weird. And from 1999 through 2001 they did not have any birds.

After that, the UFW came and they had a really big meeting, and they organized the town and a single newspaper came out; there was a lot of press and a lot of angry, angry people. The fire department was there. Agricultural Commissioner Kraft was there. "How are you going to pay for your hospital bills?" the agricultural commissioner said. "Well everybody gets money hungry, you know," he said, putting them down for talking about legal action.

One woman who was made to take off her clothes in front of her children asked Kraft and the rest of them, "Do you know how that makes me feel?"

There, for the first time, Teresa heard all of these people's stories. It makes her angry even today to see how mistreated they are when she is an American citizen and a good person whose family works these fields and helps put food on people's tables. She sends her kids off to fight in the wars this country wages. She started trying to learn about this stuff.

"I was mad at myself for taking so long to get wise."

The twenty-four who were hosed down were able to document their injuries. They got an attorney but the others in Earlimart—by far, most of the victims, who were not hosed down—did not have anyone to help them legally recover damages until eleven months into the one-year statute of limitations. The fact that they did not go to the hospital was held against them in a legal liability sense, and it hurt them in the long run that they did not receive even minimal medical help.

With help from UFW advocacy, the $150,000 fine levied against Wilbert-Ellis, an applicator company, was one of the biggest ever in the state of California for a pesticide poisoning incident. Some of that money went for the medical treatment of the hospitalized victims.

But the close to five hundred people in the languishing lawsuit received comparatively very little, especially considering that a fair assessment would clearly indicate long-term health effects, including toxic effects on the nervous system, which could never be made whole again.

These people are the salt of the earth. They don't have much, and nobody thinks about how terribly disabling the chemicals are. "The suit itself was an orphan from the start," Teresa DeAnda said. "You had hundreds of undocumenteds, not eager for any attention, often not using legal Social Security information or even a real name, and the suit went from one attorney to another and never found its advocate because there would be so many problems. The people were afraid if they acted up they would get into trouble, and so they stayed quiet because they were afraid if they were put on the stand they would say something to incriminate themselves. Most people, if they got a big settlement, received five or six hundred dollars for their troubles."

For Edelmira, her grandbaby, her daughter's son, Guadalupe, was about a month old, and he has had problems. Her daughter was harmed. All of her grandchildren experienced chronic headaches and vomiting. More of the children suddenly required glasses due to optic nerve damage, and they had more chronic ear and throat infections. Everything has accumulated and damaged their brains. For Edelmira, it feels like her head is going to split open every day. It was not this way before the accident. Everybody already took Advil or Aleve. They were taking them, running the risk of end-stage kidney disease, like vitamins, because of the constant headaches from the chemicals. Her kids said she was very different. "My grandchildren were affected," said Edelmira. "We were all affected with headaches and vomiting."

She felt like she was going to die, that she had a tumor in her head, from the chemicals, she said. It was a heavy-duty experience. It was like a rape.

We drove to the west edge of Earlimart to the Atelo School on Washington Street. New almond orchards are being planted across from the school. Almonds are heavily sprayed. Teresa talked about her children and the children they know, including one little boy one of her daughters went to school with who was missing an ear, or how at a school assembly one little girl in Delano was missing three fingers and her mother said it was due to pesticides and then there are the new victims that you do not know about until some lucky reporter tells you.

Is another cluster of cancer or birth defects lurking, undetected? She told me, "Here on my corner, my *compadre* has prostate cancer. My blind uncle had prostate cancer. My father had prostate problems. My neighbor around the corner had breast cancer. My other neighbor has cancer. There is so much cancer. Two teachers at Earlimart Elementary have died from cancer. A teenager died from cancer. There is so much cancer. My daughter knows so many people with cancer. The whole valley has so much cancer."

We drive by housing projects. Table grapes grow all around them. The grapes are sprayed. I hear rumbling from a distance. "The 99," she said. "The 99 has more semi traffic on it than any road in the United States." We drive by a huge sulfur pile. Sulfur is one of the commonest airborne pollutants.

I take my digital camera out, but she stops me. "No pictures," she says. "They don't like it when you take pictures." Then we're passing some guy on a tractor towing a spray tank and dousing the almond trees. Again, I want to take a picture. "No," she says. "They don't like it."

"Isn't this America?" I said.

"This is Tulare County," she said.

Not far from Arvin is a little barrio called Weedpatch, near Lamont, between two dirt roads that bisect cotton, carrot, and potato fields. In his great book, *The Grapes of Wrath*, Steinbeck mentioned Weedpatch.

> "We lived in a gov'ment camp a while, an' then we went north, an' when we come back it was full up. That's a nice place to live, you bet."
>
> "Where's that?" Ma asked. And she took the sticks from Ruthie's land and fed the fire. Ruthie glared with hatred at the older girl.
>
> "Over by Weedpatch. Got nice toilets an' baths, an' you kin wash clothes in a tub, an' they's water right handy, good drinkin' water; an' nights the folks plays music an' Sat'dy night they give a dance. Oh, you never seen anything so nice."[26]

Ignacio Azpitarze had been sprayed before. One of his hobbies was filming with his video camcorder. One of Ignacio's tapes was of the nights of October 3 and 4, 2003. The crop duster moving into focus as it zoomed over the roof of his home, spraying chloropicrin on him. He continued to film. It was Western Farms, which had sprayed him before. Overexposure leads to irritation of the nose and throat. The soil fumigant chloropicrin is a lacrimator, according to a medical information Web site.[27] "Exposure to vapors leads to coughing, labored breathing, sore throat, dizziness, bluish skin, vomiting, and in some instances, chemical pneumonitis and pulmonary edema."

That Saturday night, Western Farms had applied chloropicrin to the field in preparation for an onion crop. The wind shifted and went south toward the Ruben J. Blount low-income housing where farm workers lived. Weedpatch was west of the field. The farm labor camp was south of the field. The next cross street was Sunset. Ignacio immediately felt sick and called 911. Even though he was sick, he went around the neighborhood with his camcorder asking people how they were feeling. Everyone said their eyes were burning, and they were coughing. Some fifty townspeople appeared on his video, all with the same symptoms. The firemen arrived and asked the people what was growing in the fields. Some of the firefighters entered a house, sniffed here and there, and said they did not smell anything. One of the firefighters told someone it was probably something that spilled on the road and that everybody should open their windows and doors, and if problems persisted to call them back. Most of the people left. A lot of people were calling 911. Flora Bautista was babysitting her nine-month-old nephew. She had a handful of kids. Kids outside playing started running in and saying their eyes were burning, and they were coughing. When she called, the emergency operator told her to sit down and calm down. The operator had Flora on the phone for forty-five minutes. She told Flora that she was being hysterical, and that nothing was going on, even though on the playback of the 911 call you can hear the kids vomiting in the background. The baby was having difficulty breathing, and the operator kept telling Flora to sit down. She and her neighbors were desperate. They got in their cars and vans.

Favio Raygoza got his family in his van and made it to the checkpoint the sheriff had set up.

"You can't leave," the deputy said.

"My kids are sick and you are telling us to stay?" Favio said, crazy angry.

His girls were four and five.

Thwarted at the checkpoint, they retreated but talked and decided they would form a caravan. Their convoy of pickup trucks and overloaded station wagons reached the corner of Sunset and Weedpatch. There was a guard gate, and the public emergency officials, including the sheriff and members of the fire department, told them, "You can't leave. We need to find out what's going on here."

The people were so scared; the men afraid for their little children's lives. The men drivers, each of them, went up on the dirt road and busted through the roadblock.

"Okay, go to the store in Weedpatch, and we will have medical treatment for you there," the sheriff told others who began marching through on foot. It was called Weedpatch Store, a little market.

At the store in this tiny little town, the fire department put tarps on the ground. People were grouped according to their symptoms. In what they were told was an Emergency Freeze, the people were forced to sit for three or four hours without food, water, or diapers for the little ones before they received information. The babies were not given bottles. Anyone who wanted to go to the hospital had to go right now, the people waiting at the Weedpatch Store were told. But the people did not know how they were going to pay the hospital bills, and most did not go. Anthony, the nine-month-old baby, and several young infant girls, including one who was having an asthmatic spasm, went to the hospital, but the others, afraid of bills, stayed back.

Ignacio was going around with the camcorder but was ordered to turn it off, and you can even see a big hand from someone reaching out to stop him. (On Sunday, Ignacio woke coughing badly—a terrible hacking cough.)

A big macho farm worker, whose child had gone off to the hospital, came up and said he did not know how people could be treated like they are nothing.

"*Cómo sino importádanos nada,*" he said, crying, speaking of his daughter who had gone away on the ambulance.

Later, I learned that the baby never really did recover; she suffers chronic asthmatic attacks even today. None of the other children fully recovered.

"Certainly, poisonings in Kern and Tulare are underreported," Teresa told me. On March 9, 2005, two girls ran ahead of their mom and dad. They all worked for big Ag and were fixing fence posts on their own two acres on the west side of the abandoned town of Alpaugh, around avenues 50 and 30. The eleven-year-old was the first to notice the plane coming in so low that she thought it was going to hit her head. They both ducked down, and it drenched them with the pesticide Warrior (containing the neurotoxic ingredient lambdacyhalothrin). A white truck came over, and a man, whom she described as a Mexican in sunglasses, got out to feel the parents out and see if they were going to raise a stink. "Oh well, go inside your houses now," the man in sunglasses said.

They took a shower. They began feeling itchy. They did not know to go to the doctor, or else it was that, like many poor, they were afraid of the bills they would incur.

Two days after it happened, they experienced nausea and vomiting. They figured if it were so bad a chemical, the man in sunglasses would have told them.

They did not speak English well, and they were reluctant

to file a complaint. They waited nearly two months, suffering persistent rashes and recurring headaches, before Teresa helped them to file a complaint; even then they were reluctant to make waves.

"All of these horrific stories about what is happening to poor people in Tulare County in the United States are happening as we speak," she said. "These are not the past. This is today in America."

Teresa, Estevan, Edelmira, and Ignacio are as American as anybody ever was and are entitled to the same right to privacy and protection that the rest of us have. But no requirement exists in the State of California to notify people when toxic chemicals will be sprayed on a farm field across the street from them.

As a result, large numbers of our citizens, including our children, are being chronically exposed to some of the most dangerous nerve chemicals today.

In 2005, Senator Dean Flores introduced California State Senate Bill 503 that would have required some kind of notification to local farm communities when the nearby fields were being sprayed. There was nothing quite like it, and it at least would have prevented some of the poisonings of the recent past. But at an April 19, 2005, hearing of the State Senate Agriculture Committee, one of those who spoke first represented the crop duster applicators in California. She said they were the best applicators in the world, and their chemicals never went off the intended site. Best in the world, she said. The powerful agricultural lobby killed the bill off in committee.

I asked for my consciousness to be blasted. I'll never forget them, and I praise the Lord that people like, Teresa DeAnda are alive today. The earth needs some angels.

Organic Diet Makes Rats Healthier[28]

A team of European scientists found in an experiment that rats that ate organic food were much healthier than those that ate conventional diets. The scientists found that the organically fed rats enjoyed several health benefits: they slept better, had stronger immune systems, and were slimmer than rats fed conventional diets.

Organic foods are grown without petrochemical pesticides and other high-toxicity chemicals and rely primarily on biological methods of pest control. An organic farmer uses lacewings to counter aphids, and ladybugs are always welcome as beneficial predators. Organic crops are nutritionally distinct from chemically grown foods. Enough studies show them to have higher nutritional value so that we have to take seriously the possibility that organic foods are more nutritious. Certainly, you don't need a study to tell you they taste better. They are also excellent for the environment and strongly reduce our overall dependence on oil.

"What this research shows is that clearly there are links between food and health which is more to do than with just nutrients," said Dr Kirsten Brandt, of Newcastle University's School of Agriculture, Food and Rural Development, who helped colleagues at the Danish Institute of Agricultural Sciences design the experiment.

"We used to think that as long as food had adequate nutrients then it was all equally good. What this work has shown is that this is not the whole story, and we can measure differences and that they are significant. Now we need to understand what is going on. Bottom line: If people feel better eating organic food, it is probably because they are right," she said. Dr. Brandt told me in an e-mail that she suspected her animal research will pan out with population studies.[29]

We all value pure food and water for our families and ourselves. We also value consumer choice such as the ability to buy many different types of foods. As most of us ought to know, Mom was right when she told us to eat our vegetables, for a varied diet of fresh produce makes for good health. Eating well would do wonders for lowering health care costs, too.

The fact is that organic foods are a whole lot easier and less expensive than you might think. To prove this point, we sent one of our top reporters at *The Doctors' Prescription for Healthy Living* out to do a shopping survey in which she bought conventional and certified organic foods, orange for orange, apple for apple. We decided to see how true it really is that organic foods are becoming more competitively priced. We brainstormed an "average" shopping list including everything from spinach and oatmeal to mayonnaise and ice cream. Our reporter did all of her organic shopping at Whole Foods (a national chain natural market), and all of her nonorganic shopping at Von's (a national chain grocery store). We tried to compare as closely as possible, even looking at organic and nonorganic versions of the same brand where available, and comparing the price of the organic store brands at Whole Foods to the store brand of the same item at Von's. When our ace reporter returned from her shopping trip, she was pleasantly surprised by her findings.

"There is a rumor going around that shopping organic is expensive," she said. "Overall, I found that shopping organic was a little more expensive. The bill was 15 percent more for organic than nonorganic. However, this was probably due to the significant price difference on a few selected items, including cheese and fresh meat (organic lean ground beef is $7.99 per pound as opposed to $4.49 per pound nonorganic). On many items, the price difference was negligible (one pound of organic spaghetti was $1.29 compared with $1.19 for nonorganic), or the organic item was actually cheaper; for example, a ten-ounce box of Cheerios was $3.79, while a ten-ounce box of New Morning organic Oatios was only $2.69!" The conclusion to draw from this is that eating organic does not necessarily have to take a big bite out of your budget. You may want to do a little research of your own on some of your favorite items. You might just be very pleasantly surprised, too.

Product	Organic	Price	Nonorganic	Price
1 gallon milk		$5.99	Lucerne	$3.29
1 quart plain nonfat yogurt	Strauss	3.59	Mountain High	2.89
1 pound apples	Gala	2.99	Gala	0.99
1 pound oranges	Juice	0.99	Valencia	0.99
1 pound strawberries		3.99		3.49
1 bag spinach	5 oz	1.99	6 oz	3.49
1 pound broccoli		1.99		1.49
1 package sliced American cheese	Horizon 8 oz	4.99	Kraft Singles 12 oz	3.89
3 cans black beans	Westbrae	2.97	S&W	3.57
3 cans pinto beans	Westbrae	2.97	S&W	3.57

Product	Organic	Price	Nonorganic	Price
3 cans soup	Wolfgang Puck Organic	$8.07	Wolfgang Puck	$8.97
18 oz oatmeal	Bulk Organic	1.00	Quaker	3.19
1 bag frozen blueberries	365 10 oz	2.49	Von's 16 oz	3.59
1 loaf wheat bread	Rudi's Multi-Grain	3.69	Orowheat Health Nut	3.59
3 boxes mac and cheese	Whole Foods Kids	3.87	Von's	2.55
1 pound pasta	Whole Foods Spaghetti	1.29	Von's Spaghetti	1.19
1 pound coffee	Bulk house blend	9.99	Safeway Select Bulk Blend	6.99
5 pounds whole wheat flour	Bulk unbleached	4.45	Gold Medal Unbleached	2.19
5 pounds sugar	365 Evaporated Cane	6.98	C&H Evaporated Cane	3.49
1/2 gallon orange juice	365	3.69	Von's	2.19
1 pound boneless skinless chicken breast		10.99	Foster Farms	5.99
1 dozen eggs	Large brown	3.79	Large white	1.99
1 jar applesauce	Solano Gold 24 oz	2.69	Mott's 23 oz	2.49
1 frozen burrito	Amy's Bean and Cheese	2.29	Tina's Bean and Cheese	0.40
1 frozen pizza	Amy's Cheese 13 oz	5.49	Digiorno Cheese 12 oz	4.49
1 pound russet potatoes		0.99		0.79
1 jar pasta sauce	365 Marinara	2.49	Von's Marinara	1.99
1 pound lean ground beef (7% fat)		7.99		4.49

Product	Organic	Price	Nonorganic	Price
1 bag potato chips	Kettle Chips Organic 5 oz	$2.29	Kettle Chips 5 oz	2.49
1 box crackers (Wheat Thin type)	Hain 6 oz	2.29	Nabisco 9 oz	3.59
cookies (Oreo type)	Newman's Own 16 oz	3.49	Oreo 18 oz	3.99
1 pint ice cream	Ben & Jerry's Organic	4.29	Ben & Jerry's Organic	4.29
ketchup	Muir Glen 24 oz	3.49	Heinz 24 oz	2.19
mustard	Whole Foods Kids 8 oz Yellow	1.29	Von's 8 oz Yellow	0.99
mayo	Spectrum 11.25 oz	3.49	Best Foods 10 oz	2.29
shampoo	Avalon organics 11 oz	5.99	Herbal Essences 12 oz	4.59
conditioner	Avalon organics 11 oz	5.99	Herbal Essences 12 oz	4.59
1 pound butter	Horizon	5.49	Land O Lakes	5.49
1 box cereal (Cheerios type)	New Morning Oatios 10 oz	2.69	Cheerios 10 oz	3.79
1 jar peanut butter	Whole Foods Kids 18 oz	2.99	Von's 18oz	1.99
1 jar apricot preserves	Whole Foods 12 oz	2.69	Smucker's Simply Fruit 10 oz	3.49
1 jar honey	Whole Foods Kids Honey Bear 12 oz	3.49	Von's Honey Bear 12 oz	3.75
1 box granola bars	Cascadian Farms Fruit and Nut 7.4 oz, 6 bars	3.99	Nature Valley Fruit and Nut. 7.4 oz, 6 bars	4.19
Total	**Organic**	**$74.29**	**Nonorganic**	**$63.41**

Suppose you or your kids love raisins. My daughter tells me that Sun-Maid raisins are for girls and she shows me the lovely maiden in the sunbonnet on the package. Well, they certainly might be for girls but are not good for them, at least if they come from Sun-Maid. That's because Sun-Maid raisins have traces of a potential feminizing chemical agent called dicofol. according to both my laboratory data and federal monitoring data, Sun-Maid Natural California Raisins, unfortunately, contain what I would consider a dangerous chemical to have in the food supply. I mean, it is just my opinion—and what do I know? I am just a reporter without a degree in the appropriate scientific areas, the raisin growers say.

Can I tell you a story about me and the raisin growers? After I graduated from Columbia and earned a graduate degree from the University of Oregon (real degrees from two real bricks-and-mortar universities), I went on to write *Diet for a Poisoned Planet*. I mean, it wasn't that simple and all. Before I wrote the book, I served on a safe seafood committee at the National Academy of Sciences that advised Congress on legislation; conducted the first-ever pollution blood level study in humans in the Santa Monica Bay; and even testified as an expert on ocean pollution at a hearing of the Congressional Subcommittee on Health and the Environment, on February 10, 1986. Our team published its scientific results in *Environmental Toxicology and Chemistry* (8;10:951–56).

With its publication as a hardcover book from Crown, the California raisin growers voted to spend $558,000 on a campaign to counter what it was saying—all because I had the poor judgment, at least to their way of thinking, to report that they were applying a dangerous petrochemical pesticide called Kelthane (also known as dicofol, manufactured in Israel) on their raisin crops. Kelthane, identified in *Diet for a Poisoned Planet* by its generic name dicofol, was historically contaminated with anywhere from 1 percent to 20 percent DDT. The raisin growers were knowingly using DDT on a food that not only adults but children loved to eat. To make matters worse, the fresh traces of DDT were coming some twenty years after most people thought the pesticide was banned in the United States. I had the audacity to say plainly that not only was it getting into the food supply but also that raisins had what appeared to be some of the highest traces of dicofol in the American diet.

The raisin growers were also one of the main groups to have hired two of the world's largest PR firms—Ketchum and Edelman Worldwide—to sabotage my book tour. Besides a newspaper article in the *San Francisco Chronicle-Examiner* that detailed how much the California Raisin Advisory Board voted to spend on the campaign against my book, I also belatedly learned about these plans, thanks to records of correspondence to and from the White House, that the Center for Science in the Public Interest had obtained as well as from other documents smuggled out of Ketchum's corporate offices by a conscientious whistle-blower who later sent them to me anonymously. Among the documents in the White House correspondence is a letter to Governor John Sununu (who later served as President George Herbert Walker Bush's chief of staff) in which I was labeled one of those people "who specialize in terrifying consumers" and "may pose a future threat to national security." In an August 7, 1990, letter on White House stationery, Ede Holiday, assistant to the president and secretary of the Cabinet, replied that "Governor Sununu asked that I respond to your recent letter regarding food safety and especially to your comments on the upcoming publication of *Diet for a Poisoned Planet*. . . . We contacted staff at the Environmental Protection Agency to inquire about the participation of one of its science advisors in writing [the foreword] to the book. . . . EPA will contact the publisher." The White

House not only investigated how it came to be that William L. Marcus PhD, a top EPA scientific adviser, came to write the foreword for *Diet for a Poisoned Planet*. Marcus was fired not long after, even though he had clearly written the foreword as a public citizen and not in his capacity with the EPA.

According to a February 10, 1994, report from the National Whistleblower Center, in a precedent-setting ruling, U.S. Department of Labor (DOL) Secretary Robert B. Reich ordered the EPA to reinstate Marcus.[30,31] Reich's department "found EPA guilty of falsifying employment records, discrimination, and retaliation against an employee whistleblower. The DOL granted Marcus the largest compensatory damage award ever upheld under the federal environmental employee protection statutes. Stephen M. Kohn, chairperson of the National Whistleblower Center and Marcus's attorney, said, 'It's the most significant case to date for an environmental whistleblower within the EPA. The precedent is equally applicable to all federal employees.'"

"I've been vindicated," said Marcus, then an eighteen-year veteran at EPA. "My family suffered mightily. How can the public be protected when people charged with that mission are afraid that telling an unpopular truth results in their firing?"

Former Surgeon General C. Everett Koop, whose estimation in the minds of the American public has sunk along with stock in www.drkoop.com (with which he is no longer associated), and whom I once admired, trashed *Diet* in a *USA Today* interview with the conservative journalist Barbara Reynolds. Department of Agriculture staff made up a national call list to warn producers against booking me. The FDA administration issued a Talking Paper on my book and defended the very companies its own data incriminated.

The raisin growers used the politically connected legal firm of Akin, Gump, Straus, Hauer & Feld to send my publisher,

Harmony Books, a letter that threatened legal action if they did not remove every copy of *Diet* from bookstores. But I'll take the hits if it means getting my country on the right track, and I'm proud of the results that my work has generated. Among major raisin companies, Del Monte has stopped using dicofol, and sales of organic raisins have skyrocketed since the book's publication. And why shouldn't they? Selling for the same price as raisins grown with dicofol, organic raisins taste better and are quantifiably safer.

Yet, although my work helped to get dicofol out of the approved list for some brands, we had a Freedom Press reporter call Sun-Maid and ask them their policy on dicofol.

In 2006, a Freedom Press reporter asked Sun-Maid about their policy on dicofol and whether the company considered it a risk. The company told our reporter in an e-mail:

> In response to your inquiry, dicofol has been for many years on the Sun-Maid Do Not Use List. As a result Sun-Maid growers have not used dicofol for approximately 10 years. Part of our rationale is founded on the opinion of scientific leaders as well as information presented in the Reregistration Eligibility Decision hearings of the U.S. EPA.
>
> —Joe Kretsch, Technical Services Representaive,
> Sun-Maid Growers of California

However, our own laboratory testing of Sun-Maid raisins that were purchased at supermarkets in Southern California indicated that their raisins indeed contained low levels of dicofol.

The solution is simple and inexpensive, since certified organic raisins can match the raisins from Sun-Maid in terms of taste and variety. They are better though because they are grown without any pesticides, reducing the risk that our children, who eat raisins daily as a lunchtime snack, will develop cancer as their exposure to dicofol and DDE and DDT continues.

Dole, one of the major suppliers of produce in the nation, has bought an organic raisin packing house, and helped to make organic raisins mainstream. Buying organic is the way to go for raisins. Organically grown raisins have significantly fewer, if any, residues, and their price is similar to that of their chemical cousins. Despite the cute raisin singers who used to appear on television, raisins are a highly pesticide-saturated food, and consumers would be better off finding organic varieties.

I have additional concerns about dicofol. One example of the effects of dicofol comes to us from Lake Apopka in Florida. There, on its shores with their high water tables, dicofol was manufactured. At least one significant spill occurred into the lake and contaminated the entire ecosystem. Today, feminized male alligators make up almost the entire male population. They have hardly any testosterone and indistinct male-female gonads. There's little doubt as to the cause of their sexual identity problems.

Obviously, not everybody is a cop who goes around testing things and busting offending companies when they get out of hand. I can't test for everything. Are you kidding? I'm just a punk like you, caught in a jungle.

Is a little dicofol dangerous?

I'm bringing you evidence, but you're the jury. The raisin growers tell you that it is not dangerous, but Sun-Maid told us they do not use it and yet we found it on their products. It's not that I'll never eat Sun-Maid again, but they have to prove themselves to me as a consumer in a way that they have not.

Donald Malins, PhD, says the human body's DNA responds almost instantly to chemical assaults. Using techniques to view the structures of the cells' genes in fine detail, we now know that DNA is hardly the Eiffel Tower scientists once thought.

"Instead, what we're seeing is a molecule in a dynamic state of damage and repair, undergoing constant change. Rather than thinking of DNA as a rigid structure . . . DNA is more like a chemical chameleon, constantly altering its fine structure in response to changes in the cellular environment. It's a whole new way to look at DNA."

Doing a simple thing like putting good food on your table could lead to something really good for your body's DNA.

Alexandra Ramdin of Seattle was the mother of two young daughters ages two and five when her family took part in a University of Washington study of Seattle area preschoolers to determine if consuming organic foods truly reduced children's pesticide exposures.[36]

She kept a food diary for three days to distinguish between organic and conventional foods. Children were then classified as having consumed either organic or conventional diets based on analysis of the diary data (and other factors such as residential pesticide use, which were also recorded for each home).

Her children provided urine samples so levels of various known organophosphate pesticides could be measured. Organophosphates, with generic names like diazinon, chlorpyrifos malathion, parathion, methyl-parathion, and ethion are very commonly used in agriculture. Parents maintained food diaries for three days before urine collection, and they distinguished organic and conventional foods based on label information.

Urine samples were collected from eighteen children with organic diets and twenty-one children with conventional diets. Their urine was analyzed for five organophosphate pesticide metabolites, and the results were published by Dr. Cynthia L. Curl and colleagues in 2003 in *Environmental Health Perspectives*.[37]

"Significantly higher" concentrations of organophosphate metabolites were found in the urine of the children eating the conventional foods than children eating the organic foods. In fact, the concentration of organophosphate pesticide metabolites was six to nine times higher for children with conventional diets than for children with organic diets.

Eating organic fruits, vegetables, and juice can reduce children's exposure levels "from above to below the U.S. Environmental Protection Agency's current guidelines, thereby shifting exposures from a range of uncertain risk to a range of negligible risk," said the University of Washington researchers. "Consumption of organic produce appears to provide a relatively simple way for parents to reduce their children's exposure to . . . pesticides."

What else can you do?

Buy local. Buy in season. Especially when in season, organic foods are best priced. Plus, in terms of greenhouse emissions, buying organically grown and local foods grown in season cuts down on transportation costs and is part of carbon-neutral living.

Visit www.ams.usda.gov/farmersmarkets/map.htm to find a farmers' market near you. Farmers' markets are great for supporting local causes and finding organically and naturally grown foods.

If you want to be really outrageous, order your groceries with a delivery service. Felicity Lawrence reports in the *Guardian* that food "miles" have risen dramatically over the past ten years, are still rising, and have a significant impact on climate change, traffic congestion, accidents, and pollution, as well as greenhouse emissions.[38] According to the report, "Food miles increased by 15% in the 10 years to 2002. The average distance we now drive to shop for food each year is 898 miles, compared with 747 miles a decade ago. Food transport accounts for 25% of all the miles driven by heavy goods vehicles on our roads."

Lord Bach, the United Kingdom's Food and Farming

minister, said the government would work with the industry to achieve a 20 percent reduction in the environmental and social costs of food transport by 2012. He added that the report offered clear pointers to consumers: "Internet buying and home delivery can reduce road congestion and vehicle kilometers. Organic and seasonally available food can reduce environmental impacts, but these can be offset by the way they are transported to the consumer's home."

Around New York City and parts of New Jersey, more and more people are ordering foods, some of it organic, from FreshDirect home delivery service. It's a great way to eat healthy foods and cut down on transportation-related greenhouse gases. Visit www.freshdirect.com.

In Southern California, Pax Organica delivers certified organic produce once a week. Visit www.paxoorganica.com.

Nationally, Wild Oats is working with the online grocer Peapod to deliver about five hundred Wild Oats–brand foods to home delivery customers in the Chicago area. Visit www.peapod.com or www.wildoats.com.[39]

Participate in community-supported agriculture (CSA), and support local farms. Local farms in urban areas help stabilize the local environment and reduce greenhouse emissions, as well as save on transportation costs. It's also critical to our national security to have local food sources.

Essentially, you buy shares in a farm and you own the food and you come pick it up or it is delivered to you, depending on the structure of your CSA. You can go out and work on the farm, too, and pick food one day on a sort of farmer's holiday. Most require payment in advance, usually starting at about one-half or more shares, which can be a few hundred dollars.

Sharry Smith of Tampa, Floria, visited Sweetwater Organic Community Farm once to help nurture her connection with the Earth. She loved it so much that she became its education director.

"Sweetwater began with eight acres of prime agricultural land only one mile from Tampa's airport," she said. "Right now about one hundred families belong. The farm is host to many field trips for young children and intends to expand this facet to teens. We grow a huge variety of produce. The farm is unique in that it is within an urban setting, and members travel short distances to pick up their foods at what is essentially their own farmers' market on Thursdays and Sundays. People eat with the seasons, and that's different, too," added Smith. "But most of all I love influencing children with such a positive patriotic message. You see children's eyes light up the first time they come out to the farm and see someone pull a carrot from the earth. To them it is magic. They think their foods come from the grocery store," she said.

"Also, it's doing something good for my country. Not only do CSAs help get us off our petroleum dependency, we also ensure food security. Think of how vulnerable to some kind of terrorist attack our food supplies are. If transportation is disrupted, our country has only a few days of food supplies for urban and rural areas because we are so dependent on our transportation system. CSA farms encourage local agriculture. I think that is important to a country as an underlying bulwark of security." But most of all, she laments the disconnect she sees with so many people. I mentioned my trip to Kern County and the misery that I encountered there. "Most people don't realize the true cost of growing crops," she said. "They are disconnected from the harm that these same petroleum-based chemicals are doing to people's health in places like the ones you've visited. People care about these things. But they don't see the consequences of their choices or know how to change. We have to wake people up and teach them that they are the change."

Near Sweetwater is Carrollwood Village in North Tampa, a community designed around golf, but with an extra eighty acres that won't become part of golf course. Instead, the community at Carrollwood Village is working with Sweetwater Farm to turn their own land into a community farm. It is an unprecedented and fulfilling turn of events to the folks at Sweetwater when they see mainstream people turn to value-driven food choices. But it is also part of a national security network and promotes carbon-neutral living as well, so it is important to all of us.

You can learn a lot more about Sweetwater at www.sweetwater-organic.org and the CSAs by visiting the Robyn Van En Center for CSA Resources at www.csacenter.org. The Web site has a great national directory and loads of resources, referrals, and links.

Give food the importance it deserves in your life. This is what you put in your body. If you worry about some of the added costs of purchasing organic foods but you give to charity, think of organic food as giving to the most effective environmental charity today, more powerful even than the American Cancer Society or the March of Dimes, says the gifted writer and ecologist Sandra Steingraber. Your charity will show up in your food bill. Although your bill might be a little higher, your reward will be to know you are not only healthier yourself but that by protecting your children you are protecting all of our children.

FOUR
Put Good Products in Your Home

HERE'S MY TWELVE-STEP program for America's carbonholics. Call this a prescription for America's Oil Addiction, as the president put it in his 2006 State of the Union speech when he called us a nation of oil addicts.[1] Confession is always the first step, and we are, after all, a chemical nation and we have to deal with the fact that the chemicals in our lives are altering us. Me? I'm Dave, and I have an oil addiction. Oh, at first I didn't even notice. They (the vague ones) just suck you in. I was just a guy thrown onstage like an actor in an improv. America's carbonholics have to put themselves on the a path to sobriety. It's a disease, but, fortunately, through Carbonholics Anonymous, I have found that there's help for each of us from a higher source:

1. Admit you are carbonholic who is powerless to resist fossil fuels and all things petrochemical.
2. That rubber chicken in your children's closet isn't the only hidden sign. With plastic bottles in your fridge and plastic in your cosmetics and maybe even a petrochemical lurking beneath your bed, acknowledge the ubiquitous nature of the enemy; it is everywhere; it is you and me.[2]

3. Test yourself for levels of fat-loving industrial chemicals, plastics, and pesticides.

4. Discover that you are victim of bad chemistry

5. Begin detox.

6. Find out that the only detox center around is at the Scientology center. Go there, anyway; get branded as a Scientologist.

7. Throw everything plastic out of cupboards, closets, and cubbies. Discover that your furniture is made with petroleum. Donate it to a local battered woman's shelter. Home now has four walls and nothing else, not even pictures (art had to be removed because of oil-based fixatives).

8. Attend petrochemical crisis counseling when things seem overwhelming.

9. Start looking for a spiritual guide online—visit www.carbon-holicsanonymous.com or www.greensingles.org.

10. Participate in national town hall meeting. Anderson Cooper moderates.

11. Go Swiss—that is, carbon neutral; start carrying a tree around with you. Eco-invest in long-shot: jet fuel from switch grass, and make millions.

12. Get down on knees; kiss the sodden Earth. Pray to your God (of choice of course).

It's one thing to use petrochemicals. But we're mainlining. We're Tony Montana in Brian De Palma's 1983 film *Scarface* ravenously sucking up piles of cocaine into our bloated nostrils.

I am lapsed. I take my children to Jack-in-the-Box. They consume many Hershey chocolate-almond bars. We don't compost food scraps. In the living room in front of the Stickley hardwood entertainment center where the big television monitor looms like some surreal Orwellian messenger of war and violence, Chinese-manufactured petrochemical toys abound. They are in boxes, on the fireplace, by the TV, on the couch, on the beat-up coffee table where the children draw. I tell the kids they have more toys than Princes William and Harry when they are children—and they were royalty and all we are is petrochemical-sucking middle-class America. The floor always seems to be covered with happy children opening boxes and bags containing Aliens, Predators, Cabbage Patch Kids, Spiderman, Batman, Scooby-Doo, Power Puff Girls, Jabba the Hut, Beast Wars Transformers, Barbie, Big Sister, Legos, Mega-Blocks, Knex, Star Wars, and Jurassic Park dinosaurs that come in patterns of red, blue, and green. We are feeding the Great Chinese petroleum monster.

Our oldest, who is ten, sings, "I bought it on eBay" in the Chevy Suburban and means it. One night, he buys two *Alien vs. Predator* plush toys on eBay. These basically are Beanie Babies for kids who love Beast Wars, Reptilians, and Transformers. When they arrive a few days later, their tush tags reveal they were made in China for Diamond Select, of Timonium, Maryland, and that they contain polyester fiber and polyethylene pellets. A petroleum-derived polymer, polyester fiber is used not only for Beanie Babies and similar plush toys but also for other textile industry products, as well as for tires, seat belts, and heatproof jackets. They are also the source of polyethylene terepthalate (PET) packaging and bottles.

Polyethylene pellets are used as fillers in his Alien and Predator plush toys instead of petroleum-derived polyvinyl chloride (PVC) pellets. That is because polyvinyl chloride is considered to be extremely dangerous to human health, particularly to manufacturing workers who are exposed to PVC materials. According to a Beanie Baby Web site, "As a result of discussions between Ty, the manufacturer of Beanie Babies, and Greenpeace USA, regarding the toxicity of PVC (short for polyvinyl chloride), Ty has decided to use polyethylene pellets in all of its stuffed animals. This is a historic event—making toys less toxic and removing one more source of deadly dioxin from manufacturing and disposal (incineration) of PVC." (Dioxin is the name of a class of toxic chemicals, the chlorinated dioxins and furans, that are formed as a by-product of the manufacture, molding, or burning of organic chemicals and plastics that contain chlorine, reports the site.[3])

Of course, if you visit www.vinyl.com, the Web site for the Vinyl Institute, you will be told that, "Vinyl (or PVC) has been used in products for decades without any evidence of harm to human health."[4] But this is misleading, since the statement ignores the very real documented occupational risks workers face.

For skeptics and those who demand a human body count, studies confirm human breast cancer mortality among women who work with PVC and who are exposed to vinyl chloride gas.[5] These findings are confirmed by animal studies, in which the lowest concentration of vinyl chloride tested induces breast cancers.[6,7] Since vinyl chloride has an affinity for fatty tissues, such as the breast, breast cancer among women exposed to vinyl chloride is "biologically plausible."[8] On the other hand, Beanies with PVC pellets are considered rare and are more valuable on eBay (which is especially true for the Princess Beanie Baby with PVC pellets).[9]

(So let me understand this: A little girl holds Princess Beanie Baby with PVC pellets close to her breast. PVC causes breast cancer in animal and human studies, and PVC residues or metabolites [which are by-products of the original compound] are absorbed from consumer products like the Beanie Baby, possibly by little girl who is in love with her Beanie. But, nonetheless, a PVC Princess Beanie Baby is rare and fetches a higher price. Okay, that's the free market, where scarcity creates values, and it all makes sense in a weird way.)

"Do you think these toys are bad for the environment?" I ask him as he cradles his newfound friends.

"Are you crazy or something?" he says. He is holding his Alien and putting him against his downy cheek. "How could a cute little guy like this do anything bad to the environment?"

I go online and look up Diamond Select and write:

Dear Diamond Select,

My son loves your toys but I have a question:

I noticed they are made in China. What kind of assurances do we have that the factories making these toys are using fairwage labor and are trying to reduce greenhouse gases?

Seriously.

Warm regards,

David Steinman

Chris Myers, representing Diamond Select, writes back:

David,

All of our factories undergo certification and inspection. We have a fulltime person in HK that visits to ensure worker safety.

Thanks,

Chris

Which did not tell me a whole lot about their commitment to the Safe Trip ethic. So I write him again:

Thanks so much, Chris.

But my question involves a little more than that. I wonder whether your factories do anything about CO_2 emissions (greenhouse gases) and who certifies them?

Warm regards,

David Steinman

I am still waiting to hear back.

My wife is always first to awaken and rise from bed. She looks beautiful in her flannel flame-retardant pajamas.

In the bathroom, she switches on a light. She brushes her teeth with Colgate toothpaste and an electric toothbrush. Most people don't think all that much about ecological consequences of wearing nonorganic cotton bathrobes, turning on a bathroom light, or their toothpaste and its packaging. With three children, including twins, soon to rise and the two littlest needing dressing for their preschool at the Montessori on Old Canyon Road and the older needing coaxing to put his shoes on, and her husband (who she often refers to as yet another one of her children) sound asleep, neither does she. I do. It's my job.

She brushes her teeth with an electric toothbrush. The electric toothbrush is made with plastic from petrochemical-based plastic polymers and fueled by electricity generated at Southern California Edison's nuclear, coal, and hydropower facilities. The company's coal-burning power plants at Four Corners Generating Station at Fruitland, New Mexico, and its Mohave Generating Station in Laughlin, Nevada, contribute to global warming. Indeed, coal is one of the major contributors to greenhouse gases. (Interestingly, although nuclear power presents environmental problems due to toxic waste—think spent fuel rods—that stays highly radioactive for hundreds of thousands of years, the plants themselves make no contribution to global warming; nonetheless, I have to admit, I don't often take the family to the beach at San Onofre, site of one of SCE's two nuclear facilities, and I put the pedal to the metal a little faster when I am driving through the Buckeye Valley of Arizona and passing by the company's other nuclear generating station, the Palo Verde Nuclear Generating Station, in Wintersburg.)

I get out of bed and stumble into the hallway; as I said, I'm always thinking about global warming nowadays, and I make a mental note that the carpet is made with petrochemical polymers. I ask myself whether I should tell my wife that I want to rip out the carpet and replace it with an all-natural carpet. I decide that if I want to make it out of the house alive, I should not.

"Almost every plastic out there, from the polyester in clothing to the plastics used for food packaging and electronics, goes back to the use of petroleum as a building block," observes Geoffrey Coates, a Cornell University professor of chemistry and chemical biology whose discoveries for making plastics from plant-based materials instead of petroleum are paving the way for more and more companies to create packaging that decomposes back into the earth without a trace.[10]

School started at eight and, being late-night readers, artists, creators, PS2 players, and otherwise Type A personalities, none of us (except Mama) rose early enough, and no one really had the time or desire for breakfast. At least the coffee in the cupboard was fair-trade organic, although the Braun coffeemaker was made of petrochemical plastic, and connected us back to the SCE power grid. The lights were on when I got up. Someone forgot to turn off the porch light last night before going to bed. The television was on in the twins' bedroom, in the ten-year-old's playroom, and in our bedroom as well. Two TVs were tuned to the Cartoon Network, one to Fox News. The twins loved their milk and gulped from baby bottles made with polycarbonate petrochemical-based soft and hard plastics, including the presence of various estrogenic synthetic petrochemicals called phthalates and the contaminant bisphenol-A that have potentially leached into their milk. It bothered me. Phthalates and bisphenol-A, like many of the petrochemicals I'll tell you about on your perilous but safe trip, aren't quite identical to the natural hormone molecules in men's or women's bodies, but they come close enough that they occupy the same receptors on estrogen-sensitive tissues and exert their own unique effects on human health. I would love for us to avoid all exposures to chemicals that potentially interfere with the endocrine system, but it simply isn't possible, so we do the best we can and muddle on, somewhere between L.A. and Eden, hopefully a lot closer to Eden. (At least their milk was organic.) The shoes the children wore were made in China with petrochemicals. The children took lunches to school, packed in petroleum-derived vinyl-covered lunch containers that helped to keep their food cool. Their peanut butter and jelly sandwiches were packed in Tupperware, and their fruit juices were nestled beside reusable petrochemical Rubbermaid Blue Ice plastic containers to keep them cold. At least they were free of sodium-benzoate, the preservative that we now know interacts with vitamin C to form cancer-causing benzene molecules. Their lunch containers were dyed with petro-derived purple and green coal tars (despite their name, modern dyes are derived from oil).

The question every health-conscious parent must ask is where their home ends and their bodies begin. Is there really a separation between who we are and what we surround ourselves with?

The potential hazards are not only chemicals that stimulate global warming but, more immediately, chemicals that damage our health as early as *in utero*.

The largest use of phthalates is as plasticizers to soften PVC and other plastic products, including plastic food wrap, plastic toys (e.g., the rubber chickens and Spiderman action figures that the children clamor for me to buy at Toys R Us), as well as in cosmetics, particularly fragrances, hair spray, nail polish, and deodorants.

Many phthalates are used, but three in particular (dimethyl phthalate [DMP], diethyl phthalate [DEP], and dibuytl phthalate [DBP]) are used in cosmetics and personal-care products because they deliver benefits that are difficult to otherwise achieve, according to the Phthalate Information Center, an industry-sponsored Web site.

Other phthalates are used in the plastic lining of bottles, especially leaving traces of bisphenol-A, which is found in the plastic inner linings of the tiny pull-top cans of peaches and mandarin oranges that children love.

Because phthalates aren't always strongly bonded to the materials to which they are added, they can be absorbed by the human body through either inhalation or the skin. The body's largest organ, the skin is an exceptional vehicle for absorption of phthalates via cosmetics and personal-care products, enabling their passage into the body without passing through the harsh environment of the gastrointestinal tract or without first passing through the liver, the body's major detoxifying organ.

In the case of phthalates and personal-care products and cosmetics, the addition of a small amount of DBP provides just enough "give" to reduce cracking by making nail polish less brittle and more chip-resistant. When perfume fragrances are dissolved in either DEP or DMP, they evaporate more slowly, making the scent linger longer. In hair sprays, they help avoid stiffness by allowing them to form a flexible film on the hair.

Users of high-end phthalates include some of most popular perfumes. Every American and European fragrance the not-for-profit Environmental Working Group tested contains phthalates.[11,12] Every single European deodorant EWG recently tested also contains phthalates.[13]

When testing seventy-two name-brand, off-the-shelf beauty products for the presence of phthalates, the Campaign for Safe Cosmetics found phthalates in nearly three-quarters of the products tested, though the chemicals were not listed on any of the labels.[14]

A second report from the same group, "Pretty Nasty," documented similar product test results in Europe. In September 2004, the European Union put into force a new amendment to their Cosmetics Directive that prohibits the use of known or suspected carcinogens, mutagens, and reproductive toxins in cosmetics.[15] However, manufacturers have time to phase out use of these ingredients, and the directive has no power in countries outside the EU; in fact, some companies, particularly those based in the United States, have begun to manufacture one line of cosmetics to comply with the EU directive but have continued to use the suspect ingredients in products to be sold in the American and other non-EU markets.

Unfortunately for non-EU consumers, phthalates are usually ingredients in proprietary formulas and are not listed on cosmetic labels. To test for them costs about $175. Thus, testing each product, for most pregnant women, is out of the question.

Some experts, and governmental agencies such as the Consumer Product Safety Commission, say that the concern over these chemicals is overblown and that we should be confident that they are safe.[16]

No one is telling you to join the Paranoid Society for Chemical Phobias and to search under your mattress for every stinking pinko chemical commie phthalate and barbaric bisphenol-A terrorist; you will drive yourself cracked nuts doing so. But to say widespread human exposure to estrogenic chemicals like phthalates isn't worrisome and we should all go back to la-la land isn't good, either.

Let me tell you why I'm concerned, as a parent, as a husband, and as a red-blooded male of the species. The industry-funded Phthalate Information Center claims, "Once inside us, they [phthalates] break down quickly and are excreted." Okay, that sounds pretty good at first.

But, in fact, what the industry information site doesn't say is that the metabolites of various phthalate compounds could be as toxic as the parent compounds—and these metabolites are not wholly excreted from the body.

For example, if you are a male of the species, your testicles are made up of seminiferous tubules lined with Sertoli cells, which nourish developing sperm cells. While DEHP itself does not directly damage Sertoli cells, the damage is caused by a metabolite of the parent compound, monoethylhexyl phthalate (MEHP).

In one 2003 study, researchers confirmed significant and widespread presence of the phthalate DEHP and its metabolite, MEHP, in the blood of newborn infants in an Italian hospital.[17] The researchers further reported a statistically significant increase in risk of preterm birth associated with exposure to MEHP. The link between MEHP and preterm birth is important. The premature birthrate has risen 23 percent in the United States since the 1980s. Between 1992 and 2002, the rate of infants born preterm in the United States increased 13 percent.[18]

The information center claims, "And because phthalates have been around for so long, and are so widely used, they are also one of the most widely studied and well understood families of chemicals."

Not so fast, says Professor Richard Sharpe of the Medical Research Council's Human Reproductive Sciences Unit in Edinburgh. While not wanting to pronounce phthalates guilty as charged, he asserts, "If you wanted to produce a list of environmental causes of the reproductive health problems in boys, phthalates would be pretty near the top of the list."[19]

In fact, from experimental studies, we know that DEHP produces testicular toxicity at lower doses in juvenile rodents than in adults and that reproductive system development has been shown to be sensitive to breakdown products of the phthalates in rodents. This could be due to the fact that the reproductive system in juvenile rodents is still developing, he adds.

The problem is that industrial toxicology has long focused on high-level exposures with cancer as the endpoint or with occupational exposures that could cause adult infertility. The last thing the industry wants to know about are the high stakes of low-level exposures. We're not talking cancer but the effects on emotions, brain and reproductive function, and even gender behavior.

Earl Gray's laboratory at the Environmental Protection Agency is looking at the low-dose toxicity of phthalates during crucial windows of fetal development. He also thinks that chemicals in household products and cosmetics act like sex hormones or block male androgens. Gray is an androgen toxicologist with the EPA who has coauthored at least five studies on the subject, and his work reveals that male reproductive development is acutely sensitive to some phthalates.

For example, he has found that both DBP and DEHP produce dramatic changes in male sexual characteristics when exposure takes place in the uterus during pregnancy, at levels far beneath those of previous toxicological concern.

"We have found that androgens do block the action of male

fetuses so that some of them look like females," explains Dr. Gray. "We have males with undeveloped testicles and malformed penises [hypospadia] and some have even been born with a vaginal pouch."[20]

All of these points increase the level of concern and provide clear evidence that at the very least the health effects of phthalates are not as well understood as the industry groups would have us believe.

And in June 2005, bisphenol-A was linked to recurrent miscarriages among young women.[21] Scientists in Japan said a small sample study published in *Human Reproduction* indicated a link between recurrent miscarriages and bisphenol-A. Such studies could potentially expose the companies or their clients to lawsuits from consumers who may have been harmed by the chemicals. The latest study showed that women with a history of miscarriages were found to have higher levels of BPA in their bodies. The women who had miscarriages were found to have BPA levels on average about three times higher than women who had successfully given birth, according to an online food industry Web site.[22] The scientists concluded that while a high level of bisphenol-A did not in itself predict subsequent miscarriage, exposure to the chemical is associated with recurrent miscarriage. This report suggested that however it is happening, whether from baby bottles or other sources, certainly bisphenol-A is being absorbed by humans.

Puerto Rico has the highest known incidence of premature thelarche (breast development) ever reported, according to a report in *Environmental Health Perspectives*.[23] Since 1979, pediatric endocrinologists in Puerto Rico have detected an alarming increase in the number of patients with premature thelarche. Among the hypotheses proposed to explain the observed premature sexual development, the most controversial theory associated thelarche with the subject's diet. Some scientists have suggested that dairy and meat products were contaminated with anabolic estrogenic chemicals.[24] (Also, say the *EHP* researchers, a genetic predisposition of Puerto Rican girls for developing premature thelarche is unlikely. Investigation among this ethnic group in the Philadelphia, Pennsylvania, area did not reveal a similar pattern of early sexual development.)

The Premature Thelarche and Early Sexual Development (PTESD) Registry was established in 1988, collecting retrospective data to 1969 and prospective data to 1998. In this time period, 6,580 cases of premature sexual development were registered, of which 4,674 (71 percent) were premature thelarche cases.

Based on the data accumulated by the registry, the estimated annual average incidence rate of premature thelarche in Puerto Rican girls ages six to twenty-four months of age is eight cases per one thousand live female births from 1984 to 1993. This incidence is perhaps the highest ever reported in North America, if not the world. Compared with a study conducted in Minnesota, the incidence of premature thelarche in the Puerto Rican female population is 18.5 times higher.

An investigation was designed by researchers at the University of Puerto Rico and San Juan City Hospital to identify pollutants in the blood serum of Puerto Rican girls with premature thelarche.[25] Forty-one serum samples from thelarche patients and thirty-five control samples were analyzed. No pesticides or their metabolite residues were detected in the serum of the study or control subjects. However, significantly higher levels of phthalates were identified in twenty-eight (68 percent) samples from thelarche patients. Of the control samples analyzed, only one showed significant levels of phthalates. The researchers conclude, "This study suggests a possible association between plasticizers with known estrogenic and antiandrogenic activity and the cause of premature breast development in a human female population."

The phthalates found at significantly elevated levels in the blood serum of young Puerto Rican girls with premature secondary sexual characteristics were dimethyl, diethyl, and dibutyl phthalates—all identified as endocrine disruptors and all widely used in cosmetic products.

Because the federal Food, Drug & Cosmetic Act does not require premarket safety testing for cosmetic products, cosmetic safety is left largely to the industry itself. Experts for the Cosmetic Ingredient Review Board, composed of cosmetic industry scientists who are paid by the cosmetic industry to oversee the safety of its cosmetic products, have long concluded that topical uses of phthalates are safe.[26] Given the potential conflicts of interest, however, their remarks are not very reassuring.

According to a report by Molly M. Ginty from Women's eNews and posted on the Environmental Working Group Web site, here is another example of the cost of dangerous cosmetics:

When Olivia James gave birth to her son Darren seven years ago, she learned he had bright eyes and a dimple on his right cheek. She also learned he had hypospadia, a birth defect in which the urethra fails to extend the whole length of the penis. Repeated surgeries have corrected Darren's problem. But his mother, now 40 and living in Princeton, New Jersey, still can't shake the horror she felt when learned about phthalates and realized her son's condition could be linked to the chemicals in the makeup and hair products she used during her 15 years as a professional model. Every day of her career, James slathered on foundation, eye shadow, lipstick and mascara containing phthalates. In addition to wearing heavy makeup, James also had her hair straightened once a month. Like many hair products aimed at African Americans, the straightener she used contained a high concentration of phthalates.

You don't worry about these things? Tell me your secret.

Or maybe it's because I know too many secrets. Our younger son loves Scooby Doo, just like his big brother. Winnie the Pooh, Tigger, and Scooby-Doo. That's our world. And guess who makes these products? Johnson & Johnson.

The leading baby product line today in the United States, Australia, and elsewhere in the world is Johnson & Johnson's. Their Web site tells us that their products are clinically tested to ensure they are "mild and gentle enough for newborns." This is why the company says it replaces sodium lauryl sulfate, which is relatively harsh as a cleanser, with a close substitute as a cleansing ingredient. This substitute is called sodium laur*eth* sulfate. When sodium lauryl sulfate is combined with the petrochemical ethylene oxide, it is converted into an alcohol ethoxylate, turning the lauryl in sodium lauryl sulfate into laur*eth* so that we now have a chemical compound called sodium laur*eth* sulfate, which is distinctly softer and gentler.

Not only does Johnson & Johnson use ethoxylation to create gentler cleansers, many companies prefer ethoxylated alcohols, including those peddling their wares to parents. No problem so far.

In the ethoxylation process, however, a petrochemical-based contaminant called 1,4-dioxane (not to be confused with dioxin) is formed.

The evidence that incriminates 1,4-dioxane as a carcinogen is substantial. According to National Toxicology Program studies, the chemical has induced cancer in both sexes of rats and both sexes of mice.[27] "There is sufficient evidence for the carcinogenicity of 1,4-dioxane in experimental animals," notes the most recent *Eleventh Annual Report on Carcinogens*, published by the U.S. Department of Health and Human Services, National Toxicology Program.[28] The report notes that the U.S. Consumer Product Safety Commission (CSPC) "reported the presence of 1,4-dioxane, even as a trace contaminant, is cause for concern."[29]

The government's top consumer watchdog group, CSPC is not exactly the most chemical-phobic regulatory commission in the federal government, folks, but if they say this, it means they are reminding industry to clean up its act.

I first became aware of 1,4-dioxane when researching *The Safe Shopper's Bible* and interviewing high-ranking FDA officials, one of whom, Stanley Milstein, PhD, of the FDA's Division of Cosmetics, told me of his own and other public officials' concern that high levels of this contaminant were being found in children's cosmetic products. He said that the FDA "was working with manufacturers so that they would reduce the amount of contamination in their products." He also mentioned that "removal of this contaminant from the final raw material was relatively simple and inexpensive."

FDA officials say that surveys of cosmetic raw materials and finished products for the presence of the carcinogen 1,4-dioxane have been conducted by the federal agency since 1979.[30] "Levels of 1,4-dioxane in excess of 85 [parts per million, roughly equivalent to 85 drops of the chemical in a swimming pool] in children's shampoos indicate that continued monitoring of raw materials and finished products is warranted."

In 2002, I began buying kids' personal-care products that contained ethoxylated ingredients and having them tested for the prescence of 1,4-dioxane. I had learned earlier that a state public right to know law, also known as Proposition 65 and passed in California in 1986, listed 1,4-dioxane as a causable chemical if found in unregulated consumer products. Proposition 65 was cowritten by former deputy district attorney Barry Groveman, who had risen to fame as Los Angeles County's most aggressive toxics prosecutor and is the mayor of the City of Calabasas. The law requires the State of California to compile a regularly updated list of chemical carcinogens and reproductive toxins. If products, drinking water, or even workplaces or public spaces contained these listed chemicals, they were basically required to disclose to the public the presence of these substances. Not to do so left companies open to potentially costly monetary penalties that begin the day that the chemical was present. Proposition 65 also said that anybody—citizen or group—can be a toxic bounty hunter and sue a company for not disclosing the chemical exposure (although it leaves open the possibility that the state attorney general can take over the litigation for the citizen or public interest group). Proposition 65 has led companies to reformulate products that are truly safer. Thanks to this law, products nationwide became safer for all consumers; after all, if you couldn't sell your correction fluid in California, you would be missing out on one of the largest global economies. Old El Paso canned tamale chili gravy and Progresso canned tomatoes, manufactured by Whitman, eliminated their lead-soldered cans; Sears, Roebuck & Co. had dozens of products, including car wax and carburetor cleaner, reformulated to replace toxic chemicals with safer alternatives. Wine bottles sold in California no longer use lead-foil wrappers, protecting consumers from wine with unacceptably high levels of lead. Meanwhile, major manufacturers have asserted that Proposition 65, with its labeling demands, "provided an opportunity to improve product performance." The resulting products—from white-out to paint stripper—worked effectively and cost no more. They were better products, though.

I started buying brands of personal-care and cosmetic

products at Rite-Aid and other stores and sending them to the analytical laboratory. Each test cost $275.

But I knew what to look for. I knew from interviews with top-level FDA officials and published reports that many brand-products contained the undisclosed contaminant 1,4-dioxane. But there is nothing like finding things out using your own original field research. The first product I purchased was Johnson's Baby Shampoo because that was a type of product of "high concern" at FDA. My test revealed that it contained 5.3 parts per million (ppm) 1,4-dioxane, a finding confirmed by additional tests.

Tigger Bath Bubbles (the one with the phthalate-riddled orange petrochemicalized soft cap) contained 1,4-dioxane at levels ranging from 5.6 ppm to 7.9 ppm.

According to a California state health official's memorandum, "It is readily adsorbed through the lungs, skin and gastrointestinal tract of mammals."[31]

I began buying more products including Scooby-Doo Bubble Bath from Kid Care® (with its unique apparent phthalate-containing decorative topper made in China), of Phoenix, Arizona. This was an enticing product with a soft rubber phthalate-filled three-dimensional Scooby-Doo with his irrepressible smile taking a doggy bath with plenty of bubbles, holding a little ducky in his palm. Kids love Scooby-Doo. Can you blame them for loving a bubble bath? They don't know that it contains a chemical some experts suspect might cause cancer. Animal studies show a possible cancer link, although the link is largely unproven in humans.

I took the product back to my office. The label listed a number of ethoxylated ingredients, including sodium laureth sulfate, PEG-6 caprylic/capric glycerides, and PEG-15 pentaerythrityl tetrastearate. (One tell-tale sign of ethoxylated ingredients is that a product contains polythethylene glycol or PEG compounds.)

This product also contained cocamide DEA. According to

a 1998 report from the federal National Toxicology Program, two DEA-based compounds—cocamide DEA and lauramide DEA—have been demonstrated to cause cancer in at least in one species of animal.[32, 33]

Scooby-Doo Bubble Bath contained 3 ppm of 1,4-dioxane. That's a large amount of a chemical toxin to be taking in through your cosmetics. I compare it with three drops in an average size swimming pool. Low levels can have big consequences, we have learned.

Then there was L'Oréal Kids Orange Mango Smoothie Shampoo in its orange LPDE #4 bottle. Its name and bottle appeared so luscious I wanted to eat the product, packaging and all.

Its label listed at least seven different alcohol ethoxylates: sodium laureth sulfate, PEG-200 hydrogenated glyceryl palmitate, PEG-30 glyceryl cocoate, PEG-7 glyceryl stearate, sodium laureth-8 sulfate, magnesium laureth-8 sulfate, and magnesium laureth sulfate. In addition, the product contained paraben preservatives, which have been shown in test tube and animal studies to be estrogenic also. One study of breast cancer biopsies shows they accumulate in the tumors of women with breast cancer and, therefore, might potentially affect women's breast cancer risk (although most experts say there aren't enough studies at this time to make such a leap).[34] L'Oréal Kids Orange Mango Smoothie Shampoo contained 2 ppm of 1,4-dioxane.

Gerber Grins & Giggles™ Gentle & Mild Aloe Vera Baby Shampoo was tenderly packaged with a cute little baby, and fluffy teddy bear running across a green swath of grass in red rubber boots with decorative ribbons rippling breezily from a tiny stick held in its paw. Grins & Giggles contained four ethoxylated ingredients, including trideceth sulfate, PEG-80 sorbitan laurate, sodium laureth-13 carboxylate, and PEG-150 distearate. It contained 8.4 ppm of 1,4-dioxane.

Sesame Street Elmo Wet Wild Watermelon Bubble Bath

by The Village Company brags it is a new non-DEA formula, which is nice, since, as I've mentioned, DEA has been shown to cause cancer in some animal models. But they do not mention that the product contains 7.4 ppm of 1,4-dioxane, according to my laboratory study.

I bought Huggies Natural Care Baby Wash Extra Gentle with sodium laureth sulfate, PEG-80 sorbitan, sodium triceth sulfate, and PEG-150 distearate. It contained 4.2 ppm of 1,4-dioxane.

Suave Naturals Passion Flower contains ammonium laureth sulfate, PEG-5 cocamide hydroxypropyl, and cocamide MEA. It contained 2 ppm of 1,4-dioxane.

Pert Plus Shampoo contained 6.1 ppm of 1,4-dioxane.

I bought a bottle of Olay Complete Body Wash with Vitamins (normal skin). It contained sodium laureth sulfate, PEG-6 Caprylcapric glycercides, as well as cocamide MEA. It contained 23 ppm of 1,4-dioxance.

Simple Green, a product that has the appearance of being environmentally friendly, contained 0.5 ppm of 1,4-dioxance.

1,4-Dioxane Levels in Baby & Children's Consumer Products

Product	Concentration
Gerber Grins & Giggles Gentle & Mild Aloe Vera Baby Shampoo	8.4 ppm
Huggies Naural Care Baby Wash Extra Gentle	4.2 ppm
Johnson's Baby Shampoo	5.3 ppm
Johnson's Tigger Bath Bubbles	5.6 ppm to 7.9 ppm
L'Oréal Kids Orange Mango Smoothie Shampoo	2 ppm
Scooby-Doo Bubble Bath from Kid Care®	3 ppm
Sesame Street Elmo Wet Wild Watermelon Bubble Bath	7.4 ppm

1,4-Dioxane Levels in Adult Consumer Products

Product	Concentration
Dove Dishwashing Liquid	*2.5 ppm*
Keri Skin Lotion	*0.5 ppm*
Olay Complete Body Wash with Vitamins (normal skin)	*23 ppm*
Pert Plus Shampoo	*6.1 ppm*
SafeScience Dishwashing Liquid	*4.9 ppm*
Suave Naturals Passion Flower	*2 ppm*
Sunlight Dishwashing Liquid	*4.3 ppm*
Simple Green Cleaner	*0.2 ppm*

Of the total 1.13 million pounds of 1,4-dioxane released into the U.S. environment in 1992, as reported to the Toxics Release Inventory by certain types of U.S. industries, 680,000 pounds were released into the atmosphere, 450,000 pounds were released into surface waters, and 3,300 pounds were released onto the land.[35]

The tragedy is that the problem could have been averted with a few cents' worth of vacuum stripping, and not enough companies took the measures to eliminate these questionable safe cosmetic ingredients. The laboratory that was used is widely regarded as one of the best. I'm willing to acknowledge that not every product will contain 1,4-dioxane as a contaminant, but the results I obtained were compelling because they were consistent and because they simply confirmed what high-level FDA officials had earlier conceded: less than optimal manufacturing is leaving residues of a potential cancer-causing petrochemical.

Have you ever noticed how you can smell your household cleaning products even though they are all tightly sealed? These fumes are also known as volatile organic compounds or VOCs. Simply put, VOCs are carbon-based chemicals that form gases at room temperature. Examples of VOCs are phthalates, butyl cellosolve (found in Windex), formaldehyde, benzene and toluene, dichlorobenzene, acetone, xylene, vinyl chloride, naphthalene, methylene chloride, and perchloroethylene. These are all petrochemicals whose production contributes to greenhouse gas emissions and which often are used in products where petrochemicals could be replaced by environmentally safer and less costly chemicals. Thousands of VOCs are known to be capable of causing all kinds of illnesses and ailments, including neurological and organ damage, cancer, and multiple chemical sensitivities. All of these carbon-based gases are either directly alleged to be or are the end products of processes connected to global warming.

There are many sources of VOCs in your home, but certainly the products you bring into your home—from air fresheners and hairsprays to tile cleaners and paints—are a major source. In addition, VOCs are released from carpets, new furniture, and cabinetry with urea-formaldehyde resins in the wood, as well as all sorts of plastics. I remember buying the kids some rubber chicken toys the other day. They were made in China, and their colors were still sticky from the paint job. I remarked that they smelled like chemicals; that's a prime example of bringing VOCs into your home.

In one study of VOCs, the Consumer Product Safety Commission found that while outdoor air at sampled sites contained less than ten of these airborne chemical toxins, indoor air at those same locations contained an average of 150 different VOCs.[36]

Many such VOCs are the same petrochemicals implicated in global warming. VOCs evaporate easily into the air when products containing them are used. Most solvents are classified as VOCs.

VOCs have been making the news lately via a fresh round

of studies that say these chemical compounds all too easily harm humans. In the United Kingdom, when Shawn Ellis tested the air in parts of a house where cleaning agents were stored, he was measuring the concentrations of volatile organic compounds, reported CBC Marketplace.[37] A typical home might optimally have levels as low as fifty parts per billion. But levels vary within homes, depending on where cleaning products were used or stored. Ellis tested three products mentioned in the CBC report: Pledge, Clorox Wipes, and Lysol Disinfecting Spray.

Measuring the ambient air around these products, Ellis found that the levels increased significantly where they were stored. Pledge registered 273 parts per billion (ppb) VOCs, which is like a drop in a pond. (However, anything over 500 ppb could be a problem for people with sensitivities, says the report.) Clorox Wipes came in at more than 1,000 ppb. But the clear-cut indoor air champion was Lysol Disinfecting Spray, which came in around 1,200 parts per *million* (ppm), or roughly 1,000 times higher than the Clorox Wipes and equal to 1,200 drops in a pool.

In a country that values the unborn child, it is incredible that so little is being done to protect our children from poisons that are known to destroy intelligence and reproductive health and shortchange our children's future.

Perhaps this is one good reason for anti-abortion activists to be green patriots.

There is growing evidence that the solvents used in cleaning products have a deleterious effect on our children, particularly on their intelligence. Indeed, for fans of the body count, we've moved from studying rats to studying the unborn child.

At the Hospital for Sick Children, affiliated with the University of Toronto, scientists have begun to see these changes in a whole new generation of petro-babies—children who have a little less intelligence, are a little less able to deal with stress, and are a little more prone to aberrant social behavior, according to an in-depth report.

In the May–June 2001 issue of *Neurotoxicology and Teratology*, researchers compared the cognitive and behavioral functioning of thirty-three three- to seven-year-old children whose mothers worked with organic solvents during pregnancy with a control group of twenty-eight unexposed children who were matched on age, gender, parental socioeconomic status, and ethnicity.[38]

Participants were recruited prospectively by the Canadian Motherisk Program, which does research and provides counseling on reproductive risks and the effects of drugs, chemicals, and maternal disease during pregnancy. Scientists compared sixty-four children between the ages of three and nine.

Women in the test group reported contact with one or more of seventy-eight different petrosolvents from between one and forty hours each week for anywhere between the eighth and fortieth week of their pregnancies. The jobs held by the study subjects ranged across the employment spectrum. In total, seventeen different occupations were identified among the participants, including painter, photo lab worker, science teacher, lab technician, embalmer, and hair stylist. The women also said that during their work with these hazardous chemicals they took protective measures, such as wearing masks and gloves.

In spite of these precautions, however, their contact with solvents appears to have had effects on the developing brains of their unborn children that were measurable years later.

The study indicated that as levels of solvent exposure increased, children scored lower in language and motor ability. "Significantly more exposed children were rated as having mild or severe problem behaviors. The findings suggest that maternal occupational exposure to organic solvents during pregnancy is associated with poorer outcome in selective aspects of cognitive and neuromotor functioning in offspring."

But we can make up for these kinds of toxic exposures later in life, right?

A few years later, when the children were older, they were reexamined. Once again, researchers found that *in-utero* contact with petroleum solvents (which become VOCs in homes) harm mental abilities later in life. This time, children of mothers who were exposed to organic solvents tended to score lower on tests designed to measure language skills, attention, and memory.[39]

According to researchers, children born to the solvent-exposed group of women scored lower in tests measuring short-term auditory memory, general verbal information, and attention. Even when their tests scores were within normal ranges, exposed children demonstrated a reduced ability to recall sentences. The scientists also noted increased hyperactivity among members of the exposed group.

"In-utero exposure to organic solvents is associated with poorer performance on some specific subtle measures of neurocognitive function, language, and behavior," they concluded. "Reducing exposure in pregnancy is merited until more refined risk assessment is possible."

The study's authors classified both the tested and observed differences between the two groups of children as "subtle," and noted that their research did not attempt to determine how much exposure and what specific solvents caused which kinds of impairment. Instead, they said that the project was notable for being the first to establish a cause-and-effect relationship between solvents and brain damage in fetuses and that the results indicated an urgent need for further study.

"How can we, as one of the most advanced countries in the

world, allow these [Esolvents] to enter households with small children, without the appropriate testing to see whether they're safe?" said Dr. Gideon Koren, a pediatrician at the Hospital for Sick Children in Toronto, and one of the coauthors.

Koren says young children are especially vulnerable. Everything goes in their mouths, and they virtually live on the floor. And young kids are more sensitive because they are still developing the basic body systems. The brain, internal organs, and respiratory and immune systems are not fully developed until adolescence. As the researchers study the babies of women who were exposed to chemical solvents in the workplace are studied, they are found to have vision problems.

"Vision is one of the functions of the human brain, so it means that these chemicals find themselves through the mum, through the umbilical cord, into the baby, into the developing brain, and damaging functions there, and the baby is born already with a problem," Koren said.

Bucky Bailey is a member of one of eight families living near the DuPont factory in Parkersburg, West Virginia, who are suing the company over the effects of perfluorooctanoic acid (PFOA), one of the chemicals used in Teflon petrochemical fluoropolymers. His mother, Sue Bailey, was a factory worker exposed to PFOA while pregnant. Mr. Bailey was born with only one nostril and other facial defects for which he has had thirty operations. He has recently married but does not intend to have children for fear they would inherit his condition. DuPont eventually agreed to pay $50 million in cash to the plaintiffs, plus $22 million in legal costs. The company also agreed to spend $10 million on special water treatment facilities to filter out PFOA. (In spite of these enormous payouts, DuPont says it officially does not accept liability and maintains PFOA does not pose any danger to the public.)

To some, I understand, Teflon is an all-American hero, an icon. In 1990, President George Bush presented the National Medal of Technology to DuPont for the company's pioneering role in the development and commercialization of man-made polymers over the last half century. The citation given the company by the president lists Teflon as one of these very special products.

There's one problem. The EPA is trying to figure out why the chemical is showing up everywhere from remote Minnesota lakes to polar bears in Alaska and albatrosses in the Pacific Ocean to more than 95 percent of Americans' blood samples and at even higher percentages among Koreans.[40] All right, a little Teflon is cool, I guess. It isn't hurting anyone, right? Well, we don't know. You see, besides trying to figure out how a so-called inert chemical got into all of our bodies, we now also know, the health implications could be significant.[41] In worker blood studies conducted by 3M Corporation between 1994 and 2000, scientists found excess total cholesterol levels among Teflon-exposed workers, and in 2001, 3M published self-incriminating research showing that workers exposed to Teflon for between five and ten years face a risk of dying of stroke fifteen times higher than nonexposed workers.[42,43,44] The EPA says DuPont further concealed its own 1981 research showing that its pregnant workers were passing the chemical to their unborn children. In addition, the company is alleged to have failed to report evidence that the chemical had contaminated the water supply for twelve thousand people.

The EPA says that the chemicals used in Teflon and related products could pose "a potential risk of developmental and other adverse effects" on human health.[45]

Save the world? My God, I've got to save me first. Relax. Everything is going to be okay. We can get you over this. The good news is there are ways to bring sanity back to your world—

and, believe it or not, it all starts in the home. I've done the hard work and researched which companies and products you can support with your shopping dollars, all the while being assured that you are contributing not only to your own well-being but also your family's and country's. In fact, the surprising news is that so many great products are available that enable you to direct your hard-earned dollars to companies whose values include greening their love of country.

Here's what we'll do: We'll make an inventory. We'll look at all the ways we can start to make your home nontoxic and carbon neutral. I guarantee you that all this effort will result in your own vastly improved health and greater peace of mind.

We'll go through every nook and cranny, all those drawers and cabinets in your home, garage, office—everywhere—and look at everything: cleaning products, soaps, kids' stuff, appliances, electronics, cars, and we'll do a greenhouse inventory. It's important, too. A typical family of three with two cars that flies off on an annual vacation might produce fifty tons of CO_2 a year in the United Kingdom, and even more in America.[46] About 10 percent of all petroleum and fossil fuels are used for the production of household products alone. Toss in the family car, and all of a sudden you find out more than half of all energy used in America starts at home.

Consider this part of your safe trip a guide to saving your life as well as greening your patriotism. You don't need a doctor to tell you that your health and well-being will improve dramatically when you start to think about what you are surrounding yourself with, what kinds of products you put in your home and that your children and you come in contact with, often without knowing. Your children will be more likely to grow up healthy and stay that way. And although you will add years of healthy living to your life, you can also be very proud of being a true patriot and know that your actions put you in a leadership role as you lead by example. It's a good feeling to know you've done your duty, and it's a good thing for your children to see you are being a leader.

I'll share with you how to buy everything carbon neutral. I mean, it's going to be a real-life shopping extravaganza! We'll talk about pricing and what is doable for different household budgets, and what isn't. When you do transform your home, your personal health will be markedly improved. You might even stop sneezing and your allergies will be reduced, among other health benefits.

Zero waste and carbon neutral will be the underpinning of a whole new approach to the meaning of personal health.

When consumers purchase nontoxic cosmetics and household cleaning products made from carbon-neutral resources such as herbs, hemp, or corn (instead of fossil raw materials), carbon transfer to the environment is reduced. Using agricultural crops and herbal ingredients as starting points instead of petrochemicals also leads to planting more renewable crops, which store carbon dioxide instead of releasing it to the environment. Since trees and all agricultural crops are carbon sinks, they capture and store carbon.

But more to the point for being a green patriot, an equally important factor is that when manufacturers start with plant-based raw materials for their products, they reduce the country's need for oil and natural gas. The net result is that making carbon-neutral purchases can have a truly beneficial effect on greenhouse emissions, as well as reducing the country's oil dependency.

On the other hand, most products still use petrochemical-based chemicals, and most of us are adding greenhouse gases to the environment. There is a big opportunity here to direct the market toward a sustainable future with our consumer dollars.

And, beyond cleaning products, of course, are our appliances and a whole host of miscellaneous products—from cooking utensils to shaving razors—that we can purchase to make our lives healthier and simpler while doing something good for your nation's independence from foreign oil sources. I'll tell you about all of these throughout the rest of *Safe Trip*.

So what can we do? How do we do it? How do we pick out safe products from the grocery store? How to tell what is carbon neutral?

Grinning and waiting for me at the 2005 Natural Products Expo at the Anaheim, California, Convention Center, Jeff Hollender sat at the booth of his company. Hollender, the chief executive officer of Seventh Generation, an amazing company that he founded in 1988, said the name is from the Iroquois, whose belief is that, "In our every deliberation, we must consider the impact of our decisions on the next seven generations."[47]

According to the company's Web site,

> There was a small environmental organization called Renew America which had an even smaller mail order catalog of energy conservation products. It was a good idea and a good catalog, but like many worthy endeavors, the money needed to help it grow and prosper just wasn't there. Rather than see it fade away, the people at Renew America asked some people they'd been working with in Burlington, Vermont, if they'd simply take the catalog and run with it, no strings attached.

Within months, Hollender's group had packed their new catalog with previously unheard-of things like energy-saving lightbulbs and devices, water conservation items, nontoxic cleaning products, and even bathroom tissue made from unbleached recycled paper. They also started selling their products to natural food stores and coops until one day in 1995 they realized they had two growing businesses but only enough time and energy for one. So they sold the catalog to a company in Boulder, Colorado, called Gaiam, which renamed it Harmony, and it is now part of Whole Foods. Seventh Generation has since been able to "devote all our blood, sweat, and tears to filling store shelves from coast to coast with household products that are safer for you and the environment."[48]

The author of several books, including *What Matters Most*, Hollender regularly displays his wares at the Natural Products Expo, which is the world's premiere display arena for healthy living. Quite apart from the many booths touting various vitamins, minerals, and other nutritional supplements, the expo also contains areas that focus your attention on organic and natural foods, lifestyle, and home. Hollender's Seventh Generation is leading the pack in the hunt for what market analysts call Lifestyles of Health and Sustainability (LOHAS), those 68 to 78 million or more youthful boomers and cultural creatives who are maturing into ecologically conscious, and long-lived, consumers.

The *New York Times* calls the $230 billion spent to support LOHAS consciousness "the biggest market you've never heard of."[49]

According to the *New York Times* article, "In its second annual study of the LOHAS market, conducted earlier this year, the Natural Marketing Institute, a research and consulting firm in Harleysville, Pa., estimated that 68 million Americans, about a third of the adult population, qualified as LOHAS consumers, the kind of people who take environmental and social issues into account when they make purchases. That was up from 30 percent a year earlier."

And the one place where the entire LOHAS market gathers

together at its most financially potent is within these enormous halls filled to the brim with everything natural and carbon neutral as well. Carbon neutral is good, Hollender began. "Reducing greenhouse emissions is one of the biggest things we can do around the home. People want to feel good about their lives and what they are spending their money on. Regardless of party affiliation, the boomers want to make sure the legacy they leave is one of environmental responsibility. There is a consciousness in this generation that wasn't there in as high a percent of their parent's generation."

Ken Dychtwald, a Fortune 100 consultant and bestselling author said, "As more and more of the products we interact with have been manipulated, and as more and more substances we consume seem to be tinkered with and possibly contaminated, perhaps even with good intentions, what you have is a growing segment of the population that is seeking products and services, even relationships, that to some extent are less tainted than so much of what we see in the aisles and on the racks of all our retail stores."[50]

"Seventh Generation is experiencing forty percent annual growth, roughly twice what the category is growing," Hollender told me. Why not? Isn't it about time? America needs this dose of carbon-neutral medicine, and it all starts with our shopping dollars.

"People buy Seventh Generation products because it makes them feel like they are doing something good for their family and their country," Hollender said.

"If you look at the consumers and try to understand the evolution of their healthy lifestyles, what you see is that things like exercise and eating organic food are some of the activities that they adopt early on," Hollender said. "We know that buying environmentally nontoxic household products is something that is a later stage of developing." Having children helps sway reluctant shoppers, he added. "All of a sudden indoor air quality becomes a much bigger priority," he said, especially health issues like asthma, allergies, and chemical sensitivities.

Although some of Seventh Generation's packaging is made with recycled materials, the major difference is in the products themselves. "Seventh Generation chooses to start with plant-based raw materials instead of petrochemicals," said Hollender. Some of the products might then require ethoxylation, so it would be misleading to say their products are free of petrochemicals. But one thing we know from testing their products is that Seventh Generation has gone to great lengths to ensure that its products are free of petrochemical contaminants like 1,4-dioxane.

Seventh Generation is a Green 100 member; its products are found in supermarkets and health food stores. And here's where you can really become an effective green patriot and where your actions, combined with others, makes a huge difference.

For example, according to the company's literature and (they claim) verified by independent analysis, if every U.S. household replaced their current petroleum solvent–based cleaner with just one bottle of their thirty-two-ounce citrus cleaner, we could save 286,000 gallons of oil, enough to heat and cool 16,400 U.S. homes for a year. Make it a habit, and even better things happen.

Just as the mainstream household cleaning market is dominated by a few large manufacturers such as SC Johnson, Clorox, and Unilever, only a few manufacturers dominate the natural marketplace as well.

Near Seventh Generation's booth, which was lined with nontoxic cleaning products, recycled paper products, and dioxin-free diapers, companies such as Ecover and Earth Friendly also had booths with similarly touted products.

If competition is the sign of a healthy marketplace, then the marketplace for natural cleaning products is quite healthy. Cogent Environmental Solutions makes Ecogent, an all-purpose cleaner, which is part of Canada's Environmental Choice program.[51] It is classified as a "cleaning product with a low potential for environmental illness and endocrine disruption." Today, their product is used at universities, hospitals, schools, and by contract cleaners.

Michael Rochon, the founder of Cogent, said, "I wanted to develop a sustainable cleaning technology that wouldn't hurt anyone. I didn't plan on going all natural but those were the components that actually worked." He now has a patent for household cleaning products. And a much better product, he adds, than Simple Green, which he claims could "appear to create an image of being a green product and a healthy product, but it contains propylene glycol, mono butyl ether (butyl cellosolve [like Windex]). A product like that you'd never get through certification in Canada."

The U.S. nationwide franchiser ServiceMaster Cleaning has begun its own healthy-building cleaning initiative based on their *Green Clean*, which Cogent makes for them. (I think you should be wary of ServiceMaster's alliance with Chem-Lawn, a company that I think uses some very dangerous chemicals, such as 2,4-D, which is linked with cancers among agricultural workers, on neighborhood lawns.)

Meanwhile, SC Johnson is trying to offset its petrochemical dependence. The company has come out with a line of Raid bug killers that uses plant chemicals from clove and other sources for their active ingredients, although it still contains some petroleum distillates. These are certainly probably safer than the usual home and garden products containing petrochemical pesticides.

Sun & Earth, of Norristown, Pennsylvania, experienced

"major gains in grocery distribution" in 2003, and Kroger recently ordered its product for 2,500 stores. Along with Safeway and Albertson's, Sun & Earth has now been brought in 7,500 new stores.[52] Sun & Earth has grown 30 percent, with sales just under 10 million, and is potentially able to increase by a factor of ten over the next few years. To make matters worse for its competitors, consumer reporter Paul Moriarty of KYW, the CBS affiliate in Philadelphia, compared Sun & Earth All Purpose Cleaner with Fantastik.[53] In an on-air independent demonstration, Moriarty showed that the all-natural Sun & Earth outcleaned Fantastik! with its petrochemical arsenal.

The market for green cleaning products is small and amounts to less than 1 percent of the total share of an $8 billion market, probably at around $50 million. That means growth will be exponential, say LOHAS experts.[54]

You can't always be perfect. I know I can't. But it isn't as difficult as it seems, either. There is so much that we can do, and any decisions we make that bring us closer to our ideals are the right choices. The good news is that good products are so widely available. For example, take your cosmetic products. Aubrey Hampton first mixed ground ginger, peppermint, and eucalyptus leaf into coconut oil in 1967, and today his body-care company, Aubrey Organics, is one of the great American success stories of our time because it so ably embodies green patriotism and the spread of the best of American values around the globe.

"My mother would pull up a camomile plant and say, 'From the flower heads to the roots, nature works together,'" he said.

Hampton earned a doctorate in chemistry and went to work for Fabergé in New York. When asked to develop an all-natural cosmetic line for the cosmetic and personal-care company (now part of Unilever), he did. "But the company added back tons of synthetics. I went to the owner and told him I wasn't happy. He gave me a check for thirty thousand dollars and told me to start my own natural cosmetic company, and then he fired me. It was the best thing that could have ever happened to me."

Today, Aubrey Organics is a carbon-neutral company that is producing organic cosmetics without toxic preservatives.

Indiana-born—Hoosier—son of an herbalist and organic farmer—how much more American could this green patriot be?

You can go to any health food store in America and find Aubrey's cosmetics and personal-care products. Visit www.aubrey-organics.com.

Aveda is another company that I've come to admire and that I think is on the right track. The company is strongly committed to reducing global greenhouse emissions by forgoing the use of petrochemicals in its products. It is also doing good deeds around the world. Take, for example, their use of natural colors. Aveda uses uruku to produce unique lip, cheek, and eye color that is free of synthetic dyes, fragrances, and petrochemicals.[55] The color is rich, resonant—and drawn from nature.

Today, Aveda partners with the Yawanawa tribe to grow the renewable resources organically—as a way to foster community, economic independence, and cultural survival.

All of the Aveda Uruku makeup products are packaged in clamshells made from 100 percent postconsumer recycled newsprint. Using recycled newspaper instead of virgin paper reduces air pollution by 73 percent, and uses 71 percent less energy and 61 percent less water, according to the company's Web site. Even their Uruku retail displays are made from reclaimed maple, sunk in North American rivers and lakes during the logging of the 1800s. Visit www.aveda.com.

In Middlebury, visit Vermont Soapworks' Discount Factory

Outlet and Soap Museum and buy certified organic petrochemical-free soaps. Their stated goal is to provide you—"the awake consumer—with affordable alternatives to the current petrochemical-based personal care products industry." Visit www.vtsoap.com.

Avalon Organics (www.avalonorganics.com), Dr. Hauschka (www.drhauschka.com), Lily Organics (www.lilyorganics.com), Eco Bella (www.ecobella.com), Logona (www.logona.com), MyChelle (www.mychelle.com), Paul Penders (www.paul penders.com), Terressentials (www.terressentials.com), and Weleda (www.weleda.com) all offer cosmetic products available in the United States, Europe, and Asia that are purest of the pure and that eschew phthalates and almost all other petrochemical-based ingredients. (Some are even part of our Green 100.)

Does My Product Contain Phthalates?

Some of the leading beauty manufactures use phthalates in their products—such as Pantene Pro V Healthy Hold and Aqua Net hair sprays, and Arrid and Degree deodorants. Many fragrances, including Poison by Christian Dior and Coty's Healing Garden, contain phthalates, as do Cover Girl, Sally Hansen, and Maybelline (L'Oréal) nail polishes, according to the www.nottoopretty.org Web site. Check to see if your favorite products contain phthalates using this chart from the organization:[56]

HAIRSPRAY
Contains Phthalates
Aqua Net Professional Hair Spray

Clairol Herbal Essences Non Aerosol Hair-spray

Jheri Redding Finishers Flexible Hold Hairspray

Pantene Pro V Strong Hold Spray

Pantene Pro V Stronghold Healthy Hold Spray

Rave 4x Mega

Redken Cat Finishing Spritz

Salon Selectives Hold Tight Style Freeze Maximum Hold Finishing Spray

Sebastian Collection Shaper Plus

Suave Maximum Hold Hairspray Unscented, non-aerosol

Suave Naturals Extra Flexible Hold Non Aerosol Hairspray Freesia

TRESemme European Freeze-Hold Hair Spray

VO5 Crystal Clear 14 Hour Hold

Vidal Sassoon Microfine Mist Hair Spray, Aerosol

HAIRSPRAY
Phthalate Free
Aussie Mega Styling Spray

Helene Curtis Finesse Touchables Silk Protein Enriched

Helene Curtis Thermasilk Heat Activated Firm Hairspray

Suave Naturals Aloe Vera Extra Hold Hairspray

DEODORANTS
Contains Phthalates
Arrid Extra Extra Dry Maximum Strength Solid

Arrid Extra Extra Dry Ultra Clear Ultra Clean Spray

Arrid Extra Extra Dry Ultra Clear Ultra Fresh Spray

Ban Delicate Powder Roll On

Degree Original Solid Anti-Perspirant & Deodorant

Dove Solid Anti-Perspirant Deodorant

Secret Sheer Dry Regular

Secret Powder Fresh Aerosol

Sure Clear Dry Anti-Perspirant & Deodorant

DEODORANTS
Phthalate Free
Certain Dri Anti-Perspirant Roll-On

Dove Powder Anti-Perspirant Deodorant

Lady Speed Stick Soft Solid Anti-Perspirant

Secret Anti-Perspirant & Deodorant Platinum Protection Ambition Scent

Soft & Dri Anti-Perspirant Deodorant Clear Gel

FRAGRANCES
Contains Phthalates
Calgon Hawaiian Ginger Body Mist
Calgon Turquoise Seas Body Lotion
Charlie Cologne Spray
Escape by Calvin Klein
Eternity by Calvin Klein
Fire & Ice Cologne Spray
Freedom
Jovan White Musk
Lancôme Paris Trésor
Liz Claiborne Eau de Toilette Spray
Oscar
Parfums de Coeur White Tahitian Ginger Fantasy
Poison by Christian Dior
Red Door
The Healing Garden Pure Joy Body Treatment
White Diamonds Elizabeth Taylor
Wind Song Extraordinary Cologne by
    Prince Matchabelli

HAIR GEL
Contains Phthalates
Clairol Herbal Essences Natural Volume
    Body Boosting Gel
Dep Level 4 Shine Gel
LA Looks Styling Gel: Extra Super Hold
Suave Naturals Ocean Breeze Extra Control
    Spray Gel
TRESemme European Slick Melting Gel
Pantene Pro V Spray Gel Volumizing Root
    Lifter

FRAGRANCES
Phthalate Free
All of the fragrances tested
    contained phthalates.

HAIR GEL
Phthalate Free
Physique Extra Control
    Structuring Gel

HAIR MOUSSE
Contains Phthalates
Aussie Megahold Mousse

Clairol Herbal Essences Styling Mousse
Maximum Hold

Helene Curtis Salon Selectives Rise Up
Volumizing Mousse

Pantene Pro V Mousse Body Builder

HAIR MOUSSE
Phthalate Free
Finesse Touchables Silk Protein
Enriched Mousse

Helene Curtis Thermasilk
Heat Activated Mousse for
Fine/Thin Hair

L'Oréal Paris Studio Line:
Springing Curls Mousse

NAIL POLISH
Contains Phthalates
Avon beComing Radiant Long Last Nail
Gloss

Cover Girl NailSlicks

Maybelline Express Finish Fast-Dry Nail
Enamel

Maybelline Ultimate Wear Nail Enamel

Naturistics Super Shine Nail Gloss

Olay Nail Laquer

OPI Nail Laquer

Orly Salon Nails French Manicure

Orly Salon Nails Nail Color

Sally Hansen Chrome Nail Makeup

Sally Hansen Hard as Nails Nail Polish

Sally Hansen Hard as Nails With Nylon
Nail Polish

Sally Hansen Teflon Tuff Nail Color

Tropez Nail Enamel

Wet N Wild Crystalic Calcium Enriched
Nail Color

Wet N Wild Nail Color

NAIL POLISH
Phthalate Free
Kiss Colors Nail Polish

L'Oréal Jet Set Nail Enamel

L'Oréal Jet-Set Quick Dry Nail
Enamel

Maybelline Shades of Your Nail
Color

Naturistics 90 Second Dry!
Super Fast Nail Color

Revlon Nail Enamel

Revlon Super Top Speed

Urban Decay

HAND AND BODY LOTION **Contains Phthalates**	HAND AND BODY LOTION **Phthalate Free**

Jergens Skincare Original Scent
    Lotion
Nivea Crème
	Curel Soothing Hands Moistur-
	    izing Hand Lotion
	Eucerin Dry Skin Therapy Orig-
	    inal Moisturizing Lotion
	Lubriderm Skin Therapy Moistur-
	    izing Lotion
	Neutrogena Hand Cream
	Suave Naturals Sun Ripened Mois-
	    turizing Body Lotion
	Vaseline Intensive Care Advanced
	    Healing
	Vaseline Intensive Care Dry Skin
	    Lotion

Here are some more tips for staying away from cosmetics and personal-care products with petroleum-based ingredients:

Read labels. Very often what you see on the label can quickly tell you whether the product you are purchasing is good for you and good for reducing greenhouse gas emissions. For example, a label that lists preservatives such as any of the parabens (methyl, ethyl, butyl, or propyl), quaternium-15 (one of the leading causes of allergic reactions in cosmetics) or other quaternium-based compounds, diazolidinyl urea, imidazolidinyl urea, methylchloroisothiazolone, or isochlorothiaziline should signal to you that this is a product heavy on the petrochemicals and toxins you want to avoid.

Any product that contains mineral oil, petrolatum, propylene glycol, PEG compounds, or synthetic fragrances relies on petrochemicals. Get out of the dinosaur age now.

Avoid products containing ethoxylated alcohols (which often are contaminated with 1,4-dioxane). These include ingredients with the prefix, word, or syllable *PEG, Polyethylene, Polyethylene Glycol, Polyoxyethylene, eth* (as in sodium laur*eth* sulfate), or *oxynol*. Both polysorbate-60 and polysorbate-80 may also be contaminated with 1,4-dioxane.

Any products that contain cocamide DEA, lauramide DEA, cocamide MEA, triethanolamine (TEA), or diethanolamine (DEA) should also be avoided. As I mentioned, cocamide DEA, lauramide DEA, and cocamide MEA could be cancer causing, based on results of experimental studies. In addition, I reported in *The Safe Shopper's Bible* that TEA and DEA can cause the formation of cancer-causing nitrosamines in cosmetic products.

Urge companies to pledge to make safer products. Cosmetic companies should not use chemicals linked to cancer, birth defects, and other health harms in their products. Send a letter to your favorite company, and urge them to join a growing list of more than 150 other cosmetics companies that have signed the Compact for Safe Cosmetics. The Campaign for Safe Cosmetics is using the Compact to commit cosmetics companies to phasing out toxic chemicals and making cleaner, greener, healthier products for all of us. They could use your help. Here's a letter you can send:

Dear [insert company name],

Your cosmetic and personal-care products continue to use petrochemicals and are contributing to our nation's dependency on oil. In addition, some of the chemicals in your products are unsafe. I urge you to eliminate all petroleum-based chemicals from your products. Also, please visit www.safe-cosmetics.org and be one of more than 150 cosmetic companies now to sign off on their Compact for Safe Cosmetics. This pledge commits you to phase out chemicals linked to cancer, birth defects, and other health problems in your products and to replace them with safer alternatives. Our nation's health is at stake and I believe it is your patriotic duty.

Warm regards,

[sign name]

Business can get in the act, too. At Freedom Press, we are making big changes. We have begun to stock carbon-neutral cleaning products from Seventh Generation, Ecover, and Earth Friendly.

Most of our staff now are using cosmetics from Aubrey Organics, MyChelle, and Lily Organics. Our babies and children use safe shampoos from Aubrey especially. These products work truly beneficially for health and beauty and help us feel good about what we are doing as individuals who care deeply about America and who are striving to be green patriots.

I found Ecover dish soap at Mr. Moon's, the local Topanga general store.

So it's easy to go to your local store to purchase products that clean well without contributing to global warming or, even more personally, without increasing levels of toxic solvents in your blood, the tissues of your children, or some poor factory workers' bloodstream, or in the children of people living near such plants.

For many of us, being involved means being political, but how often is it that we can do patriotic things that also make us feel, look, and act better?

FIVE
Plant a Tree

FLYING INTO SAN JOSÉ, COSTA Rica, and going through customs I was suffering from all sorts of ailments, including stiffness, exhaustion, and feeling dulled, thanks to a few drinks. It had been a long day of flying from Los Angeles and changing planes at Dallas/Ft. Worth International Airport, which, like the geography of Texas, was hugely oversized—especially in my current condition.

Three days earlier I had injured my ankle playing one-on-one in a half-court pickup game at the gym in Calabasas.

It was a bad sprain, one of the worst I'd ever suffered, and my ankle was as swollen and hot as sizzling pork sausage on a grill on a hot Fourth of July. I wanted to forget everything. At DFW, I was moving in and out of the crowd with a bum ankle, hefting, lugging, and half dragging my luggage, and it wasn't any fun. I don't like using painkillers because of their side effects, but I had really needed something to quell the pain, so before I left home, I gave in and took a naproxen. I guess with the drink, too, the pill put me in an altered state, and I was someplace halfway between despair and hope. No doubt the fact that I was on my way to Costa Rica helped.

I had heard amazing things about Costa Rica but needed to

see for myself how a nation once thought of as the quintessential banana republic had redeemed itself when it finally put a value on the sometimes hidden services we obtain from nature.

I was contending with my throbbing ankle and feeling down. I thought of myself as on the brink of psychic near extinction and nullification and that nothing good could happen. I guessed all throughout the life trip, I'd been one of those desperate seekers of inspiration of the successful comeback. Costa Rica was nothing, if not the ecological comeback kid of Planet Earth.

"Where are you going?"

A DFW skyhop picked me up in his electric cart.

I boarded my flight, and we landed a few drinks later. I walked out of the terminal into the warm humid air. I saw Europeans, especially Germans, everywhere, more Europeans and Asians than Americans. I realized that everybody and their brother were coming from around the world to Costa Rica for their trip to Eden. Here, Eden was being restored and you could play it out for real. I was glad to be there. The country, too, felt peaceful. We haven't known peace in so long in America, I could feel the relaxed atmosphere of a peaceful country. I didn't even see any military because they don't have one.

Outside the terminal, brightly colored ecotourism buses and their guides awaited the new arrivals. I hailed a cab and rode to the Costa Rica Marriott, which was about twenty minutes away, in San Antonio de Belén.

It was late at night, and we traveled an empty, roughly surfaced asphalt road to the Marriott. The drive up to the front of the hotel was wide and ran alongside a coffee plantation.

The Costa Rica Marriott was a big, beautifully designed open-air hotel. I entered on one of the top levels, gave my bags and tip to the bell captain, and walked to the edge of the balcony. The dining area below was filled with people in casual attire. I heard some voices and turned around to see Herb Lewis, tanned, fit, and blond shaggy-hair, the man who was legendary in the $20 billion natural products industry. Next to him was Brian Hall, former U.S. Army reservist whose face looked like the kind of guy who might have chewed gum and played baseball or perhaps slap shot puck. I also knew him to be one of the very best national sales managers in the natural products industry, obviously a Cleveland Indians fan; the crooked ball cap set on the side of his buzz cut was quintessentially American. They both greeted me with big bear hugs and we were off, walking down to meet the rest of the crew in the bar. I began to forget my painful ankle. I was a happy guy.

Both Lewis and Hall had already been to the place where we were going, and they were very excited to tell me all about what they had planned. I was excited, too.

I am a publisher in the natural products field. I want to tell you something important: In America, with its permissive regulatory scheme, consumers should always be wary of fakes and hype—people or companies whose research consists of photocopiers and who put almost all of their money into pushing their products in advertisements, citing bogus medical studies for miracle weight loss, disappearing stretch marks, and cellulite that just seems to evaporate like magic. Their advertisements make promises no product could ever fulfill. As a publisher in the field, I wondered about some of the so-called degrees and titles these fakers hold. I've known quite a few well-intentioned frauds whose diplomas and doctoral degrees are from phony degree mills. The industry is riddled with rumors about who has real knowledge and who is faking it. It's terrible. I hate it. It's small. I've met the real thing, too: companies, good solid business people, scientists, and doctors who are involved in all aspects of the natural products field, particularly the use of natural nutrients and plant substances. These are highly successful entrepreneurs who forge new markets for their new concepts.

New Chapter, headed by longtime friends Paul Schulick and Tom Newmark, is one of the industry leaders—and all because it has discovered a natural medicine, a rain forest treasure, that might well be a viable alternative to Celebrex, Vioxx, and the other cyclooxygenase-2-inhibiting drugs.

The pharmaceutical COX-2 drugs from mega pharmaceutical corporations Pfizer and Merck once were hyped (just like any dietary supplement) for their wondrous ability to knock out the COX-2 enzyme cascade that causes inflammation and leads to many disorders, including arthritis, heart disease, and cancer. The trouble is that for users, it is like playing Russian roulette. Vioxx and other COX-2-inhibiting drugs have been alleged in articles in *The New England Journal of Medicine* and other mainstream medical journals to increase a user's risk of a heart attack.[1] The use of these drugs is now being widely curtailed. Merck pulled Vioxx from the market, and the company faces billions of dollars of liability in lawsuits from patients alleging that the drug injured them.

"To Tom Newmark and Paul Schulick, the real goal for consumers ought to be to derive the benefits of the COX-2 drugs without their drawbacks," Herb Lewis told me.

The real inflammation cure, one found to be both safe and effective, said Lewis and Hall, is in nature.

Our reporters at *Healthy Living* discovered New Chapter in 2003, and we began reporting on the company. The company's calling card was a rain forest formula called Zyflamend, available at health food stores. Hall had insisted early on that we send our reporters or, better yet, that I should come myself to visit Luna Nueva, the company's roughly two-hundred acre organic turmeric and ginger farm in Costa Rica, where several of the herbs in the formula were being grown.

Although Lewis and Hall were not medical experts and were clearly going to be perceived as biased since they worked for New Chapter, other medical experts had been impressed by the formula. Aaron Katz, MD, director of the Center for Holistic Urology at the Columbia-Presbyterian Medical Center, professor of medicine, and a skilled urological surgeon, did much of the early test tube and clinical research on Zyflamend. It was only after Katz had performed his own research, saw some of the amazing results, and was sure that the formula contained no harmful ingredients or contaminants that he began to recommend its use to possibly prevent prostate cancer among his patients. He even wrote in our publication that it appeared that Zyflamend's combination of rain forest herbs was preventing prostate cells in the so-called cancer zone from becoming malignant, and now he had the cell studies and biopsies that were providing clear-cut evidence. Roberta Lee, MD, director of The Continuum Center for Health & Healing at Beth Israel Hospital in Manhattan, told our reporters that the New Chapter rain forest formula might well outperform the pharmaceutical industry's so-called wonder drugs when it comes to helping people live pain- and arthritis-free lives, as well as protecting women from breast cancer, not to mention reducing the risk of Alzheimer's and heart disease. So impressed were we with her findings that we eventually published her lengthy report on one of the herbs in the January 2006 issue of our own publication.

And this was just the beginning. Andrew Weil, MD, the Harvard-trained physician, practioner of natural and complementary medicine, director of the integrative medical program at Arizona State University, and the bestselling author of several books, including *Spontaneous Healing*, had also spoken and written favorably about New Chapter, as well as Zyflamend itself, in his newsletter; he even mentioned the product on *Larry King Live*.

Since more men are afflicted with prostate cancer than women are with breast cancer, and we already know that breast cancer is a big concern for women (and the small number of men who are also afflicted with the disease), what was happening in Costa Rica could be a big deal—that is, if what New Chapter's executives claimed was true.

"How are you doing, my friend?" said Lewis. "Well, we have a lot to see."

"And a lot to show you. This is your first trip," Hall said. "I can tell you from my own experience the first time here you always miss more than you see. Just do your best to capture whatever your little eye might spy."

"I think my little eye might spy more than I know what to do with," I laughed.

As I sat at the hotel bar with Lewis and Hall, I met the rest of my traveling party, which included several of the Midwest's most successful natural health retailers. Dan Chapman and Ken El-Talabani of Sunrise Health Foods in Lansing, Illinois, were my old friends. Chad Beyer of Healthy Horizons in Green Bay, Wisconsin, became a new friend, as did Scott Pace of Whole Health Natural Foods in Springfield, Missouri. I could tell that it was going to be a fun, eclectic group of travelers. Costa Rica seemed to offer a sense of so much possibility. I'd heard of its vibrant democracy and its nonmilitary ways. I'd heard so much about its rainforest. I wondered if it, too, was the real thing.

For the last hundred and fifty years, Costa Rica has suffered from deforestation. By the late 1980s, the problem was really dramatic. Costa Rica, Latin America's oldest and longest-running democracy, was in trouble, with one of the highest rates of deforestation in the world. It was a catastrophe in the making. The combination of international debts at high interest rates, rising unemployment, and national economic depression brought on by stifling international profiteering as one of America's preeminent banana republics led the Costa Rican government to embark on a campaign of rapid deforestation, for cheap timber and to raise cattle, as a means of raising foreign currency. It was a road to oblivion. Costa Rica's climate was not conducive to raising cattle, and the country was destroying its real assets for short-term gains to pay off the stifling international debt.

Most everybody in the world just thought of Costa Rica as one huge forest, and the economy of the country was based on chopping down that forest, bananas, and cattle ranching. It was the terrible colonial model whereby a country's resources are extracted for the benefit of the mother. All that the world wanted and cared about was coffee and bananas.

At the same time, clearing forests was also a major consequence of the economic growth of the agricultural coffee and banana plantations.

That was during the time when the plantations were basically part of the agricultural business sector. In the 1950s and 1960s, cattle ranching for the big U.S. fast-food companies began, and the government policy was to fully colonize the country, meaning going deep into the rain forests and chopping them down and slashing and burning the debris, turning forests into grass land for agricultural activities, and allowing the ranchers to take ownership of the land. But even in the 1960s, scientists were telling the government that the land was not conducive to cattle ranching and that this was not a sustainable practice. By the 1980s, that prophecy had been proven correct. Cattle ranching was no longer profitable; other countries, like Brazil, in their own race to decimate, had entered the cheap beef market that American fast food had spawned and were easily going to outburn everybody else.

Something began to happen in the 1980s, however, thanks to people with whom I spoke, like Carlos Manuel Rodriguez, the Costa Rican surfer who had logged time at Surf Rider Beach in Malibu. The forty-five-year-old environmental lawyer and activist was not only the founder of the Ecology Federation, the organization that unites all of the nation's activists, and vice president for five years in the 1980s, but he was also appointed in 2002 to be the nation's minister of the environment.

"Costa Rica is living, breathing proof that a country can heal itself with green consciousness," he said.

We started talking earnestly about how Costa Rica had transformed itself from a nation on the brink. The key, he said, was to vault over all political barriers and to put into place as national policy the recognition of the value of nature to the country's wealth. In other words, the brilliance of Rodriguez and his cohorts has been to recognize that nature does perform valuable services in and of itself; they've been instrumental in changing the whole financial definition of national wealth for Costa Rica. Gone are the days when Costa Rica relied on bananas and cattle.

"Starting in 1969, we began trying to change the vision of our country to one of sustainability and a restorative economy," Rodriguez said. "We did so not as a party platform but as a national policy. Because this is a national policy, changes in administrations do not affect our commitment. It isn't like you in America with your Republicans and Democrats so that we never know what environmental policy America will carry out from one administration to the next. Our consistent and unwavering commitment to valuing the many services a healthy environment performs has been enormously successful. With this new policy in mind and its execution, the forests have quickly reverted back to canopy." This shows that you can recapture Eden. "When we started our land had only twenty percent canopy remaining. Today in 2005, I am pleased to say it is fifty-three percent forest canopy. That is because we have determined that Nature has a monetary value that the economic and financial models of most nations don't value. In Costa Rica, we realized before almost anybody else, that a healthy environment has financial value and it can earn its keep, so to speak. Today, as we are restoring our forests and limiting destruction by aiming for sustainability, our economy is thriving."

People today in Costa Rica make a living out of positive forest-related activities that aid in the health of the environment *and* economy—and that is what is unique about the nation. Tourism rivals bananas as the country's number one industry and will probably surpass agriculture, Rodriguez told me.

Because the country's leaders have put into place those values that recognize the value of a free-flowing river to, say, produce power, provide drinking water, and reduce erosion, power producers and others now pay landholders and the government for maintaining the natural integrity of the nation's wild waterways. At the same time, selected wood harvesting enables small-time entrepreneurial businesses to flourish and support the local economy. Another value is how the rain forest allows for the cultivation of herbs, like those found in the New Chapter Zyflamend formula.

"By the 1990s, we had developed a concept of the environmental services program," Rodriguez said.

We developed a market-based system of forest conservation; we pay for environmental services being given to us by the forests. We have found that old growth rain forest produces about thirty-two environmental services per acre, ranging from water purity to power to biodiversity to healthy soil and landscape to select[ed] sustainable wood harvesting, and much more. There were so many environmental services for the forests nobody was paying for. Today, of course, with the Kyoto Protocol, our ideas are global and a new market for carbon credits has assigned additional value to our rain forests as polluting offsets.

Costa Rica is by no means perfect, but what a comeback this country is making. I hope that President Oscar Arias Sánchez will resist free trade with America and insist on fair trade with good intentions for both nations. Costa Rica is where I came up with the title of this book. It is a land Tom Newmark fell in love with, Brian Hall fell in love with, I fell in love with, and Herb Lewis and Peter Schulick. Everybody who loves the Earth ought to visit this Eden.

Indeed, according to the World Bank, the benefits to the nation have been enormous.[2] Costa Rica, having set aside at least one-quarter of all its land for preservation, is now one of the most stable and robust democracies in Latin America, with a long-standing commitment to economic growth and social development. The combination of steady economic growth and sustained investment in human development has also led to a substantial reduction in poverty, which fell from 31.9 percent in 1991 to 18.5 percent in 2003, while extreme poverty decreased from 11.7 percent to 5.1 percent in the same period. So there are many benefits that accrue to nations that think green.

Costa Rica was a brightly burning light of sanity in a world we often think has gone environmentally insane. It wasn't perfect and the nation was still battling to maintain its biodiversity. But after learning more about the Costa Rican experiment, I felt that if Costa Rica could transform itself as it had done and was continuing to do, many other nations could as well. At least, I hoped so. I knew that the fires of rainforest destruction across the globe were burning far too brightly for me to be lured into blissful heaven.

In the morning, we climbed into an overcrowded VW bus that quickly made us feel hot and sweaty. We soon left the city behind. The road turned up thickly forested mountain slopes, and we began climbing. I settled in for the drive, drinking water and juices. It was stiflingly hot, and we were crowded together like animals. At one point, we stopped at a tourist shop for more juice and water, and I bought several cotton T-shirts for the children. It was getting hotter and steamier. Lewis told me that Newmark and Schulick "believe that nature has value and that, if approached with wisdom, there is potential for profits not only for today but in the long run, that wealth can be sustained for generations to come."

We passed through towns including San Ramon, with its tiny shops and vibrant main street. What do we have to learn from this tiny Central American nation? Many beautiful rivers flow through this land. At almost every bend in the road, I saw another wild flowing river, not like the concrete channels we have in L.A. I could almost think my consciousness was changing.

"Most people have never seen a free river like this one," Lewis said as if he knew what I had been thinking. "How do you think that affects the developing child. Not to have a concept of a natural river? To see only concrete like you have in Los Angeles?"

"Quit picking on L.A.," I said.

"It deserves it."

"We can certainly learn from Cleveland," Hall said, judiciously, coming over. "We have some tremendous greenbelts."

"Now there's a town for you," said El-Talabani, of Sunrise Health Foods. "But I like where we are in Illinois."

We were climbing higher. It was hotter and hotter in the van. The rain was falling, and we were all crowded together. And I was chasing some supposedly miracle herbal formula. Lewis was talking about his latest soul-to-soul sales experience.

"You know, recently, a very high-level executive from a large natural supermarket chain took me into one of their markets," Lewis said. "He showed me all of this wonderful organic food and even the growing number of natural cosmetics that are being made with organic herbs and without chemical additives, and their natural and organic meats and seafood and produce. He turned to me and said, 'Then, when I get to the vitamin section, all of this completely disappears.' What he meant was, the vitamins and minerals being sold today are largely synthetic. Once our vitamin and mineral supplements were fashioned from whole foods such as cereal grasses, and they were packed with organic whole food goodness. But in the last fifty years, many of the most popular vitamin and mineral formulas are derived from almost wholly synthetically created nutrients more likely to have been fashioned from petrochemical starter materials and inorganic minerals in a laboratory than harvested from the Earth." On the other hand, he said, New Chapter takes its wisdom from Nature. Instead of providing synthetic beta-carotene, its nutritional supplements, for example, utilize carotenoid-rich sources such as marigold that are then potentiated with the use of beneficial bacteria; In addition, New Chapter was the first nutrition company to receive government certification for its all organic herbal formulas. Thus, New Chapter helps the business patrons to fulfill its mission by offering nutritional formulas that truly embody the concept that nature trumps the laboratory.

We passed through a small town and ate lunch. I ordered *huevos rancheros*, which were nothing like what I expected and had different seasonings and spices than what I was used to from Mexican and Guatemalan restaurants. I did not eat them. I sat in the restaurant and drank a beer and watched a soccer game on television and felt the cool moist wind from the power of the pouring waterfall emptying the sky. In the bathroom, a single light hung down, and a spider crawled up the wall. I felt fine. People here were okay. I did not feel any paranoia, like in the past when I was in Guatemala in the 1980s and I never knew if rebels were going to stop our bus, hold us at gunpoint and demand a war tax, delay, kidnap, or kill us. I did not even see any police.

From high atop a bridge, I took pictures of the river below.

I bought some gum and went back to the cattle car. I looked out at the moistened leaves and trees of the forest surrounding the tiny town. Lewis put his hand on my shoulder and said, "A cure for every disease could be here. Arthritis, cancer, heart disease, and even diabetes—the cure is here."

But was this for real? I hoped so. There were studies coming from prestigious hospitals and institutions like Columbia University and M. D. Anderson Cancer Center. I knew that when we reached Luna Nueva, I'd be introduced to the science of these rain forest herbs and the Zyflamend formula, and I hoped it lived up to my expectations. I told everybody about my ankle. "Here, take some," Hall said, handing me three black, rich-smelling Zyflamend capsules. "This should help."

We moved deeper into the land now, and we were passing through jungle. Occasionally, I followed the contour of long cables down the mountain slopes. These were for the much touted gondola rides that were as much a part of the Costa Rican tourism business as the para-sailing boats of Alcapulco, Mexico. I noticed stately, oversized brick and stucco homes with massive lawns that stood out on the tops of the ridges like taxidermied deer. They did not seem to fit and were probably homes for the foreigners who had decided to come to Costa Rica to retire in earthly Eden.

The road changed from asphalt to dirt. With all the rain, the road was barely passable. We rocked and rolled our way down miles of jolting road. Our bodies slammed against the metal suspension seats, kidneys against bones.

The land was thickly forested. When we reached Luna Nueva, forest and farm blended completely.

Next I saw the giant conference center and lodgings being constructed from native woods that I later learned were also sustainably harvested.

We were all excited and tired as we stumbled out of the bus and assembled in the open-air eating and meeting area. Immediately, Pace, the storeowner from Missouri, said he loved the hardwood lounge chair and offered to buy several.

"It just so happens that you can," said the farm manager, Steven Farrell. "In fact, the wood comes from sustainably harvested forests and is part of one of our local businesses."

I ate a small, crooked organic banana. On the way upstairs to my room, I noticed the praying mantises and other insects, so large and beautiful and green. I took a picture of an enormous praying mantis on the side of the wall outside my room that I knew my oldest son would love. It was a lovely room, and I had a deeply invigorating rest. When I awoke in the morning my ankle still throbbed, but at least it was bearable. I showered using certified organic soap and shampoo that had been produced in Costa Rica. I realized then that the whole country was going organic. I went down to the eating area. My ankle continued to throb. I spied some bright orange turmeric roots in a bowl, cut them up, and began chewing on them. Folks were eating oatmeal and waking up with organic coffee. The turmeric was reedy and woody. I realized it was for this reason that in nations where it is widely consumed, turmeric was often fermented with beneficial bacteria that would help to liberate its healing constituents. Nonetheless, I tried to eat some and hoped it would help forestall some terrible malady. My ankle was really killing me. Now it was time for the tour, and we assembled a short distance from the open air meeting area.

Steven Farrell, the Luna Nueva farm manager, told me he began farming organically twenty-five years ago in California. His passion for organic farming spurred him to cofound the National Association of Organic Growers in Costa Rica. The more than two hundred acres of fields are not exactly as we might think of farm fields, if our only point of reference were the big farms of the San Joaquin Valley of California. Instead of geometric rows of monoculture crops, the fields are being farmed with an emphasis on permaculture so that forest and farm blend into one and nothing is lost.

Here, the farm was part of the terrain and rolled over hills, and vanilla, cacao, and sarsaparilla vines commingled on the trunks of big trees. In addition, the local people who worked there were well paid. Says Newmark, "Our workers are in fact well paid with outstanding employee benefits: medical insurance, a pension, three weeks paid vacation, a bonus equal to a month's wages, and the ability to grow food on our farm for the benefit of their families. It's a sustainable farm not just for the land, but for all species, including human." It was a good, stable situation, the kind that promoted a healthy planet, in terms of both the natural environment and the people themselves and their freedom. No wonder Costa Rica was the most democratic of all the Central American countries. Its rain forest was also in the best shape.

Ginger and turmeric mingled with wild gotu kola, a valuable circulatory-health herb growing amid smooth pebbles and small boulders. Everywhere along fallen logs and branches was mycelium, provider of powerful immune-modulating beta-glucan sugars that protect against diseases like cancer and even prolong the survival of cancer patients (and were widely used as cancer drugs in Japan, whose average lifespan is years longer than that in the United States). These lush natural areas also provided habitat for the abundant wildlife, including the highly specialized anteaters that help protect the ginger from its natural enemies. Each field was bordered by herbs, including thousands of echinacea plants, turmeric, and green tea plants to enhance soil conservation. Many of these herbs were also going to be harvested for use with New Chapter formulas. Spreading out over the hillsides were the broad leaves of the turmeric plants, exploding into white flowers with potent anti-inflammatory compounds. Walking in the rain forest, my ankle felt better. The rain fell hard and furious.

"The farm is meant to sustain the forest because the forest is our farm," said Farrell as we tramped in and out of lush vegetation.[4]

Don't think that what is going on here is simply a feel-good story for effete greenies. The potential benefits and profits from this rain forest remedy could be enormous. As I learned once we were back at the open-air meeting place, turmeric, ginger, and holy basil (tulsi) are powerful inhibitors of the COX-2 enzyme, but they don't seem to have any of the side effects of Vioxx or Celebrex.

Turmeric has been consumed as a spice for thousands of years, with a proven history of safe use. These herbs' powers could potentially help to solve a major health dilemma now confronting tens of millions of people with arthritis and other inflammatory conditions who have relied on synthetic medications like Vioxx, Celebrex, and even aspirin or ibuprofen to ease their inflammation and arthritis pain.

Like Zyflamend, these prescription drugs inhibit inflammatory enzymes in the human body called cyclooxygenase II (hence they are known as COX-2 inhibitors), but these drugs are almost too good. When COX-2 enzymes are completely knocked out by drugs, the result is less arthritis pain, but also increased risk of thrombosis (blood clots) and heart disease. It turns out your body needs some of the COX-2 enzymes, but in just the right amount, and tinkering in the lab with these various molecules creates more molecular mayhem than healing, leading to a disruption of the fine balance in the human body. For this reason, drugs like Vioxx and Celebrex, big moneymakers for Merck and Pfizer, respectively, are now either off the market or come with big black warnings that should scare the daylights out of anybody with arthritis or other inflammatory conditions who intends to use them. Unfortunately, safer, less selective, older nonsteroidal anti-inflammatory drugs like aspirin and ibuprofen help with inflammation but cause stomach bleeding and ulcers, something that the new generation of selective COX-2 inhibiting drugs was thought not to cause.

On the other hand, herbs like turmeric and ginger safely modulate COX-2 but do so without delivering a knockout punch and therefore do not cause blood clumping or stomach problems.

Of course, I know about the widespread and often warranted public doubt and skepticism that surrounds anything natural and purported to be a "cure," especially a dietary supplement masquerading as a medical drug. The 1994 federal Dietary Supplement and Health Education Act specifically prohibits manufacturers and distributors of dietary supplements from making claims that the supplements cure disease. First parties who profit from the product's sales must adhere to strictly narrow structure-and-function claims allowed within the DSHEA framework. However, third parties like *The Doctors' Prescription for Healthy Living*, that is, publishing companies and other sources of information that do not profit from the sale of the product, are protected under the First Amendment and may make stronger claims. But these claims and reports should still be balanced and objective.

As a publisher entrusted with the public good, I expect our reporting to go beyond superficial hype (and there's a lot of that kind of marketing fertilizer spread throughout the dietary supplement industry by irresponsible manufacturers and publishers). That is why when our writers and medical experts make a product recommendation, it had better be for an outstanding degree of proven health benefit and be safe. Occasionally we've erred, as does anybody who works under deadlines, but our instincts were right on target when we began following the story of Zyflamend, the herbal rain forest product being sold at health food stores and natural food markets. Some of the most compelling research in prostate cancer prevention is being done right now on Zyflamend itself, and it offers the possibility of preventing this leading cause of death among men.

In 1999, Schulick and Newmark discovered that ginger, a key ingredient in Zyflamend, had twenty-two molecules that were effective in inhibiting COX-2, 5-lipoxygenase (5-LO), another family of toxic enzymes that are detected at high levels, prostate cancer cells, and 5-hydroxyeicosatetraenoic acid (5-HETE), also found in high levels in malignant cells.[5] These three bad guys in men's reproductive systems work like a criminal gang to foul up healthy prostate function.

From that point on, says Newmark, "Paul and I both got the inspiration to find more herbs that could exert a soothing, taming effect on 5-LO, COX-2, and the inflammatory pathways in general."

However, before you start to think a simple pill can do the trick, you need to know that you make things worse by consuming foods made with highly processed and rancid vegetable oils and prepared foods that are rich sources of inflammation-causing arachidonic acid. The COX-2 enzymes in your body convert the arachidonic acid we take in from our poor diets to inflammation-causing prostaglandins. With excessive arachidonic acid, the body also produces 5-HETE, which is the fuel for prostate cancer cells.[6] In fact, 5-HETE is absolutely essential for the survival of prostate cancer cells. Inhibit production of 5-HETE, and you can literally starve the tumor. Also, according to a 2001 report in *Cancer Metastasis Review*, substances that inhibit 5-LO "cause tumor cell apoptosis, reduce tumor cell motility and invasiveness, or decrease tumor angiogenesis and growth."[7] So one smart thing for men and women alike would be to modify their diets to include low-inflammation foods such as wild salmon, organic vegetables and fruits, and the elimination of fried, greasy foods.

In other words, by moderating the COX-2 and 5-LO inflammatory cascade, we can do everything possible to stop cancer cells in their tracks. We cause these formerly immortal cells to enter into orderly programmed cell death, prevent the development of a nourishing network of blood vessels to feed the tumor, and inhibit the ability of cancer cells to disseminate throughout the body.[8,9,10]

Although Newmark and Schulick are clearly mavericks in the eyes of the staid pharmaceutical industry, their work is nonetheless brilliant and based on a solid foundation. Some one-quarter of the medicines available today owe their existence to plants. Seventy percent of the plants identified by the National Cancer Institute as useful in cancer treatment are found only in the rain forest. If you know a child who has survived leukemia, you might want to consider it likely that periwinkle, a rain forest herb, played a role. Rauwolfia is a natural plant medicine from India and was the first high blood pressure drug; it is widely known today as the medication Reserpine. The natural female hormone drug progesterone that offers women the chance for hormone balance is derived from diosgenin, a steroidal chemical found in wild yam, a dietary staple of New Guinea's rain forest natives. Less than 1 percent of tropical forest species have been thoroughly examined for their chemical compounds. A typical four square-mile patch of rain forest contains as many as fifteen hundred species of flowering plants. No doubt, your cure or mine is there, waiting. However, because these natural medicines are not readily patentable, pharmaceutical companies try to tweak the natural molecules to create a novel synthetic molecule that can then be patented as something novel and unique. Often these molecules cause as much cell mischief as the help they offer.

Having found ginger to be a COX-2 inhibitor, Schulick, a master herbalist with twenty-five years of experience, scoured all the available medical databases, including the National Library of Medicine and the U.S. Department of Agriculture, for premiere herbal candidates to combat inflammation generated by cancer. He discovered that holy basil (*Ocimum sanctum*) contains ursolic acid, a known inhibitor of COX-2; turmeric root, traditionally used in Indian foods, has been shown to inhibit COX-2, according to studies at University of California at San Diego and Seoul National University[11,12]; oregano, the herb that gives pasta sauces their aromatic odor, was a source of as many as thirty-one anti-inflammatory compounds; and rosemary has been known since 1992 by researchers from Libya, Sweden, France, and the United States to have COX-2 inhibiting properties as well.

The amount of dollars spent on scientific research that is

going into Zyflamend is not nearly the equivalent of what drug manufacturers have put into Vioxx or Celebrex. Their research dollars total hundreds of millions of dollars or billions when combined (although likely to be a far lower cost than Merck's future litigation payouts).

The few million spent on researching Zyflamend is minuscule compared with these amounts. For the dietary supplement industry, however, that amount represents an enormous investment.

Because the funds are relatively small by institutional and pharmaceutical standards, Newmark and Schulick have chosen to carefully allocate their dollars to highly focused outcome-oriented studies. Much of the research has focused on prostate (and, to a lesser extent, breast) cancer. You certainly can't fault their choice of institutions where research is being funded: Columbia-Presbyterian Medical Center and M. D. Anderson Cancer Center are tops in the nation.

What we do know is that prostate cancer begins with very small changes in the size and shape of the prostate gland cells. These changed cells then proliferate throughout the prostate. The condition is known as prostatic intraepithelial neoplasia or PIN, and it is definitely a prickly situation. However, unlike clear-cut cases of cancer, PIN alone has no apparent influence on serum prostate-specific antigen (PSA) concentration, which is measured to help gauge the severity of a cancer. Indeed, no laboratory studies, other than a tissue biopsy, can diagnose PIN. Imaging studies such as ultrasound have not proven useful either. That's because PIN isn't cancer yet. But it could well be; it's like letting a four-year-old child play with a book of matches and expecting no one to be burned. PIN has been identified as a precursor lesion to prostate cancer, says Aaron Katz, MD. This is why physicians like Katz specialize in tissue biopsies and then study them for PIN changes; once this information is obtained, he can then put his patients on a special program to prevent PIN from burgeoning into full-blown cancer. Here are the key facts about PIN Dr. Katz details in his new *Dr. Katz's Guide to Prostate Health*:[13]

- In the United States, the frequency of PIN in prostates with cancer is significantly higher than in prostates without cancer.
- PIN coexists with cancer in more than 85 percent of cases.
- Autopsy studies also demonstrate that development of high-grade PIN predates the development of clinically detectable cancer by five to ten years, consistent with the concept that high-grade PIN is a premalignant lesion.
- In a series of 249 autopsy cases, 77 percent of prostates with high-grade PIN harbored invasive adenocarcinoma, compared with only 24 percent without high-grade PIN.
- An autopsy study of European men found an association between high-grade PIN and carcinoma in the majority of cases.

For more than five years, Katz, a board-certified urologist and skilled surgeon who received his medical training at New York Medical College, has been the director of the Center for Holistic Urology at New York's Columbia-Presbyterian Medical Center. He first began learning about herbal remedies when he was doing early work at the Atkins Clinic in Manhattan, where he came in weekly "to help men with their plumbing."

"The patients there began telling me about herbs they found really helped, such as saw palmetto berry and pygeum," he said. "I also received a fellowship at Columbia to study urinary tract cancer. The use of certain herbs could help to control these cancers, I learned from patients. So I kept an open mind. This was new stuff without much scientific documentation, but when I looked more deeply, I found that a literature had developed in Europe, particularly Germany, starting in the 1960s that clearly documented herbal medicine's benefits for men's prostate health."

One of the first test tube studies on the product, titled "Zyflamend, an Herbal COX-2 Inhibitor with *In Vitro* Anti-Prostate Cancer Activity," was presented at the December 13, 2002, meeting of the Society of Urologic Oncology at the National Institutes of Health in Bethesda, Maryland. (This meeting was cosponsored by the National Cancer Institute.) The formula suppressed the growth of prostate cancer cells and caused many more to commit apoptosis, or cellular suicide. Apoptosis, in this case, is a good thing, since it is immortality and uncontrolled multiplication that characterizes cancer cells.

According to Katz, "Zyflamend's [combined] effects were found to be significantly more potent than a compound in the spice turmeric called curcumin, which is believed by many researchers to be one of the most promising molecules for the prevention and treatment of cancer." In fact, Zyflamend was found to be almost equivalent in its COX-2 inhibiting activity to the pharmaceutical selective COX-2 inhibiting drug NS-398.

"This study on Zyflamend is exceptionally promising," he stated. "This is the first known natural blend of botanicals that is showing COX-2 inhibitory activity."

In 2004, Columbia-Presbyterian's human research committee approved clinical trials to determine whether the herbal product derived from the rain forest tame PIN cells and reverse the precancerous condition so often found among men.

The ongoing study began in 2005 and is tracking some one hundred men given Zyflamend for three years, assessing disease status every six months via biopsy.

The first results have been extremely heartening, and most of the biopsies show that Zyflamend, through its rebalancing of COX-2 and other enzyme families, is reversing PIN cells and causing them to revert to normal, said Katz, although he cautions that only the full tally of all the cases, which will then be published, can be considered definitive.

Katz has been at the forefront of the development of a molecular technique to stage prostate cancer through a simple blood test. The technique, RT-PCR, has gained international recognition. He has also pioneered the use of cryotherapy for treating prostate cancer. Today, he sees more than one thousand patients a year in his Manhattan practice and makes herbal and dietary regimens a mainstay of patient care.

If Katz's results show a benefit, New Chapter is sitting on one of the biggest blockbuster medicines—synthetic or natural—today, one that not only eases the pain of arthritis but could prevent prostate cancer in millions of men throughout the world. In addition, new, unpublished research from Dr. Robert Newman at M. D. Anderson Cancer Center in Texas shows that these same rain forest herbs are also adept at inhibiting women's breast cancer cells. Once again, when the research is finally published, the benefits to humanity could be tremendous.

To me, the story of this rain forest herbal preparation is an important story for a country that I would characterize as "hyper inflammation nation" and a welcome antidote to the doom and gloom that has taken over the Vioxx and Celebrex stories, especially now that thousands of patients have begun suing Merck, the manufacturer of Vioxx, in state and federal courts over alleged links to heart attacks and other cardiovascular maladies.

That the Zyflamend product is derived from herbs grown in Costa Rica, many of which were initially discovered in the rain forests, should make us all take a hard look at how important a role the rain forest plays in our own personal lives. And while I can't say there aren't times when a powerful anti-inflammatory is needed for acute pain situations, like the immediate aftermath of my own ankle sprain, for the types of subclinical inflammation from which most Americans suffer, a product like Zyflamend could be bigger than aspirin.

The wonder is that something went right in Costa Rica and is continuing to go right. For the next several days I learned about many other rain forest herbs and visited other areas of the nation, including the remarkable resort of Tabacón. Costa Rica is a revelation. But to put more Costa Rica experiences on the map will take a lot of work and knowledge. You have to put your values to work.

Headquartered in Atlanta, BlueLinx is the largest building products distributor in the industry, with more than 11,700 customers, including building material dealers, industrial manufacturers, modular and manufactured housing producers, and home improvement retailers.[14] BlueLinx offers more than ten thousand forest products used in residential and commercial construction, manufacturing, manufactured housing, repair and remodeling, and home improvement do-it-yourself projects. Among its stated values are to "demonstrate respect" and "be ethical."[15] Also, its stated mission is to be "masters of the supply chain for those products we choose to distribute."[16] Chances are many of you purchase BlueLinx products and do not give the purchase a second thought.

An investigation in 2005 by Greenpeace and RAN (Rainforest Action Network) tie JP Morgan Chase and BlueLinx, America's largest building products distributor, to illegal logging of endangered forests.[17]

According to the RAN-Greenpeace investigation, BlueLinx has been "smuggling legally disputed, undocumented timber out of Indonesia's critically endangered rainforests [*sic*] and flooding the U.S. marketplace with artificially cheap lauan plywood."

In contrast to the actions of BlueLinx, other wood products companies have issued a voluntary corporate embargo of Indonesian forest products. These responsible actors include Centex Corporation, International Paper, and Lanoga Corporation.[18] (Both Centex and International Paper are Green 100 members.)

A case study published by DirtyMoney.org details the alleged trafficking of undocumented wood by current BlueLinx suppliers in Indonesia.[19] On a January 21, 2005, conference call, Barbara Tinsley, general counsel to BlueLinx, indicated that her client had no intention of changing its Indonesian purchasing policies. (Tinsley, a former assistant U.S. attorney with the Department of Justice for five years, was awarded some $1,546,247 in compensation from BlueLinx for 2004.)[20, 21]

"The issue here is that BlueLinx is relying on their suppliers to represent the legal origin of wood products in a country where even the government admits that at least seventy percent of logging is illegal," Brant Olson, director of the RAN Old Growth Campaign, told me in an e-mail. "We're pressing the company to provide independent and verifiable evidence of the legal origin of the wood products that they buy. So far, we have seen no such evidence."[22]

BlueLinx's suppliers cite certificates widely distributed on the Indonesian black market, RAN alleged.

In more correspondence from RAN, I was given information about the BlueLinx supplier Kayu Lapis Indonesia, which "is one of the largest plywood mills in the world. According to an annual document submitted by the company to the Indonesian Department of Forestry, half the timber procured by the company in 2001, or 299,368 out of 594,901 cubic meters, originated from sources that were either legally disputed or unknown."

JP Morgan Chase has also been condemned by RAN. "JP Morgan Chase has built its financial empire by making investments of mass destruction like BlueLinx," said Ilyse Hogue, director of the RAN Global Finance Campaign. "Illegal logging in Indonesia is both an environmental and humanitarian crisis. It is morally reprehensible that America's second largest bank is connected with corrupt timber cartels that are directly responsible for the wholesale destruction of the most fragile and endangered forest ecosystems on Earth. JP Morgan Chase's involvement in the illegal timber trade is not only a national scandal, but further proof that the company must put renewed effort into matching the environmental commitments of industry peers such as Citigroup and Bank of America."

In an e-mail to me, BlueLinx's Ashley E. Freer forwarded a message from Steven C. Hardin, the company's executive vice president. "At BlueLinx, we remain committed to sound environmental practices and sustainable forestry," he said.

We have been unwavering in our company's policies on the importation of tropical wood. To that end, we support the U.S. government in its efforts to promote legal timber harvesting worldwide. Our import operations are in full compliance with the Convention on International Trade in Endangered Species, to which the United States is a party. We are also committed to following the laws of the countries of origin for the tropical wood products we purchase, especially those laws that apply to the harvest, acquisition or export of these products. As a member of the International Wood Products Association (IWPA), BlueLinx supports IWPA's efforts to promote compliance, by all parties, with national, state and local laws and regulations pertaining to logging and forest management.

"These illegal loggers are like terrorists," said Nabiel Makarim, the former environment minister of Indonesia, referring to massive unlawful clear-cutting that has turned seasonal rains into deadly flash floods and landslides, displacing thousands, and creating a humanitarian crisis.[23] "It is difficult to combat illegal logging because we must face financial backers and their shameless protectors."

Makarim confessed to the *Jakarta Post* that the government "does not have a clue" how to combat rampant illegal logging. The ministry told the AFP news agency that illegal loggers have formed mafia-like international networks throughout Indonesia.

According to an October 27, 2003, *Business Week* editorial titled "Indonesia's Chainsaw Massacre," Indonesia's ravaged rain forests are "disappearing at a rate equivalent to the area of 300 soccer fields every hour, gobbled up by loggers eager to turn them into plywood and planks for McMansions across the U.S. and Europe."

"Certification standards in Indonesia are currently not possible . . . and will not become possible until substantial national and local legal, institutional and policy reforms take place," said a report from the Forest Stewardship Council.[24]

Don't be naïve enough to think this is just another environmental crisis without implications for those of us in the United States. What is happening in Indonesia is an international security crisis of major proportion, and we must recognize it as such. Strategies of rainforest destruction and profiteering like this can only worsen the poverty and hopelessness of people—and that, in turn, can lead to more terrorism.

According to a report prepared for the American Forest &

Paper Association, "Illegal logging is, in many respects, a symptom of corruption, graft, lax law enforcement, and poor social conditions. In fact, published measures of political and judicial corruption reveal a close correlation between corruption and illegal logging. . . . With almost 60% of its production suspect, Indonesia stands out as the country with both the highest rate of illegal activity and the most suspicious volume."[25]

In August 2005, Indonesian rain forests were burning so intensely that they smothered the neighboring Malaysia peninsula in a choking haze, threatening public health, and raising fears for its economy.[26] Malaysia sought crisis talks with its bigger neighbor as much of peninsular Malaysia, including the capital, had been shrouded in thick smog for a week, presenting the country with its worst pollution crisis since 1997, when smoke mainly from Indonesian forest fires blocked out skies across Southeast Asia. Asthma attacks soared, and tourists were holing up in their hotels or seeking refuge in air-conditioned shopping malls at one of the busiest times for the country's tourism industry. Talk about the right climate for world terrorism. My Lord, what do you want youths to do when their city is being choked off and they blame it on stupid, mindless American consumerism, buying cheap wood for what? Their McMansions? If profiteering continues and wages and earning power remain low, disillusioned youths are sure to turn to charismatic leaders like Osama bin Laden who offer hope, however false and misleading it might be, as a deadly way out of their despair. Good jobs with meaning and decent wages, the idea of hope—these are antidotes to terrorism, not more missiles and guns.

"Buyers and consumers must recognize and assume responsibility for how their actions contribute to this illegal logging crisis in Indonesia," said Lisa Curran, PhD, director of the Tropical Resources Institute at the Yale School of Forestry, which is an interdisciplinary, non–degree granting program located within the Yale School of Forestry and Environmental Studies.[27]

"We must lead by example by implementing independently verified chain-of-custody programs that document the sources of wood products and materials," she said. "Consumers have a right to stump-to-store tracking of wood products to be sure they are purchasing products that were not acquired illegally from protected areas and national parks."

There are lots of things we can do. Did you know that JP Morgan Chase issues over nine hundred different credit cards? One way we found at Freedom Press to get a little revenge on them for their irresponsible behavior is to cut up our corporate card and stop banking with them.

Visit www.jpmorganchase.com to find out if you are using one of their credit card brands, perhaps without even knowing it.[28] You might be surprised to find out your card is funding rain forest destruction. Try, instead, a card from Bank of America or Citigroup, two banks with exemplary environmental programs for protecting rain forests.

As for BlueLinx, the wood products industry is largely in agreement that most of the wood products coming from Indonesia are illegal. No matter what the company says, its actions reveal a potentially very troubling situation for an American corporation. If BlueLinx wanted to appear to be a wood products industry leader and not a predator, it would take a strong stand and severely curtail its importation of Indonesia wood products—much like Centex, IP, and The Home Depot have done. That would send a message to rain forest plunderers.

BlueLinx sells directly to building material dealers, home centers, distributors, manufacturers, and government agencies.

Do-it-yourselfers and building professionals also find their products at home centers, building material dealers, and lumberyards. If you see the BlueLinx label on your wood products, stay away from them. Instead, ask for wood that has been certified by the Forest Stewardship Council (FSC). You can easily find economically viable alternatives to BlueLinx's rain forest woods.

And you won't have to go farther than your local Home Depot, which is widely recognized as a very progressive purchaser of wood products whose stores offer environmentally conscious FSC–certified wood products that ensure forests—particularly rain forests—are logged in a manner that will promote their diversity and survival.

According to The Home Depot's own Web site, "We sell more FSC certified wood than any retailer in America and at the same time we have transitioned more vendors to FSC certified wood than any other retailer in America."[29]

Another feather in The Home Depot's environmental cap is that it has reduced purchases of Indonesian lauan (another form of meranti—high quality mahoganylike plywood—that is taken from the Indonesian and other equatorial rain forests) by more than 70 percent recently, according to its Web site.[30] "The minimal amount of lauan purchases that remain in Indonesia are strategically placed with vendors that are aggressively pursuing certification, and have been engaged in third-party audits."

It isn't so difficult to save a tree or to plant one. Many of us are certainly saving trees right now and not even knowing that we are doing so.

Many shoppers don't even know that when they shop for paper products at Office Depot and Staples, they are placing value on nature and forests. They probably think they are just buying reams of paper for their copiers and printers. But I have to tell you a little secret: these companies are going green, too. Not only is the recycled content of their papers increasing dramatically, each of these companies is increasingly able to track sourcing for their paper products, so that they are assured that they are protecting, instead of plundering, rain forests.

Office Depot recently canceled a major contract with Asia Pulp & Paper, which operates in Indonesia and has been accused of illegal logging, Scott Quaranda of the Dogwood Alliance, a southern U.S.-based forest protection group, said. "Office Depot and Staples have made great progress."

Just a few years ago, consumers would be hard pressed to find any recycled content office products. But in 2005, Office Depot published its Green Book, a catalog of environmentally preferable office products printed on chlorine-free 100 percent postconsumer waste recycled paper. The 2005 edition offered 85 percent more items than the 2004 Green Book. Today, the catalog contains about 2,500 environmentally preferable products.

In addition, Office Depot–brand recycled copy paper contains 35 percent postconsumer recycled content, which is higher than the standard required by the federal government. Staples offers a 30 percent postconsumer recycled content paper, also in line with federal government standards.[31]

The federal government defines environmentally preferable products as goods that have a reduced negative effect on human health and the environment when compared with competing products that serve the same purpose.[32] Environmentally preferable attributes include reduced toxicity, the use of recycled materials, and increased energy efficiency. The federal government is required by Executive Order to purchase recycled paper products. The U.S. General Services Administration made the decision to go one step further and purchase and sell only postconsumer recycled-content copier paper to federal agencies. Copier paper accounts for over 28 percent of all the paper purchased by the federal government, with approximately 10 million sheets being used every work hour.[33] (That's actually a little frightening, if you ask me.)

This federal program has spurred the development of recycled products by incorporating recycled content into huge government contracts and have made it easier for the rest of us to purchase postconsumer recycled-content paper.

In the case of copy paper, required recycled content has increased in the last few years from just 10 percent postconsumer content to a minimum of 30 percent. This is important.

Another key here is the difference between preconsumer and postconsumer recycled content. When manufacturers use recycled material in their product, they define it in two ways: preconsumer or postconsumer.

Preconsumer recycled content is basically manufacturing waste. For example, an envelope manufacturer might recycle the clippings left over when envelopes are cut from paper. These clippings could be made into other paper products instead of being thrown away.

Postconsumer content, on the other hand, is the material that was previously used by consumers: newspapers, magazines, office paper, packaging, paper cups, and paper plates. The efficient use of postconsumer paper waste closes the circle of recycling and also helps reduce our need for landfills, improving our community environment and health.

Among those products meeting federal standards are those from Office Depot and Staples, plus the following companies:

Aspen Xerographic™ (Boise Cascade)
Colorsource® (Unisource)
Encore 100 (New Leaf Paper) 100% PC, PCF
Envirographic® **100% PC** (Badger Paper Mills, Inc.) 100% PC, PCF

Envirographic® Bond/Offset (Badger Paper Mills, Inc.)
Eureka!™ 30% Recycled PC (Georgia-Pacific)
Eureka!™ 100% Recycled PC (Georgia-Pacific) 100 percent PC, PCF
Exact® Multipurpose Colors (Wausau Papers)
GeoCycle (Georgia-Pacific)
Great White® MultiUse 20 (International Paper)
HP Office Recycled™ (Hewlett Packard)
Multi-Purpose Recycled Paper (IBM)
New Life DP (Rolland, Inc.) 60 percent PC
Recycled Husky® Xerocopy DP (Weyerhaeuser)
Savings® DP (International Paper)
Willcopy® Recycled Paper (Willamette Industries, Inc.)
Windsor Copy Recycled (Domtar Papers, Inc.)

Note that PCF exceeds the federal requirement of 30 percent postconsumer recycled content; its claim is to be process chlorine free (PCF).

In an effort to encourage customers to recycle empty ink and toner cartridges (another smart carbon-neutral practice), Office Depot has provided a free (yes, that's right, folks, FREE) ream of EnviroCopy™ Recycled Copy Paper (500 sheets) for each ink or toner cartridge returned to their stores.

At Staples, all paper products contain at least 26.6 percent postconsumer recycled content. The company is identifying forest regions both in the United States and globally that are adversely impacted by its paper purchases and they are working with Dogwood Alliance, Forest Ethics, and the Natural Resources Defense Council to ensure that it purchases paper products only from sustainably harvested forests.

As a large paper purchaser, my company, Freedom Press, is increasingly seeking to improve its environmental record. When we directed our purchases of paper stock to a product manufactured by the Bowater Company, it was because our research revealed that Bowater was an environmentally reliable company, and by agreeing to guarantee our purchases over the long term, we also receive added discounts.

Bowater, based in Greenville, South Carolina, is one of the largest North American consumers of old newspapers and old magazines, recycling over 1.4 million metric tons in 2004.[34] So we know there is a lot of recycled content going into their paper products. The company partners with over six hundred different sources of recyclable paper in more than forty states and provinces and operates six state-of-the-art recycling facilities that rely on postconsumer recycled fiber to make paper. They offer a strong market case for environmentalism. They are saving trees, being a good corporate citizen, and the company is making money.

In fact, according to their own data, some 38 percent of their total annual newsprint production is from recovered fiber, exceeding the industry average of 30 percent. Bowater is also the largest North American consumer of old tires for tire-derived fuel. Of particular interest is that the Bowater mills at Catawba (as well as Calhoun), South Carolina, where much of our paper for *The Doctors' Prescription for Healthy Living* is manufactured, recycle around 1.6 million tires per year for energy, reducing their fuel consumption and our nation's dependence on foreign oil. The Catawba mill has also been officially recognized for being one of the cleanest in the world and is one of only four facilities to meet the EPA's Voluntary Advanced Technology Incentive program Tier 1 requirements. What all of this means, in plain talk, is that facilities like the Catawba mill have cut adsorbable organic halide emissions to less than half the minimum requirements of standard facilities.[35] Since these emissions are a marker for use of dangerous chlorinated fossil fuel hydrocarbons that can cause cancer, reproductive harm, and other maladies, lowering them is a good thing. The amount of toxic chlorinated fossil fuel hydrocarbons, found in pulp and paper effluent discharge, goes down remarkably when you are more efficient and produce less waste; it also leads to less dioxin and other troubling chlorine-based toxins in our fishing streams and in our own bodies. Not a bad thing.

On the other hand, Bowater also manages and buys timber from private landowners.[36] The company has a history of clear-cutting and then replanting and intensively managing thousands of acres of one-species pine plantations. In doing so, the company engages in herbicide and pesticide spraying.

Sometimes, twenty to thirty loads of chemical fertilizer pellets are dumped on one area by the dangerous, treetop-level flights, according to forest preservation advocates.

In the Cumberland Plateau area of Tennessee, residents became ill when a plane dumped its toxic chemical load on private homes, and people were standing in their yards. It all reminded me once again of the kids of Alpaugh and Earlimart.

Creeks and wildlife were also in the path of the aerial chemical pellets.

I don't like this, and I don't like supporting such business practices. Fortunately, Bowater acknowledged it could do things better when it responded to activist pressure organized by the Dogwood Alliance and Natural Resources Defense Council (NRDC). On June 29, 2005, Dogwood Alliance, NRDC, and Bowater announced the signing of an accord to increase protection for hundred of thousands of acres on the Cumberland Plateau and across the South that Bowater owned, managed, or purchased timber from. Highlighting the agreement is the fact that Bowater agreed to end the conversion of hardwood forests to less biologically diverse single-species pine plantations on its lands and said it will stop purchasing fiber from private landowners that convert their land into single-species pine plantations after 2007. Because Bowater is a major purchaser of privately owned timber, the company influences tremendously the buying habits of many other companies, as well as how private landowners manage their lands. "This is a major win for hundreds of communities throughout Tennessee and the South that have been living with the impacts of paper production for generations and have been calling for change," said Danna Smith, policy director for Dogwood Alliance. "We believe that other paper companies can and must follow Bowater's lead."

There are currently 32 million acres of pine plantations in the South comprising over 15 percent of the forests.

Look closely at where you buy your paper. It's easy to buy the right paper, and it usually won't cost much more. Here are some good companies:

- Potlatch (founded in 1903 in Potlatch, Idaho) harvests wood from over a million acres of forest land in Arkansas and Idaho that are certified to the rigorous standards of the Forest Stewardship Council.[37]
- Fraser Papers can now apply the FSC recycled logo to its 100 percent postconsumer paper products.[38] Fraser Papers operates nineteen paper machines at mills in Maine, New Hampshire, and Wisconsin in the United States, and in Quebec and New Brunswick in Canada.
- Visit www.greenerprinter.com. This sheet-fed printing company, based in Berkeley, California, now enables us to do *The Doctors' Prescription Healthy Living* reprints on 100 percent recycled New Leaf paper stock with soy-based inks at competitive prices. When our clients now purchase reprints from our magazine, they can further enhance their own corporate image by stating that their papers are completely recycled, use soy-based inks, and are printed in the good old United States of America—and we know from consumer surveys that more and

more consumers are looking for companies who are more than simply selling nutritional supplements and that they want companies that make them feel good about their purchases. In a very real way, we are adding brand value to and our clients. That's good business. Their client list includes ClifBar, Del Monte, the accounting firm of Ernst & Young, Hewlett-Packard, and The Breast Cancer Fund, to name just a few. All finished print jobs at GreenerPrinter are shipped Climate Cool, as certified by the Climate Neutral Network. This means that the climate emissions associated with shipping by truck or air-freight are certified by an Environmental Review Panel to achieve a net-zero impact on the earth's climate. (To learn more about shipping this way, visit www.climateneutral.com.) Also visit www.newleafpaper.com, a company that provides high-quality business papers.

- Airborne Express, DHL, FedEx, United Parcel Service, and the United States Postal Service have also introduced reusable packaging, higher postconsumer recycled content, and unbleached paper. Switching from using 100 percent virgin (nonrecycled) bleached paperboard envelopes to envelopes made from around 80 percent postconsumer recycled content (which FedEx, USPS and Airborne Express did) cuts greenhouse gas emissions by 39 percent, toxic effluent flow by 81 percent, and solid waste by 60 percent.

- FedEx Kinko's has taken action to dramatically reduce its ecological footprint by increasing the recycled content of the paper used behind the counter at more than eleven hundred U.S. FedEx Kinko's Office and Print Centers.[39] FedEx Kinko's introduced a new paper line in 2004. The new paper increased the overall annual postconsumer recycled content average to an estimated 26.2 percent, close to achieving the company's goal of 30 percent. (However, while this is a good first step, I think they can do a lot better.)

How about your checks? Check Gallery is one of America's leading environmentally friendly bank check printers. Their personal checks are printed with soy-based ink on recycled bond paper. They produce personal bank checks, address labels, contact cards, and checkbook covers featuring beautiful, wildlife-inspired designs. Visit www.checkgallery.com.

For the home, I visited a supermarket on Mulholland in Calabasas to buy paper towels. I compared products from Seventh Generation, Earth Friendly, Green Forest, and Bounty. According to www.quickerpickerupper.com, "Bounty paper towels are made from virgin wood pulp," usually spruce or pine.

I went to the Web site for Green Forest. "Green Forest is Paper Made From Paper. State of the art papermaking technology transforms office paper, magazines, and boxes into clean and sanitary Green Forest paper products."

Green Forest was 100 percent recycled content but only 10 percent postconsumer paper—well, that could be better.

I also researched Seventh Generation, which is the company that has the most transparency and what would appear to be the very best product. According to Seventh Generation, their products are 80 percent postconsumer recycled. By using Seventh Generation paper products, here is what they say we can do to help reduce our impact on global warming:[40]

- Replacing just one three-pack of white 70-sheet, two-ply paper towels with Seventh Generation paper products in all U.S. households would prevent the release of almost 63,000 tons of greenhouse gases.
- If every household chose just a single 500-pack of their one-ply napkins over their usual nonrecycled brand, we would save 120,930 tons.
- Doing the same with a 12-pack of 400-sheet, two-ply bathroom tissue would save 170,317 tons.

- According to Seventh Generation's Web site, "Altogether, from bathroom tissue to facial tissue, if everyone from coast to coast replaced their non-recycled paper products with the recycled equivalent version, the Earth would achieve a savings of 666,369 tons of greenhouse gases."

Starbucks, the coffee empire, has more than eight thousand stores worldwide. More than one-half of all the paper the company uses goes into hot-beverage cups. It doesn't take a brain surgeon to figure out that replacing even a small percentage of all that paper with postconsumer recycled fibers will save a lot of trees, and that saving intact forests anywhere has a positive effect on climate.

By the end of 2005, the company converted all its hot-beverage cups to 10 percent postconsumer recycled content. This was a small first step. Yet, just this one step in the right direction will save 5 million pounds of tree fiber annually. That won't save the world, but it is certainly a start.

So what took Starbucks so long? The FDA had concerns over the safety of food contact with postconsumer recycled papers in hot serving ware due to potential leaching problems of chemicals into edible portions, and government and private industry had to work together to alleviate such concerns.

In November 2004, when Starbucks announced FDA approval to make the first coffee cup from postconsumer recycled fibers, just getting that approval was clearing a big hurdle.

Yet, since food and beverage containers are a major part of today's trash, the old regulation significantly weakened the market for postconsumer recycled paper. According to *Non-Toxic Times*, "Without high-volume demand destinations like food and beverage container markets to support our recycling efforts, less demand is created for recycled paper, it's worth less, and not all the paper we're dutifully recycling can find a place to be reused. When that happens, our waste paper ends up in landfills despite our best efforts to reuse it. On the other hand, if our used paper could be made into new food containers, we'd make giant leaps and bounds toward more fully closing the recycling loop." [41]

Who would have thought that having a latte at Starbucks was an example of green patriotism? Meantime, what about your cereal? The Kellogg Company, of Battle Creek, Michigan, uses more than 2 billion Kellogg's packages a year that display the "100% Recycled Paperboard" symbol. [42] According to Tony the Tiger, that's "grrreat!"

General Mills has a strong commitment to recycled paperboard packaging, as well as offering organic cereals with its Cascadian Farm brand. [43]

Nature's Path, the British Columbia–based Canadian manufacturer of Nature's Path, EnviroKidz, and LifeStream foods and snacks, uses ecopackaging called EnviroBox for its cereal boxes. From Cascades Boxboard, Inc., it's made out of 100 percent recycled and recyclable clay-coated fiber, eliminating over seventy-five tons of paperboard per year compared with its original box. It saves over 700,000 gallons of clean water, and more than 500,000 kilowatt-hours of electrical power. It also reduces total packaging by 10 percent, which removes over three hundred tractor trailers and trucks from highways per year, since more cases can be packed per load.

Natural Collection from the Neil Kelly Company is another modern-day example of green patriotism. The Portland, Oregon, based cabinet company uses wheat straw, sustainable harvested FSC-certified wood, and petroleum-free particleboard. Their new Naturals Collection, which is drawing national interest, is made with double-sided, melamine-laminated wheat board, an industrial grade particleboard. Because it is made with wheat straw, wheat board is an annually renewable product and helps to reduce carbon dioxide emissions.

Cabinet interiors in standard maple plywood also come with FSC-certified CollinsWood particleboard and plywood.

Here's the irony: all this great kitchen cabinetry comes from a company whose president is a retired U.S. Army colonel, Rick Fields. Visit them at www.neilkelly.com.

Poliform, an Italian company, adheres to greenhouse reducing guidelines. Its Varenna cabinets are part of the suite featured on NBC's *The Apprentice*, which might or might not say something about the meaning of green beyond dollars in the world of Trump. (However, when we contacted Trumps Organization, they refused to discuss the issue with us.) Visit them at www.poliform.com.

How about something very cool: bamboo kitchen utensils ($5.75 for a set of six at www.greenfeet.com) are from a renewable resource. Bamboo is easily replanted, grows very quickly, and renews itself in a few years.

When you're exhausted and don't want to do the dishes, go to Wal-Mart to pick up some recycled paper plates from Chinet with 95 percent total recycled content (only 88 cents for a pack of fifteen, we hear).

Environmental Home Center (www.environmentalhome center.com) in Seattle is the "ultimate source for green building materials" with revenues that have grown 40 percent a year since 2001.

Carrefour, IKEA, and Lowe's are all creating business models that aim to support companies' wood products only from well-managed logging lands. Visit them at www.carrefour.com, www.ikea.com, and www.lowes.com.

Endura Wood Products offers a wide variety of certified and rediscovered woods and wood products for homes and business. Visit www.endurawood.com.

At Eco Friendly Flooring, their reclaimed Yellow Heart pine and Douglas fir flooring deserves consideration when you are looking for a truly distinctive and warm floor. These timbers are purchased from demolition companies and Wisconsin area farmers taking down their old barns. The huge beams used in construction in Wisconsin in the early 1900s are now being reclaimed for use in flooring. Visit www.ecofriendlyflooring.com.

Also visit www.ecotimber.com for FSC-certified floors.

Here are some more tools for performing inspirational acts of green patriotism:

- At eBay.com, search under "recycled" and you will find pages and pages of items, including wood flooring and colorful scarves hand knit with recycled silk.
- You can file your treasured pictures or CDs in boxes made from recycled newspaper for only $14.99 to 19.99 at www.containerstore.com.
- Find a stool made from renewable water hyacinth at Pier 1 for $78.
- Plant a memory tree. Fill your local park with a memory in honor of someone dear in your life. *Giving a tree* makes a marvelous, long-lasting gift for anyone. Plant a tree to honor the birth of a child or mark a sad occasion with something that completes the cycle of life. Visit www.give-a-tree.com, www.treepeople.org, or www.arborday.org.

The heart accounts for less than 1 percent of the weight of the human body, yet without a healthy heart the body cannot survive. Rain forests cover only around 2 percent of the Earth's surface and 6 percent of its landmass, but they store vast amounts of carbon dioxide. In a recent article in *Scientific American*, Stuart L. Pimm and Clinton Jenkins, conservation, ecology, and extinction investigators from the Nicholas School of the Environment and Earth Sciences at Duke University, wrote that the world's three remaining tropical forests and twenty-five "hot spots" harbor "most of the world's species of plants and animals."[44] Indeed, more than half the animal species in the world live in rain forests.[45] Only a single square mile of Amazon rain forest is home to up to fifteen hundred species of butterfly. In contrast, we have only 750 species in all of the United States and Canada.[46]

The Amazon, African Congo, and Indonesian rain forests are being destroyed at staggering rates. Almost half of Earth's original forest cover is gone, much destroyed within the past three decades, according to a 1997 World Resources Institute report.[47]

The Amazon has been described as the "lungs of our planet," because it provides the essential environmental world service of continuously recycling carbon dioxide into oxygen. More than 20 percent of the planet's oxygen supply is produced in the Amazon rain forest, according to The Nature Conservancy.[48,49] The Amazonian rain forest covers over a billion acres, encompassing areas in Brazil, Venezuela, Colombia, and the Eastern Andean region of Ecuador and Peru. If Amazonia were a country, it would be the world's ninth largest.

In an article in 2000 in *Nature*, Peter M. Cox of the Hadley Centre and coresearchers tell us, "About half of the current [greenhouse] emissions are being absorbed by the ocean and by land ecosystems."[50,51] By 2050, his team expects that if we continue to release carbon dioxide into the atmosphere at current and projected rates, the rain forests will be afflicted with drought. At that point, the vast amounts of carbon dioxide being stored in rain forests like the Amazon will be released. This could lead to global warming increases of 1.5 degrees C., which would cause tremendous climate change. "Of course, this could be accelerated, and may be 'short-circuited' by direct human deforestation," say the researchers in the *Nature* article.

Wangari Maathai wanted to create a sustainable supply of fuel wood for rural African women while halting soil erosion and other threatening forms of environmental degradation. Her Greenbelt campaign, which enlisted more than fifty thousand poor rural women to plant more than 30 million trees in Kenya and neighboring nations, eventually broadened its focus across the region, advocating broader provision of greater freedom, improved health care, and women's rights—which is why she won the 2004 Nobel Peace Prize.

Where is the trigger point that sends human life careering into the big black void? At what point of species loss on Earth do we render ourselves obsolete and give back what we've taken with so much unconsciousness? Are we sleepwalking into oblivion?

I don't think so. I think most of us are awake, and that a lot more people are awakening to the fact that we have only one planet. Once people awake, it's hard to go back to sleep. In every facet of their lives, people are hungry to meet the challenges. They just need the tools and the vision.

Each of us can plant a tree knowing we are individually and together creating the vision of the forests of tomorrow that will keep our planet healthy.

SIX
Be Kind to Animals

I GOT BACK on the carbon highway. If we're going to ensure our future, we have to ensure the future of the most vulnerable species around us. Did Americans have the foresight to recognize they need the wild salmon as much as the wild salmon need us? Or, how else can we respond to the global warming crisis?

I arrived November 1 at Seattle-Tacoma airport and began my roughly two-hour drive to Bellingham. It was raining hard, and I wondered how hard it would be raining tomorrow when I went fishing. Great. I hoped I could borrow some skins, since I hadn't brought my own.

I was on my way to Bellingham, Washington. On the battleground to win the war against global warming, the salmon of the San Juan Islands where I was headed were ground zero.

These were the waters of prime American wild salmon, and I was going to visit David Barlean, founder of Barlean's Fishery. Barlean was a reef netter. He was one of only eleven licensed reef netters still plying their nets in Washington State. He makes a fine living catching wild salmon, which is rare.

I learned about the Barlean's Fishery from my work as publisher of Freedom Press and our reporting on another aspect of the Barlean family's business operations. The family name, Barlean, is not only the name of the fishery but also Barlean's Organic Oils, the largest buyer of organic flaxseed in North America, the portion of the company that David's son Bruce began and runs.

With financial interests in wild salmon and organic flaxseed, you might say the Barleans are trading in two of the hottest foods in America today. More and more doctors recommend that essential fatty acids be part of everybody's diet, and salmon and flax remain two of nature's richest sources of the all-important omega-3 fatty acids. Indeed, experts say that we need both salmon and flax, since each supplies a slightly different member of the omega-3 fatty acid family, and each has its own unique health benefits.

By purchasing organic flaxseed on long-term contracts, Barlean's Organic Oils has played an important role in creating and growing the market for what had become an almost totally forgotten cereal grain: organic flaxseed, and that's an important story in and of itself.

The story that intrigued me and made me want to visit the Barlean family on their home territory in Whatcom County, Washington, was their legendary commercial reef netting operation, which yielded those fish that are richest in omega-3 fatty acids—the Chinook or king salmon. I have to admit I have always loved fishing, and I have fished both commercially and recreationally at one time or another. So I couldn't resist talking Barlean into taking me out reef netting with him.

Think about what everyone wants more of these days: excellent health.

The hottest topic in health today is inflammation. Good health depends on low levels of inflammation and flowing blood that doesn't clot abnormally, which could cause a heart attack, stroke, or dementia.

Besides the herbs such as turmeric in the rain forests of Costa Rica, another key to great health, say medical experts, is to consume optimal amounts of omega-3 fatty acids, which are found abundantly and healthfully in wild Pacific salmon and organic flaxseed.

Unfortunately, the American diet is high in omega-6 fatty acid intake. These devils that stimulate inflammatory cascades throughout the body are found in vegetable oils and prepared foods like potato chips. Being gluttons as so many people are, you can imagine then that a lot of us are on fire with high inflammation.

Our diets are so rich in prepared foods that they are thought to cause a whole host of health problems, including arthritis, Alzheimer's, cancer, and diabetes. One of the remedies is to change our diets and use more of what nature has given us: the omega-3 fatty acids.

Low risk for arthritis, cancer, and heart disease are all linked to high intake of these rare fatty acids. When Freedom Press brought out one of its books on omega-3 fatty acids, *The Omega-3 Miracle*, the authors reprinted a lengthy statement from the American Heart Association that strongly recommended eating foods, such as salmon and trout, with high omega-3 fatty acid levels twice a week.[1]

The Barlean family taps into the sea and the land for their purely natural yet uniquely different forms of omega-3 fatty acids. What's more, this is a story about a family that with reef nets and organic farming puts a value on nature and on the way we obtain our foods. Just like Costa Rica, this is another spiritual experience. In providing us with wild salmon that is reef netted, and flaxseed that is grown organically, the family certainly epitomizes what it is to be kind to animals and, along the way, has captured the market on two of the foods richest in a highly sought nutrient.

So, you say that we don't need wild salmon and that you like your salmon farmed? Farm-raised salmon contains higher levels of petroleum-derived organochlorines—such as polychlorinated biphenyls (PCBs), toxaphene, dieldrin, dioxins, and polybrominated diphenyl ethers (PBDEs)—than their wild counterparts, according to a study in the January 9, 2004, issue of the prestigious journal *Science*.[2,3]

"Having analyzed over 2 metric tons of farmed and wild salmon from around the world for organochlorine contaminants, we show that concentrations of these contaminants are significantly higher in farmed salmon than in wild," said the article. "European-raised salmon have significantly greater contaminant loads than those raised in North and South America. . . . Risk analysis indicates that consumption of farmed Atlantic salmon may pose health risks that detract from the beneficial effects of fish consumption."

In a 2005 study reported in *Environmental Health Perspectives*, several of the same researchers from the *Science* study added this further caveat: "Consumption of farmed salmon at relatively low frequencies results in elevated exposure to dioxins and dioxin-like compounds with commensurate elevation in estimates of health risk."[4]

Omega-3 fatty acids have been traditionally supplied in the diet by wild cold-water ocean fish (herring, cod, salmon, mackerel, sardines, anchovies, black cod, albacore tuna) whose original food source is at the bottom of the food chain in the form of phytoplankton, said an expert. "If the tissues of ocean deepwater fish did not contain such a large amount of omega-3 fatty acids, they would become stiff and would not survive in the very cold water," said Dr. Tom Saldeen, chairman of the Department of Forensic Medicine at the medical facility of Uppsala, Sweden, and one of the world's leading experts on the health benefits of fish oils.[5] "Omega-3 fatty acids also keep cells supple and flexible in humankind, helping to maintain joint suppleness and skin and blood vessel elasticity. Such supple, flexible cells are said to be signs of youth."

It was pitch-black when I checked into the Hampton Inn. I could barely see the mountains, and the San Juan Islands were beyond a few more hills before the coast. It was cold, and it rained intermittently. I didn't feel like going out to eat and just went to my room, looked at CNN, and fell asleep.

By the next morning the weather had cleared, and it was a perfect day without much wind for this area, and was as cold as a bitch. Barlean jumped out of his blue Dodge Ram 2500 Cummins Turbo Diesel. He stood six one. He wore blue jeans, work boots, a thin jacket, and a drab army-colored hat. His teeth were bright when he smiled, and his eyes were green, like the ones I'd seen once in a Tennessee walker. He wanted to show me his fish market and led me across from the original home he and his wife Barbara lived in to a tall red barn. In the corner was a sign that said it all: FISH MARKET HERE.

Forget Pike Place Market in Seattle. Barlean's, nearly two hours away, near Bellingham, is the most popular little fish market in Whatcom County and quite possibly in the Western United States, and anybody who goes there for fresh fish ends up buying their seafood from Barlean's the rest of their lives.

Barlean found that putting his fish in hands of consumers within hours after catching is a big draw. "In truth," he said, "fish labeled 'fresh' in food stores are already four or five days old. Consumers know the difference and are willing to pay for Barlean's freshness. Plus, they know about my secret freezing methods—and even our frozen fish is fresher than what passes for fresh. I know it's amazing, but only when you understand the secret of cold-water bacteria do you realize that one of the reasons frozen fish loses its fresh taste is due to the actions of cold-water bacteria, and the only way you stop these little critters is to freeze your fish at lower temperatures than anybody else."

Using what would be considered advanced telemarketing techniques for their time, Barlean and his wife Barbara set up a direct order concept. Consumers often committed to purchasing fish before they were caught.

Barlean's staff called the network when he was coming in with a catch. The lines of cars from their customers created noteworthy traffic jams on these otherwise empty rural roads. The locals would see the traffic jams and they would stop to find out what was happening, and pretty soon, Barlean was looking like a pretty savvy small-town businessman. But then in the 1970s and 1980s came some inopportune federal court rulings and international fishery treaties that provided the First Nations peoples with greater fishery rights, as well as limiting what Barlean could do. The government made things a lot tougher, he said. It was still profitable but it was during this time his son Bruce became interested in the omega-3 oils while working at a nutritional company, and they began investing in organic flaxseed, which was practically unheard of in America. Today, however, organic flaxseed is just as important as the fishery, if not more so, since flaxseed is far more abundant than wild Pacific salmon and results in a higher dollar volume. In addition, their flaxseed has won seven straight Vity Awards, the nutrition industry's version of the Emmys, for taste and purity from *Vitamin Health Retailer*, and the product is available throughout America's health food store networks in the refrigerator sections (think of flaxseed oil as a perishable food requiring refrigeration in order to maintain its freshness and rich omega-3 content).

Great health coming from nature aside, the flax side of the business and fishery employed many people for a small county like Whatcom. Clearly, this was an important business, important to the economic vitality of a region. This was also a carbon-neutral business of first-rate national importance.

The twelve-acre Barlean's farm in Ferndale bustles with activity. Trucks from Canada and the Dakotas pull up to deliver flaxseed; forklift drivers haul pressed flax meal into storage containers; fresh pressed, the flaxseed oil is bottled, labeled, and air shipped to health stores. The orders for Barlean's organic oils pour in from stores nationwide, and the always friendly support staff provides the excellent service for which the company is known.

"I aim to make everyone in the world healthy and strong with omega-3s. No laboratory or pharmaceutical company can supply what we do through our natural sources."

He pulled me aside. "I'll survive. I know how to make a living. But I'm concerned for the region that we're losing the fishery," he said. In modern times, the salmon's decline is attributed to industrial activities today alleged to be linked to global warming, including accelerated logging in the headwater areas of the Nooksack Basin, erecting small hydroelectric dams on salmon streams, ground and water pollution from industry and agriculture, decline of wetland and nursery areas, and the rapid development of lowland areas of the river.

As a result of such exploitation, the North Fork of the Nooksack River has dropped over eight feet in the past ten years; more than 60 percent of the salmon streams have been destroyed due to logging practices; and the critical portions of the South Fork of the Nooksack River average over 70 degrees F, which is a lethal temperature for salmon.

Indeed, it is this last factor, the rising temperature of the Nooksack, that might indicate the greatest threat to the salmon of Puget Sound.

As the temperature of the earth rises, the chilly streams and rivers that provide homes to salmon will grow increasingly warmer. With rising temperatures, salmon and trout are going to disappear.

According to a study by the NRDC and Defenders of Wildlife, global warming is likely to spur the disappearance of trout and salmon from as much as 18 to 38 percent of their current habitat by the year 2090. The study also found that habitat loss for individual species could be as high as 17 percent by 2030, 34 percent by 2060, and 42 percent by 2090 if emissions of heat-trapping pollution such as carbon dioxide are not reduced.[6]

Regardless of location, the disappearance of cold-water fish will come at a significant cost—to jobs, recreation, and regional culture. Each year roughly 10 million Americans spend an average of ten days angling for salmon and trout, and the estimated value of the combined fisheries ranges from $1.5 billion to $14 billion a year. Trout are also central to the culture of the Rocky and Appalachian mountains, while salmon are an integral part of the Northwest culture.

The first time Barlean went reef netting, he called the world-famous Pike Place Fish Market in Seattle and told the buyer he had some freshly netted kings in perfect condition and asked if he wanted them. "The buyer told me he could get the salmon for thirty cents less and hung up. I couldn't make a living at that price. I just put a sign out on the front yard and I began selling people on the concept that they could receive their fish direct from the fisherman.

"You see we don't make it look like a fish market at all," he said. "I told my daughter Cindy, who runs the fishery, that the best way to drive away business is to put in a refrigerated counter with all the fish laid out. That way, people will know they are five or six days old. When we started out early on, my brother comes in and tells me we have to open up a market in Lynden, a nearby Dutch-founded town; we'll sell the fish for twenty cents a pound less, he tells me. So we did that and the people came in and said they already had their favorite market. We weren't different. Our strength is that I am a fisherman. People want to feel like they are getting their fish direct from the fishermen. They want to see us filleting a wild-caught King and know that everything is direct from the fishermen themselves."

I looked around the fish house. Little Neck clams in the tank had just been brought in by native fishers. The Dungeness crabs in a tank were local. So was the halibut. All of the salmon—pink, chum, Sockeye and King—were caught by Barlean. The wild reef pink was $1.50 a pound, and the wild whole sockeye was $4.99 a pound. The smoked king was $8 a pound, and the smoked Coho was a dollar less.

At some point, I asked him about his military service. I asked because I saw his left hand; the little finger was almost completely gone and his ring finger was gone, and it just struck me that it might have happened in Korea or Vietnam.

"That was a childhood accident," he said. "I was chopping wood with my brother. I reached for one that had fallen from the stump and down came his ax. It was an accident. If I hadn't moved my hand quickly enough, I'd have lost everything."

It was time to go fishing. The tide was right, he said. We were lucky. The wind might have been blowing and it was bitter cold, but at least the rain was not falling. No clouds were present. It wasn't warm. But at least it wasn't wet, and that was my good thing for the day.

When he walked stiff-legged to his turquoise Dodge Ram, I remembered how someone told me he had a wooden leg—from a motorcycle accident. I looked in the back, and noticed there were no lifejackets.

I got in the cab and said howdy to big Jason, his deckhand, who was helping out this late in the season and who sat in the middle of the pickup truck. Jason was big and strapping and at around six-six was the size of an NBA small power forward. He looked like he could have come from one of the Columbia River tribes like the Umqua, if he were Indian, but he said he was not.

Barlean stopped at a service station, and Jason got out and bought some sunflower seeds and water. We ended up on a ferry, which we took to Lummi Island, one of the San Juan Islands. The Lummi tribe celebrate "schelangen" (pronounced *shlay-n-gun*), or way of life, as one intertwined with salmon. It's what I liked about this whole area, the connection to the Earth being so dominant. But their way of life was disappearing with the warming of the rivers around them. In the past decade, the Lummi fishing fleet had fallen from three dozen boats to fewer than six.[7]

According to an online information site devoted to Lummi culture, "For thousands of years, the Lummi and other tribes had fished using reef nets without adversely affecting the salmon runs. Ceremonies and legends related to salmon and salmon fishing, with names such as *The First Salmon Ceremony* and *The Tale of the Salmon Woman* have been passed down through generations and provided evidence of the sacred relationship between the Lummi history and culture and the salmon.[8] Beginning with the white man's arrival, however, the salmon population went into sharp decline."

"I started out working in Kodiak dragging for King and Dungeness crab," Barlean told me.

That's where we had our first children, Bruce and Cindy, and that was the kind of town where if you were not an alcoholic you would not do well. I come there after the big wave of 1964, and when they rebuilt it, they built one food store and one church and one of this and one of that and seven bars. All drinks were a dollar then. Did not matter what you ordered. All were a dollar. Those were the days when you could make a lot of money fishing in Alaska but my wife, Barbara, you know, she wasn't a drinker, and she had our oldest, Bruce, and now Cindy, and she didn't like being home alone, you know, five or six days at a time while I was out fishing and she was going to leave or we were going to have to go back down to Washington. So I took up with my cousin down here fishing for Dungeness crab and I have to tell you I think that boy spent every night figuring out how many things he could do wrong the next day because he had to be the worst crabber I ever seen. But he was breaking even. I figured if he could break even, I could do a whole lot better. So I went out and decided I was going to buy my own boat. I ended up buying one of these long flat canoes the Indians were using; that boat was not for crabbing; it was for reef netting. I'd done reef netting when I was fifteen or sixteen with my brother. I knew how to do it and I liked it and those were days when a reef netter could make a good living. So I began reef netting. I love it. I loved sport fishing, but this is so close to sport fishing I love it even more, and I've never felt the need to go sport fishing since I began reef netting in 1972.

We sat in the truck, Jason smoking, David talking. "I bought a set of canoe-style boats, and when they were so old, they leaked like a sieve. I got so tired of driving out there and changing the marine batteries that I looked at a different way of doing things. I came up with an idea of a catamaran-style boat on pontoons."

The ferry smacked up against the quay at Lummi Island. We drove our pickup truck onto Lummi Island, along Granger Highway to Legoe Bay. Now the wind blew hard against my shoulders, and I had a hard time standing while slipping on my rubber skins and boots. An oil tanker escorted by two tugs, a requirement ever since 9/11, steamed at sea through the narrow island corridors. The sky was clear right now, but it could change any moment.

The rain had been falling for weeks. This late in the season, most of the reef netters had pulled in their boats, and they were on the beach. Today, I suspected, he, Jason, and I were the only men in North America about to go reef net fishing in waters anywhere in North America. I jumped down off the seawall and walked up to the water. The beach was made up entirely of seashells, big balls of kelp, smooth stones, gravel, and not much sand. I heard crunching under my boots. I was glad I had on a set of skins.

The wind was blowing so hard it made me want to hide. The water rushed in against the shore in cold little mean waves.

I looked far out to sea and saw the little catamaran pontoons. Barlean jumped into the smallest dinghy I'd ever seen. It wasn't even five feet long. Instead of using oars, he used a long ocean branch he'd picked up off the beach and quickly made it out to his skiff. It was bobbing up and down hard. I pulled up my boots and stepped into the water. Jason slipped on his boots and smoked.

Fifteen minutes later Barlean was back in his skiff, and we stepped in and went out to sea. He turned around and we were going bam, bam, and bam.

I felt the spray hitting me, and my natural instinct was to stay dry as long as possible, so I put my back to the bow and looked at Barlean in the stern grinning. He held the stick of the Johnson outboard with one hand and pushed the boat along at about fifteen knots. We were headed out toward the maze of the green and forested and mountainous San Juan Islands. I knew all this jazz about warming waters was coming true, but the waters where I was were cold. Before us appeared two long pontoon rafts, bobbing hard. The waves slapped hard against the tires that lined the sides of the rafts. A buoy bell clanged farther away. I heard lines slapping against bridge towers and thought about my own time as a kid on the sea. We bumped up against the side of the first pontoon, and the water dumped into the skiff and Jason began bailing. I started singing "Sloop John-B," the jaunty folk song about a mythical drunk adventure in Nassau town. But at least there, around Nassau, the water was warm.

Reef netting is an art. It is celebration. It is kindness. The first peoples of the land practiced the art by stringing out a net between two canoes or, in this case, pontoons, in the path of migrating salmon. The nets created a funnel held in place by large stone anchors. Sometimes the nets were even woven with wild sea grass. You can start to see how beautiful this practice was and how it blended so closely with its environment so that technology was even then mirroring the genius of nature. The salmon swam into the funnel or were pushed by strong tidal action directly into the traps, and when the desired number of fish was in, the fishermen raised their net and pulled the sides up into the canoes. After this, the anchors were loosened, and the two canoes or pontoons could drift together as the net was hauled in and all fish were brought up live. Only the desired fish were caught, and none of the other fish were harmed but gently released to the waters.

Commercial reef netting began in Whatcom County around 1935 as a modernized version of Salish Indian fishing methods. At first square-ended boats that were forty or so feet long were used and required eight to twelve fishers.

Today, with diminished stocks and fewer and fewer fish, Barlean, a fine mechanic and welder, turned his pontoons into heavy-pulling winching stations. Big marine batteries on the deck powered the handmade winches. Instead of needing a crew of eight to twelve, he could work his net with Jason alone.

"Be careful on this deck," Barlean said.

Jason jumped up on the pontoon raft. I followed, carefully.

Jason tied down the line on the cleat. Barlean jumped up on the raft.

I'd been on boats all my life, but I'd never been on something like this. This was a small thirty-foot raft bobbing up and down in the middle of Puget Sound.

Killer whales and big sharks lived in these waters, along with the vaunted Sockeye and Chinook, and here I was freezing, and wondering how I was going to get these boots off, if and when I was going to go over into the soup, and it was cold and filled with strange soft things. My sailing lessons from my father always included the use of life vests, and, in retrospect, I had to admit, I kind of liked that. But, somehow, I don't think the thought that a life vest might be nice had crossed anybody's mind around here in a long time, and I was not about to ask for one now. I'd just have to get my boots off fast if I went in.

On a pole I saw all of his registration decals for licensed reef netting from the Washington State Department of Game and Fisheries from the 1980s into 2000 and beyond.

We lost a pin for one of the mooring lines. I held on to the line and helped to twist a new pin into the shackle. Jason and Barlean jumped back in the skiff. They powered to the other nearby raft and left me alone on the first pontoon to mull things over while the wind slapped me silly. The net was on the second raft, and I had wanted to go there, but, had to watch them out of the slits of my eyes. It had been dropped into the water the other day and was tangled. So untangling took a long, wild, windy while. Leaving Jason on the raft to fix the net, Barlean returned in the skiff back to the first raft where I was standing, freezing and looking for something useful to do.

Reef netting was a different way of catching fish. It was artistic in a way that a pursue seine or gill net could never be.

More to the point, it was a very kindly way of interacting with nature. The men with the square-rigged nets snagged gills; hence, their name was gill netters; it was a cruel practice that severely depleted local fish stocks. There were lots of problems with it, Barlean said. Gill nets killed everything—the fish species the fishers desired and the ones they did not. In fact, about a quarter of all marine life caught every year in gill nets were species the fishermen didn't want, he said. Worst were the wild shrimp trawlers. Everything was dead by the time the nets were hauled into the boat. "Gill nets," he said, "are one of the worst things to happen to the ocean.

"Since only the small fish can pass through, a gill net catches all of the large fish," he said. "The genetically smaller strains are the ones most likely to survive gill nets and therefore to repopulate. As generation after generation of larger salmon is slain, those gene pools are eliminated. That's one reason the average size of the salmon we catch today is so much smaller than ever before."

The purse seine, he said, which wrapped around the fish much like a purse with a drawstring, brought fish to the surface in schools. But still it was difficult to throw out the species you didn't want.

"Nothing compares to the reef net," he said. "We use the gentlest way of catching fish. We catch only what we need."

After Jason untangled the net, we dropped it into the sea. Weights took it down about thirty or forty feet.

I'd worked on the *Janie II*, a commercial purse seine ship out of Monterey and San Pedro. I knew what it was like to work on a purse seine ship. But on a ship like *Janie II*, you were a few feet above the sea unless you were listing with a big haul. Here, the sea and my toes met inches below the soles of my rubber boots.

Even though the wind was blowing hard and the waters

were washing over the rafts, Barlean moved deftly and assertively. Once the net was set, Barlean got back into the skiff and fetched Jason back to our raft.

Jason climbed up into his tower; it was tall and narrow. Barlean climbed up into his tower on the other end of the raft that I was on. Both men were high up in the sky and looking down on the rippling surface. Barlean began calling out the fish he saw in the transparent waters. A big school of flounder was swimming past. "I didn't know flounder school on the surface," Jason shouted.

"Hell, yes," Barlean shouted back.

Barlean was first to see the salmon schooling and swimming into the net. In moments, he slid down the pole and began raising the net. Jason quickly followed, sliding down the pole. We began pulling in the nets and the fish came to the surface. These were large chum salmon (*Oncorhynchus keta*), also known as "dogs."

Chum salmon have the widest distribution of any of the Pacific salmon. They range south to the Sacramento River in California and the island of Kyushu in the Sea of Japan. In the north they range east in the Arctic Ocean to the Mackenzie River in Canada and west to the Lena River in Siberia. Chum salmon are the most abundant commercially harvested salmon species in arctic, northwestern, and interior Alaska and are a traditional source of dried fish for winter use.[9] A mature adult chum like the ones we netted were usually around twenty-five inches long and weighed ten pounds. Their snouts were bluntly pointed and greatly extended, compressed, and turned down in the breeding males; the lower jaws were enlarged and turned up at the tips, making it impossible for them to close their sharp-toothed mouths. Looking at their snouts with their big canine fangs, I understood why they were called dog salmon.

The strong, thick fish were flipping on the surface, steely

blue backs gleaming. Their upper sides had fine black speckles. Their bellies were silver-white. We carefully fished out the flounders that schooled with them and tossed them back into the sea, taking only the salmon.

I helped transfer them into the holding tank at the end of the raft, between the pontoons. All the salmon we netted were swimming live to the end.

When we crossed back over the rough waters, we landed the skiff on the beach, and unloaded our catch.

David Barlean is the vulnerable species of American we need to preserve. It's a crime that we have only eleven reef netters left in the Northwest. We need people like Barlean and other men and women who put a value on nature. I don't care if Barlean's interests are proprietary. We need what he values: wild salmon. We need reef netting and flourishing, healthy wild salmon populations in our rivers in Washington and Oregon, or we are going to be in trouble. I left Bellingham uncertain about whether we could win this war. But I did know the right thing to do, no matter what the outcome.

Ultimately, what we do to animals comes back to haunt us; what happens to our pets, our farm animals, wildlife, and in the laboratory is an early warning sign of what is happening to us. And the chemicals of global warming are certainly having an impact on the animals around us. We ought to be looking a little more closely at what is happening to our wildlife, and we just might see also what is happening to us.

Joe Thompson of MASS MoCA (Massachusetts Museum of Contemporary Art) said of an exhibition in North Adams, Massachusetts, "Becoming Animal: Contemporary Art in the Animal Kingdom," that it was a half-art, half-science show. The thirteen artists in the exhibition "are acutely aware of the diminishing space between human and animal existence, and the extraordinary opportunity—and mutual threat—this shrinking space provides."[10]

"Research projects, for instance, have proved how close human genes are to those of animals, even those of insects," Grace Glueck wrote in her *New York Times* review of the exhibit. "The subject of legal and ethical rights for animals is no longer easily dismissed. And studies of animals communicating within their own species, as well as with humans, are seriously pursued. Bears and other mammals are invading villages to reclaim turf seized by suburbia. On the darker side of the subject, humans are increasingly susceptible to animal diseases, among them mad cow and avian flu."

If that's the case, maybe we should not be eating fish with cancers, sexual abnormalities, and reproductive difficulties. Could these tumors and scars resulting from the chemicals of global warming be passed on to us?

Some of the most basic chemicals of global warming are the polycyclic aromatic hydrocarbons, or PAHs, which are produced by the incomplete combustion in the burning of fossil fuel, particularly coal and petroleum. When scientists mention the first link to have been established between fossil fuels and cancer, they went back to 1775, when Sir Percival Pott determined that scrotal cancers among England's chimney sweeps were likely being induced by their exposure to soot, a rich source of PAHs.[11] Today, we know that where there are combustion engines, either in harbors or on roads, we are likely to find PAHs. These environmental contaminants are especially prevalent in heavily industrialized inland waterways, estuaries, and bays where contaminated finfish and shellfish are harvested both for commerce and by recreational and subsistence fishers. Not only are several PAHs known to be potent inducers of breast cancer in rodents, they exert profound estrogenic effects.[12]

As early as 1962, T. L. Dao, writing in *Cancer Research*,

noted the "unique similarity" between natural human hormones and PAHs. Around the same time, researchers observed that PAHs may act on the same receptor sites as the estrogen molecules women's and men's own bodies produce.[13]

That means that petrochemicals like PAHs can attach themselves to women's and men's estrogen-sensitive tissues that would normally be receptive to endogenous estrogenic influences from the natural estrogen molecules circulating in both men's and women's bodies. The trouble is that PAHs stimulate toxic cell activity that can lead to an increased risk of breast cancer.

These chemicals are widely found in flesh foods, particularly nonorganic beef products, some types of seafood (particularly fish from the nation's inland waterways), and cuts of pork, lamb, and other more exotic flesh foods such as walrus blubber and polar bear and whale meat. Scientists have known about these estrogenic effects for decades. Today, we are paying a price for ignoring these early warning signs.

Knowledge of the wide range of dietary contaminants with estrogenic effects dates to the late 1940s and 1950s, when it was shown that DDT decreased testicular growth and inhibited the development of secondary sex characteristics in the cockerel.[14] In 1952, a DDT analog was shown to maintain estrus in rats that had had their ovaries removed.[15] In 1961, methoxychlor was found to increase uterine weight in mice.[16] In 1981, more than thirty years after it was first known that DDT was highly estrogenic, researchers writing in the journal *Carcinogenesis* noted: "Because of their fat-solubility and tendency toward long-term deposition in body fat, particularly in the female breast, and the apparent ability of DDT to promote tumours in the mammary gland of the male rat, such agents might be considered possible contributors to the high incidence of breast cancer among women."[17]

The body's endocrine system is responsible for sending hormonal mesages to our glands and organs. When everything is operating without interference, fetuses, babies, and children grow to become healthy adults. But when the endocrine system is influenced by outside chemicals such as DDT, confusing messages are sent to our cells, leading to genetic malfunctions that result in gross or subtle cellular changes that can cause many problems. In male babies, this could mean a child born with undescended testicles or who is susceptible to testicular cancer. In adults, such influences can translate into diminished sperm quality and higher rates of prostate cancer. In women, such changes can promote breast and ovarian cancer.

"Behavioral and developmental problems in children are among the most pervasive sociological issues in the United States today," said Charles W. Schmidt, one of America's top science writers.[18] "Learning disabilities, intellectual retardation, dyslexia, attention deficit/hyperactivity disorder (ADHD), autism, and propensity to violence are eventually diagnosed in 3% of all children born in the United States. . . . *Evidence is mounting that, in some cases at least, these disorders may be linked to exposure to chemicals in the environment* [emphasis added].

"With the focus in toxicology shifting toward the study of low-level effects, researchers are finding that neurobehavioral end points in exposed children and animals can be observed at doses far below those that cause more obvious signs of toxicity."

In 1984, a major work of epidemiology with direct implications for public health policy became available from Dr. Greta Fein and her fellow researchers, who tracked 313 infants born in Michigan hospitals to mothers documented as having eaten fish from the Great Lakes before or during their pregnancy.

According to the published study, the babies born to the mothers with the highest levels of petrochemicals—in this case PCBs—in their bodily tissues went through a relatively short gestation period and were shorter, weighed less, had smaller heads, and suffered from behavioral disorders in their reflexes at birth.[19] These were not just little events. These differences persisted throughout childhood, according to the follow-up study, published in 1996, that the husband-and-wife team of Joseph and Sandra Jacobson, from the Department of Psychology, Wayne State University, Detroit, Michigan, conducted and published in *The New England Journal of Medicine*.[20]

Taking up the research after Fein, the Jacobsons have continued to follow this cohort of children who, while still in their mothers' wombs, were exposed to PCBs from contaminated Great Lakes fish. A battery of IQ and achievement tests was administered when the children were eleven years old. Concentrations of polychlorinated biphenyls in maternal serum and milk at delivery were only slightly higher than in the general population. This worries me, too, because these effects are so widespread over the population, I just feel very strongly that people are being affected by these chemicals. I mean, I remember the levels of PCB in some of the fishermen and women of Venice Pier when I was researching contamination of the Santa Monica Bay as a reporter in Los Angeles. They had such high PCB levels. I remember one woman who had a level of DDT that was about 150 parts per billion in her blood, and she was nursing a baby and eating the fish that she had caught right off the pier and barbecuing them. Real people. Real consequences.

In the study, prenatal exposure to polychlorinated biphenyls was associated with lower full-scale and verbal IQ scores after control for potential confounding variables such as socioeconomic status. The strongest effects were on memory and attention. The most highly exposed children were three times as likely to have low average IQ scores and twice as likely to be at least two years behind in reading comprehension.

Women in the "high-exposure" category ate about fourteen pounds of Great Lakes fish per year for six years or more.[21] Average fish consumption in the United States was seventeen pounds per person per year. Most seafood choices, fortunately, aren't as contaminated as the fish from the Great Lakes, and health officials are encouraging us to eat higher quantities of fish instead of red meat. But most people won't even know if the fish they are purchasing is highly contaminated with these chemical toxins, and we know there will always be a small number of people affected by even very low toxic exposures. Perhaps this higher consumption level will burden consumers and their offspring with equivalent chemical toxicity or at least reach a threshold level to trigger such neurological damage.

How many more kids' native intelligence and ability to cope with the complexities of life are being shortchanged because of their exposure in utero to these chemicals? How many such children does it take to significantly weaken the fabric that holds our society together?

After publishing the results of her study, Dr. Sandra Jacobson told Janet Raloff of *Science News Online* that one of the big surprises was that most of the children who were affected by PCBs were middle-class.[22] In other words, their learning or IQ deficits cannot be blamed on economic poverty, she said.

"I thought that once they reached a structured school environment, whatever minor [PCB-induced] handicaps they had would be overcome. So I was quite surprised to find that, if anything, the effects were stronger and clearer at age 11 than they had been at age 4."

Raloff quoted Bernard Weiss, a neurotoxicologist at the University of Rochester, who said these effects could have a profound impact on the native intelligence of future generations. The population's mean intelligence is 100, with half scoring higher and half lower, he told her. Ordinarily, for every 100 million people tested, he said, 2.3 million lie above 130 on the IQ scale, and another 2.3 million score below 70—a level "at which most school districts would consider [offering] remedial education."

In the Raloff article, Weiss calculated a five-point downward shift in IQ for the United States as a result of PCB exposures. This "could move nearly 6 million children who had been above an IQ of 130 to below 130, and push an equal number of children into the below-70 category."

So when you look at populations, he said, even small reductions in IQ come to represent "very substantial shifts." Moreover, he argued, the financial consequences "could be stupendous." Economists have developed relationships that correlate IQ and earning power. "Over a 30-year working lifetime, each IQ point earns [an individual] something like $5,500 (in 1990 dollars)." Multiplied across a population, that differential would be large.

Jacobson's work has since been confirmed with recent peer-reviewed scientific work published in *Pediatrics* on the intellectually damaging effect DDT is having on American children.[23] In a critical piece of scientific sleuthing, researchers at the University of California at Berkeley's Center for Children's Environmental Health research say babies born in the United States to mothers who have emigrated from Mexico demonstrate significant mental and physical impairment due to exposure to pesticides derived from petrochemicals.[24]

Scientists measured levels of DDT in 360 pregnant women now living in the Salinas Valley, but almost all of whom had come to the United States from Mexico in the last five years. In Mexico, chemicals banned in the United States are used for crop production, and I detailed the extensive contamination of Mexican produce with chemicals banned in the United States in *Diet for a Poisoned Planet*. Marla Cone reports in the *Los Angeles Times* most of these women were exposed to DDT through recent applications of the compound, noting that DDT was used on farms until 1995 and for mosquito control until 2000. DDT continues to be used worldwide today as protection against malaria.

According to the study results as reported in a *Los Angeles Times* article, for every tenfold rise in DDT exposure, the children's scores on mental tests dropped 2 to 3 points. Their motor skills were also reduced. In the worst cases, the highest DDT doses were associated with a 7- to 10-point drop in the mental scores of 24-month-old children compared with those who were not exposed.

Making these declines in intelligence more notable is that the average score in the study was only 86. Yet scores below 85 are strongly linked with developmental delays and learning disabilities. These children will find it difficult if not impossible to learn how to think and to solve problems. In addition, one of the key indicators of a breakdown in problem-solving skills is violence, whether it is in the neighborhood or around the globe. If problem-solving skills are being impaired in America and Mexico, they are certainly also being impaired in society today. Maybe a little dust doesn't gum up the clockworks, but too much will. If we're busy dusting the IQ off our kids for a few dollars more and they can't apply intelligence to solving tomorrow's problems, then what's the point of having kids? It is likely that more violence will be substituted instead, thanks to the chemical dusting.

With current migration trends favoring population movement

from south to north, such studies, although small in scope, have enormously important political and societal implications. What's more, the statistical demographics of a changing America mean that more and more of our population is going to be made up of Mexican immigrants. If their children are being poisoned in the womb, our whole national IQ is going to take a dive. How will America compete if more and more of its population has had its intellectual and reproductive future stolen? President said that we can't afford to leave a single child behind when it comes to education, but he never mentioned the link with toxic chemicals, and it is time for our next president to do so.

We need healthy children to win the war against terrorism.

Conversely, is it possible that reducing exposure to toxic chemicals could raise the national IQ? State University of New York (SUNY) at Oswego is on the shores of Lake Ontario. In the 1980s, the state began stocking salmon that would make their way up the Oswego River to spawn. The stocking program stimulated a vibrant sport-fishing industry as anglers lined the banks of the Oswego River to catch some of the monstrous fishes making their way upriver. But researchers such as the psychologist Helen Daly, of the Center for Behavioral Effects of Environmental Toxins at SUNY, worried as more and more families began consuming significant amounts of the Lake Ontario salmon, which were highly contaminated with chemicals, particularly PCBs. To determine the effects of such consumption on these families, Daly began a series of experiments in which she fed rats Lake Ontario salmon and a control group either less-contaminated Pacific salmon or a diet without any salmon whatsoever. Here's what happened—and the consistency of the results are both frightening and discomforting—but, also for those of who are awake or trying to awaken, they offer profound hope that with fewer chemicals of global warming in our bodies we will indeed be smarter and healthier people. As long as the rats' lives were relatively nonplussed and stress-free, no differences could be found between the two groups. But when negative forces (such as mild electric shocks or withholding chow at feeding time) were into these rats' lives, the rats consuming the Lake Ontario salmon showed a remarkable inability to deal with the stress. Daly said the rats eating the contaminated salmon were "hyper-reactive." But the rats given the purer wild Pacific salmon were much more comfortable with the stress and followed normal routines.[25]

The studies haven't been done on the children of the fisherman catching these fish from this region yet. These studies need to be done, but no such studies are being funded. Still, we need to heed these early warning signs. This could point to a very dangerous trend in society. To avoid a modern-day body count, we should take a societal leap of imagination, as difficult as that might be for supporters of a human body count–based public health policy. Think of the impact on a nation's ability to be competitive, to innovate, to handle stress on a societal level. We all know that it is how we react to stress that determines our fate. If a nation can't handle stress, if a nation is dumbed down, perhaps its people won't be as effective when it comes to making important decisions about war and peace. Perhaps they will be less likely to ask important questions before becoming embroiled in foreign entanglements.

Another disturbing trend is for xenoestrogens to blur the differences between male and female. For example, scientists are now finding male fish with ovarian tissues in their testes off the contaminated waters of Los Angeles and Orange counties in California.[26] It is believed that their intersex condition are the result of xenoestrogen-tainted sewage and other forms of pollution, since no other such fish were found elsewhere in cleaner waters. Such sexual blurring has been found in Missouri River sturgeon, the Florida panther, alligators of Lake Apopka, Florida, and elsewhere as well.

If animals are becoming feminized from these chemicals and their sexual organs are becoming blurred, does that mean our children's sex differences are, too?

At Erasmus University in Rotterdam, The Netherlands, researches have found that prenatal or perinatal (via breast milk) exposure to PCBs is associated with changes in the behavior of children at play.[27] While nobody wants to pigeon-hole boy or girl into a set of socially prescribed behaviors, researchers find some behaviors to be more typically male or female. Such ways of assessing male and female behaviors is to look at the sum total of a child's activities, as is done in the Pre-School Activities Inventory. This standard test is used to evaluate the gender aspects of play behavior in young children. A Dutch version of the same test was used in the study. It consisted of twenty-four questions addressing three aspects of play behavior: type of toys, activities, and child characteristics. The authors of the Pre-School Activities Inventory state:

> The questions assess either feminine or masculine play behavior from which 3 scales are derived: a composite scale, integrating both masculine and feminine play behavior, and a masculine and a feminine scale. The composite scale is essentially defined as the difference: feminine scale minus masculine scale. A negative score on the composite scale implies masculine play behavior and a positive score feminine play behavior. A higher score on the feminine scale indicates more feminine play behavior, whereas a higher score on the masculine scale indicates more masculine play behavior.

Using recognized scales to assess typical male or female behavior, the researchers found that, "In boys, higher prenatal PCB levels were related with less masculinized play . . . whereas in girls higher PCB levels were associated with more masculinized play. . . . Higher prenatal dioxin levels were associated with more feminized play in boys as well as girls. . . . These effects suggest prenatal steroid hormone imbalances caused by prenatal exposure to environmental levels of PCBs, dioxins, and other related organochlorine compounds." These effects were seen with "background levels" that result from consuming foods typically found in the diet.

The play-behavior study results are truly important. Dr. Theo Colborn, coauthor of the landmark book *Our Stolen Future*, analyzed the Dutch studies and wrote about them on her Web site at www.ourstolenfuture.org.[28] First, they clearly implicated hormonally active contaminants in disruption of the development of gender-specific human behavior, even if they fell short of establishing causality, she said. Second, the affected behaviors, sex-specific childhood play, have been linked speculatively to later patterns in adult sexual choice. While highly controversial, some research suggests that "childhood gender nonconformity (e.g., play behavior typical for opposite sex) is a predictor of same-sex sexual choice in adulthood," said the study authors.

"We have a longer life span than animals, so you can see these changes more easily in animals, but, in humans, our generation times are over twenty years so it can take a lifetime or two or more to see what is happening," said Colborn in an interview with me.[29] "I think of how many male children today are born with hypospadia, the problem of external genitalia in which the penis develops without the urethra at the end; the urethra may be down in the shaft, in the perineum, or in the scrotal area. The closer the hole is to the rest of the body, the more severe the problem. One in 125 American boys today is born with this condition. The rate has doubled over only twenty years. In Denmark, it came out to one in 118 boys, very similar to America." The condition is probably more prevalent than reporting suggests, she added. "Hypospadia is underreported. Doctors often don't report it as it may be a stigma for the child or family. Insurance won't share this information with public health officials. These problems are laid down before the children are born."

Jeremiah, the bullfrog, was a friend of mine. But now I'm not so sure if he is a boy or girl; his croaking speech may be more likely to be in the soprano than the bass range. The intersex rate among frogs in central Illinois, where atrazine (a restricted pesticide) is used, is twice as high as in the southern areas, where atrazine use is low, according to a recent study.[30] Talking about adding insult to male injury, researchers also found that mature male frogs exposed to atrazine had a decrease in testosterone to levels equivalent to that found in females. "I was very much surprised at the impact of atrazine on developing frogs," said Tyrone B. Hayes, professor of biology at the University of California at Berkeley. Hayes's study has gotten a cold reception from agricultural interests. *Environmental Health News* reports: "The Minnesota Pollution Control Agency last fall canceled Hayes' keynote speech on atrazine scheduled for a conference this month. The agency asked Hayes to downplay the word atrazine and he refused. A *Minneapolis Star Tribune* story showed that some state officials deemed a spotlight on atrazine to be politically risky (One of the most popular agricultural herbicides, atrazine is sprayed on fields, but most of it runs off into aboveground streams and eventually drinking water, ponds, reservoirs, and wells. A U.S. Geological Survey study found that more than one-quarter of samples of water from the

Mississippi River basin contain atrazine at levels exceeding the EPA's maximum contaminant level.[31])

The scary part of what Hayes found is that the doses at which atrazine profoundly feminizes frogs were as low as 0.1 part per billion. "As the amount of atrazine increased, as many as 20 percent of frogs exposed during their early development produced multiple sex organs or had both male and female organs. Many had small, feminized larynxes."

Hayes's research team said that the effect on the frogs could have resulted from atrazine causing the body to produce more of the enzyme aromatase, which is present in vertebrates. Aromatase is used by the body to convert the male hormone testosterone to the female hormone estrogen.[32]

Although these effects are being found at a fraction of a part per billion in tiny vulnerable amphibians, we are consuming water with amounts around three parts per billion.

So what happens when millions of men and women drink traces of atrazine in their tap water and inhale it into their lungs at holiday time when atrazine is sprayed on Christmas trees?[33,34,35,36]

Although human research is limited and poorly funded, the herbicide has been incriminated in two of three published reports in a threefold increase in ovarian cancer risk.[37,38,39] Funding for such studies is difficult for researchers to come by, but the risks are real both for our immediate health and because atrazine is another petroleum-derived chemical that feeds off our oil addiction.

It isn't only the fish of the Northwest or frogs in the Midwest that face tough times. Polar bears don't have it any easier. The same chemicals that produce endocrine disruptions and genetic mutations in the Midwest's wildlife are part of the fossil fuel mentality that is also having an impact in the Arctic. Think of the high levels of flame retardants researchers are finding in polar bears as markers for increasing global temperatures. Polar bears are having difficulty reproducing, and these same chemicals are certainly being considered as a cause of or contributor to their reproductive woes. Now, "flame retardants originating largely in the United States are building up in their bodies, according to an international team of wildlife scientists," reported Marla Cone in a January 9, 2006, report in the *Los Angeles Times* (she is also the author of *Silent Snow* from Grove Press).[40] Polar bears are "walking on thin ice," according to the World Wildlife Fund (WWF), the international environmental group (www.wwf.org). "The demise of the polar bears will be a foretaste of the devastation that climate change could bring to all of nature's top predators, including humans," warned Dr. Richard Dixon, head of policy at WWF Scotland. "We have only a few years to curb our polluting ways and save the Arctic, including the polar bears. This is a challenge to the generation of people running the world today—the last generation that can prevent the worst of climate chaos."[41]

Unfortunately, the Arctic "is now experiencing some of the most rapid and severe climate change on Earth," according to the Arctic Climate Impact Assessment, which was unveiled at a scientific conference in Reykjavik, Iceland in November 2004.[42] The report stated out that the average temperature in the Arctic has risen almost twice as fast as the rest of the world over the past few decades. Over the next hundred years, winter temperatures are expected to rise by up to 10° C over the oceans. In the past thirty years, the annual average area of Arctic sea ice has shrunk by nearly a million square kilometers, an area larger than Norway, Sweden, and Denmark put together. Before the end of the twenty-first century, the report predicted, 50 percent of summer ice could be gone, with "some models showing near complete disappearance." The international team blamed "heat-trapping gases from tailpipes and smokestacks around the world [that] are contributing to profound environmental change."

The only way we can be sure we're doing what is right is to see tangible results. If we start seeing levels of fossil fuel residues declining in polar bears, and healthy populations of wild salmon and amphibians, we will know we are hedging our bets against global warming. But that's going to require some major changes in our consciousness. Part of that change has to involve our being kind to animals, even farm animals. So what are we going to do? How are we going to make a difference?

Let's start with the animals that are closest to us, those that we raise on our ranches and farms. Mel Coleman, a fifth-generation Colorado rancher, found his calf-selling business floundering in the late 1970s. There was just no profit in selling off calves anymore because the megacorporations controlled the prices. Yet, at the same time, he was gathering some important insights into a market that was not being served. Although estrogenic hormones enhance the growth of livestock by as much as 20 percent, many consumers were becoming wary of the use of hormones and other animal drugs.[43]

"My brother and sister-in-law were shopping at a health food store and they found that a lot of their friends and acquaintances were looking for beef that was raised without hormones and antibiotics," he said. "So we took some calves and fattened them naturally, and we called them natural beef."

Initially, they met opposition from the U.S. Department of Agriculture, which argued that there was no definition for natural beef. It took two years to hammer out a memo of understanding with the USDA on a definition for the natural label and to put together an audit trail that would ensure the integrity of their product.

In a very real way, family ranchers are helping to maintain

wildlife habitat, Mel Coleman said in an interview. "Some 70 percent of all wildlife lives on ranch and farm lands. The American Farmland Trust reports that we are losing 3,000 acres a day to development, such as housing developments, malls, parking structures and roads," he said. "Over a year this is an area the size of Delaware. While we call this working land, I think of it as prime wildlife habitat that is crucial also to stabilize our global climate.

"What we really are is grass managers," said Coleman.

Grass is a natural resource that, with a little rainfall and energy from the sun and when managed properly, can actually increase in density and promote tremendous biodiversity. Grass is the basis for the entire food chain. If you are a cattle rancher and you don't manage your land right, you won't be able to raise as many cattle on it. My father [Mel Coleman, Sr.] pioneered the concept that we are essentially grass managers. When we increase grass density, we provide more forage for wildlife and reduce erosion, which improves watershed quality. A majority of ranchers are paying more and more attention to the grasses that they have. But I've found in my experience that the small family rancher, who won't feed his cattle at any point any growth stimulating hormones or antibiotics, does the best job of grass management. If you manage the whole process in a more sustainable way, we don't have any environmental messes to clean up.

"Our program does so much more than market natural beef," Coleman added. "It impacts everything from the sustainability of grasslands to the well-being of small ranchers to the very quality of the beef we sell. We feel we're making a difference in all of those areas."[44]

So do his growing number of customers. Speaking to the growth of the LOHAS market, he said, "Years ago, we marketed to the 'purists.' Now, we have the chance to appeal to a much bigger percentage of people. They're more sophisticated about issues such as sustainable agriculture, and we can give them a product that not only delivers the eating experience they want but one that speaks to the problems they're concerned about improving."[45]

Similar to Coleman's experience, Doc and Connie Hatfield, founders of Oregon Country Beef, were broke back in 1986, when instead of "whining about how tough things were," said Connie Hatfield, "we found out about the market for antibiotic- and hormone-free beef."[46]

From 1995 to 2005, the Oregon Country Beef brand has gone from processing 3,400 head a year to 40,000. "Since the mad cow scare in 2003, production has more than doubled, with a 73 percent increase over the past year."

Oregon Country Beef made a key move in 2004 when it made a deal with Burgerville, a Vancouver, Washington, chain that is dedicated to locally produced and sustainable foods, to produce all the beef for their hamburgers.

Jack Graves, chief cultural officer for Burgerville, told the *New York Times* the chain was looking for a safe source of beef after the mad cow scare in 2003, and held back sales to give Oregon Country Beef time to meet Burgerville's demand of 35,000 pounds a week. (Visit Burgerville at www.burgerville.com or any of its thirty-nine locations in southern Washington and Oregon. Visit Oregon Country Beef at www.oregoncountrybeef.com.)

In 1985, Laura Freeman, of Winchester, Kentucky, founded Laura's Lean Beef Company on her family's farm, with two goals in mind: to improve the financial stability of medium-sized cattle operations, and to improve the nutritional qualities of beef. Today Laura's Lean Beef is naturally raised, with distribution in more than five thousand grocery stores in forty-six states. In 2005, company sales are expected to reach $135 million, according to the company's Web site. And because they believe healthier beef is leaner beef, Laura's raises breeds of cattle such as Limousin and Charolais, whose cuts are naturally lower in fat than beef from other breeds. Visit www.lauraleanbeef.com.

Also in the Midwest, Dakota Beef's cattle are raised on certified organic ranches and processed at Dakota Beef's certified organic facility in Howard, South Dakota. In October 2004, Raley's and Bel Air supermarket chains began offering Dakota Beef's certified organic beef in 117 of their Northern California and Nevada stores. Visit Dakota Beef for an Internet source of excellent quality organic flesh foods (www.dakota beefcompany.com).

Green Circle Organics launched its branded premium quality organic beef products, including Organic R-T-E beef entrees, based on recipes created by renowned organic chef and Washington, D.C., restaurateur Nora Pouillion. Be sure to visit Pouillion's next time you are in Washington, D.C. Visit www.nora.com and www.greencircleorganics.com.

"From the very beginning, Green Circle has been dedicated to help creating a healthy ecosystem, and we're equally committed to producing the best and most wholesome beef," said Bill Cole, president of the company and the son of one of the founders of AOL, David Cole. "The flavor, the marbling, the texture—our beef can be marketed to top chefs, and our retail products offer the same level of eating experience."[47]

Beyond our food choices, we have many ways to express our love for and caring of animals; this simply requires us to be thoughtful in other areas of living. Here are some suggestions for what you can do to feel inspired.

- Stop using chemical pesticides to kill weeds and pests. These products can even give your dog cancer.[48,49] Try friendly remedies for your lawn and garden. Beneficial bugs and soaps and other natural alternatives to chemical pesticides are available at most gardening centers and nurseries.

- Make ecotourism part of your vacation plans. Ecotourism is the practice of touring natural habitats in a manner meant to minimize ecological impact. "Ecotours can accommodate any taste," said Gerard "Ged" Caddick, who has led tours for WWF, the National Geographic Society, and the American Museum of Natural History, and founded Terra Incognita Ecotours in 2004. Typical ecotours are available to the Amazon, Costa Rica, Africa, and the Arctic, or they might be close to home and in your own state or region. "We change the places we visit for the better, and we hope to change ourselves for the better, too," Caddick said. "We share and become involved in the wonder of learning, seeing, and discovering new places, people and problems. We are part of the solution. All this in some of the most beautiful places on Earth. Of course you can do these trips on your own, especially if you have large quantities of time, money, patience, and you are willing to take some risks." Visit www.terra-incognita-ecotours.com. Another good site is www.earth-foot.org, where you can get in touch with a number of geographically diverse hosts and guides. *Sierra* magazine, from the Sierra Club, and *E: The Environmental Magazine* feature ecotours. Visit www.emagazine.com and www.sierraclub.org.
- Buy a federal duck stamp offered by the National Wildlife Refuge System. The Federal Duck Stamp is a U.S. program to generate revenue to protect wetlands. In 1934, the Migratory Bird Hunting Stamp Act, popularly known as the "Duck Stamp Act," was passed by Congress. The Act requires the purchase of a stamp by waterfowl hunters. Revenue generated by the stamp is used to acquire important wetlands. Since its inception, the program has resulted in the

protection of approximately 4.5 million acres of waterfowl habitat. For every dollar you spend on Federal Duck Stamps, ninety-eight cents go directly to purchase vital habitat for protection in the National Wildlife Refuge System. By your contribution, you benefit more than 200 species of birds at the nation's 92 million acres of wildlife refuges. At $15, it's a bargain. Displaying this stamp admits you free to all national wildlife sanctuaries, too. For details, call the Federal Duck Stamp office toll-free at (877) 887-5508 or check out their Web site at www.fws.gov/duckstamps/Conservation/conservation.htm or www.duckstamp.com.

- Drink tea from a mug purchased from the World Wildlife Fund and toast the lions, tigers, and host of other animals whose wild habitats you're helping to preserve. Check out their Web site at www.wwfus.org or contact them at (202) 293-4800 for more details.

- Buy organic, fair-trade, or shade-grown coffee. According to Maria Rodale's excellent *Organic Style* magazine, clearing land for large conventionally grown coffee plantations ends up destroying wildlife habitat. "Farms with reduced shade in Colombia and Mexico have 97 percent fewer bird species than those with crops under natural tree canopies."[50] Audubon Coffee is Audubon-branded and 100 percent organic, shade grown, and habitat friendly. Visit www.auduboncoffeeclub.com. Café Canopy at www.shade-coffee.com offers shade-grown, organic coffees certified by the Smithsonian Migratory Bird Center's standards.

- Put on a Greenpeace Defending the Ocean organic cotton T-shirt and earn some love from tunas and whales. Visit www.greenpeace.org.

- Purchase a desk calendar with stunning wildlife and landscape photography from the Sierra Club at www.sierraclub.org, and benefit this important environmental organization.

- Buy only wood products with Forest Stewardship Council certification, which helps maintain and improve wildlife habitat. Visit www.fsc.org.
- Adopt wildlife. This is a great gift. For fifty to a hundred dollars or more, an acre of land can be protected by the World Wildlife Trust. I love elephants, so let me tell you about the Wild Lands Elephant Corridor Project. "The Wild Lands Elephant Corridor, located in the Garo Hills, protects an important population (thought to be approximately twenty percent of all the Indian elephants), by addressing the problem of forest fragmentation, which is a serious threat to the elephants' survival," according to their Web site. The Wild Lands Corridor has gentle sandy beaches on both sides of the river, where elephants can cross easily, said the site. To choose from more than two dozen low-cost but big-time projects all over the world, visit www.worldlandtrust.org.

Animals are us. We eat them. It is so primal. But even eating should be sacred. If we get more involved in being kind to animals and thinking more about them than whether we're going to have beef, lamb, or chicken for lunch or dinner, we can come to the realization that being kind to animals is about more than their value to the human belly.

Being kind to animals means making sure they have a place on earth. When we do good things for animals, our overall health is stronger. Our nation's moral health will be stronger, too. A planet that is healthy for animals is healthy for all of us. Our future depends on their future and making sure that vulnerable species like wild salmon, frogs, and polar bears survive.

Let's be kind to animals. Let's be kind to ourselves.

SEVEN
Drive a Cool Car

LENEXA, KANSAS, WAS FREEZING. All of the hotels were booked. The guy on the bus taking me to the only room I could find on late notice told me that the hotels were always overbooked on Mondays and the car rental agencies were always totally out of cars on this day, and that's the way it was and the way it had always been, and it had not been a problem anyone felt was worth paying attention to until I brought it up. So I shut up. The bed I slept in had bugs, and the Chinese food wasn't very good either.

Although I'd flown into Kansas, the actual Ford assembly plant that I was being driven to the next cold morning in a deluxe Ford limo bus with a gaggle of Detroit auto-beat writers was a short distance from the airport at 8121 NE U.S. Highway 69 in Claycomo, Missouri. Today, November 16, 2005, was serious business for Ford, the United Auto Workers, and American manufacturing. If there was one common denominator to the comeback of the American auto industry, it was to go lean, and the color green.

I wasn't one of the auto-beat writers. I didn't work for the *Free Press* or *Ward's Auto News* and know all of the players like they did. I wasn't sure what to expect when I got off the bus at the red-brick entry and walked inside Ford.

About all I knew was that the company founder, Henry Ford, invented the assembly line or at least received much of the credit for doing so. Fortunately, I had armed myself with Douglas Brinkley's excellent one-volume history of Henry Ford, the man and the company, in *Wheels for the World*. So I knew just enough about Ford to know that I knew next to nothing. I was one of the customers Ford lost sometime ago to the Japanese carmakers, anyway. I liked Toyota.

I was opening up and becoming much more receptive to the possibility of buying Ford, however, because I'd begun to hear something about the company going green. A "green" Ford intrigued me—it would be good for the environment and good for America.

Ford, like General Motors, couldn't deny it was in trouble; major workforce reductions would be announced a few months later, and after that William Clay Ford would step down as CEO of the company while announcing even more plant closings and accelerated retirements. Both companies were losing market share to the Japanese and, unlike the Asian companies, both were dealing with bloated worker benefit and pension systems that could be the millstones that would drag them down, no matter what they actually did—unless, of course, they went green and advanced fundamental changes in the engines and fuels used for transportation. I hoped they would do it soon.

Ford was in a race for its life. Since 1995, Toyota, Nissan, and Honda had seen their American market share go from 18 to 28 percent. Ford, GM, and Chrysler had seen their market share dip from 73 to 58 percent in the same time.[1] On August 25, 2005, *USA Today* reported: "The debts of General Motors and Ford Motor were lowered to junk status by Moody's Investors Service."[2]

Conversely, not going green soon enough could already have been the death knell tolling. It might already be too late for GM. It was GM that rejected the hybrid concept and lagged years behind Toyota by the time its first consumer version came out in 2006. But it wasn't too late for Ford—or the well-paid blue collar working men and women in Claycomo, Missouri, where Ford was building its future.

Suddenly, the music turned upbeat; the plant doors swung open; and in rolled a burgundy Mercury Mariner hybrid. We were all in a tizzy, snapping images with our digital cameras. It was everything that a Ford should be; it was everything you could want. It represented the very best technology coming out of the American car industry. (Ford itself has some 139 patents now for its own hybrid technology breakthroughs, although some of the technology used for their hybrids is licensed from Toyota.)

Thomas Brewer, the general manager of Lincoln-Mercury, in blue tie, shirt, and jacket, stepped up to the podium where the lectern was adorned with UAW, Ford, and Mercury logos, with the UAW logo first.

Ford hybrid models were in "high demand by our dealers," he said. "One of the most important components of our future is that we have to win the hearts and minds of a new generation of consumers. We've found that our hybrid models do just that."

So popular has the hybrid Mariner been that five hundred were presold via the Internet even before production began, in a tradition dating all the way to Henry Ford's time, when purchases were made before production, cash on the barrelhead, according to Brinkley.

From the early presale data, "the average age of the Mercury Mariner hybrid consumer is fourteen years younger than a typical Mercury buyer," Brewer said. "But what is even more impressive is that the Mariner attracts fifty percent of new buyers to Ford, and one in five is a convert from an Asian car company."

So environmentally conscious has Ford become that they

have even received a strong endorsement from the Sierra Club, which only a few years ago criticized Ford's greenhouse emissions record. The Mercury Mariner hybrid was voted best compact SUV by the Texas Auto Writers Association.[3]

The Mercury brand had to "shake off the brand's stodgy, oldster image and attract a new generation of customers," wrote Bryce G. Hoffman in the November 27, 2005, *Detroit News*, only a few days later, after attending the Lenexa event.[4]

And leading the charge, Brewer said, was the Mercury Mariner. I could tell he was very proud of what the Claycomo plant workers had accomplished. I had the feeling it was a good workforce. A lot of the men and women were there in the folding chairs in their Ford blue overalls, listening to their boss. This was important to them.

Next to speak was Nancy Gioia, who only weeks before had replaced the highly regarded Mary Anne Wright as director of Sustainable Mobility Technologies and Hybrid Vehicle Programs at Ford; Wright, an engineer, left "for personal reasons," according to an associate.

"We had our best sales month ever in September," Gioia said. "We believe hybrid technology is a key technology for the world."

"Let's go inside," I said. I put on my noise blockers and began walking down the most amazing industrial sight I have ever seen, following my guide, who was speaking to me via audiophones. This assembly line with auto bodies and chassis and shells and engines and hammers and screwdrivers and pneumatics went on for what appeared to be miles. I was inside Henry Ford's world, and it was pretty cool in this noise-deafening 4.45 million square foot manufacturing plant. I spoke to an accompanying union official. He said the average wage was $26 an hour plus equal value benefits. I thought that was great pay, and the benefits were something big, too.

From my visit to the manufacturing plant and talking with union leaders, I learned that the workers there loved hybrids because they were insuring their future jobs and livelihoods. Although they were going to manufacture only four thousand Mercury Mariner hybrids there (and thousands more at a Ford hybrid plant in Mexico), the company planned to be manufacturing 250,000 annually by 2010, according to David Cue, Ford's chief hybrid engineer. Most of the work was in the planning, he said. It was a matter of retooling the plants. But even his prediction of a quarter of a million hybrids by 2010 might be just the beginning of what it will mean to drive climate-cool cars.

For the new beginning of the new American auto industry the color has to be green. The hybrid gamble of 1994 that turned an admired so-called imitator company into an industry leader has already paid off for both Toyota as well as Honda, and will for Ford, too, and even possibly GM. Hybrid technology might be a bridge technology, but it is the immediate future (no matter how much GMC tried to deny this throughout the last decade, when their competitors were gaining strategic market share). All I knew was that I was standing in the midst of the most complex assembly line I'd ever seen, one that made me proud of what an American company had accomplished, and the workers there were building a solid employment future in their lifetime. They had been handed a plum like no other American car plant in the United States. Here was where UAW and Ford engineers teamed up to make sure there was "seamless integration" on the assembly lines so that both hybrid and nonhybrid Mariners could be built flawlessly, said Brewer. This is where quality control was number one. I met men and women who went over every single aspect of every single hybrid Mariner to ensure that it was perfect when it left the Claycomo plant.

These cars would be solid performers because Ford was doing such an excellent job and had anticipated the future.

The Mercury hybrid would also emit more than 90 percent fewer greenhouse gas emissions than conventional autos and get 33 miles per gallon on city streets and 29 on the highway. (See explanation on page 228.) That's the beginning of a new green American future that we should all value.

I felt bullish about Ford. I liked the Mariner. I'd buy one. It was a great car and really showed some vision. And it was just the beginning.

Ford is going to be America's first green motor company, and that will save its future.

I'd been following Ford for some time. I first came to know Ford's future plans when I was invited to test drive one of their first hybrids at the Lifestyles of Health and Sustainability Conference at the Ritz-Carlton Hotel in Marina Del Rey in 2004. I was on the streets of L.A. It was hot. The 2005 Ford Escape Hybrid which was about to be introduced looked like, well, your typical small, four-door SUV. It was small and compact. It was also a year late, according to *Car & Driver*.[5]

Michael F. Hollander, a PR specialist for Ford, had a big smile not only because he was genuinely excited (which helps in PR) but also because he was showing a virgin—his first hybrid.

"I'd say public awareness of hybrids is like the Internet twenty years ago," he said.

Hollander said he observed all kinds of reactions from test drivers. "They are all over the map," he said. "Some people think the hybrid is quieter than they expected. Others say it is faster or has better performance. Gas mileage is a big thing. You want to drive it?" I liked the feel and the quiet that, without an internal combustion engine, set in immediately. The car shifted imperceptibly from gas to electric.

"We're not like Toyota," he said. "They made the Prius to look the way it does so that it screams, 'Hey, I'm an environmentalist. Look at me! Look at what I am doing for the environment.' We didn't do that. We created the Escape to look like any other car. We did this on purpose."

I asked him if we could drive free form, but he told me, "Dearborn gave us a prescribed route we have to take."

"What's the difference in price between a nonhybrid Escape and this one?" I said.

"Well, that can vary," he said. "You could pay an additional three thousand dollars, or more, if you really add on the extras. It depends on what you want. Most people who buy the hybrids have money and want all the gadgets. There's an option package that comes with a navigation system. That's the fun part of the car because you get to show all your friends how it works. You have this display in front of you and you tend to drive better because you can see visually on the dash when the car is shifting into its electric motor, is using gasoline, or both. You can develop a really good feel for the vehicle and find its sweet spot."

Car & Driver said, "Our hybrid Escape was delivered with an eye-bulging $32,450 price tag. Ford compares this hybrid with a well-equipped V-6 model, so that big number is the result of a $3,000 hybrid premium and $3,855 worth of options, including navigation, leather seats, and extra airbags. Discount shoppers can delete four-wheel drive to save $1,625 but will still pay the extra $3,000."[6]

There's some good news for hybrid drivers stuck in freeway gridlock, Hollander said. "You will save on gas. Under twenty miles per hour you are running on electric," Hollander told me. "That means basically you have unlimited mileage; you're sitting there in rush hour; neither motor nor engine are running; it starts right up with the electric motor and with full torque." That's good for city driving, too, which is why hybrids can actually get better mileage by three or four miles per gallon in the city.

At the time, neither Daimler Chrysler nor General Motors had a hybrid on the market. Ford was selling hybrids as fast as they could make them.

"So you think being first with a hybrid gives you an advantage over GM?" I said.

"You think?" he said.

Early on with my awkward stopping and going, the car's 29 miles per gallon were impressive. But it could do much better, 7 or 8 mpg better, he said. "The actual rating is thirty-six to thirty-seven."

But I needed to touch the sweet spot that experienced hybrid drivers talked about when their cars were in the fossil fuel–free zone and they were liberated from the dinosaur age. I could tell that people were going to have fun getting to know their hybrids, and it would be a fun time for the American auto industry if it would only become a world leader in green transportation. I sure hoped so.

"You have to learn how to drive the car," Hollander said. "When people learn how to drive with the electric motor they can really increase mpg."

I turned away from the beach on Venice Boulevard, passing a tiny strip mall with ethnic food shops. I felt the engine turn off, the motor slip on, and then silence, except for the sound of the wheels coasting. "You ever hear the sound of wheels coasting?" he said. Driving was a quiet experience, which I preferred.

"We might need a few less sound barriers along the freeways when everyone starts driving hybrids," Hollander said, softly.

I turned on Lincoln; we passed Bali Way.

The sales were phenomenal, Hollander blurted out enthusiastically. "We can't make enough," he added.

I turned down Fiji Way.

"People really love them?" I said.

"Absolutely."

Bearing out my assessment that the hybrid was the future—at least in the immediate decade—of the auto industry, hybrid sales have risen consistently since the Honda Insight debuted in the American market in 1999.[7] In that year, only a couple of hundred Insights were sold. The sales of U.S. hybrids have generally doubled every year:

- 2000:   9,350
- 2001:   20,287
- 2002:   35,000
- 2003:   47,525
- 2004:   88,000

According to the Bloomberg news service, 35,474 hybrid vehicles were sold during the first quarter of 2005, with the Toyota Prius accounting for the greatest amount of sales—22,800, up from 9,918 for the comparable period of 2004. Honda's hybrid sales for the first quarter of 2005 numbered 9,025, up from 6,169 for the same period last year, with the hybrid Civic's 8.2 percent quarterly drop attributed to the automaker's introduction of the new hybrid Accord. Ford sold 3,569 Escape hybrid SUVs during the quarter. Sales are going to escalate from here, and then branch out into a number of diversely fueled types of vehicles.

But we also have to be aware of diluting the environmental integrity of the product. Today's hybrids have sacrificed miles per gallon for performance. The old hybrids demonstrated superior mpg. In December 1999, when Honda introduced the Insight with its "aerodynamic teardrop shape," it received a 70 mpg rating.[8] But newer models, like the Escape, obtain from

29 to 33 mpg (its nonhybrid counterpart gets around 19 to 22 mpg).[9]

The Korean carmaker Hyundai announced it was entering the hybrid game, but unlike GM, Ford, or Daimler, which are licensing technologies to catch up, Hyundai was going on its own technologies, which already did not match up to Toyota.

According to *Business Week*, "Hyundai has a long way to go on fuel economy. Its hybrid burns 5.3 liters for every 100 kilometers (44 miles per gallon) of city travel. That's better than the 8 liters per 100 km (29 miles per gallon) the gasoline-engine-powered Accent needs, but it's worse than the low 4.7 liters (50 miles per gallon) the Honda Civic hybrid gets by on."[10]

The new hybrid Saturn that GM released in summer 2006 would only provide a 10 to 12 percent fuel improvement, which was hardly inspiring.

But these are the hazards of coming in a distant third or fourth in the hybrid game. Today, increasing mpg and offering consumers a wide choice of fuels is the winning formula and one Ford and GM must adopt. All of the auto companies need to be creating flex fuel infrastructures with more ethanol fueling stations to be constructed in the Midwest and hydrogen stations in California. This is part of green strategic thinking and is very exciting from a market perspective, since we are essentially creating new world markets that bring more competition and innovation.

These companies all have a chance to win if they understand that mpg and driving a carbon-neutral cool car matter to most consumers. They must reinvent themselves.

The big automakers are going to have to become almost regional in their thinking for a short period as they grow their markets for alternative fuels. That is because we have tons of competing flex-fuel highways operating right now, and that is exciting but fraught with peril.

In California, Governor Schwarzenegger wants a hydrogen highway with hydrogen filling stations every twenty miles. This works for Ford's and GM's fuel cell technologies.

The Midwest is home to ethanol (E85).

Texas and the Southwest are home to biodiesel.

Expect successful companies to find a way to participate in a whole eco-mall of different green car choices. Expect to see flex-fuel Suburbans that run on Nebraska and Illinois corn and switchgrass; diesel trucks running on vegetable oil; hydrogen-powered sedans; and, of course, hybrids, which represent the first major breakthrough since the Stanley steamer.

Actually, let's get off our high horse. America is way behind Brazil. In Brazil, the nation's millions of vehicles almost all run on nonpolluting and non–greenhouse gas emitting sugarcane fuel. Of course, Brazil grows a lot of sugarcane, a lot more than we can.

But, in the United States, we have wood chips, prairie switch-grass, corn stubble, and processed food waste; all of this can be turned into fuel that could compete extremely well with peak oil.

Green fuels are different than petrochemical fuels. Some green fuels are created by biomass with use of fermentation and the novel enzymes that the bacteria produce, instead of with use of chlorine and other chemical catalysts. Yet, so powerful are these naturally produced enzymes that they break down the tough carbohydrates in these plants' cell walls. We use bacteria to turn hard fibers and what otherwise would be waste into liquid gold. Many experts say that ethanol will never compete with oil in terms of production, but if American use of ethanol even approached 5 percent, which is reasonable, it could have a significant impact on the market. Critics of ethanol have said that if we use all our corn for fuel we won't have enough to eat for food. But advanced enzymatic technologies can make fuel from most any kind of biomass. On the other hand, some technologies also involve the fossil fuel methanol, which should be eliminated by the industry as soon as possible. Although the fuel produces fewer pollutants than regular gasoline, some fuels right now emit more nitric oxide gases into the atmosphere, and this must also be curbed quickly.

General Motors Corporation and Ford Motor Company have both partnered with energy companies to promote the use of ethanol as an alternative to gasoline in Illinois and Missouri. GM has teamed up with Shell Oil Products U.S. and VeraSun Energy Corp. to add twenty-six ethanol fuel stations in the Chicago area.[11] Ford and VeraSun said they would convert forty gasoline pumps in Illinois and Missouri to dispense E85, a mixture of 85 percent ethanol and 15 percent gasoline.

GM sold 270,000 flex-fuel vehicles last year and plans to make 400,000 this year, according to Bloomberg News. "Ford produced 250,000 of the autos in 2005 and has said it may build 280,000 this year."

You might not even know you are driving a flex-fuel vehicle. Suburbans Tauruses, Explorers, and Stratuses have had flex-fuel engines and can run on both gasoline and ethanol. The trouble is that the carmakers' executives never thought it was a big deal and expended little effort to educate consumers. This is a case where the carmaker absolutely should have blown its own horn in advance of the current oil crisis. They should have been talking up the green game years ago.

No one believed when Bill Ford took over the company of his great-grandfather from the flailing times of Jack Nasser that Ford was serious about the environment. Yet the company had been producing a highly praised environmental report card since 1999. Ford was the first North American automaker to make being carbon neutral part of their business philosophy.

In 2005, Ford issued a first-of-its-kind comprehensive report that examined the business implications of reducing greenhouse gas emissions from Ford vehicles, as well as the facilities that produce them.[12] The new reality that began to emerge in 2005, however, "really hurt everybody who was making the big bucks selling SUVs," said Mary Anne Wright, director of Sustainable Mobility Technologies and Hybrid Vehicle Programs at Ford. (Wright, who left in November 2005, to be replaced by Nancy Gioia, was responsible for all present and future hybrid, fuel cell, and alternative fuel technology development. Wright had assumed her position only in April 2004 and reported jointly to Product Creation and Research and Advanced Engineering.)

She told me at the LOHAS conference that Bill Ford was totally behind her efforts. The company was one of the first to produce a green sustainability report, she added. "I give the credit to Bill Ford. In the late 1990s, we were riding high, selling SUVs by the trainload. All that money coming in. . . . But I doubt we will ever see twenty-five dollar barrels of oil again. The price is more likely to reach one hundred dollars before twenty-five. But Bill Ford is behind us. Totally committed. We have to be here and be profitable and be conscious of the new carbon-neutral reality. If we aren't, we are not going to thrive as a car company. We will lose ground. This is the future for cars because cars can make the most profound difference dollar for dollar when it comes to influencing the effects of global warming." Think of this, she said. "Our cars are responsible for around one-fourth of U.S. greenhouse gas, and transportation consumes seventy percent of U.S. oil."

Dr. Michael Tamor, manager of Ford's Sustainable Mobility Technologies, stated, "If you think about the 15- to 20-year timeframe, you could argue that all vehicles are going to be hybrids. It's just a matter of which power plant is used in the hybrid system." Tamor added, "To freeze time and pretend that hybrids are not going to happen doesn't make sense."[13]

"Hybrids are different than most technologies," said John German, manager of Environmental and Energy Analyses for American Honda. "If an OEM is sitting back on developing diesel engines, he won't be in too much trouble. But with hybrids, it's becoming more and more sophisticated. You just can't turn it on. If you don't make the system now, as Toyota continues to make hybrids much cheaper and in greater numbers, the others won't be able to catch up."[14]

German thinks that hybrids could reach 50 to 70 percent of the market in ten years. "I live in Detroit," he added. "I don't want to see the Big Three go out of business. But that's a possibility."

"But most of all you feel it with the employees," said Wright.

You go to Kansas City where the Escape is being made, and the employees are really proud of what they are doing. They know they are building not only their future for the company but also a future for their families. And Bill Ford is totally accessible. Most of all, he listens. He has his ideas, but he listens like no other executive at his level. Sure, we made mistakes. You know, at first all we thought about was making one hybrid and that we might do it but no one thought it would catch on and so we did not build the necessary structures internally to mass produce this vehicle. Pricing was astronomical at the start. But with the demand that is exceeding all expectations, the prices will go down, and the hybrid will simply be what people drive.

The most conservative estimate for 2010 and beyond has J. D. Power forecasting a plateau of 3 percent hybrid penetration in the U.S. market. The most optimistic and forward-looking prediction comes from Booz Allen Hamilton, a global strategy and technology consulting firm. They predict that hybrid cars will make up 80 percent of the overall car market by 2015. I don't think the actual number will be that high, but it will someday be significantly higher than what J.D. Power predicted; plus, you can expect many more fuel variations to emerge rapidly and far greater mpg with the hybrids spawning new add-on technologies, reflecting greater consumer choice in preferred fuel.

Here are some reasons why getting yourself into a more fuel efficient car makes sense.

Right now, the auto industry accounts for at least 20 percent of U.S. and 12 percent of global greenhouse gas emissions.[15] (Other sources say transportation carbon dioxide emissions account for one-third of all carbon dioxide emissions, "more than from factories, homes, and all other individual sources."[16])

The industry's emissions are currently on track to rise by over one-third over the next fifteen years and double worldwide by 2050. If this happens, some experts say they will exacerbate the current global warming trend.[17]

It doesn't take a Ralph Nader to know that federal officials and consumers have shown a decided lack of leadership when it comes to fleet fuel economy standards in the nineties. The late nineties and early new millennium surge in SUV and minivan sales meant that combined fuel economy averages for cars and light trucks ebbed to their "lowest point in nearly 20 years."[18]

The industrial age is with us. The information age is too. This is also the green age. Yet we can invent ourselves only if political and business leaders embrace new green-shaded economic models. Instead, many leaders have pretended the new green model of the car of the future didn't even exist or wouldn't be wanted (even though Paul Hawken, Amory and L. Hunter Lovins detailed the "hyper-car" in their own important book *Natural Capitalism* some time ago). Why did Toyota become the world leader and overtake Ford and GM? Toyota was first to recognize that the business model and the new consciousness today are part of the green age.

Despite short-term setbacks, America customers can still transform themselves by 2020—if they take energy efficiency seriously and see it as a vision for economic recovery, taking on a global leadership role.

Fuel cell technology propelled the next car, a Focus, which I drove at the LOHAS conference. I was with Kip Mushisky, Ford's vehicle engineer manager. I turned the key in the ignition. Inside the car was highly pressurized liquid hydrogen, extracted from natural gas, a fossil fuel.

First, hydrogen fuel flowed into one electrode. The electrode was coated with a catalyst that strips the hydrogen into electrons and protons. The movement of the electrons generated electricity to power the motor, and the protons passed through a proton-exchange membrane into another electrode. In flowed oxygen; it came in contact with hydrogen. Hydrogen plus oxygen produced water vapors, which were emitted from the vehicle.

"There are some twenty-four of these vehicles now here at Ford," said Mushisky. "We have a partnership with BP, which is refueling the cars at three different centers in the United States. This car is refueled at BP's plant in Sacramento."

"There is no infrastructure," he said. "So it is difficult."

This car's inner workings sounded like waster sloshing through a tank.

"There are going to be lots of things on this journey that won't work," said Mushisky, "and we don't know that hydrogen is the future. The hybrids are real. They are now. They do not demand a new infrastructure. But hydrogen fuel cell cars do. It isn't there yet. It might be there someday. But it might not matter. We have to explore hydrogen like we have explored electric vehicles, although, ultimately, the EVs [electronic vehicles] did not catch on the way some people thought they might. We found people did not like the inconvenience of finding special limited sites for charging them; again, no infrastructure existed."

So was I driving the car of the future? Or was I in an engineering relic, a wrong turn, and evidence of a mutation on the genetic transportation highway?

GM nonetheless in the first five years of the new millennium put most of its eggs in the fuel cells basket and pledged to have mass-produced fuel-cell vehicles by 2010, although *U.S. News & World Report* wondered if "GM engineers have been inhaling too many fumes."[19] With not even two dozen hydrogen filling stations in the United States and with most of these expected to be in or near L.A. and San Francisco, 2010 might have been overly optimistic.

(Not to be left out, Daimler-Chrysler's retired board member Jürgen Hubbert put the total percentage of hydrogen fuel cell cars at about 1 percent by 2012—and he said Daimler aimed to be building most of them.[20])

Hydrogen derived from natural gas would be profitable to Big Oil and was going to be part of the energy future.

But hybrids were now, and the mistake that GM had made was to ignore the consumer market for hybrids. It was a real miscalculation to have put most of its eggs in the hydrogen basket and so few into the hybrid, as if its best futurists had the prescience to know which basket of eggs would survive the jostling of the ultracompetitive auto marketplace.

On the other hand, GM was making inroads with major

commercial transportation fleets, and that was promising. If many of the largest U.S. cities replaced their conventional buses with GM hybrid-powered buses, there would be far fewer ER visits for pollution-induced asthma and heart attacks—this switch should have a positive impact on all of society, and that would be good. So, I like what GM is doing there. GM's diesel electric hybrid system buses were being used in Seattle, Philadelphia, Houston, Minneapolis, Portland, Aspen, Charlotte, Springfield (Massachusetts), and Honolulu. According to the company's Web site, "In Seattle/King County alone, there are 235 GM hybrid-powered buses, and a fleet will soon be operational in Yosemite National Park. . . . At GM, we've launched a hybrid program that is focused on the highest-fuel-consuming vehicles such as mass transit buses, full-size trucks and SUVs. We are helping to preserve the environment, one city at a time."[21]

The technology in these buses has served as the starting point for GM's codevelopment with DaimlerChrysler and BMW of a two-mode hybrid system that GM will launch first in the Chevrolet Tahoe and GMC Yukon in 2007.[22] I'm glad to see GM in the game. It's late, though.

Innovations also have to be made in design and materials. In 2004, the Pentagon cosponsored a report issued by the Rocky Mountain Institute that found that "artfully combining lightweight materials with innovations in propulsion and aerodynamics could cut oil use by cars, trucks, and planes by two-thirds, without compromising comfort, safety, performance or affordability."

What will the cars of the future look like? How aerodynamic will they be?

Using ultralight bodies could double the fuel efficiency of today's hybrids, and a greater per-unit ability to absorb crash energy would make such cars as safe as or safer than today's cars.

Do we have the will to succeed and break the chains that bind us? We did once. Why not again? The National Resources Defense Council (NRDC) report *Dangerous Addiction* observes that, in response to the Organization of Petroleum Exporting Countries oil embargoes of the 1970s, Congress passed tougher fuel-economy standards that helped double the average gas mileage by the late 1980s.[23] However, since that time, we've actually worsened our fuel consumption habits by buying bigger cars like the SUVs.

Here's how much oil improvements in fuel efficiency will save Americans (while also cutting billions of tons of global warming pollution), according to the NRDC:[24]

A 40-mpg standard would save more than 50 billion barrels over the next 50 years, more than 15 times the likely yield of economically recoverable oil from the Arctic Refuge. A 55-mpg standard would save more than 20 times the Arctic Refuge's likely yield.

Raising our mpg to 55 by 2020 would cut our projected oil demand in half, and save consumers almost $30 billion per year.

Raising fuel economy standards to 40 mpg would save car owners $3,000 to $5,000 at the gas pump over the life of their car, more than offsetting increased vehicle costs. U.S. emissions of heat-trapping carbon dioxide would be reduced by nearly 900 million tons per year by 2020.

Even interim steps toward the 40-mpg and 55-mpg targets would have huge benefits, according to the NRDC. A three-mile-per-gallon improvement in fuel economy saves one million barrels of oil per day. We would save $25 billion in reduced fuel costs. We would also help reduce carbon dioxide emissions by 140 million tons per year. Our health would improve, too.

The answers are out there. We can have the energy equivalent of a Manhattan Project that creates our independence—what a great and laudable goal. But that will take a president who can excite people about the possibilities.

"There is really no need going around starting wars over oil," said Willie Nelson, the country singer who organized Farm Aid two decades ago to focus on the plight of American agriculture and traditional family farms.

Not when we have BioWillie, a biodiesel fuel made from vegetable oils that is ready to go into your tank without any modifications. BioWillie is the name of the biodiesel product that is named for the redheaded stranger. Nelson found out about biodiesel in Hawaii, where he has a home, after his wife bought a biodiesel-burning car.

Thanks to Willie's celebrity fuel, biodiesel stations are popping up across the country. They offer pure biodiesel and biodiesel/petroleum blends.

"While diesel technology alone can make big strides toward helping us meet our national energy, environment, and security objectives, when you add biodiesel and other biofuels, it gets really interesting. We think biofuels are a win-win proposition. Biofuels represent a huge opportunity to reduce our consumption of conventional petroleum-based fuel (and our dependence on foreign oil). Biofuels reduce lifecycle CO_2 [greenhouse gas] emissions, because the plants from which they're derived absorb carbon dioxide from the atmosphere during growth. Biofuels reduce tailpipe emissions of particulates, carbon monoxide, and hydrocarbons, compared with conventional diesel fuel. And biofuels support the American agricultural economy."

This amazing quote came from a speech by Chrysler Group President and CEO Tom LaSorda on January 23, 2006, at the Detroit Economic Club.[25]

Meantime, Bill Ford said that his company is now going to shift its focus to flex-fuel vehicles, where he thinks Ford could outpace or compete with its Japanese rivals (who thus far had no flex-fuel vehicles to speak of in the United States). "This is not a lack of commitment to hybrids," Ford said from Dearborn, Michigan. "It's an expansion of our commitment to other technologies."[26] It's smart business. It's green patriotism, too, even though it fulfills his first commitment in a plain business manner to the shareholders to maximize their profits.

Of course, we will have to scrutinize sourcing of biofuels since we don't want sugarcone, soy- or other crop-based biofuels obtained from recently cleared Indonesian, Amazonian, or other precious rain forests. These would be a negative net impact that would only hurt the environment. In addition, the use of fossil fuel catalysts should be replaced, and nitric oxide emissions reduced. What's more, use of biofuels should also include much improved mpg. They are still not an excuse to continue being spendthrifts with mpg.

Additionally, if biofuels really take off, we will have to find ways of growing crops without toxic pesticides. So there are issues here, too, to watch out for. But it is a good move in the right direction.

Look for BioWillie at Carl's Corner Truckstop outside Dallas and in California, Georgia, and South Carolina. Biodiesel costs about $2.30 per gallon for a 20/80 vegetable-oil and diesel blend, and $3.20 to $3.50 for pure biodiesel. For more information, visit www.biodiesel.org and www.wnbiodiesel.com.

Canola oil, of course, is a favorite of biodiesel fanatics. I liked the story that Margaret Juhae Lee wrote in the *Green Guide* about her future mother-in-law, who collected canola oil and used it to fuel her car. "One afternoon a week, Carol drives to a restaurant-supply company in her hometown of Lafayette, Louisiana to fill her car's gas tank with canola oil.[27]

"Each five-gallon jug of canola oil costs $20, which works

out to $4 a gallon. It's more than what I would pay at the gas station, but I get around 32 miles per gallon for city driving," Carol told the *Green Guide*. "And I can relieve some of my guilt about being an American oil glutton."

Of course, if you go the canola oil route, your car will need a conversion kit. Diesel-engine conversion kits cost up to $700 (plus installation) and require a storage tank and a small pump. See www.elsbett.com and www.greasecar.com.

But the real breakthroughs might come from out of left field. *Business Week* reports that Greg Hanssen's company EnergyCS converted a Toyota Prius that now achieves from 100 to 180 mpg in a typical commute.[28]

"These vehicles are quickly becoming the darlings of strange bedfellows: both conservative hawks and environmentalists, who see such fuel efficiency as key to ensuring national security and fighting climate change. Reducing dependence on the turbulent Middle East 'is a war issue,' said former CIA Chief R. James Woolsey, who calls the cars' potential 'phenomenal.' What's the secret? It's as simple as adding more batteries and a plug to hybrids such as the Prius."

The plug-in hybrid electric vehicles are superhybrids with larger batteries. "This gives drivers the ability to run entirely on electric power at highway speeds for 20-plus miles. For long trips, the battery never runs down."[29]

In New York City, the big question, however, is how much legroom commuters expect from their taxis. Environmentalists in New York City were keenly interested in seeing some of the taxi fleet converted to hybrids. The hybrids approved for use, for now, however, had smaller foot and legroom than the other roomier fossil fuel cabs.[30] These included the 2006 Ford Escape hybrid, 2006 Mercury Mariner hybrid, 2006 Toyota Highlander hybrid, 2006 Toyota Prius,

2006 Honda Civic hybrid, 2006 Honda Accord hybrid, and the 2006 Lexus RX 400H.[31]

Ten inches "is approximately the difference in backseat space between a standard New York taxi and the new hybrid SUVs that environmentalists would like to see added to the city's fleet of 12,760 yellow cabs," said a wire report.

What would New Yorkers decide? People like their comforts. Would they go for a smaller ride or for a nostalgic ride in the fossil fuel past? According to the report, "Mark A. Izeman, a lawyer with the Natural Resources Defense Council, said he is certain hybrids will be embraced by cabbies and customers alike." He added that converting the entire fleet would be like taking twenty-four thousand cars off the crowded, polluted streets of the city and would help reduce global warming.

No doubt, hybrid taxis soon will be as roomy, but it will take taxi and limousine commissions from different cities and jurisdictions to act together. Other private and public hack companies and commissions have been slow to embrace hybrids, but if the New York experiment gains momentum, it will stimulate additional interest in hybrids from other cities' taxi and limousine companies and commissions.

In the meantime, New Yorkers should contact the New York City Taxi and Limousine Commission at www.nyc.gov/html/tlc/html/home/home.shtml to say they do like having hybrids in their fleet.

The shift in consciousness is occurring globally. The Health Secretary of Mexico said that more than one-third of Mexico's disease burden is the result of environmental factors, the most serious of which is air pollution. Mexico City ranks among the most polluted cities in the world. Its ozone levels exceed World Health Organization standards three hundred days a year. Exhaust fumes from Mexico City's estimated 4 million motor vehicles, many of which are old and especially environmentally damaging, are the main source of air pollutants. The Mexican government is providing incentives for using cleaner fuels and smog control measures. But the state-owned oil company Pemex is also contributing to pollution and has yet to eliminate production of leaded gasoline. We should expect more from our southern neighbor.

Mexico City signed an agreement in January 2006 to take delivery of five hundred Civic Hybrid sedans. José Luis Luege Tamargo, Secretary of the Environment and Natural Resources, said at the signing that Mexico City alone consumes 26,000 tons of gasoline and diesel daily—208,000 barrels or 8.7 million gallons of fuel. The five hundred hybrids are a nice start but really just too little for a city with this type of fossil fuel dependency. And we need to get the lead out.

We don't know with any certainty about the outcome of this warming period, its causes, or how long it will last. Larry David drives a Prius hybrid for his fantastic HBO comedy *Curb Your Enthusiasm*, which so ably spoofs all of us on L.A.'s Westside. It is so L.A. Toyota engineers must have been thinking of L.A. when they were designing the Prius. You know, movie stars. If that's not your bag, try the Mercury Mariner or Ford Explorer. The Ford hybrids are great to drive, and you won't stand out as you would in a Prius. If all of us together break the shackles the oil industry has on the auto industry, it will be critical to our national security, as well as curbing greenhouse emissions. It will also help to create a more diversified and competitive marketplace—and we hold the power with one of the most important purchases, financially, most of us will ever make.

We are all talking about the hydrogen highway, but we can't get on it until we take a test drive. So, if you haven't, go drive a hybrid or buy a flex-fuel vehicle and support your local farmer. See what it is like to drive a cool car. If enough of us do so, we'll free ourselves from reliance on Middle Eastern oil in our own lifetimes. I've prepared a guide to what's out there, based on 2006 fuel standards. Happy driving.

Vehicle	Seats	Gas engine, transmission	City/highway mpg	Approx. base price
Ford Escape SUV	5	4 cyl., CVT	36/31	$28,000
Honda Insight ('05)	2	4 cyl., MT, CVT	61/66, 57/56	$20,000
Honda Civic	5	4 cyl., CVT	50/50	$22,000
Honda Accord ('05)	5	V-6, AT	29/37	$31,000
Lexus RX 400h SUV	7	V-^, CVT	31/27	$49,000
Mercury Mariner SUV	5	4 cyl., CVT	36/31	$30,000
Toyota Prius	5	4 cyl., CVT	60/51	$21,000
Toyota Highlander SUV	7	V-6, CVT	33/28	$34,000

EIGHT
Stop Being Toxic

My flight into Omaha, Nebraska, was not even half full. Nobody flies from L.A. to Omaha unless they're returning home, of course, from visiting friends on the coast or running a telephone network operation, since Omaha is the telemarketing capital of the nation.

It was nighttime and warm when I trotted off to my next destination. I got in a petro cab and took it to the hotel. This time I kept quiet and just dug being in the Midwest again.

I stopped at the front desk in the homey lobby at the Carlson Country Inn & Suites (which is actually in Carter Lake), Iowa of Abbott Road and presented my ID and credit card and checked in. I went up to the third floor. I dumped my luggage on the bed.

Although this trip had come up quickly, I had done online research on which hotels near the Omaha airport had the best environmental records. Carlson appeared to be one of my better choices.

Carlson Hotels Worldwide said it was a member of the International Tourism Partnership (ITP) and had agreed to voluntarily follow the International Hotels Environmental Initiative. The ITP has even published guiding principles—with the strong support of the Marriott, Hilton, and Starwood (Sheraton) groups—on how to build more properties without causing damage to the environment, by using green technologies.[1]

It was a nice room and there were no crabs or dust mites in the sheets, so I could not complain from the comfort or friendliness standpoint, and that was important. I liked the people, I liked the hotel, and I liked my room, but I could find little evidence that the company was seriously implementing innovative environmental practices. They told me that to save water they wouldn't wash my towels or change my sheets every day unless I requested it. But in the bathroom, the usual swag consisted of the same old petrochemical junk in the usual wasteful plastic packaging.

I sent an e-mail from my laptop to the Carlson corporate Web site, asking them, "What is your company's environmental policy? Do you offer organic foods for breakfast? Do you use organic materials for your towels? If you would fill me in, that would be great." Eventually, the company sent me back a really disgusting note. "Dear Mr. Steinman, Thank you for contacting us via the office of Betsy Day, Director of Public Relations & Communications. Thank you for your feedback. We do research information for our environment on a regular basis and we will be forwarding your feedback to our Corporate Purchasing department. Thank you for allowing us the opportunity to assist you. Janet, Corporate Customer Service Specialist, Carlson Hotels Worldwide, 11340 Blondo Street Omaha, NE. 68164; www.regenthotels.com; www.radisson.com; www.parkplaza.com; www.countryinns.com; www.parkinn.com."

I sent another e-mail: "Message to management: I'm not talking about tomorrow with your environmental commitments. I'm talking about today. Why doesn't your hotel offer any organic foods or use less packaging?"

I just thought they sounded kind of bland, the kind of bland that waits to follow about ten years after something has already happened. I went in the bathroom and slapped water on my face to wake myself up. This was all a bad dream. I should have had my trusty pesticide water test kit available to do some field research. Nebraska drinking water was routinely contaminated with atrazine, acetochlor, and alachlor, three chemical herbicides with a record of causing either ovarian or other cancers, endocrine disruption, and other serious health problems.[2,3,4,5]

That night as I lay down to sleep, Sioux Indian thunderclouds clapped above me, shook the room, and made me feel like a leaf on the prairie. All night, lightning and thunder filled the sky, and the rain fell furiously like arrows into the earth. I turned on CNN halfway through the night and listened to the news. It was August 23, 2005. Farther south, Hurricane Katrina was waiting offshore. Meanwhile, on Fox, reporters said Katrina was going to be a big one—the mother of all storms. But no one knew for sure when it would make landfall.

In the morning, I went downstairs to the breakfast buffet. Nothing there was organic. Carlson, I had to say, disappointed me. What an opportunity it had to be a leader in the organic movement. How about some organic fruits and vegetables, an organic fruit spread, or some Organic Valley dairy? What they offered was part of "dead" unconscious living. I didn't want that anymore.

Barely any life anyplace for me right now, it's too early, and the food is uninspiring. Why can't these people be inspired? What a drag.

• • •

NatureWorks' publicist Mary Rosenthal had flown in the previous night from Minneapolis and met me in the lobby of my hotel. NatureWorks, she told me, was part of Cargill.

Founded in 1865 and based in Minneapolis, Cargill is the largest privately held company today in America, according to *Forbes* magazine, and a global agricultural force, particularly in corn and soy.[6]

Members of the Cargill and MacMillan families jointly own common equity for the company. (Warren R. Staley, Cargill's chairman and chief executive officer, is only the third nonfamily chief executive in the company's 140-year history.) Its 2004 revenues were $66.67 billion, an increase of 6 percent over the previous year, with net profit of $1.525 billion, according to *Forbes*.

An international provider of food, as well as agricultural and risk management products and services, it has 124,000 employees in fifty-nine countries.[7] A short description of what this company is about is easy: expand the markets for corn and soy products.

The people at Cargill are agricultural innovators whose projects are based on scientific research. The company is liquid, agile, and moving quickly into profitable agriculture ventures. Besides producing and distributing crop nutrients and feed ingredients to grow foods and process grain, oilseeds, husks, and other agricultural commodities, they're also big producers of ethanol- and vegetable-based machine oils.

Rosenthal had a strong pleasant smile and careful eyes. She greeted me warmly with a handshake. She had her roller suitcase and, for a moment, I thought of a stewardess from the sixties or the entertainment director on the *Love Boat* or something like that. I knew I was in capable PR hands and in for a special trip.

"We want to get the word out about what we have here," Mary Rosenthal said as we left the hotel and walked outside. "This is something we are totally passionate about and committed to." The car heater warmed me up and she headed away from the hotel.

"It's just an amazing thing that is happening here and so important to the nation. We all feel this way."

We passed through Fort Calhoun on U.S. 75 and drove past cornfields with six-foot stalks. If you think Nebraska is flat, its terrain will surprise you. Bluffs and hills covered with thick brush ran up to the horizon.

Fort Calhoun's elevation was actually eleven hundred feet. Lewis and Clark met with the Oto and Missouria Indians near where present-day Fort Calhoun is now located. This meeting locale was called Council Bluff. Clark's journal noted the merits of "Council Bluff" as a location for "a Trading establishment & fortification."[8] Gradually, the name Council Bluffs was used by traders and explorers to describe the entire area on both sides of the river.

We passed the Lutheran, Catholic, and Baptist churches that line U.S. 75, and then Mormon Park. A sign said, "God Loves North Omaha."

Amber waves of future plastic shimmered in the Nebraska sun, and a giant conglomeration of smokestacks rose up from the prairie, as well as all sorts of silos and distillers.

Most intriguing to me, and the reason I was on my way to Blair, was that Cargill was the first company in the world to launch large-scale production of corn-based plastics and polymers as a replacement for those derived from petroleum. This was a big step forward for America's oil independence.

We neared the plant and passed through the small town of Blair, population around eight thousand, along the Missouri River, and the westernmost edge of the Nebraska-Iowa Corn Belt. Rosenthal said it was not by accident that the plant was here on the edge of the Corn Belt. This locale put Cargill's finished feed products close to the cattle feedlots of Colorado and the Western states, as well as the many hog farms of nearby Iowa.

I'd forgotten that towns like Blair existed. Most of us in L.A. wouldn't give one thought to Blair, unless we came from there, and most of us now come from farther south. In the Big Enchilada, most of us couldn't grow our own food, if we even tried. Our town is so baked in asphalt, I doubt we could even find the naked earth to plant a seed.

As is so important for any true journalist, I always try to take an evenhanded approach. So I don't claim Cargill to be the number one environmental agricultural company in the United States, and I'm not out here to be their booster.

Certainly, other large agricultural companies such as Kraft and General Mills have made significant investments in organic food production, which is the ultimate form of carbon-neutral agriculture. Archer Daniels Midland dominates the ethanol market.

Cargill's Web site doesn't mention organic agriculture; however, it does discuss the company's current investments in genetically modified agricultural crops. This was disappointing.

Yet, here in Blair, Nebraska, the company was actually doing something profoundly important for the environment—and so you really have to judge companies in their totality and strive to be an honest reality broker.

The shift from petrochemical-derived plastics and polymers to those made from corn or other domestic renewable plant sources not only contributes to reducing the nation's dependency on foreign oil but also, if implemented on a large scale, would greatly reduce the amount of pollution, including greenhouse gases. America would not have to rely on unfriendly enemy governments for oil.

In the rapidly changing world of green business, Cargill, a company not primarily known for its environmental record, could quite suddenly become a global leader—and knowing the ripple effect green business practices and innovations have within organizations and how they inspire people, I am certain that what is going on at NatureWorks is going to invigorate other aspects of Cargill's operations, infusing the company with a sprig of green consciousness. Indeed, Cargill is also one of the nation's leading producers of ethanol, another nonpolluting fossil fuel substitute from corn that has become important to American carmakers. But what Cargill is doing at NatureWorks is so profound for, and unique to, my country that I think it is like taking a large, powerful step into the green river of environmental consciousness.

The Cargill plant is huge, and it was hard to make sense of it all. It is an industrial facility that processes corn into many different products, from hog and cattle feed to biofuels such as ethanol, animal feed nutrients like lysine, and, now, plastics.

The entire industrial plant covers more than four hundred acres. Drab industrial buildings and countless distillers, silos, and metal buildings are spread out against the backdrop of cornfields. Corn-carrying cars line the railroad tracks within the complex. They were off-loading raw materials into the corn-mashing machines. A truck with "Sweet Brand" emblazoned on its door drove through the gate. We passed security, got out, handed over our IDs to a guard who had a Jimmy Durante–sized nose and was about sixty. I signed in, and watched a movie on plant safety.

From toys and servingware to flexible and rigid packaging, our world is filled with plastics and polymers. Since the post–World War II petrochemical explosion, these have almost always been made with petrochemicals, including polyvinyl chloride, styrene, polyethylene, acrylics, elastomers such as butadiene, and phthalates.[9] These toxic molecules often end up in the tissues of workers, consumers, and in the local environment in our lakes, streams, and underground aquifers, as well as the air and aquatic life.

It doesn't take a brain surgeon or even environmental extremist to make the connection and see that these same toxic chemicals are part and parcel of global warming processes as well. When we buy plastic products, we end up perpetuating more global warming processes. But, until recently, we haven't had all that many choices. Our products are almost all packaged in, or made from, plastic. We have so many plastic molecules in our tissues by now, there might be some truth to the phrase that someone is plastic; we are, more and more, made from plastic molecules, too. We have had no choice but to be toxic.

Yet, NatureWorks and Cargill are giving consumers and businesses powerful and radically new choices, the real sign of a vibrant economy, and more and more people and businesses are taking nature up on these new choices.

The proposition is mind shattering. NatureWorks is attempting to defy the common belief that we cannot produce goods without toxic molecules—that toxicity and conversion of raw materials to finished products must result in pollution.

But this is old-line thinking. "From the perspective of the chemical industry, pollution and progress are not synonymous," American Chemical Society President William F. Carroll said at a ceremony for 2005 Presidential Green Chemistry Challenge Awards winners.[10] "Pollution is waste, and waste means cost."

Green chemistry is defined as the efficient, pollution-free production of industrial chemicals, pharmaceuticals, and consumer products. The genius of green chemistry is to find ways "to develop ever-better chemical products and processes that require fewer reagents, less solvent, and less energy to produce, while being safer, generating less waste, and increasing profitability," said *Science & Technology*.[11]

The concept of green chemistry was formally established at

the Environmental Protection Agency about fifteen years ago in response to the Pollution Prevention Act of 1990.[12]

But green chemistry didn't achieve American media consciousness until October 2005, when we began to hear another term, particularly important to the organic chemists whose starting materials are fossil fuels. That term is *metathesis*.

Metathesis is a concept of organic chemistry that involves the efficient swapping of groups of atoms between molecules. In essence, metathesis is by definition a double decomposition reaction between two compounds in which parts of each are interchanged to form two new compounds. We start with AB and CD, but in the reaction we end up with AD and CB, explains Word Reference.com.[13] However, whenever we change molecular couples there will always be waste and toxicity, which we want to minimize. The key is to produce few if any toxic-waste by-products—and that's where green chemistry is now getting its due.

On October 5, 2005, Robert H. Grubbs and Richard R. Schrock of the United States and Yves Chauvin of France won the Nobel Prize for discoveries with metathesis. In essence, their discoveries, using various newly recognized metal compounds as catalysts, will enable chemical reactions to occur far more efficiently (with fewer reaction steps and resources required, as well as less toxicity). As the Royal Swedish Academy of Sciences suggested, think of a ballroom and couples dancing and changing partners effortlessly, smoothly, endlessly. Fewer waste by-products add up to stronger plastics, purer medical drugs, and safer food ingredients.

"This represents a great step forward for 'green chemistry,' reducing potentially hazardous waste through smarter production," the Nobel committee said.[14,15] "Metathesis is an example of how important basic science has been applied for the benefit of man, society, and the environment."

After the safety movie, we drove to the NatureWorks building in one corner, passing corn silos that looked like giant scarecrows. I saw distillation towers rising from the 85-million-gallon-per-year ethanol production facility.[16] Another plain red brick building was owned by Degussa, an Italian agricultural company that distributes lysine from corn for the pharmaceutical and veterinary markets, especially for hogs. (When hogs are fed lysine, they metabolize the amino acids in corn significantly better and put on weight faster.)

We arrived at 700 NatureWorks. The company certainly wasn't a film studio, but what was happening here was cool enough to be a Hollywood feature.

Here, green chemistry was changing the consciousness of America. The plant manager Carey Buckles, a handsome, trim engineering whiz from the Gulf region of Mississippi, met us inside a conference room to give us a PowerPoint presentation. Buckles, who reminded me of a dark-haired Scot, graduated magna cum laude in 1983 from Mississippi State and he worked for Dow for eighteen years. He was about six-three. His family belonged to Faith Family Baptist Church. (Cargill and Dow together built NatureWorks.)

Even though Buckles had worked in the Gulf petrochemical industry, it was his experience with Dow—not really thought of as a green company—that had enabled him to make more of a difference to our environment than many other people who claim to be deep ecologists and other serious environmental types.

Mary Rosenthal removed various corn-based NatureWorks products from her suitcase. The conference table was soon covered with a whole host of shirts, comforters, packages, mugs, beer cups, and more, all made from corn. A Bud Light beer container was being used at more large-scale sports events than ever. In May 2004, the Oakland Coliseum, home of the Oakland Athletics, was the first ballpark in the United States to adopt corn-based cups and serviceware. The same crop of corn-based containers found their way into the hands of music fans attending the June 2004 annual Telluride Bluegrass Festival in Telluride, Colorado. There, an estimated forty-one thousand meals with cups and serviceware made from corn were used exclusively during the five-day event.[17] After the festival, 49 percent of the waste was either composted or recycled. This was a 20 percent increase over the previous year.

Also during the summer of 2004, Belgium's second-largest brewery, Alken-Maes, served more than 1.5 million beers in the new corn cups at the three main music festivals in Belgium. Alken-Maes was the first Belgian brewer to use the Nature-Works cups. Not only was it environmentally correct, with the compostable packaging reducing the amount of waste generated at large music festivals, it was also smart business and helped to position Alken-Maes as the industry leader in the highly competitive Belgian brewery industry.[18]

The advantages over petroleum that had once been latent were now glaring at us with gleaming eyes. When corn-based containers are used at large corporate and sporting events, they can be collected and industrially composted just like table scraps to produce soil amendment. We're talking corn here.

"These corn-based polymers degrade like corn or tomatoes would if you compost them," Rosenthal said.

"In addition, NatureWorks also purchases back its own materials and easily turns them back into lactic acid for reuse," Buckles said.

Buckles handed me several more containers, including packaging perishables for the natural supermarket giant Wild Oats is using for fresh produce and perishables. These "corntainers" are also being used now by the leading French hypermarket chain Auchan, which recently introduced fresh salads packaged in the containers at all of its 116 stores throughout the country. The company has positioned itself as more than just a retailer, adopting a "quality-driven philosophy geared toward improving its customers' quality of life." Natural packaging is the way for them to take their mission to the next level.

Cargill's Ingeo is the registered brand name of "the first man-made fiber made from 100% annually renewable resources," according to the Ingeo Web site.[19] Rosenthal picked up a pillow and blanket made from corn fibers and handed them to me. "How much easier could it get?" she said. "You can buy these at Target."

So how do you get plastic from corn? The process is almost completely nontoxic and uses ancient natural methods such as bacterial fermentation instead of chemical catalysts. This is generally thought of as environmentally far more benign.

The process itself uses several fermentation steps that follow almost the same sequence as the human digestive tract: corn comes in from the farmer and is converted first to complex starches and then to simpler sugars such as dextrose; dextrose can be coaxed into milk sugar polymers or polylactides and then into various chemically controlled and fermented patented resins, films, and filaments. When the product's useful life has come to an end, it can be industrially composted and used to enrich the soil, instead of sending toxic molecules into underground aquifers. This is full-cycle green chemistry at its best. And since corn is a supplier of carbon atoms, this is clearly a case of the effortless ballroom dancing of metathesis—and one eschewing even metal catalysts.

Throughout the PowerPoint presentation, Buckles was eager to tell his company's story, because it showed the direction of the modern environmental movement and where so many new recruits are coming from. "Most of the people I know consider themselves strongly pro-environment and view environmental issues as neither extreme right nor left," he said. "Part of our story here at NatureWorks is about the people in the company—and that's the great story that has never been told." He thought about his own life and where he had worked.

You get all these environmentalists criticizing Dow, but, frankly, the company has played a key role in helping to revolutionize polymers—which are a major global industry and user of petroleum—and shift not only the nation's but the world's focus from oil to corn. I spent eighteen years at Dow and loved my work there. In fact, Dow and Cargill originally partnered to build NatureWorks, and both companies were in it together until 2002 when Cargill bought out Dow. I've been with this project from the start, and I love it. When this opportunity to manage the NatureWorks project came about, I jumped at it. Just like anybody else, I wanted to make a difference and do something good for my country. Here, I had a chance to work in an industry that was developing a new raw material base and greatly impact the environment in a very positive manner by eliminating the need for petroleum and by reducing pollution to virtually nothing. But not only are we lessening our nation's dependency on foreign oil, we are also having a powerful impact on the local community. We're an economic asset to the region. At NatureWorks alone, we purchase 650 million bushels of corn from farmers 100 miles around the plant. We hope to double this number in the next few years. In fact, since start-up only a few years ago, NatureWorks has added 150 new jobs in the area.

(This was not insignificant for Washington County, which has an overall population of around eighteen thousand.)

Buckles finished his PowerPoint presentation with images of all the finished products that were beginning to flow into the market.

It was inherently risky to make the move—I liked my job at Dow—but the draw of being able to be in on the ground floor of something so profound piqued my interest. We've created the first new polymer from a truly new raw material in thirty to fifty years, perhaps since the inception of the polymers industry. That whole concept that you are developing a new raw materials base is what makes this so exciting and worthwhile. Every day you go to work knowing you are making your community and your country better and stronger. The support in the local community is amazing, and it makes people who work at NatureWorks feel really good to know they are part of a plan to cut the country's foreign oil dependency and significantly reduce our environmental footprint.

Anyone you speak to in the community—and I've spoken to hundreds if not thousands of people—all say, "Yeah, this is a good thing. This is what we should be doing [for the community and for the country]." They get it. And that's what I mean about environmentalism: we're not just talking about change; we are the change; it isn't left; it isn't right; it's right here in Blair, Nebraska, smack in the middle of the country, which as far as politics goes is about as "the middle of the country" as you can get, and everyone working here is living the change.

After all, he said, what you want is to derive carbon no matter whether it is extracted or grown.

"You can obtain carbon with almost any organic matter, but oil has obviously been the economic cheap choice for half a century or longer," Buckles said.

Indeed, long before the current oil crisis, Cargill scientists had been working to develop new markets for corn and soy. One such market that existed theoretically but had yet to be implemented practically on an operational level was deriving polymers from corn sugars.

Always on the lookout for new uses of soy and corn, Cargill's agricultural scientists teamed up with Dow's chemical engineers. Said Buckles, "Our engineers had the practical know-how to set up a complex polymer plant."

"It isn't easy," he added. "We've had to move rapidly from being predominantly a research company with more than one-hundred doctorate level employees to one implementing that research into operations and becoming profitable. We are finding our niche in the enormous plastics and polymer market and growing out from there."

It was ironic than an engineer with Dow Chemical, a company long reviled by environmentalists, should be in the vanguard of the new green movement. It makes you shake your head and go wow. Everybody has a chance to be good. Maybe every company. But can we escape our past as individuals or as corporations? After all, it was Dow that manufactured such toxic compounds as Agent Orange, the birth defect–causing defoliant used during the Vietnam War. Furthermore, the active ingredients in Agent Orange, 2,4,5-T and 2,4-D, are also known to be cancer causing; in fact, although 2,4,5-T was banned from further use in the United States in the early 1980s, the herbicide 2,4-D continues to be widely used both in commercial agriculture and on lawns. It is widely known to cause human cancer, according to a host of epidemiological studies. I reported on the hearings held in Oregon in the late 1970s in which the EPA tried to ban 2,4,5-T and 2,4-D from further use. Dow attorneys ripped apart the testimonies of the women of Alsea, a local logging community in Oregon. There, these phenoxy herbicides were being sprayed to control brush, and traces had been found in the community drinking water. At the same time, childbearing women experienced unusually high miscarriage rates. The link between the herbicides and their miscarriages seemed strong, but I remembered how the attorneys for Dow used a line of questioning that made it look like anything could have caused the women's miscarriages. It was humiliating and unfair.

The largest chemical company in the United States, Dow Chemical is a leading producer of pesticides, plastics, hydrocarbons, and other chemicals. Its production processes and practices have poisoned the environment as well as consumers and workers, sometimes with dire consequences for entire communities.

The company is responsible for hazardous pesticides (such as 2,4-D, Dursban, Telone, and DBCP), as well as by-products such as dioxin, ozone-depleting chlorofluorocarbons, and Agent Orange and napalm used during the Vietnam War. In 1999, Dow acquired Union Carbide, whose pesticide plant in Bhopal, India, released methyl isocyanate and other chemicals in 1984, causing one of the worst industrial disasters in history. Recently Dow has positioned itself as one of five corporations dominating the market for genetically engineered seeds.[20] How could any company escape a past like that? Were they murderers? Did they make weapons of war? Did they profit from the war? I was shaking my head yet feeling very positive about this present experience. Sanity, I'm sure, is doing a balancing act between opposing thoughts in your brain, and that was what I was doing with all of the thoughts going through my head.

We left the conference room and walked down the hallway. It seemed that everyone who worked at NatureWorks was about the size of an NFL tackle, and I began to understand the reason for the long-standing national dominance of the Corn-husker football teams. Corn-fed beef and corn-fed kids. They were big. Buckles and Rosenthal and I donned our own form of protective gear and stepped outside, back under the big gray prairie sky. The first thing that struck me was the way the huge amount of industrial machinery, pipes, silos, vats, and distillation towers that dominated the plant shrank the sky. Everything was dirty-beige, gray, and black. Yet the company's investment in metallurgy and pollution-free manufacturing was implementing the kind of innovative technology that should make the rest of the world green with envy—this was America at its peaceful and technologically innovative best. We were using our capital to become strong from within. Already, NatureWorks's corn-based plastic and polymer technologies were being embraced in Europe, Asia, and Mexico.

In one area of the factory, Buckles showed me giant fermentation vats where friendly bacteria, nourished with simple vitamins and minerals, were used to produce biological enzymes that catalyzed initial reactions that turned corn to starch and eventually into polylactides that became the coagulated and smoothened polymers.

I realized that what I was seeing here in Blair, Nebraska, was a plastic distillation and manufacturing plant not unlike those in the chemical corridors of Texas, Louisiana, Delaware, and New Jersey.

The twist, of course, was that here corn was the starting material, and the factory was virtually nonpolluting. That's what got me. The no-pollution reality was real and happening in Blair, Nebraska.

There were no mutagens, carcinogens, or neurotoxins, and virtually no long-term health risks to workers. The danger of fire and explosions was almost nonexistent. I was even more shocked when Buckles reminded me that besides manufacturing plastics and polymers, NatureWorks is host to one of the country's largest ethanol plants. That meant Cargill was playing a role in the resurgence of American auto manufacturing as the fleet switched to more crop-based fuels. It was exciting to see the new strength in America emerging from here in the Corn Belt, and it was about time that folks in Nebraska and Minneapolis got their props.

We stepped outside, and the clouds were bright and sunny, although farther south loomed Katrina; we didn't know how big it was going to be.

I saw another big stack of silos.

"You know something," I said, "out here you don't need foreign oil, do you?" Buckles said simply, "Nope.

"In 2006, we will be completely greenhouse neutral," he said. "Not only are we investing heavily in wind credits, but from cradle to grave we use 20 to 50 percent less fossil fuel and produce 35 to 70 percent fewer greenhouse emissions than would be required with fossil fuels as raw materials."

"Don't take pictures here," he said as we entered the heart and soul of the manufacturing facilities, with pipes bent at right angles that carried the materials through a cadre of vats where carefully controlled reactions occurred that changed individual dextrose molecules into complex polylactides.

"During the processing, there are some waste bacteria left over, which can be settled out of the wastewater, and there is pure gypsum, which is used to help break down high-clay soils or to remediate open strip mines," he said. "This level of pollution, if you can even call what we produce that, certainly is not even close to what you would get out of the smokestacks of a petrochemical polymer factory, and everything is used and reused; in effect, there is no waste."

Yet, for all of the innovative work going on at Nature-Works, the transition from research to profitable entity has required patience. Cargill, parent company, recognizes it is developing not only a technology but also a market, Buckles said. The plant is producing a mere 300 million pounds of corn-based polymers in a $300 billion global polymer industry.

"It takes time, because for the biggest customers, you have so many layers and so many purchasing agents with their own sets of specifications and needs. Each buyer has his or her concerns. They do drop tests to make sure that the new packages won't break; they need to see how the containers palletize, how much each weighs, how they can be recycled and reused, everything . . . before they commit. These things take time."

Although NatureWorks showed that plastic can be profitably made from any kind of carbon donor, the properties of each starting material go on to create slightly different polymers with characteristic properties that make them suitable for some tasks and not others. In essence, then, corn-based polymers are not identical to the petrochemical polymers. They're very close and have roughly the same feel but, molecularly, are held together differently, and what we can't see with the naked eye can determine at what temperature the materials melt or how they "breathe," even how they go through converting machinery. All of this has had subtle effects on the marketability of the polymers and led to some early roadblocks.

Initially, NatureWorks started making fiber polymers for the textile industry that could replace nylon and other synthetic fabrics. But textile industry buyers and experts said that this was a long-term process requiring several years of testing and refining. How would their fibers work in the mills, for example? Fibers made from corn would have to be spun on a large scale, milled, dyed, and heavily processed, and all of this would have to be done over and over in the beginning so that mills could make sure they could work with the new fiber. The industrial and institutional hurdles were enormous.

"That was when we realized that introducing corn-based fibers was going to take time," he said.

On the other hand, turning the same raw materials into clear plastic film for perishable food items, and other types of packaging, could be done now. Because the corn-based polymers are not precisely identical to petroleum-based polymers, handling them can require changes in manufacturing platforms, however. Fortunately some of the manufacturing converters who would be turning corn pellets from NatureWorks into plastic packaging found that if they were already working with polystyrene materials, they could easily work with corn-based polymers with just a few adjustments in processing temperatures.

Still, other hurdles became apparent because of the differences in molecular structure. Corn-based film can be used for bottling natural spring and other "flat" waters that lack carbonation, but the microscopic gaps between corn-based polymers are greater compared with fossil-fuel films. As a result, corn polymers don't work well for containers intended to hold bubbly, carbonated waters, which would lose their carbon dioxide (the source of their carbonation) through the microscopic gaps in the film.

On the bright side, polylactic acid polymers made from corn can be used for the windows in cake and doughnut boxes, where their "breathability" provides a clear-cut benefit: Because the corn-based plastic "breathes," condensation does not form inside pastry boxes; during one such test, retail doughnut sales increased.[21]

We walked into the packaging area where the corn polymers were being spewed out in the shape of popcorn-sized pellets that could be shipped to various plastic processing plants for reprocessing into products.

In 2002, when Wild Oats became one of the first companies to embrace the new technology, the cost of the "corntainers" was high. As one of the first customers, the company paid about 50 percent more for takeout containers made from the bioplastic instead of fossil fuels.[22] Nonetheless, Wild Oats found that its customers liked the new corntainers, and the natural food retailer credits the corntainers with increasing deli sales by 12 percent. Today, the company has switched to corn-based plastic in eighty of its Wild Oats Natural Marketplace stores.[23] (Earth Fare is another chain along the Eastern seaboard that is using them.)

Another reward was the bottom line. At the same time that NatureWorks has increased its manufacturing know-how and increased efficiency, oil prices have risen dramatically. Indeed, even before the devastating consequences that hurricanes Katrina and Rita wrought on the petrochemical industry in the Gulf of Mexico, the "corntainers" in its deli cost Wild Oats 5 percent less than traditional plastic, said spokeswoman Sonja Tuitele.

Also flexing their economic patriotism is Newman's Own, the natural foods company the movie actor and race car driver Paul Newman began with his daughter Nell. The company is packaging its new perishable baby salad vegetables in corntainers, too. This should give them a big marketing advantage as they move from cookies and popcorn into perishable produce.

In January 2005, Biota Brands of America, which offers premium Colorado spring water, became the first U.S. water company to use bottles molded of a natural plastic from NatureWorks.[24]

In November 2005, Naturally Iowa Dairy of Clarinda, Iowa, announced it would use corn packaging for its natural and organic milk products in its Rolling Hills Organic Farms and Naturally Iowa all-natural milk brands.[25]

Coop Italy and Auchon, a supermarket chain in France, are also using corn-based plastics from NatureWorks.

The textile market is beginning to embrace corn-based fibers as the natural alternative to fossil-fuel-derived fabrics. Pacific Coast Feather Co., the Seattle-based manufacturer of comforters and pillows, has found that their Natural Living brand made with Ingeo corn fibers from NatureWorks is a marketplace powerhouse. The company has tripled the number of stores that distribute their Natural Living brand, including both Linens-n-Things and Marshall Field.[26] Indeed, a visit to the Linens-n-Things Web site shows a wide range of Natural Living brand products that are quite competitively priced with their petrochemical cousins. Factor in your improved personal health from your reduced exposure to petrochemicals, and you've got a bargain. An Ingeo mattress topper filled with Ingeo natural fiber was on sale for only $59.99 for a twin bed compared with $69.99 for a Novaform Ultimate Mattress Topper made with petroleum raw materials.[27] Meanwhile, at Target.com, an Ingeo fiber Natural Living Comforter was listed at $59.99 to $89.99, which is competitive with the polyester-filled Waverly comforters on the Web site.[28]

But the most important deal has been with Wal-Mart, the nation's largest grocery seller. In November 2005, Wal-Mart began using the corn-based polymers to replace 114 million clear-plastic clamshell containers that are used annually by the retailer for cut fruit, herbs, strawberries, and Brussels sprouts in its 3,779 Wal-Mart, Sam's Club, and Neighborhood Market stores in the United States.

"With this change to packaging made from corn, we will save the equivalent of 800,000 gallons of gasoline and reduce more than 11 million pounds of greenhouse-gas emissions," said Wal-Mart executive Matt Kistler, vice president for product development and private brands for the company's Sam's Club division. Kistler said the new plastic was now being used for telephone calling cards and holiday season gift cards sold at Wal-Mart.[29]

The benefits to each of us for being less toxic to those around us are enormous. Let's take a hypothetical thousand packaging bottles made with either corn or oil. A corn plastics plant uses 1,606 megajoules of fossil fuel resources, compared with 2,493 megajoules for a petroleum plastics plant (per thousand bottles).[30] In terms of greenhouse gases, the corn plant produces only 62 kilograms compared with 111 kilograms for the petroleum plastics plant per a thousand bottles, according to a report in the March 28, 2005, issue of *Forbes*.[31] Carbon-neutral efficiency engenders lower costs. Put another way, take those same thousand bottles and compare the raw materials used in producing them from either oil or corn. Since 1975, assume the real cost for oil-based raw materials has gone from under $30 to over $40 (as of spring 2005 before Katrina and Rita). The cost of corn-based raw materials has gone from over $60 to under $20, according to the U.S. Department of Energy.[32] Now factor in oil at $70 a barrel, and OPEC is going to be pricing itself out of existence as the new technologies evolve that allow America to replace oil with home-grown resources.

By the time Carey Buckles and Mary Rosenthal finished showing me the plant, I was truly impressed. I know it is easy to take a black- and-white view—good guys versus bad guys—and a lot of us have loved to hate Dow and probably hadn't thought too highly of Cargill either. But this was a new picture, and I could not wait to report what I'd seen and heard.

I spoke with Buckles and Rosenthal about using organic corn. They want to do it, they know it is important, but they are business people, they said. Their plant uses so much corn and the amount of organic corn is so minuscule that they are not set up to handle it. I know where they are coming from, and I think that criticizing them when this is a moment of triumph is unfair. If you'd seen these corn monsters sucking it all in, you'd know they are telling the truth; right now, I agreed, it was impractical, but maybe down the line, I said, Cargill would put its considerable research and innovative technologies into this area as well. But if you put what's happening here down because of this you're certainly missing the big picture. Cargill has just taken a dip into the clear waters of their future, and I think they liked this green consciousness thing. I saw potential global, positive change emanating from the Corn Belt. I saw big agriculture's consciousness being transformed. I saw corn coming into a plant from local farmers and how this helped the local economy. From there, the corn was being turned into plastic in a process developed in America that one day the whole world would want. The licensing fees alone will create tremendous wealth for the company and for all nations and promote a green technology. With greater demand, more high-paying jobs would be created, more corn would be planted, and less fossil fuel was going to be required. There will be almost no toxicity where these plants are located, and there will be good paying jobs so there will be much less NIMBY (Not In My Backyard) opposition manufacturers and waste operations often face.

When we parted company, we were friends. Maybe there were a whole lot more green-conscious people than I had thought existed and maybe lots of them were between the coasts. I felt better than when I woke up earlier that day, dreary and tired from the flight. I felt like the world was my friend. That was nice.

Rosenthal and I drove back to the airport. She told me how thankful she was to be able to wake up each morning and do a job that really meant something. I told her I felt the same way.

The winds were blowing the trees, and the amber fields of

potential polylactic acid plastic pellets shimmered under the midafternoon heat. "People today want to know they are making a difference," she said. "They just need to be better informed and know that being green is easier than they might think."

Wal-Mart? Target? Dow? Cargill? You mean, these are the companies that are strongly influencing America's environmental movement, taking us by leaps and bounds into the realm of green patriotism?

But why are these big companies going green? Is it altruism or financial interests? Maybe it is both. Maybe this is a time in business history when being a good corporate citizen is profitable.

Amory B. Lovins writes in *Scientific American* that there is "more profit with less carbon." [33] He says Americans now use 47 percent less energy per dollar of economic output than they did thirty years ago, lowering our costs by $1 billion a day. This might not sound like much in today's world where our gas and electric bills are rising precipitously. But think of it this way: without these energy efficiencies, our current energy bills and the prices of a whole host of consumer goods would be even higher, and our skies would be darker with pollution.

"These savings act like a huge universal tax cut that also reduces the federal deficit," Lovins said. "Far from dampening global development, lower energy bills accelerate it. Once, compact fluorescent lamps ran $20. Today, they cost two to five dollars and compete nicely with incandescent bulbs—except that the compact fluorescents use 75 to 80 percent less electricity and last 10 to 13 times longer."

No wonder, then, in May 2005, General Electric promised to raise the company's overall energy efficiency by 30 percent by 2012 "to enhance the company's shareholder value."[34] Five other megacorporate powers—IBM, British Telecom, Alcan,

NorskeCanada, and Bayer—have collectively saved $2 billion since the early 1990s by reducing their carbon emissions by 60 percent, said Lovins. That not only means a lower cost of living but also less toxicity to the environment and to you and your friends and neighbors and loved ones.

We can all stand to be a little less toxic to our environment and maybe to our friends and loved ones, too; and even if you're a big bad polluting guy, gal, or company, you can really change. At least, that was the message I took home with me from Nebraska. This time, from I-99, I veered west into the coastal range of Central California. I drove through the town of Taft. After my earlier visits in the spring to Earlimart and Weedpatch, these towns appeared to be positively wealthy. In fact, most of the towns in this part of the San Joaquin Valley were quite prosperous. Oildale, although small, with a population of around 27,885 according to the 2000 Census, was not like the fruit-picking farmworker barrios of Weedpatch, Earlimat, and McFarland, where the poverty screamed obscenities at my consciousness.[35] Here in Taft, I passed the Chevron Valley Credit Union and an oil museum. My slow passage along Main Street took me past buildings with facades dating to the 1950s and '60s, with models of miniature oil rigs in front and paintings of oil rigs on their walls.

Soon, I ended up near Fellows and stopped at the Derrick Café, post office, and Town Market, and that was almost the whole town. Skyrocketing oil prices had breathed life into even formerly abandoned wells, and the Midway-Sunset oilfield was humming with happy men and women. I drove down Highway 33, past Berry Petroleum, Conoco, ExxonMobil, and a host of independents' signs.

I took Shale Road down toward the coastal foothills. I was surrounded. You do not know what an oilfield is until you have visited the Midway-Sunset field, and you are driving down Shale Road, and the oil pumps become ever more numerous. I turned off the radio, which was now nothing but static. Grating pumping sounds surrounded my brain like a thousand buzzing wasps. It was what I imagine it would be like being in the midst of a herd of thousands of wildebeests. Only instead of animals, there were wells. The pumps seemed almost to have faces, but the eyes were actually mad holes drilled into the metal. Near some of the wells were steam injectors. The crude here was thick, and it needed to be thinned. To reduce the viscosity of the oil, steam was being injected into the ground and used as a heat source. The steam was being piped to the Midway-Sunset Cogeneration Plant, saving tons of greenhouse gas emissions from going into the environment. All around me, the oil pumps moved steadily, rhythmically. The pumps were everywhere. I took pictures, but it was futile. I needed a 180-degree panoramic lens, and even then it was only a small piece of the picture. Everything became clear in the midst of the squeaking and swirling heat and dust and dryness. The beast was us. We drove dinosaur cars and ate foods packaged in fossil-fuel plastics, and we were the beasts, and we demanded the oil from fields over the mountains.

These tens of thousands of wells were pumping for David, Terri, Spenser, Hunter, and Sharla, and Denise and Cassie and Jeanne and Kim and Jodey and Rubel and Benny and Pat and Michael and Jay and Jim and Joanna and Dennis and everyone driving someplace in L.A. today. Much of the oil here was flowing south, like our water, to the Chevron El Segundo refinery to become gasoline. We were living, breathing, carbon-based creatures.

I came down the I-5 and took Highway 119 west to Taft to Highway 33. I saw a traffic light at Highway 119 and the intersection with Midway Road. I went about six miles and saw a stop at the Highway 33 intersection. I made a right and less than a mile later on the big flat fossil plain I saw the Chevron sign on my left and two big white water tanks on my right and this was the final turn on this leg of my journey. I arrived at Chevron around nine A.M. Hermann Ng, facilities supervisor for Chevron, was talking on his cell, hardhat jauntily on his head, in the parking lot of Chevron's row of one-story field offices.

Although this world of mining and energy production is truly a world away from Los Angeles, on the other side of the Tehachapi mountain range, we were only around 150 miles from the Chevron refinery in El Segundo where much oil from this field, which is now more than one hundred years old, would journey before it powered the L.A. car scene.

I got into Ng's half-ton truck. He said he could give me half a megawatt of energy—which he said could power 250 regular homes, "not movie stars' homes, regular people's homes"—without fossil fuel, coal, or any other earth exudation, with virtually no overhead or oversight, maintenance, or upkeep (except for a little dusting)—and without much residual workforce effort *right now*, and he said he would bet the house that what Chevron has done here where we were standing right now in the heart of Midway-Sunset Oil Field in the desert shale of the western ridges of Kern County, could be the future of your home's energy needs. Was he feeling cool? Yes, because he knows the power of solar firsthand. And so does Chevron. It is all about being carbon-neutral, being less toxic—and more profitable.

Chevron has not always been an environmental leader. The company's Ortho division (purchased by Dow Chemical and later sold to Scott's, maker of the Miracle-Gro line of gardening products) has long been a leading purveyor of 2,4-D and other potentially dangerous lawn and home pesticides. A Chevron Chemical

Co. Inc. (Ortho Division) superfund site is located in Orlando, Orange County, Florida. The site covered approximately 4.39 acres in an industrial area at 3100 Orange Blossom Trail. There, Chevron Chemical Co. operated a chemical blending facility for pesticides and other crop sprays between 1950 and 1976. The facility formulated a variety of liquid and powdered pesticides, including some truly dangerous ones (now largely banned in the United States) such as chlordane, lindane, dieldrin, and aldrin. Soil samples indicated the presence of pesticides, benzene, toluene, xylene, chlordane, naphthalene, and metals. Groundwater samples contained metals, benzene, toluene, xylene, pesticides, trichlorethylene, and chlorobenzene.[36]

I have no interest in being a Chevron booster, either, and, more recently, they were experiencing serious criticisms from a region in Ecuador where they have oil fields they inherited from their merger with Texaco. But, as I learned with Cargill, I think you have to look at not only a company's history but also where it is headed. In that sense, Chevron was remarkable, and one of the good guys, even if they were an oil company. I liked them. I purposely seek out their stations, too, when I need some dinofuel.

"We could not sit around and wait for everybody else when it comes to solar," Ng said. "If you do that, nothing will ever advance. Chevron is taking a leading role in solar."

Solar mining, as the company refers to its use of solar here, could be the future of office- and home-based energy systems throughout the world, in both industrialized and developing nations.

"The main postal facility in San Francisco is solar powered, thanks to Chevron," he said, over his shoulder. "One of our most important profit centers is conservation and solar. It is going to be a bigger and bigger part of our future. The writing is on the wall."

With our homes accounting for about half of all oil consumption and greenhouse emissions in the world today, mining the sun could make a distinct and significant difference in our lives, literally brightening everybody's future. We might even increase our empowerment quotient and take back some of our independence.

We drove a short distance to Pipeline Delivery Station 31, a quiet fenced-in site not far away on Randall Road. On one side were crude storage tanks several stories high and a maze of oil pipelines. Crude oil arrived from nearby rigs by truck and pipeline to this distribution center from where it was delivered via pipeline 150 miles south to the Chevron refinery. We pulled up at a gate.

Ng got out, unlocked it, got back in, and drove forward. When we got out, I was in the midst of row on row of sturdily mounted aluminum modules, like trays, one after another, angled south to capture the power of the sun.

It was not a very sunny day, but nonetheless, the SolarMine array was performing well above expectations.

"Almost all the oil here goes to Los Angeles," Ng said. "With oil at fifty dollars a barrel, it's worth a lot these days, and even many of the least productive fields around here are back in production." The irony, of course, is that the energy of the sun was sending all of that fossil fuel to the oil-greedy universe that was Los Angeles.

We walked over to the array of aluminum mounts. They looked like giant multilegged silver beetles.

Thin cells—dark, adhesive, and flexible—lined the aluminum trays, each facing the sun.

The black film looked like the surface for the eyes of a fly.

In total, forty-eight hundred Uni-Solar cells, each about 1.3 feet wide and 18 feet long, covered nearly three acres.

"So many breakthroughs are represented in the SolarMine

project," he said. "When I worked for Amoco sometimes our facilities were so far away from the grid, when we needed to set up monitoring equipment, its energy source was power from solar photovoltaic cells." He grinned as if he was about to let me in on a big secret. "Now, do you know what one of the most popular things for hunters to shoot at was where we were? That's right. You wouldn't think so, but they loved using our solar cells for target practice. Well, in the old systems, if one solar cell was destroyed, this knocked out the whole system. No more. Not with these babies."

Ng rubbed his hand on a strip with a solar cell. "With these here, even if one is damaged, the system continues to operate."

"What's upkeep like?" I asked.

"None. We don't even have to dust them. We did once. Recently, with the rains, we haven't even needed to do that. But even when they are dusty, they are still highly productive."

"I am a big believer in solar," he said. "I think one day soon every new home in California will have a solar roof. The good thing we are doing here at Chevron is that we are not waiting for someone to do this first. We are pioneers. If everyone waits around until the technology is perfected and the price lowered, nothing will ever happen.

"Someone has to go out there and take chances. That's what we did, and I have to say it has paid off for us. With energy prices the way they are now, we save around a hundred thousand dollars a year."

In 2001, when United Solar Systems signed an agreement with Texaco (which merged in 2000 with Chevron to become ChevronTexaco and then, once again, in 2005, Chevron) to design and install the photovoltaic system, the first meeting was scheduled for September 12, 2001, but with all aircraft grounded due to the terrorist attack on America the day before, the meeting was rescheduled for a week later. The system was quickly completed on December 18, 2002, the largest solar array in the state of California. The cost of the project was $4.86 million. But with a California Energy Commission's Emerging Renewables Program offering a 50 percent rebate, the cost was reduced to $2.43 million, a great example, by the way, of how to make green taxes work well for society and encourage a company to do the right thing (see also Chapter 9).[37] Because solar energy is totally environmentally friendly, the SolarMine project saves 850 tons of carbon dioxide and 1,950 pounds of nitric oxide annually. As so often happens, bottom-line savings are achieved with technologies that not only reduce greenhouse emissions but also put American technology in a leadership role (although Europe now has an even larger and more impressive solar array near Leipzig).

"No upkeep. Consistent power. I'd say this is a good thing."

But three acres is, well, three acres, I said, and it does not seem very productive to require three acres to power the equivalent of 250 homes. Ng touched the cells, inspected them, and then turned to me.

"For pure efficiency, there's nothing that compares with fossil fuel. But I am telling you we have something very unique here. You see, Uni-Solar is now using thin-film solar cells to make roofs for homes."

He told me that Uni-Solar was using a proprietary thin-film, vapor-deposited amorphous silicon alloy to reduce the materials cost of building solar cells. Amorphous silicon cells absorb light more efficiently than crystalline systems, so the thickness of its solar cells could be one hundred times less, he said. But with improving technology, of course, the thickness could eventually be a thousand or more times less than today, extracting and compressing the solar rays of the sun.

These systems are thin, unobtrusive, and easily installed.

The filmmakers Campbell Dalglish and Catherine Oberg wanted to escape their Manhattan apartment, and they found a wooded lot in East Patchogue, Long Island, near wetlands, a lake, and bordering on a bird sanctuary, according to their success story posted on the Uni-Solar Web site.[38]

Early on, Campbell and Catherine decided their home would feature solar technology. "Solar is really catching on," said Campbell. "But most people are conservative about the look of their homes. When you mention solar, they picture unsightly panels that are snuffed out by a passing cloud. We wanted to show that solar has come a long way."

Campbell and Catherine set three criteria for the solar energy system they would choose. It had to be effective, it had to be attractive, and it had to be affordable.

They were also determined to have minimal environmental impact. "We didn't want to cut down any extra trees." But time and again, they were told they'd have to cut down trees to ensure that sufficient sunshine reached the solar panels. However, the Uni-Solar system wouldn't require the felling of a single tree. Once installed, the system was almost indistinguishable from the standing seam metal roof. That's because the cells were so thin they were part of the roof.

On days when the home uses little electricity, the extra power generated by their solar roof is sold back to Long Island Power Authority, turning the electric meter backward.

Who would have thought that Coca-Cola was going green? Can we really equate the two? Or is just a company doing what it thinks is smart business? When Coca-Cola Bottling management faced the decision of whether to replace their existing roof with a standard membrane roof or opt for a more environmentally and economically sound choice, they decided to follow the green business vision and opted for a solar roof for their Los Angeles plant.[39] Completed in January 2004 with Uni-Solar's thin flexible solar cells and the technological help of Solar Integrated Technologies, their system provides 100 kilowatts of clean solar power daily. The use of solar power benefits everybody, including the surrounding community. Having a solar roof allows the facility to generate its own electricity cost effectively and helps increase the stability of the region's energy supply as well. Not only will Coca-Cola save millions in energy costs over the life of the system, it will decrease its carbon dioxide emissions, by example, shifting an entire company philosophy to acknowledge that the goal is to be carbon-neutral The bottom-line energy savings are sure to prove it was an economist's smart choice as well.

For many homeowners today, the economic incentives are there and only getting better. I went to John Schaeffer, president of Gaiam Real Goods Solar Living Center, in Hopland, California, and told him I was especially interested in costs of solar and what rebates are available nationwide. He told me, "In California, the rebate is $2.80/watt plus a 7.5 percent tax credit from state and $2,000 federal."[40] This all translated into about 40 percent off the retail price, he said. "In Colorado, the rebate is $4.50/watt, plus fed tax credit." This takes about 60 percent off retail costs, he adds. "New York and New Jersey have lucrative rebates amounting to 60 percent off retail pricing."

"Is business picking up?" I said.

"Hugely," he replied. "It doubled in 2005 over 2004, growing 50 percent on average per year over the last five years."

"How much would it cost to put solar into a 2,500-square-foot home?" I said.

"Approximately twelve to fifteen thousand dollars, depending on your state."

"What else can people do around the home for energy saving?"

"Solar hot water, instantaneous hot water heaters, better insulation, energy efficient refrigeration, compact fluorescent lamps. See our catalog for more."

I love the Real Goods catalog. There's so much you can personally do with solar in your home or business. Their catalogs make great shopping and reading.

Check out the Real Goods Solar Living Center in Hopland, California. If you can't make the road trip to 13771 South Highway 101, visit their Web site at www.realgoods.com.

Although solar systems can be expensive, federal, state, and local programs help to substantially offset these costs in the form of tax credits, rebates, grants, loans, leasing, and direct equipment sales. States that are offering or have offered any of these incentives include Arizona, California, Connecticut, Massachusetts, Nevada, New Jersey, New York, Pennsylvania, and Rhode Island. A complete and up-to-date list of state and local programs is maintained by the Database of State Incentives for Renewable Energy at www.dsireusa.org. Visit www.akeena.net for additional help with a solar system and information about state and federal programs.

"Today, in California, where we are famous for the sun, we are going to put the positive benefits of that sun to good use," Governor Arnold Schwarzenegger said in February 2005 when he announced his political support for SB 1, the state solar power bill that offers California a great deal of energy independence. His ambitious plan has been the passage of legislation that would invest billions of dollars in tax credits and private funds to put electricity-producing solar panels on a million California rooftops.[41] The governor's plan called for increasing the state's total solar output from about 101 megawatts to 3,000 megawatts by 2018. Such progress would have resulted in enough solar power for some 2.25 million homes and eliminated the need for building half a dozen large natural gas–fired generating plants.

Although passed in the State Senate, unfortunately, on September 9, 2005, the California Assembly failed to pass the Million Solar Roofs bill. Hopefully, the State of California will do the right and the smart thing and put into place a powerful incentive program that benefits the citizenry and allows them to keep more of their money in their own pockets by effortlessly producing their own energy.

To show you how extensively green consciousness has begun to permeate America, particularly institutional building design, Albany County in the state of New York is using solar energy at the county's hockey facility in Colonie. Albany County partnered with the New York State Energy Research and Development Authority, which provided $240,000 for the project, and ETM Solar Works, which installed the 40kW photovoltaic system on the roof of the facility.[42] "The use of alternative energy sources, such as the PV system being installed at our ice rink, is a wise investment that will reduce our reliance on traditional energy sources," said Albany County Executive Mike Breslin. "The implementation of this renewable system will save energy and protect our environment, while resulting in cost savings to our taxpayers."

Although California is usually a trendsetter, even without full legislative support from the State of California, demand for solar home units throughout the United States is blindingly bright, perhaps even too bright for the industry to supply consumers' needs. An August 5, 2005, report in the *New York Times* noted that shortages of photovoltaic panels are seriously stifling eager home owners and businesses.[43]

Although the federal energy bill passed in 2005 provides for up to $2,000 in tax credits, a shortage of solar panels "has led to long waits and inconvenience for many Americans who are ready to spend $10,000 to $20,000 for residential solar power systems of 2,000 to 5,000 watts," according to the *New York Times* article.

That Spain, Italy, and Portugal are also implementing solar incentive programs means that there will be greater incentive for more companies, particularly in the United States, to enter a potentially fertile international arena.

The German Solar Industry Association enjoyed a growth rate well above 50 percent for 2004, the latest year for which results are available.[44] On a former lignite-mine ash deposit in Espenhain, near Leipzig, Shell Solar (of the Royal Dutch/Shell Group of Companies) officially opened the world's largest grid-connected solar power plant, comprising of 33,500 solar modules, with an output of 5 megawatts, or roughly tenfold America's largest array in the Midway-Sunset oil field. The power generated from the solar park is being fed into the grid to meet the electricity demand of some eighteen hundred households. The solar power station saves 3,700 tons of carbon dioxide emissions annually and makes the Shell project completely carbon-neutral.

Ng and I walked around the array, and he looked up at the sun. He took me inside the conversion building where DC was converted to AC and "stepped up" to 12,000 volts to feed the oil field power distribution system. Since all power is used immediately, no battery backup is required. The inverters and transformers were humming.

"The key to the future of solar is to concentrate more power per millimeter," he said.

"Does Chevron really take renewables seriously?" I asked.

"Well, that's a policy question for someone else to answer," he said, tactfully.

I knew just who to talk to. After chatting with Ng, I spoke to James C. Davis, president of Chevron Energy Solutions.

Davis had been involved with energy solutions for many years. He was senior vice president of Integrated Solutions for Pacific Gas & Electric (PG&E) Energy Services.

There, Davis conceptualized PG&E Energy Services' integrated energy solution model for major commercial, industrial, and institutional accounts, then developed and managed the supporting marketing, sales, deal structuring, finance, and operations functions.

When Chevron purchased Integrated Solutions in 2000, Davis became president of the new company. (In the interim, PG&E, the holding corporation, filed for bankruptcy protection on April 6, 2001.[45]) Chevron Energy Solutions is one of the top five environmental service companies in the United States today.

The vast majority of his new company's customers are major public institutions. According to Davis, "The largest consumers of energy in the United States are the federal government, and city, county, state, and school districts, and all of them have performance contracts. They can use their anticipated savings to avoid the need for additional upfront capital and make immediate major purchases of energy conservation, efficiency, and renewable energy technologies.

"If we were to think about what is the cheapest, most plentiful source of energy there is, it is energy conservation," Davis said. "We as a country have done a very poor job of conserving energy. In the United States, every time we achieve a big gain in energy efficiency, rather than just taking that gain and continuing on, we use that to build a better house, or a bigger automobile, ultimately using more energy than before. We are seeing more and more companies interested in conservation. I can tell you that running out of customers is not a fear of mine."

For example, the U.S. Postal Service has been a major customer that is now using solar almost exclusively to power its main processing facility in Northern California and is renovating all of its other Northern California facilities to run on solar power.

A lot of the things we do at Chevron Energy Solutions involves bundling of energy efficiency solutions, along with alternative and renewable technologies. The unique bundling makes the alternative energy investment possible. On the demand side you have energy efficiency and conservation—how to reduce your consumption of power . . . lighting . . . more efficient boilers, chillers, and HVAC [heating, ventilation, and air-conditioning] systems; these can all significantly reduce power consumption. On the supply side, there is also the need for power, the production of power that typically happens at the utility, but there are now more and more solutions on-site for an institution to generate or cogenerate its own power or at least to reduce the power required to operate. The demand side and the supply side both ultimately reduce the amount of power that needs to be produced by the local utility, and an integrated approach does this best. It is a value-added service. We're the only oil company affiliate we're aware of that focuses on energy efficiency and renewable power solutions.

We are very serious about being carbon-neutral at Chevron. It makes sense from our own needs and from an internal systemic and business perspective. The way we think about the answer to your question about being carbon-neutral is how close it is to our chairman Dave O'Reilly's philosophy. First of all, Chevron has a huge energy expenditure of three to four billion dollars annually worldwide. Finding ways to operate our own facilities more efficiently is simply good business. When you reduce your energy consumption, it is also good for the environment. We win every way. This is why we think it makes good business sense from an internal perspective. Our chairman feels that if we are going to do something on an external basis, it has to be something more than saying Chevron is throwing one hundred million dollars at this, meaning it has to be a profitable business to be in, and, also, that we act systemically. Our direction was to build a profitable business based on energy efficiency and conservation. Today, Chevron Energy Solutions brings in over 200 million dollars in annual revenue; however, its own proprietary systems implementation knowledge saves the company much more on the bottom line with systemic internal energy efficiency.

"The convergence of renewable technologies with energy efficiency projects is the future of building," he said. "We help to see that both of these are integrated into a customer's facility whether new or retrofitted. That's what is so exciting about our capabilities: we see supply-side with demand-side solutions."

The innovations are impressive, too. For example, the City of Millbrae, California, is working with Chevron Energy Solutions to start construction of facilities at Millbrae's Water Pollution Control Plant (WPCP) to generate on-site electricity from restaurant kitchen grease and other organic matter.[46]

Attached to the wastewater treatment plant is a cogeneration plant that captures energy from what would have been dumped into the rivers and groundwater.

The upgrades to the waste plant make it one of the first treatment plants in the United States to receive and process inedible grease in a comprehensive system specifically designed to control odors, generate reliable power, reduce energy costs, and provide a new municipal revenue stream. The new system will efficiently create and use a free biofuel—

digester gas produced from grease—and increase the amount of "green power" generated by the cogeneration plant by 40 percent.

The electricity generated from so-called waste actually reduces the city's requirement for about 1.5 million kilowatt-hours from the local utility each year. Of course, this in turn reduces everybody's dependency on oil. This lower demand also translates to 1,178,000 fewer pounds of carbon dioxide emissions annually, equivalent to planting 166 acres of trees, according to a Chevron Energy Solutions press release.[47]

The upgraded system will produce about $264,000 in combined energy savings and revenues from its grease receiving facility each year to effectively pay for the $5.5 million facility improvements at no new cost to the city's ratepayers.

Industrial America is aging and has not been investing capital in this infrastructure, and if energy prices stay high and interest rates stay low, these types of projects will finally make the private sector budget cuts. Another motivation is one of social responsibility. "Everyone you meet now wants to say they are doing something important about being carbon-neutral and energy conservation," Davis said. "They are greening their facilities. But at the end of the day, most companies in their very competitive world of financial performance must look at things through strict economic terms.

"Our prospects for the future look more promising than ever before. I have always been a strong believer in the fact that we cannot build our business around government rebates and tax incentives. We have to build our business by adding value for our customers. That is not to say that we don't take advantage of the tax rebates. It certainly helps to improve a project's chances of successful funding."

Americans can fill themselves and their world up with toxic

molecules, or we can shape a carbon-neutral, toxic-free future. Seeking redemption for being toxic is one of the good things we toxic talkers and wastemongers can also do in our own personal lives. How many of us are toxic? How many of us are really saccharin? But isn't saccharin a fake sweetener? Maybe our real sweetness also comes with a little toxicity. We have toxic habits, toxic relationships, toxic foods, and toxic cosmetics. We're all toxic. We're just trying to minimize our toxicity, which I suspect is a good thing.

But what about what we can do to initiate change? How can we become catalysts instead of junking up the gears?

One of the best ways to start being less toxic is using less energy to do things, both in your personal actions and activities and around the home. The opportunities for us to stop being so wasteful and therefore less toxic to the rest of the world are so great that the legendary resource analyst Amory Lovins of the Rocky Mountain Institute estimates that the United States could run its entire economy on about one-fourth of the current electricity used, saving us billions of dollars every year. We should consciously seek carbon-neutral appliances and high-tech products. We can do a lot in these areas alone. But we also need to be less toxic to the people around us, maybe nicer.

Carbon-neutral thinking fosters innovation and puts high tech back into American towns; it supplies good jobs. Come with me to Northern California's Humboldt County, the sparsely populated, heavily forested home of the California redwoods where the cash crops are timber and marijuana. This is a land of rivers—the Eel, Mad, Trinity, and Klamath—and off-the-grid communities in the scattered mountains.

With a population of around 128,000, more than half of the people here live outside cities in unincorporated areas where no electrical grids are present.[48] Although a part of heavily populated California, Humboldt is one of the unique regions in the world to embrace solar power not out of luxury but due to sheer necessity. If there is a solar hub in the world today, it is the Trinity Alps Wilderness, parts of Shasta-Trinity National Forests. Here, you find more solar panels per person than anyplace else in the world. Without a power grid, people need to be much more creative, and this demand has led to Sun Frost refrigerators.

"A lot of people live back in the woods and they are powering their homes through solar," said Larry Schlussler, PhD, owner of Sun Frost Refrigerators and Freezers, a small American company producing some of the most energy-efficient home appliances today. "But, when you are using solar systems that stand alone and that are not part of the electric grid, producing power can be very expensive, so you want to be sure whatever you're powering is as energy efficient as possible. Refrigerators and freezers are some of the biggest electrical hogs in your home. We saw a real need throughout the region. If you can get an energy-efficient refrigerator, it makes your entire home that much more energy efficient."

Although Schlussler's Sun Frost appliances are more expensive than less efficient mass-market models, their energy efficiency makes up for their added cost; he said a standard refrigerator can cost almost twice its price after adding the cost of power to run it. Even in a home using conventional utility power, energy consumption for refrigeration is typically cut by a factor of five, he said. In addition, the company provides good jobs in a county that once was so dependent on logging the last of its redwoods.

So if you're on the road for the American portion of your Safe Trip, you might want to visit the Sun Frost factory, which is 275 miles north of The Republic of San Francisco on California's Redwood Coast in the town of Arcata.

My libertarian and neoconservative friends tell me government is bungling and inefficient, an evil intrusion into our lives, and that the nine most fearful words in English are, "I'm from the government, and I'm here to help." Okay, they are right a lot of the time. But, in this case, Sun Frost, like many of the very best appliance and computer companies, participated in the U.S. government's Energy Star program. This program represents government at its best.

With Energy Star we get our money's worth. This government program is achieving amazing results, helping businesses and individuals go carbon-neutral far more quickly. Over the years, a lot of books have mentioned the government's Energy Star program in passing but gloss over it, really.

A government-backed program that has received "only" about $50 million annually, Energy Star is a voluntary partnership among the U.S. Department of Energy, EPA, product manufacturers, local utilities, and retailers to promote energy efficiency and conservation education. Products certified by Energy Star meet strict energy efficiency guidelines set by the EPA and U.S. Department of Energy.

The program deserves more attention, especially as the Bush administration has announced its intention to reduce the program's funding by roughly 30 percent.[49]

"While the Bush administration talks up its voluntary efforts to address climate change, these backroom cuts show that this is mostly hollow rhetoric," said Steven Nadel, executive director of the American Council for an Energy-Efficient Economy. "This is a big step backward at a time when the United States needs to show forward motion on energy efficiency and climate change issues."

To date, the EPA estimates that Energy Star programs have prevented more than 150 million tons of carbon emissions from reaching the atmosphere and that American consumers using Energy Star products saved over $6 billion, with reduced energy bills in 2001 alone. According to the EPA, each Energy Star dollar generates more than $15 in private investment. So Energy Star is not only a pollution prevention program, it also has an economic stimulus effect.

In 2004 alone, with the help of Energy Star, Americans saved enough energy to power 24 million homes and avoid greenhouse gas emissions equivalent to those from 20 million cars—all while saving $10 billion, according to the Energy Star Web site, www.energystar.gov.[50]

One of the best features about the Energy Star Web site is its Home Energy Analysis. If you have five minutes and your energy bills are handy, you can find out if your energy use is above average. You will need to enter some common information about your home such as age, square footage, number of occupants, and energy bill totals for a consecutive twelve-month period. If you don't keep your bills, contact your utility for a twelve-month summary.

Another great feature is the Web site listings of Energy Star–certified appliances. Before you visit your local Sears or Best Buy, go online first to Energy Star and search your Energy Star–rated models. Take this information and cross-reference it for pricing at your favorite brick and mortar or online retailer.

Some states offer rewards for buying the most energy-efficient appliances. Connecticut and California, for example, have rebate programs that will refund part of the purchase price of certain new energy-efficient appliances. Maryland eliminates sales tax on some appliances with the Energy Star label. Check with your local utility and the Energy Star Rebate Locator to find out if cash rebates or other incentives are available in your area.

Testifying to the power of Energy Star to aid consumers,

Margaret Suozzo writes on the Co-op America Web site (www.coopamerica.org) that a typical small business, with ten computers, ten monitors, one printer, one fax machine, and one medium-volume copier, can use Energy Star–certified equipment and save more than 3,500 kilowatt-hours of electricity per year, worth at least $265 at today's average commercial electric rates.[51] The EPA estimates that if all Americans did this with small offices alone, we would save some 21 billion kilowatt hours and 2.3 billion pounds of carbon dioxide. That is equivalent to taking 807,000 cars off the road, she said.

The typical household spends $1,500 a year on energy bills. With Energy Star, you can save up to 30 percent, or more than $450 per year. Besides saving families about a third on their energy bill, the environment will benefit from similar savings of greenhouse gas emissions without sacrificing features, style, or comfort. If you are looking for new household products, look for ones that have earned the Energy Star label.

Energy Star has provided us with great direction when we have had to purchase new appliances for our home and when Freedom Press has as well. We found our refrigerators (for home and office) and Bosch washing machine and dryers, thanks to Energy Star. I've learned with Energy Star that it is easy to find energy-efficient, less toxic appliances and electronic gear that meet strict energy efficiency guidelines (set by the EPA and DOE).

One of the shortcomings of the Energy Star appliance and electronics gear energy efficiency listings is that they do not give you the full story about shopping for carbon-neutral appliances. Some companies are going to great lengths to green their business and manufacturing practices.

Although a company might manufacture highly efficient appliances, some of the companies pollute more than others, and that also should matter to consumers who are greening their patriotism.

Some of the leading manufacturers of popular brands in the United States and elsewhere in the world today are Mitsubishi, VestFrost, GE, Whirlpool, Maytag, Bosch, Miele, LG, Samsung, Hewlett-Packard, and IBM. I've looked at these companies to give you a sense of where they have been, some of their past environmental misdeeds, and where they are headed, so you can make a decision that works for your values and sensibilities. Some of them, like Maytag and Whirlpool, with poor pollution records from only a few years ago, are taking important steps to stop being toxic.

Since to varying degrees we all use appliances from washers and refrigerators to microwave ovens, as well as high-tech electronics gear like laptops, cell phones, and digital music players, it pays to know more about the companies manufacturing these products and from whom we are purchasing them if we want to extend our good acts into the world at large. Most of these companies manufacture throughout the world so our shopping dollars have a lot of power to prevent or foster destruction.

Let me tell you what I've learned about many of our most popular brands of kitchen and high-tech appliances.

Japan's Mitsubishi Electric's latest models look at the entire life cycle of the refrigerator, from raw materials to disposal, to create an environmentally friendly fridge. The very small amount of energy consumed by its newest model with a non-chlorofluorocarbon refrigerant reduces carbon dioxide emissions to help reduce global warming. Meantime, Mitsubishi's entire production facility works toward sustainability, promoting zero emissions, and reducing greenhouse gas and chemical emissions. Mitsubishi presents some startling refrigerator facts at its Web site: "In fact, in Japan alone, the combined savings in electricity from use of Mitsubishi Electric's latest model refrigerator throughout its full product lifecycle can yield sufficient energy savings to serve approximately 72,000 average-sized homes in Tokyo—a major metropolis with more than 13 million inhabitants—for a full year."[52] Visit www.mitsubishielectric.com.

The Danish innovator Vestfrost makes ConServ units that retail for $1,149 to $1,399. The Vestfrost Group was the first company worldwide to obtain the Community Ecolabel, adopted by the European Union to alert consumers to those products meeting the highest standards for environmental friendliness and carbon-neutral production.[53] Each of Vestfrost's ConServ refrigerators not only offer super energy efficiency but are also built with all recyclable parts (and this is information you won't obtain at the Energy Star Web site). Vestfrost is the first in the industry to document compliance with all EU energy and environmental criteria.[54] Visit www.vestfrost.com.

When we recently purchased our new washer and dryer, I learned that to qualify for Energy Star status, a washing machine must clean clothes using 50 percent less energy than a standard washer. This means that a full-size, Energy Star–qualified washer will use anywhere from 18 to 25 gallons of water per load as opposed to 40 gallons per load in a standard washer, as well as show a significant reduction in the use of electricity (measured in kilowatt hours per year). According to Energy Star, the reduction in water and energy use per load can save you up to $110 per year on utility bills.[55] Factor in the ten- to twelve-year life span of a truly quality washer, and the savings start to add up.

As usual, even more good things happen when you do one right thing. A standard washing machine spins at 400 to 500 revolutions per minute, whereas high-efficiency machines spin at a whopping 800 to 1,000 cycles. The increased spin speed saves you time, energy, and money. A high-efficiency model extracts enough water to allow you to dry a load of towels in twenty-three minutes in your dryer, a little more than one third of the time it took with an old washer and dryer. Believe me, if you or a loved one does a lot of laundry, this is a big deal.

Maytag is one of the market leaders for washing machines, dryers, refrigerators, and other home appliances. When I was looking for a new refrigerator for our home, I saw a 20.3-cubic foot bottom-freezer refrigerator from Amana that was Energy Star rated and priced from $1,999 to $2,225, depending on the extras. I also looked at Jenn-Air models that were Energy Star rated. Eventually I learned that both Amana and Jenn-Air are brands that Maytag manufactures. (The company's other brands include Maytag, Hoover, Dixie-Narco, and Jade.) The bad news, however, is that the Maytag refrigeration products manufacturing plant in Amana, Iowa, is ranked in the seventieth to eightieth percentile in the nation for dirtiest facilities, spewing out toluene and 1,1-dichloro-1-fluroethane, with toxic effects on the nervous system and blood, according to the authoritative www.scorecard.org Web site.[56] A company that pollutes with organic compounds pollutes with greenhouse emissions as well. The good news is that Maytag is doing better now. In fact, according to John Daggett, external communications director at the company, "The latest Maytag data that was reported to the EPA show that those chemicals have been eliminated from use in our process. We changed our process and eliminated those chemicals in 2003."[57]

Whirlpool, of Benton Harbor, Michigan, is the world's leading manufacturer and marketer of major home appliances, with annual sales of over $12 billion; it has 68,000 employees and nearly fifty manufacturing and technology research centers around the globe. Its brands include Whirlpool,

KitchenAid, Brastemp, Bauknecht, and Consul, and they are sold in more than 170 countries. In the United States, Whirlpool has been an active partner of the Energy Star Program since August 1998 and has been honored with the Energy Star Partner of the Year Award five times (1999–2002 and 2004). At its Fort Smith, Arkansas, plant, however, Whirlpool's facility ranked in the one hundredth percentile for the dirtiest and worst facilities in the country.[58] In 2002, its Toxic Release Inventory (TRI) pollution air releases included 380,000 pounds of suspected cardiovascular and blood toxicants and 380,000 pounds of suspected nerve-system damaging chemicals. In Evansville, Indiana, Whirlpool had further releases of xylene and 1,1-dichloro-1-fluoroethane and some 605,000 pounds of suspected cardiovascular or blood toxicants; 44,000 pounds of suspected developmental toxicants; about the same amount of suspected immunotoxicants; kidney, gastrointestinal and liver, reproductive, respiratory, and skin or sense organ toxicants; and some 605,000 pounds of suspect neurotoxins.

The company was, to put it mildly, disappointing in the amount of poisons it released into the environment. However, on January 1, 2003, the 141b foam-blowing agent was replaced with the less toxic 245fa foam-blowing agent. From 2002 to 2003, toxic emissions decreased by nearly 100 percent at both plants in Arkansas and Indiana, and they have remained at those lower levels since then. The 141b foam-blowing agent was used as a stepping-stone process to eliminate chlorofluorocarbons (CFCs) beginning in the mid-1990s and its use reduced emissions by nearly 90 percent during its substitution; so, in fact, the 141b foam-blowing agent, as bad it was, was a necessary stepping-stone to an even better process. The end result of the move from CFCs to 141b to 245fa has led to a dramatic decrease in emissions.

"For example, toxic emissions at our Fort Smith plant have decreased from approximately 1 million pounds in 1988 to 37 pounds in 2004, during a time when production increased by 40 percent," according to Jody Lau, Whirlpool global communications director, in an e-mail.[59] "Our Evansville facility received the Indiana Governor's award for environmental excellence in 2004 for its change to 245fa." Additional releases at their Evansville facility decreased by approximately 50 percent from 2002 to 2003. "Additionally, in 2004 the Fort Smith Division made several efficiency improvements, including installing an energy management system on HVAC equipment, adding a power monitoring system on the electrical service and replacing lighting with more efficient systems. The Evansville facility also replaced lighting with more efficient systems," according to the company. Give them some credit. Whirlpool might not be perfect, but a reasonable person can see they are striving to make the transformation to a green company, as difficult as it might be for a large corporation. Still, the company will need to be pressured to make an even greater environmental commitment.

Not only has the entire line of Bosch appliances been awarded the Energy Star label, making Bosch even more compelling, but also this German-based company (with extensive manufacturing facilities throughout the world) ranks as one of the cleanest companies overall in terms of petrochemical and other dangerous emissions. Bosch's worldwide facilities and plants, including in the United States, rank in the top 10 percent of the United States for cleanest, least toxic emissions. At its Anderson, South Carolina, plant, Bosch ranks in the top 10 to 20 percent for the cleanest, best facilities for air releases of recognized carcinogens and developmental and reproductive toxins, and in the top 10 percent for total environmental releases.[60] Similarly, at its Broadview, Illinois, plant, Bosch ranks in the top 10 to 20 percent cleanest best facilities for releases of lead, nitrogen dioxide, and ozone.[61] It also ranks among the cleanest, best facilities for the least pollution, which means during manufacturing they are more efficient and less likely to produce as much greenhouse gases, either.[62,63,64,65,66] Visit www.bosch.com.

By using only a small amount of water, Miele also reduces energy consumption. Every Miele dishwasher made for North America qualifies for the Energy Star Program, meaning it exceeds government energy standards by over 25 percent. This means that Miele dishwashers qualify for a variety of rebate programs available throughout the country. Contact your local energy supplier for rebates in your area. Additionally, every Miele washing machine made for North America also qualifies for the Energy Star Program, meaning they are also at least 50 percent more efficient than minimum federal government standards.[67] Visit www.miele.com.

LG Electronics is quickly emerging on the scene as a major manufacturer of home appliances and electronics, including air conditioners and cell phones. Although LG Electronics, based in Korea, doesn't have manufacturing plants in the United States and I could not use the information at Scorecard.org, the company has earned Korean ECO Label accreditation for its air cleaners and power-saving computers, among other products. The Eco Label Program, operated by the Korean Environmental Labeling Association, certifies environmentally friendly products considering their entire life cycle perspective, which includes reducing pollution and saving raw materials and energy. The company is also producing products that do not contain ozone-depleting or greenhouse gas–related refrigerants, PVC, lead, chromium-6, cadmium, or mercury, and that do not use flame-retardant substances such as polybrominated biphenyls and PBDEs. Its

DIOS refrigerators use environmentally friendly refrigerants and blowing agents that do not harm the ozone layer depletion or contribute to global warming, and that also use compressor technologies to reduce power consumption by up to 40 percent. DIOS refrigerators were the first refrigerators to earn the Korean Environmental Declaration of Products (EDP) certification under which all environmental impacts during production must be disclosed to customers. Their new microwave ovens use less than one watt of power. Their WHISEN air conditioners employ an environmentally friendly twin-power system to reduce power consumption by up to 65 percent and use ozone-friendly refrigerants. Visit www.lge.com.

Samsung produces DVD recorders, cell phones, TVs, and many other high-tech products. The Samsung semiconductor plant in Austin, Texas, ranks in the top 30 percent for lowest total environmental releases and had no harmful releases of carcinogens, neurotoxins, blood toxicants, or other harmful chemicals.[68] Another Samsung technology breakthrough is use of U-shaped cold-cathode fluorescent lamps to lower their mercury content. Samsung Electronics began to switch over from straight tubes to U-shaped tubes as the backlight in its LCD module for 23-inch televisions in January 2004. Use of the new backlight was expanded to include the new 17-, 19-, 20-, and 26-inch LCD TV modules. The brightness of LCD modules has not been affected by the change, but the amount of mercury in the lamps has been halved. The result has been a reduction in resources used, as well as hazardous substances in the LCD modules. Another example is complete removal of hexavalent chromium in screws. Hazardous hexavalent chromium was previously added to screws to make them rust resistant, but Samsung Electronics completely switched over to using the benign trivalent chromium in 2004, increasing the environment friendliness of its LCD products.[69] Visit www.samsung.com.

Although Hewlett-Packard, the nation's leading manufacturer of high-end printers, servers, and other computer equipment, has a ten-acre Superfund site in Palo Alto, Santa Clara County, California, that was contaminated with a number of chemical toxins such as 1,1,1-trichloroethane, toluene, and xylene, the company seems, in some ways, to have redeemed itself with a very clean record for its Boise, Idaho, manufacturing plant, which ranks in the top 10 percent for cleanest facilities for overall releases (and in the top 20 to 30 percent for releasing the least amount of developmental toxins).[70] Visit www.hp.com.

Apple produces the world-famous Macintosh computers and family of iPods. Although we could not find data on Apple's toxic emissions for where its computers or other electronics gear are manufactured, since October 2002 Apple has partnered with the City of Cupertino—home of Apple's worldwide headquarters—to develop an electronics recycling program. Through this program, the city's residents can return their used or unwanted computer systems and selected home electronics (regardless of manufacturer) to Apple's Cupertino recycling collection facility. The service is provided to residents free of charge. This recycling program is an outstanding example of business and local government working together to reduce the impact of electronic waste. It has been so successful that Apple and the City of Cupertino have signed an agreement to extend the program for another year, with three one-year options to follow. For more information, visit www.recycleapc.com/apple/index.asp, or call Apple Computer's recorded information line at 408-862-2667.

However, this local program aside, Apple has come under heavy fire from environmental groups. Unfortunately for Apple, the Silicon Valley Toxics Coalition (SVTC) has some strong criticisms of its environmental record. Although Apple has implemented a $30 buyback recycling plan, the SVTC said it is ineffective. In this plan, consumers must pay $30 per component, or $60 to send back a system (monitor and tower). Apple is now taking back iPods, according to Barbara Kyle of the SVTC, because these products contain the same kinds of highly toxic materials you'll find in a home computer, but they are small enough that people will actually throw them into trash cans.

"The design is also poor," she said. The battery wears out somewhat quickly, sometimes within a year, then it is $100 to replace it. Although customers can take them back to Apple stores for no charge to be recycled and receive a 10 percent discount on the next purchase, "people are surprised at how quickly the product wears out and aren't really sure they want to invest another $100 to replace the battery. Our question is, why can't customers bring back any product to the store? Apple should continue what they started with the iPod. They are in a unique position to implement such a program because they have retail stores. But they don't prioritize recycling and they aren't trying hard enough to stop being toxic. Even though they offer the $30 buyback, it seems like this is a program that was just put in place so they can say they have a recycling program. This is not just an environmental issue, but also a values issue.

"Apple is a company that promotes an image of being forward thinking, continued Barbara Kyle, "but it doesn't really seem like the company is acting that way. We'd like to see Apple implement a program that shows they are really taking steps to be responsible for their products at the end of the product's life. In my opinion, it is really just Steve Jobs being stubborn! Apple has an interesting corporate culture in that if Jobs doesn't want to do something, it doesn't happen, and it really seems that he has dug his heels in on this issue. They will usually just not comment or engage in anything with us. You could call them to talk about their recycling/environmental policies and more than likely, you will not get any answers."

Indeed, on several occasions when our reporters at Freedom Press contacted Apple for their response to these criticisms, they would not even return our calls.

Dell, the SVTC Computer TakeBack Campaign's original target, has begun implementing a variety of programs to encourage recycling. Dell will take old computers and donate them to the National Cristina Foundation to help disabled and economically disadvantaged children and adults in local communities. The foundation will pick up your computer at your door and put it to good use. Visit www.cristina.org/dsf/dell.ncf to learn more about this worthwhile service.

To educate consumers and businesses about options for disposing of unwanted computers, the Rethink Initiative coalition created a Web site (www.ebay.com/rethink) that includes information on how to safely sell, recycle, or donate used computers.

At Freedom Press, we've made some important breakthroughs, too. Our new computers come with lead-free motherboards and contain voltage regulators that reduce the actual power the machine requires to run.

Just in your home, there is so much you can do for free, and that is easy to do. I just got up and turned down our water heater to approximately 120° F (instead of the usual 145° F). With this one move, according to the Rocky Mountain Institute, I will save 212 pounds of carbon dioxide per year. If you use air conditioning, increasing your thermostat by only 3° F will save an average of 339 pounds of carbon dioxide per year.

Choosing to wash clothes in cold water saves 327 pounds of

carbon dioxide per year; drying clothes outside in the fresh air and sunlight not only lengthens the life of your clothes but also saves energy and 1,386 pounds of carbon dioxide emissions. Turning off any unneeded lights in your home would not only save 376 pounds of carbon dioxide a year but also about $21.04 per year in energy costs. All these measures cost nothing to implement, and actually save you money over the long term while reducing your impact on the environment.[71]

Some 40 percent of U.S. greenhouse gases come from electricity-generating plants. Replacing a 75-watt lightbulb with an 18-watt compact fluorescent bulb gives you better-quality light and uses so much less electricity that you save over $35 in the end—and reduce carbon dioxide emissions.

There's a lot more on the horizon that you should know about. The sooner you can take advantage of these breakthroughs, the sooner you will be saving money on your energy bills, and the sooner our country will cut its dependency on foreign oil. Plus, these breakthroughs are part of the new green economy and portend great news for American workers being employed in good jobs.

Sometimes the small things we could do give us our biggest payoffs, and we don't even realize what we can be doing until somebody tells us. Most of us don't really think all that much about the fact that when we supposedly turn off our home electronics devices that they aren't actually turned off but continue to suck up what is called "standby power," otherwise known as a big drain on our already bloated monthly energy chits. Some 15 percent of your home's total energy bill is for standby power, according to the spring 2004 online edition of *on earth* from the NRDC. Think of what you could save on the family budget by being a green patriot—and you'll see why this is all so cool.

Alan Meier, a senior energy analyst at the International Energy Agency, an intergovernmental policy group, estimated that U.S. households use 45 billion kilowatt-hours in standby electricity every year. That's a cost of $3.5 billion.

"Put another way, these sleeping gadgets keep the equivalent of seventeen 500-megawatt power plants running year-round, just to keep your light-emitting diodes glowing," he told the magazine.

Meier, however, has come up with several innovations that should help to reduce electricity consumption by replacing the more wasteful adapters with the more efficient switching power supplies, and redesigning the software in electronics devices such as printers to automatically turn off everything but the most essential components. Combined, these and other changes could reduce the standby power consumption of appliances to less than one watt.

Our good friends at the government Energy Star program have been involved with NRDC scientists and industry executives to develop standby power specs based on his work, and major manufacturers such as Sony and IBM plan to reduce standby power consumption in all products. Once again, government is seeding the market first with its vast purchasing powers, as federal agencies are now required to buy only these new power-stingy appliances. We're even making headway in Beijing. Overseas, the Chinese government has pledged to reduce the standby power for the 40 million TVs the country manufactures annually.

Of course, in your own home and office, be sure to use power strips or surge protectors and turn off electric power completely by using their cut-off capabilities.

The article also said even with duct tape, most of our homes lose about 20 percent of heated or cooled air that travels through air ducts due to holes and cracks. In California alone, these leaks cost consumers some $1 to $2 billion annually in energy consumption.

Scientists at Lawrence Berkeley National Laboratory have developed an innovative aerosol sealant that reduces leaks by 90 percent. A certified technician will come to your home, cover all of your homes' vents, and then blow a "fog" into the ducts that finds all of the holes and cracks and plugs them with polymer particles. The sealant, now recommended by the Energy Star program, is available from Aeroseal (www.aeroseal.com).

Beginning in 2005, new regulations in California required most homeowners who replace their central air conditioning to seal these ducts. Other states, including New York and Texas, have also passed legislation or altered building codes to encourage the practice. Aeroseal now has seventy franchises nationwide. A new energy breakthrough leads to a new market. This is green patriotism at its best, and it does involve some government help in the marketplace.

Most homes require power in the range of 114 to 126 volts, a range of more than 10 percent. However, because power must be delivered over longer and longer distances on highly inefficient grids, nine of ten homes receive significantly more volts than are needed. The facts are that almost all of our electric appliances and high tech run quite well on around 114 V. So anything above this results in excess heat and wear and premature appliance failure. MicroPlanet's Home Voltage Regulator comes to the rescue by attaching to the electric meter at your home. MicroPlanet's ingenious gizmo uses feedback methods to step down the amount allowed into the circuits and returns the rest to the grid, reducing home and business energy costs.

Based in Edmonds, Washington, MicroPlanet estimates that its devices could reduce household energy usage by as much as 20 percent by eliminating wasted voltage.

Install them in a million homes nationwide, and you could

reduce carbon dioxide emissions from power plants by 640,000 tons a year. Eventually, MicroPlanet hopes its device will become the standard for all U.S. households. Visit www.microplanet.com.

How many chargers are plugged in your wall socket or under your desk or table to the power surge protector strip? I counted seven or eight under my desk alone. We live and travel by the charger and converter. To the charger we connect our wired world and convert alternating current (AC) to direct current (DC) to power cell phones, laptops, answering machines, and tons of other appliances. But many people leave charger and converter black boxes plugged into the wall all of the time. Then there are the many chargers hidden within computers and other appliances. One estimate is that 3.1 billion charging boxes are in the United States, and 400 to 500 million more are sold every year.

These black-box vampires use only one-quarter of the energy they draw. One estimate puts that at about 100 billion kilowatt-hours per year wasted.

The good news is that much more efficient designs are coming to market that convert up to 90 percent of the electricity.

The implementation of this powerful new technology came about thanks to the green-tech patriots Chris Calwell and Travis Reeder at the environmental research firm Ecos Consulting. Calwell and Reeder teamed up with Noah Horowitz, a senior scientist at the NRDC, and they met with some of the most important companies in electronics today—including Apple, Canon, and Sony—and convinced them of the importance of using these far more advanced technologies. Making the transformation complete, Intel, which provides chips for 80 percent of the desktop computer industry, will feature new more efficient power-supply technology.

Horowitz teamed up with U.S. government officials to

convince China's energy agency (where 85 percent of the world's power supplies are manufactured) to adopt their own high efficiency standards for the tens of millions of external power supplies manufactured and sold there each year.

Potential energy savings from desktop computers could equal *16 billion* kilowatt hours a year. That is, said Horowitz, "roughly enough power to supply all the homes in the city of Chicago for one year."

Be sure to follow these money-saving green tips from the NRDC Web site (www.nrdc.org):

- Unplug seldom-used appliances. You can save around $10 every month on your utility bill.
- Unplug your chargers when you're not charging. Every house is full of little plastic power supplies to charge cell phones, digital cameras, cordless tools, and other personal gadgets. Keep them unplugged until you need them.
- Use power strips to switch off televisions, home theater equipment, and stereos when you're not using them. Even when you think these products are off, together their "standby" consumption can be equivalent to that of a 75- or 100-watt lightbulb running continuously.
- Enable the "sleep mode" feature on your computer, allowing it to use less power during periods of inactivity.
- Configure your computer to "hibernate" automatically after 30 minutes or so of inactivity. Allowing your computer to hibernate saves energy and is more time efficient than shutting down and restarting your computer from scratch.
- Be sure to set your thermostat in winter to 68 degrees F or less during the daytime, and 55 degrees before going to sleep (or when you're away for the day). During the summer, be really energy efficient; set thermostats to 78 degrees or higher.

- Speaking of being energy efficient, during the heating season, leave shades and blinds open on sunny days, but close them at night to reduce the amount of heat lost through windows. On the other hand, close shades and blinds during the summer or when the air conditioner is in use or will be in use later in the day.
- Set the thermostat on your water heater between 120 and 130 degrees F.
- Set your refrigerator temperature at 38 to 42 degrees F; your freezer should be set between 0 and 5 degrees F. If your model has one, use the power-save switch. Be sure the refrigerator door is tightly closed. To be sure your seals are working, put a dollar bill put between the door gaskets. It should be difficult to pull out. If it slides easily between the gaskets, replace them.
- Wash only full loads in your dishwasher, using short cycles for all but the dirtiest dishes.
- Use the Internet. Several Web sites contain additional useful information. Besides the EPA's Energy Star Web site at www.energystar.gov, the American Council for an Energy Efficient Economy at www.aceee.org publishes a yearly list of the most energy-efficient appliances. The Consortium for Energy Efficiency at www.cee1.org has information on programs promoting energy efficiency in the home.
- Turn off the lights when you leave a room.

Really, the ways we can stop being toxic in life, as a nation, individuals, consumers, and as inhabitants of Planet Earth are as myriad as our relationships and consciousness itself.

I went away from my environmental roots for a long time. I saw myself as a hard-nosed businessman, nursing martinis and bulging stomach, along with all my other corporate friends, most of whom were Republicans. Or maybe I just treated people and the Earth as dismissively as any corporate guy would. The corporation fed me, and I fed my woman, and I was a pretty basic guy.

I was in your face, in his or her face, ready to displace. Anyone or anything could become a target. But it was not a very good me. But, then, that's what a lot of us thought being part of a corporate culture allowed us to be.

When I came back to civilized society, I knew I was a sinner, a fossil fuel drunkard on bended knees, and a seeker of green salvation.

After attending my first meeting of Carbonholics Anonymous, I learned I'm not alone. Most of us have been pretty destructive in our lives and we're trying to come back to our environmental roots, or maybe we're just putting down eco-roots or roots of goodness for the first time.

I do know this. I'm excited. I'm learning how to live and to be a little, or maybe a whole lot, less toxic.

NINE
Put Your Money Where Your Mouth Is

NOTHING ABOUT THE roads of Vancouver, British Columbia, had made sense since I slid into my fossil-fuel Enterprise rental. I was totally lost. But, at least, I was there. Even as a child I wanted to live in what I always thought of as the Great Northwest. Maybe the fuel for my imagination was growing up watching all of the made-for-TV movies and animated features from *The Wonderful World of Disney* on the living room floor on Sunday nights with my youngest sister, and loving but never quite getting over the tragic, yet inspiring (to a kid), animated tale of Paul Bunyan and his great blue ox, Babe (the short had even been nominated for an Academy Award in 1958). Even today I remembered everything about Paul Bunyan, and, for some reason, driving around Vancouver, I began recalling details from my childhood I thought I'd forgotten. I knew that his occupation was a lumberjack and his closest kin, of course, was Babe. His buddies included Cal McNab, Chris Crosshaul, Shot Gunderson, Pecos Bill, John Henry, and Daniel Hackett. But his foes were the powerful J. P. Styles, Joe Muffaw, and the modern industrialists—the loggers using their newly developed lumber machines. I even recalled that his height was sixty-three ax handles, and that his favorite pastimes were eating flapjacks and roughhousing with Babe.[1] I was terribly distraught that Paul, with his old-fashioned ax lost the contest against modern chainsaw loggers to see who could fell the most trees.

As I became more and more lost and traveled on a road lined with grand homes with manicured dark-green moist lawns and coiffed trees, I finally got it, what the trip was all about. It was spiritual, whatever that word meant. And to grow spiritually in the context of whatever religion or God you believe in you had to be an environmentalist. And even green patriotism has to go through God. So everyone would have to go on this journey. But I also had to free myself; or, rather, open myself up to a different kind of influence on spirituality and religion and maybe even my super-critical spy-eye way of seeing things. I was trying to apply an American Midwest street-grid mentality to a city, region, and people that defied straight lines. After all, I'd grown up in LA, a town that was laid down in grids of a certain Midwest geometry and mind-set, and I absorbed all of this as a full-fledged child of the military industrial complex and Aerospace and Hughes and all of that. But here, equipped with map on lap, it did me little good. This road, like all the roads in Vancouver, was following nature; its contours curvaceously clung razor-close to the edge of tiny bays and inlets of the Fraser River, undulating over forks of the river and through forested inlets, sloping down through urban evergreen forests into the wet rocks and sand and seashore. Nothing about the town had anything to do with a grid mentality.

All these pretty green gardens filled with roses and coiffed evergreens, looking like schoolkids all dressed up for picture day, made me think of tea at four, British upper-class customs, and Christianity. Sure, people here were quite rooted in British Christianity, but the land was not Christianized. I liked that. The LA basin had been beaten down with so much dogma and its land so absolutely paved, but Vancouver had a natural wild heart.

I can't, of course, make you change your consciousness; I can't even make you read these words. But even a virtual road trip can help you and me to become part of the change, because what I've been talking about incessantly on this road trip was perhaps your own seismic tectonic consciousness shift from grids to opening up to the whole world. A man who has lived here his entire life, the geneticist-turned-environmentalist David Suzuki, whom I had come to meet on this trip, embodied this change in consciousness in his living, in consciousness, at a core level—but he was tired of talking and he was ready to carry the entire nation of Canada on his own safe trip. I'd met Indians in Campbell River and Port Hardy whose traditions, and particularly their transformational multicolored masks, initiated me into the interconnectedness between themselves, salmon, killer whale, raven, bear, and other living things, which constituted their total being, experience, and religion; the belief wove together the fabric of their societies when they were strong and dominant. Indeed, while researching Suzuki's past, I learned he credited his deep excursions into the wilds of British Columbia as a child with his father as key to his own change in consciousness. Everything he did sprang from a religious consciousness, including how he used money. You might say one facet of Suzuki was that he was a scientist who had gotten religion.

I was here because of what Suzuki was attempting to do, and not enough people knew about his efforts. Suzuki was attempting to transform the very consciousness of a nation to make it entirely carbon-neutral within twenty years.

Unlike the United States with its nearly 300 million souls and Byzantine bureaucracies and laws, Canada is smaller with around 32 million people (similar to the population of

California but in a land larger than the continental United States) and simpler in government. With Canada, I could actually get a handle on how one man with a vision was changing an entire nation, the ninth largest emitter of greenhouse gases in the world.[2]

In Los Angeles you could forget your environment, forget the San Gabriel or Angeles Crest mountains, because the mountains, often removed or made into ghostly unreal images by a film of smog, looked like papier-mâché props on a giant set. Everyone knew this was a set.

In Los Angeles, man was huge, and his selfish dreams were nourished because everyone took their cut. Everybody here gets that you have to hustle to live in LA, and just about everybody—except for those innocents who might turn up as saints in a Forest Gump movie—stoops to conquer at one time or another and has a lot to answer for. But on the other hand, for a brief time, where else can an immigrant rule like a sultan and create his own celluloid kingdom?

Yet here in Vancouver, mountains ruled. Once in the mountains, nature ruled. Bear ruled. Bear ate man if man was not careful. Man was little.

My driver from the airport to the car rental agency told me he had moved to BC from the east coast of Canada because "things are freer here. Everything that happens in British Columbia happens on the East Coast a few years later," he said.

Rounding a curve along an inlet on Southeast Marine, I passed by the Quebecor World printing facilities. Quebecor World is one of the largest printers in the world, and my company, Freedom Press, occasionally used their services. Quebecor World was making changes that not only reduced pollution but also would have a positive impact on their bottom line. They were proving going green was a concept that was good for both the environment and profits.

Quebecor World, for instance, installed a brand new regenerative thermal oxidizer (RTO) in their 16,000-square-meter printing plant in Recife, Brazil, in 2001. This RTO destroys air toxins and volatile organic compounds that are otherwise discharged in industrial process exhausts through high temperature thermal oxidation, converting the VOCs to carbon dioxide and water vapor, and recycling released energy to be reused.[3] The Recife-based printing plant is the largest in Latin America, and Quebecor's commitment to RTO technology significantly reduced greenhouse and other toxic air emissions, while recovering 95 percent of the possible energy produced. The company was also planning to install RTOs in Mexico, Peru, and Argentina, part of a program that would eventually see all of their plants in Latin America equipped with pollution-control devices that it claims will "far exceed the levels of environmental performance that are required by the local authorities on air emissions."

However, beyond this, my visit to the Quebecor worldwide Web site revealed little about their environmental policy, and I'd uncovered some serious problems in my own research. Quebecor's Buffalo, New York, plant ranked in the top 90 to 100 percent among all such plants for total environmental releases and releases of environmental developmental toxicants, according to information from Scorecard.org.[4] In Richmond, Virginia, the Quebecor publication rotogravure printing facility, located at 7400 Impala Drive, was issued a consent order by the state Air Pollution Control Board for "excess emissions" and the inability to properly maintain emission control systems.[5] I kept on driving, realizing that for all its surrounding beauty, Vancouver itself was a center of heavy industrial activity. No wonder Suzuki was concerned.

I took the elevator up and stepped into a geothermal-heated building, home to the David Suzuki Foundation. On the wall was a painting of Suzuki as a boy looking into the reflection of a pond and seeing the wise scientist he was destined to become. Suzuki came in and greeted me, twinkle in his eyes, backpack slung casually over his shoulder. He looked like Pat Morita, the late actor whose role as sensei in *The Karate Kid* did so much to elevate martial arts to a spiritual as well as physical quest for millions of American children. I wanted to meet Suzuki for a long time. He is a seminal figure in the global environmental movement; yet, because he is considered to be a man of wisdom and vision, he has astutely avoided politicizing the environment. Being neither left- nor right-wing, he has been revered as Canada's top science broadcaster since 1979, whose *Nature of Things* is seen in over forty countries—including the United States on the Discovery Channel and PBS.[6,7] In 2004, Suzuki was nominated as one of the top ten "Great Canadians" by viewers of the Canadian Broadcasting Corporation.

A third-generation Japanese-Canadian ("Canadian Sansei"), Suzuki and his family suffered internment in British Columbia during the Second World War from when he was six (1942) until after the war ended. In June 1942, the government sold the Suzuki family's dry-cleaning business, then interned Suzuki, his mother, and two sisters in a camp in the Sloan Valley in the BC Interior. His father had been sent to a labor camp in Solsqua, two months earlier. Suzuki's sister, Dawn, was born in the internment camp.[8]

After the war, Suzuki's family, like other Japanese-Canadian families, was forced to move east of the Rockies. The Suzukis moved to Islington, Leamington, and London, Ontario.

In 1954, a year after the pivotal discovery of the DNA structure by Watson and Crick, Suzuki started his first year of undergraduate studies at Amherst College, which was about seventy-five miles from Boston. It was here that he was first introduced to genetics and completed his honors thesis, which focused on a rare genetic event of the fruit fly, the phenomenon of "crossing over," the physical exchange of parts between similar chromosomes during production of eggs.

His scientific future assured, Suzuki did something unusual for the times; he rebelled against the ethos that science could do only good, and he began questioning the impact of science not only on people's lives but also upon the environment.

"I was motivated by Rachel Carson in 1962 when I first read *Silent Spring*," he said. "The prevailing philosophy then and today is that we can control chemical toxins like DDT through regulation. Now, I know that this is completely wrong in the sense that regulating our toxic inputs into the environment actually legitimizes environmental degradation. Even with regulation, no one knew about the phenomenon of biomagnification [whereby compounds become magnified as they are ingested up the food chain and found in biological tissues in ever increasing concentrations]. It is false comfort to presume that if we put into place certain regulations that these will solve problems. How could we possibly have set effective limits on DDT in the early 1940s when we didn't even know about biomagnification as a biological process until birds began to disappear?"

I found Suzuki to have an engaging, accessible style that immediately resonated—not off putting, not academic— someone who truly was intent on transcending polarizing factions.

"Today, with global warming, we are facing what I think is the most profound challenge to our existence in modern times," he said. "But, once again, government is trying to regulate what industry is doing as if regulations can solve this problem." Although Suzuki reluctantly agreed that regulations certainly have helped, he stated.

More than regulation, there has to be a transformation that moves more deeply into the human psyche, and that is almost religious in consciousness changing. It has to be reflected in science, business, industry, and economics and how and what we accrue value.

The mistake all of us make—but particularly those who craft regulations—is to think of the environment as something that is out there. In truth, whatever we do we are doing to ourselves. We are the environment. We breathe the air. We drink the water. We consume foods from the earth. We are the earth, water, and air. There is no demarcation, no impregnable wall of separation between us and what we pour into the environment. When you see that we are the earth, water, air, it becomes unacceptable to just throw toxic wastes into our environment.

"I just read an article that Ray Anderson [CEO of Interface Inc., the world's largest flooring manufacturer and board member of the Suzuki Foundation] sent me that was the most terrifying article about peak oil," he said.

Once you exhaust all of the oil there is no more to discover. From that point on, you are just exhausting the reservoirs that there are. There are others who say it is going to be a drop in reserves. Paul Roberts makes this point in his book *The End of Oil*. We are now pumping amounts higher than almost ever before, and with China and India's economies galloping, we are gulping more fossil fuel than ever before but we have more nations than ever with declining production. Right now, things seem to be okay. But if we are truly nearing our peak, that kind of collapse would change things quickly. You will find that much more of what you eat is going to be grown locally because of prohibitive fuel costs.

The fact is, we're already seeing this emphasis on local foods to keep prices down.

"But do we have to enter a state of collapse to make change?" I asked.

"Change comes from necessity," he replied. "And we might be reaching the point of near collapse, particularly as people feel it in their pocketbooks when they have to fill their vehicles up with gasoline."

"American moms and dads are not going to keep sending their sons and daughters to fight more oil wars," I said. "They just won't."

They don't have to if we take these warnings from nature seriously and start to change our ways. Climate change is with us. A decade ago, it was conjecture. Now the future is unfolding before our eyes. Look at the change in the permafrost. Here in Canada, the Inuit peoples see global warming now as Arctic ice and permafrost begin disappearing. We have extensive records by bird watchers of the arrivals and departures of birds on their migratory pathways. It is crystal clear that our species are traveling north 10 to 14 days sooner than ever before and leaving 7 to 10 days later. We see the distribution of frogs, a sentinel creature with implications for the birthing areas of earth, changing dramatically. The range of abalone species is changing. We see problems with salmon because of rising water temperature. All is congruent with the notion that the planet is warming up. I think the most frightening piece of evidence is the carbon dioxide levels in the layers of ice in Antarctica. Every layer of snow contains bubbles of atmosphere trapped within which provide a nice record of carbon dioxide levels through the ages. The frightening thing is you get some jiggling of

CO_2 levels going up and down that correspond to the ice ages and warm periods. But you see the CO_2 rising in the nineteenth century, and then it just leaps straight off the page in the twentieth century.

But climate change isn't enough, I say. "It's abstract. It seems so far away to most people. They don't realize that climate change is happening now, as we speak, that glaciers are disappearing at an unprecedented rate."

"I know. I know." Suzuki stroked his beard. "Ironically, our foundation worked on global climate change and all of its frightening implications for seven or eight years without moving anyone or anybody emotionally.

"Then we had an idea," he continued. "We discovered that, in my father's time, the word asthma was almost unknown. No one here had asthma. Today, one in five Canadian children has asthma."

I listened to Suzuki's discussion of asthma with great interest. An article by experts at the Division of Pediatric Pulmonary, The Children's Hospital, Denver, Colorado, in the June 2003 issue of *Pediatric Clinics of North America* said, "Asthmatic children living in low-income families in United States inner city communities continue to have disproportionately high rates of hospitalizations, emergency department visits, disability, and death."[9]

"We know it's the air pollution," he said.

Our climate change group tried to educate Canadians on global warming and its basis, and we got very little traction, and then we found that Health Canada showed that 16,000 Canadians [and tenfold more U.S. citizens, according to government estimates] die every year from air pollution.[10] We recruited doctors from across the country to speak out. We took a film crew to an emergency room at a hospital and showed children and adults being brought into the ER who were unable to breathe, believing they were dying because of asthma attacks, and it was very powerful and real and brought the truth home and aroused so much interest in air pollution. You have to move the people. It is hard to make people think about the future. Most people are scanners. All they think about is what they see immediately in their surroundings. That is how much in the future they think. But with asthma, it was something they felt, and that they saw immediately.

So you're right, Dave, in that the immediate concerns like toxic effects of these chemicals on people are important. Our asthma reports showed that people act out of enlightened self-interest. But now we see things happening that are frightening people—the extreme hikes in oil prices, vast portions of the Arctic that are melting, evacuations of South Seas island nations [like Tuvalu], due to the rising tide. People are ready for the next big leap. I want to see change accelerate, and most of the deep thinkers on the topic like Amory and Hunter Lovins and Paul Hawken know there has to be more, something more fundamental, because otherwise all we are ever doing is lobbying for this side or that. That's pure power money politics where you pay for phones and campaigners. But, the David Suzuki Foundation can't win playing that way because, then, all we would be is a lobbying group and lobbying groups can always be outspent by the other side. The idea here is to bring everyone together.

Most businesses today are just beginning to integrate their human, natural, and social commitments into their other bottom-line markers. What business requires is a new definition of wealth. It makes sense from any nation's self-interests. Countries with the most environmental destruction have the lowest levels of living and most political strife. That, clearly, was not what Canadians wanted for their country or what we wanted for ours.

Canada's overexploitation is a problem for the United States, too. Canada is running out of natural gas. Canada is America's biggest supplier of this vital resource. Canada currently exports about 55 percent of its natural gas production to the United States; yet, the nation's major gas producing province of Alberta has "only has about nine more years of conventional reserves," according to Moneycanoe.ca, a publication of Quebecor Media.[11]

That's frightening because without Canada, the United States will be even more dependent on Middle Eastern sources for natural gas. That can't be a positive prognosis for any nation, much less one as addicted to oil as America.

Reducing consumption does not mean reducing our quality of life. To shift to a sustainable economy, we need to focus on generating genuine asset-based wealth rather than continuing to measure progress exclusively in extraction terms as in how much gas or oil we take from the Earth. Certainly, in Canada and many other small-is-beautiful nations, improving energy efficiency standards, shifting to renewable energy sources like wind, solar, and micro-hydro, can help.

Suzuki looked me straight in the eye and expressed his need to get things done. "I want to see the transformation of Canada to a wholly sustainable economy in my lifetime," he said. "Do you understand?"

Suzuki and foundation board member Jim Fulton (himself a House of Commons veteran) met with Canadian Prime Minister Paul Martin for an environmental summit at his office in Ottawa in February 2004.

Fulton, with dark bushy brows, graying dark hair, and a dashing mustache, was dressed casually to see an old friend. Martin and Fulton were comfortable with each other. After all, Fulton himself was a fifteen-year veteran of the House of Commons. Martin and Fulton had sat on environmental committees, traveled to Rio de Janeiro for the Earth Summit, and gone to many other conferences on climate change. And there was Suzuki. It didn't hurt that Martin's children loved watching Suzuki's *Nature of Things*.

Also, the political zeitgeist in Canada was ripe for an environmental makeover. Although Martin's Liberal Party had lost overall seats in the 2004 federal election, the majority of voters had supported political parties with strong environmental sustainability positions. Despite disagreement on other hot-button issues, the Liberals, NDP, and Bloc Quebecois shared common ground on a number of environmental issues. Suzuki told the prime minister about the program, which he called Sustainability Within A Generation or SWAG. "That unusual combination of the broad appeal among voters, my being a former legislative colleague, and David being a recognized and admired science broadcaster gave the PM a sense that SWAG was something that was intuitively correct and achievable," Fulton told me in an interview.

Martin stunned both Fulton and Suzuki next, however, when he demanded copies of the SWAG publication in French and English and ordered them distributed across the government to various deputy ministers, ranging from health and environment to Natural Resources Canada.

Soon, "We were quite surprised to find people who were personally familiar with SWAG because it had been sent to them by the PM and they had been told to read it," Fulton said. Martin was the kind of sensitized leader who would be receptive to their message.

"The prime minister was well versed and knowledgeable when it comes to environmental issues. He understood why Toronto had 140 smog alerts last year. He has an eye for these sorts of things. Because he was minister of finance for so long, he realizes that to change our nature of relationship with the environment, it takes a while."

At first, Martin told Suzuki, "I've read your sustainability-within-a-generation manifesto, and I am going to do everything you are asking in this document—except in the energy area. That would mean taking away subsidies from the oil and gas producers in Alberta, and that would lose crucial party support."

"Okay, then level the playing field," Suzuki countered.

Canada had just received a $3 billion windfall from the sale of its national gas company [Petro-Canada] to private industry.

"Use some of that money," Suzuki said.

Suzuki got a call from the PM only days before the 2004 all-important Throne Speech.

"You're not going to get credit for this but I am going to take all of your recommendations, including energy, and include them in my speech," he told Suzuki.

On October 5, 2004, Martin told the world Canada had embarked upon SWAG or sustainability within a generation:

As the ethic and imperative of sustainability take deeper root worldwide, human ingenuity will turn increasingly to ways to produce and use energy more cleanly and efficiently; to eliminate toxins from our air, water and soil; and to build more sustainable communities. Here lie great new opportunities for the world economy. Canada's entrepreneurs must aim to be at the leading edge. To that end, the Government will work with the private sector to improve the commercialization of the best new environmental technologies. . . . Major investments funded out of the proceeds of the sale of the

Government's Petro-Canada shares will support their development and deployment.[12]

"We spent $3.5 million on our climate committee here at the Foundation and we leveraged that amount into one billion dollars of renewable energy subsidies," Suzuki told me. "Of course, we're just at the beginning of the transformation."

The Suzuki Foundation has discussed SWAG with the Union of Concerned Scientists in the United States and Australian Conservation Fund to spread the message. The message is sweeping over the world. The issue is how fast we can go.

Stephen Meyer of the Massachusetts Institute of Technology concluded, "Anecdotes notwithstanding, the data compel us to reject the argument that higher numbers of endangered species are associated with poor economic performance."[13]

Meyer went state by state to simultaneously rate states by how strict their environmental regulations were and how much economic strength they exhibited in terms of job generation and building and construction projects. When he put the two analyses side by side, state by state, it showed a remarkable relationship between environmental standards and prosperity: "States with stronger environmental policies consistently outperformed the weaker environmental states on all the economic measures."

A similar outcome was seen in another independently conducted study from the Institute for Southern Studies in North Carolina. Once again, the report noted: "States with the best environmental records also offer the best job opportunities and climate for long-term economic development. The best stewards of the environment also offer workaday citizens the best opportunity for prosperity."[14]

Pollutants are us. They are building up. They are changing us. I tried to get across the river and tell you this. But as much as you and I know that the chemicals and processes of global warming also pose immediate health and long-term security threats to our nation, when I came out with *Diet for a Poisoned Planet*, and I said that we ought to protect ourselves from these chemicals' known and unknown effects, I was the menace du jour who came at the right moment when the cold war was over and the libertarians and neoconservatives had just begun to substitute the "green menace" for the "red menace." The George Herbert Walker Bush administration, with its cronies at the American Council for Science and Health (ACSH, an alleged science-based organization whose mission seems to be to defend the worst polluters in the land) together with Ketchum and Edelman (two whorish worldwide PR agencies), labeled me a threat to national security for revealing the pesticides and industrial chemicals in our food supply and particularly for pointing out that the raisins in your child's lunch contained fresh residues and metabolites of DDT. In a July 12, 1990, letter by Elizabeth Whelan, the head of the ACSH, to Governor John Sununu who was then the president's chief of staff at the White House, I was labeled as someone who "may pose a future threat to national security." A reply came from Ede Holiday on White House stationery that they were looking into the matter of how it came to be that one of the EPA's own top scientists had written the foreword for my book. At one point, cronies working with industry even tried to paint me as a Scientologist, which I never was or have been (although I would defend everybody's right to freedom of belief) and, in fact, I forced one of the overzealous hacks to retract such a statement in a dossier being distributed about me. These people are evil because they are telling you lies. I am here to tell you the truth.

I felt then, as now, that I was a patriot. As individuals, we have to shoulder some of the burden, too. We don't have to get everything at Wal-Mart or other places where discounts are so deep they actually end up discounting our environment and human dignity as well.

That freedom goes along with green patriotism and high environmental standards is explicit in the work of Pulitzer Prize–winning author Jared Diamond who takes us to New Guinea to two oil fields in his classic best-selling tome *Collapse*.

One represents the best in environment and ecology. The other represents the worst. "I found these experiences instructive, because I had previously assumed that oil industry impacts were overwhelmingly harmful."[15]

His experience occurred in divided New Guinea. A portion of the island is ruled by Indonesia, and a portion as an independent democracy. Salawati Island is off the coast of Indonesian New Guinea. He was asked to conduct a bird survey of islands of the region. Much of the island was leased for oil exploration by Pertamina, the national oil company of Indonesia. Visiting as a guest of Pertamina, which even provided him with a vehicle, Diamond reports, "In view of that kindness, I am sorry to report on the conditions that I encountered. From a long distance, the field's location could be recognized by a flame shooting out of a high tower, where natural gas obtained as a by-product of oil extraction was being burned off, there being nothing else to do with it." He encountered a complete lack of even a try at having a green fossil fuel facility. The roads were cut extremely wide, wider than needed, and were severely damaging mammals, birds, frogs, and reptiles because it was too wide to safely cross. "There were numerous oil spills on the ground." He found only three species of large fruit pigeons, a staple food, when other regions contained as many as fourteen species.

In contrast, he visited Kutubu oil field located near the Kikori River, Papua, New Guinea (the freedom-loving democracy). This oil field was owned by a subsidiary of the former international oil giant Chevron Corporation. From 1998 to 2003, he made four visits, and he found something entirely different. The Chevron oil field was being so well cared for environmentally that it was the best place on the entire island for diversity. The roads were narrowly cut. Oil spills were assiduously avoided. Part of the reason things worked so well is that Chevron itself is run by personnel who see their company's environmental commitment as a key to long-term success. But give credit to the people of Papua. Their government was run from the ground up by councils from local communities knowing how to count trees and pigeons. The police force and army were relatively benign as well, and the central government did not run the country as an autocracy. With freedom come expectations for behavior. Chevron's environmentally sensitive executives knew beforehand they would have to do a lot to impress the Papuan government and immediately enlisted the aid of the World Wildlife Fund to guide them in preparing a comprehensive wildlife and ecological plan for the entire watershed. Chevron was going to take, but also give a whole lot more back and, in turn, deliver an oil field for many generations.

"As my airplane flight from Papua New Guinea's capital of Port Moresby droned on towards the field's main airstrip at Moro and was approaching its scheduled arrival time," Diamond said he looked out the window and saw only a road narrow enough for two vehicles to pass side by side going for more than one hundred miles from six thousand feet altitude on Mt. Moran, site of an oil field, to the coast. The next day walking this road he found an abundance of animal life. This was his introduction to the company's "extreme concern" to do things right for the long run. In contrast, as a national oil company in a corrupt island-nation that is already burning down its rain forests, Pertamina faced no credible public opposition. Chevron was also a profitable company, yet doing things right. The people who lived within the Chevron oil field enjoyed a much higher quality of life and standard of living. The right thing to do was the better thing in so many ways. Not only is it a hardcore geographer like Diamond who sees this. Additional research shows that no matter where you look—in America, Europe, or Asia—environmental protection has a positive effect on local and national economies and standards of living, as well as being part and parcel of freedom-loving societies.

Paradoxical though it might seem, we enjoy a better standard of living when we invest in our environment competitively. Of course, it is stupid to think that any nation can be great without a manufacturing base. So we don't want to lose that and go back to some forsaken preindustrial era. But what do we want to manufacture? Rubber chickens or hydrogen engines, solar panels, and pollution scrubbers? Great nations should have vital and active manufacturing bases that are busy leading us into a better future and, from a financial standpoint, building markets. Forget the Internet revolution of the '90s; that's all passé. The new revolution is in the manufacturing sector with a green consciousness. This is also major crux of my journey, I realized, to see that business and manufacturing must become the embodiment of the environmental movement. Innovative manufacturing stimulated by the valuing of natural assets is transforming business, technology, and our very economy. Americans can be world leaders and get excited about their green future, or they can remain stuck in the petroleum-contaminated New Orleans mud.

I don't want trade wars, either. But the power of people—that is, the worldwide environmental movement—to work with indigenous populations to build popular support for fair and humane working conditions and environmental policies is the key to freedom and less terrorism. Once people start asking environmental questions, it is a natural progression for them to begin asking about concepts like freedom, fairness, and responsibility, and to feel empowered in a positive manner. Bill McKibben, author of *The End of Nature*, recently took a trip to China where he reported in the December 2005 issue of *Harper's* on the powerful outrage of villagers over polluted rivers. This is the fuel of democracy there, he said. Their large numbers of protestors over the recent chemical contamination of a river are democratizing China, and we'd be politically foolish to turn away from this powerful movement. Protests over environmental rape today are as politically energizing and the modern global equivalent to the historic anger over taxes on stamps and tea, invasions of privacy, and as forced lodging of the crown's soldiers in patriots' homes were to our own American founders. If people globally force governments to tow the line here, America benefits in every way by promoting ecologically based social stability. We will be bringing the playing field up instead of sinking down to the lowest depths of ecological depravity. Environmentalism as I'm talking about is a president's biggest weapon for building strong international relations; it goes so far beyond politics. So that's why America needs a president who gets it.

Because we lack leadership, we are trying to regulate our way out of a mess that requires a complete national change in consciousness and spirituality.

That takes placing a value on nature. We must start to put a value on nature in our balance sheets, and, if we do this, we can fuel the new green movement. It just makes sense. Suzuki and Paul Hawken were right. They both state clearly that we have to value our natural assets to measure our wealth, our gross national assets. There has to be a place on the balance sheet for these.

For example, hydroelectric-power producers in Costa Rica pay $57 million annually to landholders and government to receive services provided by healthy flowing rivers and naturally strong river banks where the sediment and natural structures and beds stay in place. After all, a healthy flowing river can produce much more electricity than one that is degraded with erosion.[16]

"When a piece of natural habitat is ploughed, for example, the conversion may make sense to the land owner, but it may also damage fisheries downstream, increase flooding and clog rivers with sediment," said the April 23, 2005, edition of *The Economist* in its article, "Are You Being Served?"

In September 2005 in *Scientific American*, Herman E. Daly, professor at the School of Public Policy, University of Maryland, reported that "man-made capital cannot substitute for natural capital. Once, catches were limited by the number of fishing boats (man-made capital). Today the limit is the number of fish in the ocean—building more boats will not increase catches. To ensure long-term economic health, nations must sustain the level of natural capital (such as fish), not just total wealth."[17]

Of course, weak sustainability could mean building more and better fishing boats to squeeze the last fishes from the sea. That is what we are doing with the gill nets that kill all the fish over large swathes of the sea, including commercially nondesirable yet ecologically important species. Strong sustainability involves support for growing and maintaining fish populations. All the fishing boats in the world cannot sustain or save an industry; in the end, only the fish in the sea can.

That means we have to put a value on populations and what the oceans hold in reserve as our assets.

If any industry knows about having something in reserve, it is insurers. These businesses are certainly forcing other businesses to recognize and deal with global warming and environmental issues. This is causing changes in business practices and pushing even reluctant industries into the green business consciousness.

Here's an example. John Fogach, chairman of ForestRe, a London-based forest insurer working with clients in Panama, is putting together a collaborative effort to save vast regions of rain forest. The Panama Canal requires large amounts of freshwater to operate its locks. Yet, this freshwater is disappearing due to rain forest degradation.

To this end, Fogach's ForestRe has expanded its concept of the value of forestry from "pure" timber, pulp, and paper to broader "environmental" markets.[18]

New values in forestry, according to ForestRe, include carbon credits that will be sold to private industry and governments as offsets to their own pollution and carbon emissions, water quality services, soil quality services, biodiversity protection schemes, and ecotourism. This is not pretty or merely cosmetic. It is critical to profits to look at natural assets as a great source of wealth or liability. The insurers are going to make companies spend vast amounts on environmental projects to protect their own investments. Fogach is currently putting together companies that use the Panama Canal to fund reforesting the entire region and restoring its ecological system. Researchers at the Smithsonian Tropical Research Institutes in Panama "think that reforesting the canal's denuded watershed would regulate the supply," said the *Economist*.[19]

After all, a healthy forest would make expensive dredging and other water projects unnecessary. "Environmental entries are starting to appear on the balance sheet," the magazine said.

While global warming may not be the sole cause of the extreme number of hurricanes in 2005, a growing number of insurance companies have come to the conclusion that climate change, caused mainly by human activity, could well increase the intensity of hurricanes and other weather disasters. This also has insurers extremely concerned. No amount of money is available now to deal with another hurricane season like 2005 when the Gulf Coast flooded and we lost major portions of New Orleans.

"We think it's a serious problem and it's something we have to pay close attention to," Andrew Castaldi, head of catastrophe and perils for Swiss Reinsurance Co.'s Americas division in New York, told a reporter in a 2005 article in the *Globe and Mail* of Toronto, Canada. "We'd be remiss if we didn't take it into account."

It's the domino effect in motion.

Swiss Re is looking at incorporating climate change into its modeling and investing in green companies with a $350-million clean energy fund.

By 2080, the costs from hurricanes, typhoons and windstorms will jump by two-thirds to $27 billion (U.S.) a year, the Association of British Insurers said. (Ironically and sadly, in the United States, the National Association of Insurance Commissioners had organized a climate change symposium on the issue in September in New Orleans. The meeting was canceled due to the disaster wrought by Hurricane Katrina.)

Insurers are "only going to become more articulate and more active on these issues in terms of encouraging clearer government policy on climate change and encouraging their clients to better protect themselves from potential climate change risk," said Brigid Barnett, a senior research analyst who focuses on financial services at Innovest Strategic Value Advisors, in the *Globe and Mail* article.[20]

Whole international markets are now devoted to carbon credits. Developing nations and industries can comply with international treaties and standards by buying portions of intact forests in Australia, Costa Rica, or elsewhere and helping to preserve these carbon "sinks." It isn't pretty, to be sure, and Mark Lynas, author of *High Tide*, condemned global carbon trading as a scheme in the worst way because it allows polluters to go on polluting.[21] But at least it is a start to placing bottom line value on being carbon neutral

The world trade in greenhouse gas emissions is heating up as carbon dioxide prices surge and companies buy and sell credits worth hundreds of millions of euros in expectation of tightening global standards, said a July 13, 2005, analysis in Reuters.[22] The EU scheme caps CO_2 emissions from about twelve thousand factories and power plants, and allows firms to trade credits. This is big business in Europe. According to *BusinessWeek*, "The system is helping foster green investments in countries that are home to some of the world's biggest polluters."[23] For example, JGC Corp. and Marubeni Corp. teamed with a chemical maker in China's Zhejiang Province to recover gases released in making refrigerants. The estimated carbon savings was 40 million tons of CO_2. Now, with this reduction, the company owned credits worth $200 million, which it could sell to other companies that can't meet the required caps. Says *BusinessWeek*, "Sumitomo Corp. and Rabo Bank of the Netherlands have a similar contract with Gujarat Fluorochemicals in India for three million tons of carbon credits. And Paris-based chemical maker Rhodia is cutting nitrous oxide emissions at its plants in South Korea and Brazil. Rhodia will likely sell those credits, equivalent to as much as thirteen million tons of CO_2."

Prices for CO_2 credits for the first phase of the scheme (2005-2007) had "surged off a low of just over six euros a ton in mid January 2005 to nearly thirty euros seven months later," said Reuters.

You'd almost think this was all the fantasy of an underground man, his jaws gnawing, as he typed away in his lonely basement—someone like a Patrick Henry, Dostoevsky, or, more ominously, Leon Trotsky. But I'm not alone in what I'm thinking. Not anymore. Paul Hawken and Amory and Hunter Lovins tell us in *Natural Capitalism* that Wal-Mart found out that being sensitive to your environment meant more profits with its Lawrence, Kansas, "Eco-Store." To save energy, the company fitted a day-lighting section in half the store and used normal fluorescent lighting in the rest. At corporate headquarters in Arkansas, Wal-Mart inventory experts saw that the naturally lighted side of the store was producing significantly higher sales rates than other stores without the energy-saving design innovation. Today, Wal-Mart operates several more eco-stores and is really trying to take a leadership role in its environmental initiatives.

When it comes to the environment, CEO Lee Scott speaks plain and direct: "As we have worked on innovating our company, we have seen a whole host of opportunities to do more and better with much less. But we still have a long way to go."[24]

The coauthors of *Natural Capitalism* say that Boeing put in new lighting systems in its design and manufacturing areas. Quite apart from reducing lighting-related energy use by up to 90 percent (and recouping their outlay in less than two years), product quality improved. Why? With this green consciousness, an added bonus was the technology for light itself was better, and workers also were able to more clearly spot defects in aircraft they were constructing.

A really good case example is NaturaLawn of America, located in Frederick, Maryland, the nation's first organic-based lawn care franchise service.[25] According to a case study from the Green Gazelle project of the Center for Small Business and the Environment, NaturaLawn of America now has over seventy-three independently owned franchise locations servicing over forty-five thousand environmentally concerned customers in twenty-seven states and generating over $24 million in annual revenues. In 2002 alone, NaturaLawn of America reduced the usage of petroleum derivative fertilizers by over 2.5 million pounds, and reduced petroleum-based pesticides from entering into our environment by over 1 million gallons when compared with traditional chemical lawn care. NaturaLawn of America is not a start-up business that's untested. To the contrary, the company has shown that its organic-based systems not only work, but also are safer than chemical-based systems.

You might be surprised to learn that NaturaLawn of America has grown to be the fourth-largest lawn care company in the United States. Do something great for everyone in your neighborhood and start incorporating nontoxic lawn care. This is a big deal for everybody's health. Lawn chemicals are among the most toxic cancer-causing chemicals to which adults and children are exposed. I see people applying these chemicals to lawns as being as, if not more, dangerous to our children as the actions of other kinds of criminal acts. Visit www.nl-amer.com.

Thanks to the sweeping green consciousness, companies are dramatically reducing greenhouse gas emissions, often exceeding the Kyoto Protocol targets.[26]

Alcoa, a world leader in aluminum manufacturing, committed to reducing emissions by 25 percent from 1990 levels by 2010, and by 50 percent from 1990 levels over the same period if their inert anode technology yields anticipated energy savings. "A key factor in reducing greenhouse emissions is energy efficiency," according to John Pizzey, Aloca executive vice president in a September 30, 2002, speech to his employees. "Because of the amount of energy required to make aluminum from ore, any increase in energy efficiency—through process improvements and through the use of recycled feedstock—can make Alcoa both greener and more competitive."

Pizzey set a goal for Aloca and a benchmark for the industry to make 50 percent of their fabrication metal from recycled aluminum by 2020.

BP, one of the world's major petroleum companies, achieved its carbon-neutral target eight years early, reducing emissions 10 percent worldwide below the company's 1990 levels, and all of this happened at no net cost.

DuPont, the chemical manufacturer, has reduced emissions worldwide by 45 percent and improved energy efficiency by 15 percent over 1990 levels. It now uses renewables for 10 percent of its global energy use. After studying the data on climate change, "we came to the conclusion that the science was compelling and that action should be taken," DuPont Chairman and CEO Chad Holliday said in a press release.[27]

IBM, known for its information technology, has reduced energy consumption worldwide by 25 percent, through conservation, pocketing $527 million.

"While some assume that cutting CO_2 emissions costs businesses money, we have found just the opposite. Addressing climate change makes business sense," said Wayne Balta, vice president for Corporate Environmental Affairs and Product Safety. "We have saved more than one hundred million dollars since 1998 by conserving energy. When you consider the significant environmental benefits also achieved, cutting emissions is a win-win proposition."[28]

Interface Inc., the world's largest commercial flooring manufacturer, has been striving to be a fully sustainable enterprise and has saved $262 million since 1994 by consuming less raw material and energy, managing waste, and conserving water. These measures have already had an enormous effect. The company has reduced its number of smokestacks by over one-third and almost halved its greenhouse gas emissions.

Ray Anderson, CEO of Interface, Inc., is a board member

of the Suzuki Foundation. He said, "If we get it right, our company and our supply chain will never have to take another drop of oil."[29]

Nike, the shoe and garment manufacturers, reduced carbon dioxide emissions worldwide from business travel and from facilities and services to 13 percent below 1998 levels in 2005. Nike's initiatives include the Considered product line, which is "the driving force and ethos behind a newly established team committed to integrating sustainable product innovation across all Nike branded products," said the company's Web site.

"Considered" is Nike's "response to the growing consumer demand for products that tell stories about a product's materials and design intention," said John Hoke, Nike's vice president of Footwear Creative Design and codirector of the Considered team. "We saw it as an opportunity to create product that speaks to both premium design and sustainability. It was the natural next step for us to take based on more than a decade of rooting our environmental commitment. . . . This is obviously a huge challenge—one that will inspire us for years to come. As a company, we've developed programs around shoe recycling, reducing greenhouse gas emissions, reducing toxics in the manufacturing process and continually looking for ways to reduce waste in the design and manufacturing processes."[30]

Employees in the United States who travel for Nike business have the option of choosing Delta Air Lines to allocate a portion of their ticket cost to a fund established by Nike and Delta Air Lines. The Eco-Class fund is aimed at mitigating the annual climate impact of Nike's air travel on Delta flights by offsetting the equivalent carbon emissions.

PCBs and the Hudson River go together like, well, GE and superfund. Besides being responsible for PCB pollution of the Hudson River Valley, GE contributes to some seventy-five to one hundred Superfund sites. The company's long list of alleged environmental misdeeds can be traced back to 1949 and were publicly highlighted during 1995 with the establishment of a Presidential Advisory Commission on the full extent of our nation's environmental and humanitarian misdeeds with nuclear radiation.[31] GE ran the Hanford Nuclear Reservation in Richland, Washington, as part of America's weapons program and is alleged to have deliberately engaged in releases from the plant to see how far downwind the radioactive material would travel. "One cloud drifted four hundred miles, all the way down to the California-Oregon border, carrying perhaps thousands of times more radiation than that emitted at Three Mile Island." The company is also alleged to have conducted what were clearly unethical studies on prisoners on the effects of radiation on their testicles. In 1998, GE agreed to a $200 million settlement with the EPA and the Department of Justice for claims linked with PCB pollution of the Housatonic River due to the company's plant in Pittsfield, Massachusetts. (GE no longer uses PCBs in manufacturing, although former CEO Jack Welch has been quoted as saying at an April 22, 1998 shareholder meeting that "PCBs do not pose adverse health risks.")

GE has left some big carbon and chemically sticky footprints on Earth.

How do we forgive? And how do we change? We change through actions, and actions are inspired by greening our religion and how we handle money. Say hello to GE, the new environmental company.

Jeffrey Immelt, GE's CEO, affirmed on May 9, 2005, at the George Washington University School of Business, that GE is going green, and I applaud them for that visionary changeover, especially because they hold so much potential to change this world and usher us technologically into the carbon-neutral age. GE is "taking a long look around, and here's what we see: a diminishing domestic oil supply and natural gas reserves . . . our continued dependence on foreign source of energy . . . increasing scare resources, like water, in an ever more populated world . . . and the signs of global climate change."[32]

"Ecomagination is driven by our belief that applying technology to solving problems is great business," said Immelt. "We're launching ecomagination not because it's trendy or moral, but because it will accelerate our growth and make us more competitive."

"Imagine if we discovered a new resource," GE said in its October 17, 2005, two-page advertisement in the *Wall Street Journal*. "One that could help solve the problems of energy-hungry world. At GE, we think we've discovered just that. We call it ecomagination. It's already helped us create some very forward-looking technology that, maybe, in time, can help make the water a little clearer, the trees a little happier, the sky a little bluer, and the world a little closer to the way it was made. Just imagine it."

This was not just the soggy feel-good drizzle of PR pitter-patter, either. Take a trip with me to the Irish town of Arklow, near the Irish Sea. There, a pioneering GE wind farm, located six miles off the Irish coast, was providing the electricity to a nearby grid to power as many as 16,000 homes. Not only did the Arklow Bank windmill farm save Ireland, which is 90 percent dependent on fossil fuel imports, some 15,000 tons of fossil fuels annually, it also brought Ireland closer to being a carbon-neutral nation, by preventing release of 68,000 tons of carbon dioxide emissions. That was like taking 16,000 cars off the road. Public officials now say that by expanding the Arklow windmill farm, it could supply 10 percent of all of Ireland's electricity needs.[33] But that's nothing new to GE, at least. The company expected its wind turbine sales to private and public utilities and businesses to generate in excess of $2 billion in revenue in 2005. Interestingly, during the height of the Enron meltdown in 2002, when GE picked up the bankrupt company's business, wind power was producing "only" $500 million in revenues. Wind power is growing 30 percent a year in Europe and America, and it is quite likely that the wind can provide up to one-fifth or more of the United States' total energy needs—and that's what makes GE's involvement super smart from a business viewpoint. But it is a good thing, too, from an environmental and do-the-right-thing perspective. Selling for around five cents a kilowatt-hour (which includes federal tax credits), wind power has reached the point where it actually costs less now or is competitive with coal, oil, gas, hydro, and nuclear, which generally run six to seven cents per kilowatt hour. The fact is, GE scientists say, there's enough wind along the eastern slopes of the Rocky Mountains to supply the power for all of the United States!

Meantime, at its Global Research Center near Schenectady, New York, GE scientists are in the midst of developing nanodiodes—1/80,000th as thick as a human hair—that convert sunlight into electricity. These could soon bring solar power into a new realm of technological applications—imagine running your digital camera on solar power instead of also having to power up with batteries. One of the drawbacks to photovoltaic cells that GE has been producing and selling is that they are only 20 percent efficient in terms of converting sunlight to power. That's because the silicon materials used have too many impurities and imperfections still, but the nanodiodes might counter these imperfections. To this end, GE has assigned fifty nanoscientists to work on the new technology. Imagine the clarity of our skies and purity of our landfills with nanodiodes in our solar collectors.

Moving from the minutiae of nanotechnology to the

grossly visible metal mammoth steam engine, a GE-designed hybrid locomotive uses less fuel and produces fewer toxic and greenhouse emissions than today's current crop of locomotives, and that's another market advantage and real sales leverage. Enthused, GE's Vice President of Advanced Technology at the Global Research Center Michael Idelchick said to *Fortune* magazine, "The hunt for clean, sustainable energy will be the defining story of the 21st century."

GE and Dow Jones, the publisher of the *Wall Street Journal*, said they were offering seed money to great business ideas that combine environmental innovation and profitability, because they believed "green" business is good business. So if you're a university or MBA student, or a confident entrepreneur, submit your business idea. You could win $50,000 in start-up money. Visit www.dowjones.com/ge to register online.

The Business Roundtable is an association of CEOs from leading U.S. corporations whose combined workforce represents more than 10 million men and women. In September 2005, the Business Roundtable launched its SEE Change Initiative. An acronymn for social, environmental, and economic, the SEE Change Initiative was developed thanks, in part, to the leadership role of Chad Holliday, chairman and CEO of DuPont. "SEE Change is not just about improving the environment or being socially responsible. It's about growing your business, growing jobs, and growing the economy—and doing so in a way that will leave society a better place for future generations," said Marian Hopkins, director of public policy for the Business Roundtable.[34] The Business Roundtable has also launched its Climate Resolve program, which has put on national workshops to help companies implement carbon-neutral practices, including use of cogeneration and renewable energy sources at plants themselves and also how to start entering savings on greenhouse emissions into the balance sheet.[35]

Waste Management, the largest trash, toxic waste, and environmental service company in North America, has a new slogan, "Think Green," that it claims goes deeper than the color of its refuse collection trucks.[36] Waste Management has been developing landfill gas-to-energy projects for more than fifteen years and that currently provide than 250 megawatts of energy, which is enough to power 225,000 homes and replace more than 2 million barrels of oil annually. This kind of innovation has definite synergistic ripples that everybody profits from, both financially and environmentally. Instead of drifting into the atmosphere as a pure greenhouse emission, the methane gas from the company's Next Generation Sainte-Sophie landfill near Montreal is now powering the local Cascades paper mill and supplanting 75 percent of its use of natural gas.

Greening your patriotism—carbon-neutral business practices—or just a good environmental ethos—whatever you want to call this shift in consciousness—clearly, says Boston-based environmental and sustainability consultant Andrew Savitz, the tipping point has arrived.

Savitz said he loves to tell the story about Toyota's early foray into hybrid technology. "Back in the 1980s, there was a senior engineer at Toyota who came up with the idea for a hybrid engine. Many people thought it was environmental lunacy, but Toyota made two bets when it decided to pursue that idea. One was that environmental concerns would grow in importance, and the other was that gas prices would go up over time. And they won on both bets. This has gone from being a niche business for Toyota to being a centerpiece of its growth efforts. And it's a perfect example of what can happen when there's a public interest and a business interest in protecting the environment. They coincide in a marketplace opportunity that can make a difference for all of us."

Again, I don't want to sugarcoat, either. We're definitely seeing business moving in the right direction. The question is in how directed a manner and aggressively business moves—and, as I've said, that also depends on us and how much we expect of ourselves.

Not everybody is happy with the progress. We might still be heading over the cliff into the abyss of global climate change if we don't make green consciousness go even more deeply into our finances and economy.

Green Life, a sustainability group, is deeply critical of the Business Roundtable's initiatives.[37] According to Green Life, "Climate Resolve's expectations are set low, while its spotlight is turned on only when participants are flattered by it. Take General Motors, which not only qualified for participation in Climate Resolve, but was noted in the Exemplary Company Actions listed in the program's first progress report . . . for initiatives including 'the removal of bulbs illuminating the front panel of over 100 vending machines.' Meanwhile, General Motors' fleetwide fuel economy—the truest gauge of an automaker's impact on the climate—is the same as it was ten years ago. . . . America's leading corporations aren't kids learning how to play ball. They should be treated like marquee players, whom much is expected of and on whom the spotlight always shines."

Can an entire nation go green? In 1989, Dr. Karl-Henrik Robèrt of Sweden founded The Natural Step organization to address the systemic causes of environmental problems, according to the program's Web site.[38] The Natural Step is based on Robèrt's heartfelt experience treating children with cancer whose sickness he realized was often environmentally related. He began a systemic cancer-prevention program that included root thinking to transform the way that we perceive manufacturing. Sweden has taken the natural step to a systemic level in some seventy municipalities that range in size from small farm villages, to Stockholm in the center of an urban region of some 1.76 million souls.[39] Today more than sixty Swedish corporations, including IKEA, Electrolux, McDonald's Sweden, and Scandic Hotels, are actively using The Natural Step's principles and approach to sustainability.

McDonald's embraced The Natural Step program in Umeå, Sweden, to become part of its "Green Zone," a public-private enterprise comprising a Ford dealership that was selling mostly hybrid vehicles, an environmentally conscious car wash, and fast-food place. (This green zone is not to be confused with the governmental one in Baghdad.) All buildings were constructed and made from locally harvested, sustainable woods, topped by green-sod roofs, creating a rooftop garden effect (one that many visionaries see happening all across the skyscrapers of Manhattan someday).

Seventh Generation CEO Jeffrey Hollender and coauthor Stephen Fenichell reported in *What Matters Most*, their green business book, that three-quarters of the 160 McDonald's franchises in Sweden served organic ice cream. All served organic milk, and half ran on renewable energy. All newly built sites use piping made with recycled material. The McDonald's in Sweden recycled 97 percent of its solid waste.[40] One McDonald's in that country sells biodiesel made from the cooking oil used for their fries. So why don't we get organic ice cream and all-natural beef at McDonald's in the United States?

Because we're slobs, and we don't care. We just keep getting fat on the chemical beef and corn that we're being fed while our health declines rapidly after age fifty.

If we were really to act like a bright and enlightened society, we might say the answer could be found in our federal and state tax schemes as well as in law and order. Polluters are criminal trust passers, as well as trespassers.

Viewed by an economist, those who pollute without paying the full costs are depreciating a "public trust resource" that belongs to society at large, said Peter Montague, editor in chief of Rachel's Environmental News, which is perhaps the most widely read environmental news report today (www.rachel.org). They are appropriating ("taking" or "privatizing") a resource that belongs to everyone, without paying compensation, he said.

"Normally when a public servant embezzles or steals financial capital from the public, society imposes penalties including disgrace, monetary fines and, in rare cases, imprisonment," said Montague. "But when polluters appropriate and degrade public-trust resources, such as water and air, they often get away scot-free."[41]

The reason farms producing chemically grown crops and hog barons sell their wares for only one dollar and the organic farmer or rancher must charge three is because chemical farmers and ranchers "externalize" the costs of pollution to the public at large. Take the pesticides and fertilizers that farmers use.

Dead fish dot the shores of the Gulf Coast. Dead pelicans lay scattered among them. The lines of dead fish are constant and extend across hundreds of miles of beaches all of the time. This is the Dead Zone in the Gulf of Mexico. It provides an unsettling example of the cascading chain of environmental destruction. An unprecedented rise in nutrient and sediment pollution, most of it from agricultural chemicals linked with global warming, flowing down the Mississippi River causes explosive growth in phytoplankton in the ocean. Photosynthesis initially produces much oxygen near the surface, but when the tiny microorganisms eventually die, they fall to the bottom to be consumed by bacteria, a process that uses up most of the oxygen in the water, especially near the bottom. The hypoxia then suffocates the shrimp, fish, and other aquatic life. The annual death zone has expanded to eight thousand square miles, an area the size of New Jersey. The people of Louisiana and Texas are up in arms about the dead fish swamping their shores, underscoring the terrible economic consequences to the Gulf Coast commercial shrimp industry, which employs more than seventy thousand fishermen

Upstream along the Mississippi and its tributaries, in the corn belt of the Midwest, farmers who fertilize their crops with nitrates and manure are often oblivious to the faraway impacts of their actions. They have gotten used to giving their crops "insurance" levels of nutrients, knowing that some will be lost due to spring melt, evaporation, and torrential spring rains. Fertilizer has been cheap (until this year), so it made sense to heap plenty on to ensure a good crop.

Then there is pesticide use, or, should I say, misuse? Many studies published in medical journals link pesticide exposures with higher cancer and birth defect rates. Parkinson's disease is linked in studies with such exposures. Asthma, premature delivery, birth defects—these are just some of the documented results of pervasive pesticide exposure. No one wants unsafe chemicals in our food supply or in the neighborhood, including our schools (where, as I have seen in the San Joaquin Valley, they often sit beside sprayed fields).

Not only does our current system of agriculture violate concepts of private property and personal responsibility, but the chemicals we use are poisoning our environment and the very intellectual capabilities of our future generations—and their schools.

Given what we know about the ecological impacts of pesticides and fertilizers, particularly on our drinking water, it might seem incredible that some twenty-nine of fifty U.S.

states provide exemptions from sales taxes for agricultural chemicals such as pesticides and fertilizers. According to one report, states lose at least $674 million each year as a result of the exemptions.

"People traditionally think of taxation and the environment as two separate spheres," said Janet E. Milne, director of the Environmental Tax Policy Institute at Vermont Law School.[42] "Government engages in taxation to generate the revenues it needs to function. Government gets involved in the environment to protect the public interest, usually using regulation," said Milne. "But there is tremendous potential to have taxes do some real work, even do double duty—generate the revenues government needs and encourage business to adopt pro-environmental policies."

Some experts say that green taxes could replace personal income taxes with a net gain in public health. The basic idea is shifting taxes from labor to criminals, those who violate private property rights with their deadly toxic pollution.

In simple terms, a green tax puts the burden where it belongs; it actually decreases the taxes on labor and shifts them to the polluters. The scheme encourages good companies to invest more, employ more people, and therefore contribute to creating more jobs, say experts.

For fiscal conservatives and libertarians, some experts say a green tax on polluting businesses can ultimately replace an income tax and end up saving us all in taxes.

Such a tax could stimulate a move to produce eventually zero toxic waste and totally carbon neutral effects.

Reports from Europe, where a green tax is growing in popular appeal, show that such taxes seem to accomplish their goals and are actually good for society.

In Ireland, a green tax was recently introduced on supermarket bags and has already cut the country's use of nonrecyclable bags by more than a billion and earned 3.5 million euros for the Dublin exchequer.

In Sweden, pesticide use in the early 1980s was similar to that of Oregon, about five thousand tons per year. In 1985, the Swedish government used a 30 percent sales tax on pesticides to fund reduction efforts, with an overall goal of reducing pesticide use by 50 percent. That goal was met in 1990—thanks in large part to research that showed that pesticides could be used effectively at much lower doses—and the government promptly set an additional 50 percent reduction target.

But Sweden is run by a pack of pinko socialists, I hear the American neoconservatives and libertarians argue. Yet, in 1987, Iowa responded to widespread nitrate contamination of groundwater by imposing a small tax on fertilizers and dedicating the resulting revenue (about $1 million per year) to the Leopold Center for Sustainable Agriculture. In the ensuing years, the Center and other state efforts helped reduce nitrogen fertilizer use by 12 to 15 percent relative to neighboring states while maintaining high crop yields.

Milne said there are many ways green taxes are critical to advancing markets and social goodness (not to mention our carbon-neutral future):

- Reflect Real Costs. If a factory farm operation in North Carolina or a manufacturing plant in Louisiana is polluting the groundwater with dangerous chemicals and everybody knows it, that farm or plant ought to pay a tax, instead of shifting the burden to consumers.
- Influence Behavior. Providing tax credits for conservation and renewable energy sources has had tremendously positive influences on consumer behavior and corporations. Many of society's leading-edge conservation projects today were initiated, in part, as a response to societal rewards via

credits and deductions. Consumers right now often receive rebates for buying energy-efficient appliances, solar panels, or a hybrid; this stimulates the market and encourages manufacturers to adopt even higher standards. It's a good way for government to give citizens back some of their money.

- Achieve More Cost-Effective Results. Think of the savings to public health and the environment with fewer toxic molecules running around and cleaner air for all of us to breathe.

Reach More Types of Behavior:

- Influence Everyday Decisions. Certainly, the chemical pesticides used in growing cotton are as dangerous to people as cigarettes, which are heavily taxed. You can bet if we taxed chemical cotton, we'd see a significant new market for cotton overall. Everyone would win with this new market, too. It just makes the pot larger and the game more competitive. It's a good thing for society. Taxes can influence everything we do, including our supermarket shopping decisions, how we get to work, and what kind of clothing we wear.
- Spur New Technology. Thanks to tax credits and federal rebates, we might be on the verge of creating more and more domestic energy from agricultural refuse, ending our extreme dependency on foreign oil. The Department of Energy, in particular, has funded basic scientific research on converting biomass to fuels.
- Reform Other Taxes. Taxes on labor would go down, and our own personal taxes might even be lowered.

Can we really have green taxes in America? The answer is, of course, we already do. One reason that there is so much interest in ethanol, which could be the answer to our foreign oil dependency, is the government's tax credits for its manufacture. The Department of Energy has funded basic research on the process of manufacturing ethanol from agricultural wastes such as stalks and husks and other forms of biomass, and such credits were part of the 2005 energy bill to the tune of 51 cents for every gallon manufactured.

Federal green tax credits covered some of the costs for both residential and commercial solar installations. Grist-Magazine.com reports that tax credits and other incentives have inspired many U.S. companies to install solar power systems at their facilities. Among the adopters are Johnson & Johnson, Lowe's, Toyota, BJ's Wholesale Club, and UPS.[43]

Johnson & Johnson, for example, recently installed a 500-kilowatt solar array at a facility located in Titusville, New Jersey. "Incentive programs," states Johnson & Johnson's John Subacus in the GristMagazine.com report, "made the project financially neutral, and we felt it was the best time to jump in and do something good for the environment."

The problem, quite frankly, is that Washington isn't providing any type of vision or inspiration to the country and hasn't tied being a carbon-neutral nation with national security, a fresh idea which everyone can agree on. Neither the president nor Congress has articulated this inspiring vision, and we need that from our American leadership.

I'm trying to initiate this call to action; my neighbor, who is president of the Malibu Surfing Association and runs an FDA-compliant print business, joined the one percent club where one percent of his sales go to support charitable and environmental projects (www.onepercentclub.org).

The way we do business, if we're religious, ought to be imbued with some social good for sure, and our religion ought to be imbued with our world in mind and how we spend and use money. This is something we can all take part in—my neighbor pounding away with an annoying hammer nearby could be buying FSC-certified wood products. It's within everyone's realm to do all the time. Here are ways you can put your money where your mouth is at your own business:

- Look for ways to recycle in your processes. You can always find ways to reduce your electricity use, water, and other materials that are going down the drain, up the smokestack, or into the garbage. Many small companies have found that initiating strong office recycling programs improves worker morale and retains higher-skilled laborers.
- One of the interesting by-products of looking for waste is saving money by making adjustments.
- Spread the message from within that you're an environmental company. Reward employees and departments for meeting and exceeding environmental goals. Set up award programs. (IBM has set up internal environmental technology competitions between divisions to spur innovation.)
- Learn from your competitors. Use their environmental strengths to leapfrog and become an industry leader yourself.
- Use your suppliers to do your research. Let your suppliers know that you are looking for environmental quality, and they will do the work for you and get you best pricing. We ask for quotes on 100 percent recyclable paper now routinely, which is a big and welcome change for us, and our suppliers are only too happy to do the research for us.
- If you use industrial products, seek those made without petrochemicals. This can be in the area of shop solvents, cleaners, sudsing agents, and other materials. Not everything, of course, comes petrochemical free. Building managers can order green cleaning products from companies like Seventh Generation.
- Add brand value to your clients. As an added bonus to those

companies and institutions purchasing our reprints, we offer 100 percent New Leaf recycled paper and, with a certification logo on each item, we make our clients look good, too. In every business today, customers have environmental needs that your company can help solve either through better processes or better products with which you can supply them. You wind up strengthening valuable business relationships. I'll bet there are ways for almost every business to assess what they are doing to help the environment and what they can do to improve.

When you have the extra cash you might want to consider strategic environmental investing. In the Green 100 at the end of this book, I've listed a number of publicly held companies whose environmental progressivism might surprise some. Eco-investing, when done expertly, pays off and might have some surprising picks. Today, when you invest in GE, you're also investing in fuel cells, wind turbines, and photovoltaic technology. Buying shares in Chevron—with its energy conservation and renewable energy divisions and its widely recognized high environmental standards—or BP and Shell, both of whom are investing heavily in solar, is buying green equity.

It isn't that these companies are by any means environmentally perfect—and in this book I've tried hard not to sugarcoat—but they are leaders, nonetheless, and they are likely to be a good investment if they implement carbon-neutral consciousness and business practices. This makes them socially responsible allies and solid investments.

With mutual funds, experts do the screening for you. Look for socially responsible investment or SRI funds. These funds are dedicated to doing good things for society with intent through avoidance: eschewing tobacco, military, pornography, animal cruelty, bad labor practices, and environmental abuses.

"There's now a very large body of evidence that documents that investors do not pay a 'conscience penalty' when they invest in companies that are socially responsible," said Timothy Small, president of the Social Investment Forum and senior vice president at Boston-based Walden Asset Management, which manages $1.4 billion for institutional and individual investors. "In fact, they may very well do better over time, which is what I believe based on our firm's investment experience over 35 years."[44]

Besides visiting www.waldenassetmgmt.com, here are some other funds to look at. Be sure to check out their latest returns and get expert advice:

New Alternatives Fund invests 25 percent of its funds in renewable energy such as wind power, fuel cells, ocean energy, solar, hydrogen, biomass, and geothermal. Visit them at www.newalternativesfund.com.

The Domini Equity fund is based on the Domini Social Index 400 (whose companies include McDonald's). So why did Domini pick McDonald's? "When I look at McDonald's versus the fast-food industry, I see them on a path toward human dignity and environmental sustainability," said the forward-looking Amy Domini who picks her green companies from the Standard & Poor's five-hundred-stock index.[45] Visit www.domini.com for more information.

Over a decade, the Green Century Equity Fund has averaged just over an 8-percent-a-year return. The environmental criteria used for selecting the stocks include each company's performance record on waste disposal, toxic emissions, fines or penalties, and efforts in waste and emissions reductions, recycling, and use of environmentally beneficial fuels, products, and services. Social criteria examined include a company's employee relations, corporate citizenship, product-related issues, and attitudes regarding consumer issues, according to the company's Web site. Its holdings include not only Microsoft,

Intel, and Cisco, but also Green Mountain Coffee Roasters, Inc., based in Waterbury, Vermont. For several years, the company has been a leader in the effort to establish better social and environmental standards in the coffee growing industry. Visit them at www.greencentury.com

Green banking is another way of putting your money where your mouth is. Green banking, said *GreenMoney Journal*, "is making major strides today across the United States."[46] According to the magazine, Chittenden Bank's Socially Responsible Banking Program, of Brattleboro, Vermont, allows depositors to benefit conservation by lending money to local green businesses. Beeken Parsons of Shelburne, Vermont, designed and created handcrafted furniture with wood harvested from sustainable forestry, and was helped by just such a loan. Visit www.chittenden.com

Candice and Dan Heydon of Oyster Creek Farm & Mushroom Company in Damariscotta, Maine, came to Coastal Enterprises, Inc., of Wiscasset, when they needed financing for their mushroom business. The nonprofit community development corporation and community development financial institution provided start-up financing. Today the company not only grows thousands of mushrooms on logs in sheds and lean-tos on their property but also buys wild mushrooms from foragers throughout Maine. Among the environmental aspects of the business are its reliance on the sustainable harvest of a renewable, nontimber forest product and its virtual elimination of any waste products; what does not sell fresh is sold dried and what does not sell dried is ground and sold as powder, says the publication. Visit www.ceimaine.org.

I like this example a lot. In Durham, North Carolina, Self-Help, a nonprofit credit union and community development lender, helped out Lea Clayton to buy fifteen acres of farm land in Alamance County, not far from the Haw River. The money helped develop an organic farm to become part of the CSA national food security network. Visit www.self-help.org.

In addition to www.greenmoneyjournal.com, which I love to read, also be sure to visit www.socialfunds.com, a Web site dedicated to socially responsible investing.

Admit it. You might be a Republican but you're also a proud, if closeted, environmentalist. So be a green elephant, and bust out of that closet. Hold your elected leaders' feet to the fire or be a leader in your own local, state, or federal government. Neither party is doing enough. Just as some Democrats are trying to take over border security as their issue, Republicans ought to be falling all over themselves to be green elephants and to have a vision, have something new and interesting and inspiring to say. Tell your Republican local, state, and federal officials that you will support them far more strongly when they take strong proenvironmental positions.

Republicans for Environmental Progress, also known as REP America, has done a great deal to keep the environmental flame alive in the Republican Party and is building stronger support every year, according to their political strategist David Jenkins in an interview with me.

Check out www.repamerica.org to learn about the Republican Party's deep-rooted environmental ties that go all the way back to Abraham Lincoln, who set aside portions of what would later become Yosemite National Park. According to Jenkins," Teddy Roosevelt established our unmatched system of wildlife refuges and national parks. Barry Goldwater, the father of conservatism, was a lifelong conservationist (and also a REP America member). Richard Nixon signed the Clean Air Act, the Endangered Species Act, the National Environmental Policy Act, and also established the Environmental Protection Agency."

● ● ●

You have to stand for something or you will fall for anything. So figure out what you stand for and don't back down, especially with your back at the gates of hell. But be smart. Here's a story that will illustrate what I mean. George Simeon was chief executive of Organic Valley, a cooperative of mostly small organic dairy, cattle, hog, and livestock farmers. For some three years, Organic Valley had been Wal-Mart's primary supplier of organic milk. When Wal-Mart demanded another 20 percent price cut in the company's pricing structure for its organic dairy products, well, a 20 percent cut can be hard for a company. Simeon decided his dairy cooperative could only provide the kind of pricing the retail leviathan was demanding if they diluted the integrity of their organic milk by crowding animals and feeding them more grains than pasture grass.

"Wal-Mart allows you to really build market share," Simeon told the *New York Times*. "But we're about our values and being able to sustain our farmers. If a customer wants to stretch us to the point where we're not able to deliver our mission, then we have to find different markets."[47]

Wal-Mart began working with mega-food giant Dean Foods's Horizon Organic, the country's largest organic dairy marketer, which was willing to meet Wal-Mart's pricing. Horizon produced about 20 percent of its milk from a fairly large four thousand–cow organic dairy in Paul, Idaho, as well as some 305 family farms. Although the Paul, Idaho, farm was small in comparison with other super factory dairy farms, it was still large, and its animal husbandry practices appeared to blur the line between factory farms and ideally humane organic farms—at least according to its critics.

The Cornucopia Institute, which represented small organic farm interests, filed a formal complaint in 2005 with the USDA's Office of Compliance asking them to initiate an investigation into alleged violations of the federal organic law by the Horizon dairy in Idaho. Grass is the end all and be all of cows. The complaints asked the USDA to investigate whether it was legal to confine cows in an industrial setting, without access to pasture, and still label milk and dairy products organic.

"According to reports, both the Idaho and California operations differ little from conventional confinement dairies other than having their high-producing cows fed certified organic feed," said Mark Kastel of Cornucopia. "Real organic farms have made great financial investments in converting to pasture-based production—enhancing the nutritional properties of the milk and for enhancing animal health—while it appears that these large corporate-dominated enterprises are happy just to pay lip service to required organic ethics."

Two other suppliers of organic dairy for Dean/Horizon were two large farms run by Aurora Organic Dairy and a California farm owned by Case Vander Eyk Jr. with ten thousand cows split between its organic and conventional operations. Although Aurora's farm in Platteville, Colorado, might have been at the foot of the Rocky Mountains, according to the *New York Times*, "Of the 5,200 cows on the farm, just a few hundred—those between milking cycles or near the end of their lactation—were sitting or grazing on small patches of pasture."[48]

The Cornucopia Institute filed similar complaints with the USDA concerning management practices at the Aurora and Vander Eyk dairies.

In August 2005, the USDA dismissed these complaints.

But the situation brings up the real issue: the Wal-Mart effect when pricing pressure dilutes the integrity of what it means to be certified organic.[49]

All of these large farms probably were blurring the clear-cut distinctions between organic and conventional dairies if you believe that organic certification should represent the highest ideals of humane treatment of farm animals and that crowding animals and denying them normal pasturing is never an ideal.

To its credit, Aurora Organic has added 550 acres of grazing land to its farm and is building a new dairy in a layout conducive to putting thousands of cows on pasture and still milking them three times a day.

As for Horizon, it is developing initiatives across the country to support the conversion of more and more family-run dairy operations to organic products, relieving pressure on their larger farm. (In fact, small family-run farms provide 80 percent of the dairy products sold under the Horizon brand, according to the company's spokesperson.) "We want to meet the regulations," said Kelly O'Shea, Horizon's director of government and industry relations, "and see integrity in the organic standards."

Buying Horizon and Aurora dairy products is certainly better than purchasing dairy products from conventionally raised animals given regular subtherapeutic doses of antibiotics and sulfa drugs that government reports show appear in their finished milk products, and I have no problem as a consumer in supporting either of these companies.[50] But you, the consumer, ought to have inside information. The 10 million gallons of milk Aurora farm produces each year goes to the supermarkets where you probably shop and is being sold under store brands such as Safeway Select, Kirkland at Costco, and Archer Farms at Target, according to the paper.

To find Organic Valley's products, go to their Web site at www.organicvalley.com and use their "Where to Buy" store locator service.

Anyone and everyone ought to put their money where their mouth is. Reggae artist Tego Calderon said no to P. Diddy when the entrepreneur offered him the opportunity to be part of the prestigious Sean John spring collection ad campaign, because of alleged human rights violations in Central American clothing factories, reported eco-fashion model and journalist Summer Rayne Oakes.[51] Meanwhile, according to Oakes, the British model Lily Cole said no to modeling for DeBeers, the global diamond company, after she learned of the company's alleged role in the persecution and dispersion of the Bushmen of the Kalahari to further their diamond mining interests.

Now if we could just have Paris Hilton do for carbon-neutral living what she did for Carl's Jr. Spicy BBQ Six Dollar Burger, that'd be very cool.

But until then, you and I hold the power with our wallets. We don't have to spend every last dollar on being green. But every time we put our money down we have a chance to make it stand for something we believe in, and every time we do so we are becoming part of the solution.

TEN
Think Seven Generations Ahead

> *We are instructed to carry love for one another,*
> *And to show great respect for all beings of the earth.*
> *We must stand together, the four sacred colors of man,*
> *as the one family that we are,*
> *in the interest of peace. . . .*
> *Our energy is the combined will of all the people*
> *With the spirit of the natural world,*
> *To be of one body, one heart, and one mind.*
> —Chief Leon Shenandoah (*Onondaga*)

Sometimes the only thing that carries you through is not the personal but the vision. Sometimes everything personal is screwed up and all you have left is a vision. I have to go, I told my kids; they're clinging to me and I feel terrible, leaving them behind. But Daddy has to make a living, and sometimes he has to travel. I left home on June 18 at around 10 A.M. It was crazy getting out, just crazy. I was trying to get my oldest son to his martial arts class for his fourth green belt test in Tang Soo do Tony Do Khan, which is not bad for a ten-year-old.[1] Our three-year-old son knew I was going, and he was holding onto me like a little cloying monkey. Only my daughter (the twin) was sanguine, and she made going easy, but, then, she had Mama at her side, the older woman's hand absently in her hair. Terri was going through tough times with the passing of her father and her mother's lung cancer and other crises.

But, finally, I dropped Spenser off at the dojo, bowed to Sensei Benny Castaneda, and I was on my way to Burbank Airport. I used to fly out of LAX, but, lately, I'd changed and much preferred Burbank because it was much less crowded, the parking was easier, and security never made me wait in long lines. Besides, LAX was farther away from home with gas at $3 a gallon there in the big enchilada. Anyway, Burbank had the best flight to Albany.

I'd been thinking about this trip for some time—ever since I learned about an 8,400-acre forest purchase that took place in the Adirondacks of northeastern New York State. The deal, which involved state government, private industry, and the Nature Conservancy allowed for sustainable logging and a long-term employment picture; yet it also accomplished every imaginable sensible ecological goal in a way that I don't think would happen without cooperation among citizens, government, and business.

The flight was uneventful, which was to say I was happy just to be there. I didn't meet anyone to save my life, and nobody paid much attention to me, either. Even the stewardess didn't offer me free beverages, thinking I was asleep or out of it. It was a little bumpy over Las Vegas, our one stop. I got out and switched from Southwest Flight #2894 to Flight #1685, which flew straight over Lake Michigan and on to Albany, the capital of New York State. I was headed to Shaker Country.

I sat between a couple that had gone to Las Vegas with their daughter and son-in-law, all of whom stayed and ate at one of the top hotels, and who were now all very sick with a bout of food poisoning. They were sleeping or making frequent trips to the bathroom, but otherwise they were nice folks. I was in the middle of them, trying to be as thin as a slice of bologna, typing madly on my laptop.

I arrived at Albany at 10:45 P.M. The Albany airport was simple to navigate and relatively small. I stood in line at Avis, feeling slightly tired, but the woman there was nice, and my Chevy midsize was close by. Sad fact: I'd called for a hybrid, but none of the rental agencies offered one. Happy fact: They're in such high demand, if there are any, they're usually the first choice of discriminating consumers, and car rental agencies are investing on purchasing more for their fleets. I realized times changed rapidly.

I picked up my luggage, walked out of the terminal, and got in my car. I drove a mile or two to the Hilton Garden Inn at 800 Albany Shaker Road.

I checked in, made a few calls. I remembered good times in New York from when I went to school.

I was okay with everything, just tired, and in this mood, I visited Wolf Road Diner, looking at Mohawk country from a late night diner, eating a delicious patty melt and onion rings. A patty-melt? I certainly was not living up to the safe trip ethic. Sometimes I let my own self down. What was I doing in this diner? Wasn't I supposed to be some die-hard environmentalist? I went back to my room, saddened. I spoke to everyone in my family on the phone and slept easily with no one beside me, not the kids, not my wife, no one. On the other hand, I awoke on June 19, Father's Day, in a hotel room in Albany, New York, far from my loved ones. Soon, I was in the car and driving north to the Adirondacks.

In this part of the journey, I was in Saratoga County, near the Mohawk River. A sign said, WELCOME TO SOLARTOWN. The sky was long, and land flat. I passed by The Ripe Tomato

American Grill, open since 1934. You don't see these kinds of things in LA, and the ones you do see along the highways usually end up being roadhouses for motorcycle gangs. I was near the Hudson River and Queensberry. The land was inundated with water.

Eveywhere were rivers and streams, and the big river was the Hudson. In my research work at the National Academy of Sciences on the safe seafood committee where I represented the public interest, I received a report from the New York Department of Environment that detailed the extent of chlordane contamination in fish from New York State inland waters, and one of the things that stunned me and now saddened me is that it was virtually impossible to find any fish in New York State (except perhaps for where I was headed) that did not have significant contamination with the pesticide chlordane, which is cancer causing and was banned in the 1980s but was widely used for home termite control. Everywhere I looked now I understood so clearly how close to the surface the water was there. A single molecule can flow through these waters and reach creeks that run into large bodies of water.

Because of the high surface water and the ability of chlordane to diffuse into the water where it remained inert and fat loving, it was quickly carried everywhere the water flowed and eventually absorbed into the fatty tissues of fish and people. This is why there were no safe fish anymore from New York's inland waters to eat. I loved New York all the more for the wounds it had suffered and grown past.

The land was beautiful. In a past life, I might have reminded everyone that it was contaminated but might have forgotten to mention its beauty.

Let's go on to new things. Let's go on to hope.

Moving past the lowlands, I headed up into the highlands

and the mountains of the Adirondacks. I could never forget them. These were not the tallest peaks, but they had their own amazing rock formations and rivers, which were fairy-tale perfect. The land was heavily covered with unbroken forest canopy and rocky peaks that piked up out of the forest, and the Ausable River ran up against them, ice on granite, majestic and white. The highway entered the wilderness.

Dirk Bryant was holding a map while he waited for me at a small-craft airport outside Lake Placid. Bryant was with the local branch of the Nature Conservancy in Keene and had taken the time to get to know this land better than almost anybody else involved in the deal. Part of his job at the Nature Conservancy was to become a part of the land and a member of the community, to know the lay of the land and everything about the land, and the people, and the community so that the transformation to a green land was seamless. He held a topographical map of the region and showed me the territory we were going to be covering. "You can't possibly get a feel for the massive size of this land unless you do a fly over," he said.

Pilot Phil Blinn met us at a yellow Cessna 172 N7962G, and we strapped ourselves in. I sat in the copilot's seat, and Bryant sat aft.

"It's a perfect day for flying," Bryant said.

"Not much cloud cover at all," Blinn added.

The engine revved up and we quickly went up.

"We're flying over Whiteface Mountain and Mirror Lake," he said into the headphone set.

"Somebody pulled a twenty-eight-pound Lake Trout out of Lake Placid," Bryant told Blinn.

"Mirror Lake has some big ones, too," Blinn said.

We passed over Mirror Lake, the tiny lake next to which the city of Lake Placid was located. Then, we passed over Lake Placid, which was west of the town with three islands.

"We started working on the deal three years ago," Bryant told me. "We closed it on the last day of the year 2004."

Lyme Timber Company, a New Hampshire–based sustainable forestry company, had just purchased slightly more than eighty-four thousand acres from Domtar Industries, Inc., in the "Sable Highlands" region of Clinton and Franklin counties in the northeast corner of the state near Vermont's Lake Champlain.[2]

Domtar is widely regarded as an ideal forest products company, and Lyme Timber is known for sustainable forest management specializing in creating value out of intact lands.

The agreement represented the third largest land acquisition in the state's history, according to the state Department of Environmental Conservation (DEC).

According to the DEC, Governor George Pataki, a conservation-oriented Republican, had committed to the protection of more than nine hundred thousand acres of land across New York since 1995, nearly a 20 percent increase in state-protected open space during this time period "and an enduring outdoor legacy for all New Yorkers."

The Lyme Timber Company, a private timber investment company headquartered in Hanover, New Hampshire, was going to continue harvesting timber on the property. But New York State acquired working forest conservation easements on eighty-four thousand acres of these lands that required sustainable forest management and timber harvesting, prohibited residential development and restricted subdivisions, and created a balance of public recreational access and continued traditional private recreational leasing on the property. Yet, importantly, the easements honored all of the traditional hunt clubs so that none of the local people were deprived of their own outdoors heritage.

This was a new model for all of us where government,

business, and environmental groups were making our world a better place.

From private industry, Domtar acquired the lands in 1962 and, in a move of environmental and economic foresight, acquired Forest Stewardship Council (FSC) certification as early as 2000. Raymond Royer, Domtar president and chief executive officer, explained that conservation, sustainability—that is, thinking seven generations ahead—worked financially and economically. Although the lands were protected for the future, "at the same time, this land will remain productive forestland, supporting local jobs and the important forest products economy."

Domtar and Lyme entered into a twenty-year fiber supply agreement that guaranteed continued timber harvests and the jobs associated with them. Because Domtar was focusing on creating the next generation paper products and their paper products needed to be FSC certified, its market share would continue to grow, and its products acquire added value, while its supply was protected and assured.

The whole move brought a new economic stimulus to this poor area of the state. Not only had Lyme Timber Company hired between thirty and fifty foresters, loggers, and truckers to harvest and transport timber from its 84,040-acre working forest ownership, maintaining jobs for contractors previously employed by Domtar, these initial jobs, in turn, supported a variety of forest products businesses in the Adirondack region, including log buyers, sawmills, and equipment sales.

The Nature Conservancy also purchased an additional approximately 20,000 acres from Domtar. Later, these 20,000 acres are to be transferred to the state of New York as a deep ecology preserve. That will up the total to some 104,000 acres.

I doubt all that many folks realize that Manhattan's pure drinking water is the result of having placed a value on nature—and that doing so required enlightened self-interest by government, property owners, and business. In the 1980s, New York City faced a dilemma. Because of encroaching development, the state had the choice of either building new treatment plants to clean up the growing pollution of its drinking water that flowed from upstate in the Catskills, at a cost of billions, or to try something else, something innovative, that would prove to be not only less expensive, but also more valuable. It wasn't easy, but public officials began working with residents of the Catskills to purchase watershed and forest easements to limit development near the pure pristine waters. Not all residents liked the imposition there or anywhere else, what they generally called a "taking." But enough New Yorker landowners actually saw value in not developing certain areas and began working together in enlightened self- and social interest.

When we think of New York, most of us think of New York City, but the Adirondacks that roll below our plane, to the St. Lawrence River Valley in the West, Lake Champlain in the East and Lake Erie in the North, represent the largest intact wilderness area east of the Rocky Mountains. And their integrity is also critical to the quality of New Yorkers' drinking water. So it's important to New Yorkers to keep up this environmental tradition whether under Republican or Democratic leadership.

We flew over logging roads, disappearing beneath renewed forest canopy. Then, we soared over Saranac Lake where rumor has it you can find the rare and elusive spruce grouse. Bryant confirmed its existence. "The spruce grouse needs very dense unbroken canopy and we have the largest stretches of unbroken canopy east of the Mississippi." But that unbroken canopy has been threatened for years. This was old land known to Europeans long before the West was explored.

"The whole area we are flying over was extensively logged at the end of the nineteenth century," Bryant said. "Much of the logging of hemlock was done for the raw materials needed to tan hides, and the white pine was logged for pulp and paper."

Climate change and acid rain were two big threats today, he said. I asked Blinn if he'd seen examples of a warming trend in this region. "We are starting to see much earlier ice outs on Lake Champlain. I have noticed a big difference in temperature, too. It seems much warmer, overall. We used to get twenty-five below weather two or three weeks at a time. We don't anymore."

I looked down on pristine Ingram pond where all nearby logging was certified by the FSC. There were no breaks in the canopy of trees around the pond, and as a result there were no bogs that resulted when the forests near ponds were cleared. "They are doing a lot of selective harvesting, but you can't even tell," Bryant said.

Moose disappeared from the Adirondacks between 1870 and 1970. "The demise of moose was a result of hunting and the changing nature of Adirondack forests," notes New York State's Adirondack Park Agency. "Once the mountains were opened up by lumbering and agriculture, deer, preferring to browse on young trees and shrubs in areas recently cleared, invaded the region in much greater numbers, and the moose were in trouble."[3]

The huge amount of nineteenth-century lumbering threw the ecosystem off balance. Unfortunately, the deer harbored a nematode parasite called brainworm, which is comparatively harmless to them. But the moose picked up the parasite from the snails and slugs (which acted as its host during part of the worm's life cycle), with disastrous consequences, said the park agency. "The nematode settles in their brains, inducing the 'blind staggers' and eventually, death."[4]

Today, with return of the deep forest with trees older than one hundred years, moose are making a comeback. With its high standards of forestry and conservation, the Domtar-Lyme Timber Company property, all privately held, had the highest density of moose in the Adirondacks Park. Rare bird species like the Bicknell's thrush survived, thanks to the enlarging deep ecology. If there were no FSC-certified forest, this would be a much different land with roads and clear cuts.

Not all land was FSC certified, however. "What some non-FSC-certified companies do," said Bryant, "is log their lands and sell them for home development. Without this joint effort, all the lands would be heavily logged with clear cuts, and most every pond would eventually end up being developed for second homes. There would be less public land and less access to the many lakes and rivers and streams."

I saw what he meant below. In areas where logging was recent and less regulated were swathes of gold bog grasses and, farther away, brown-earthed potato farms. Beneath, logged lands had been overtaken with bogs, broken trees littering streams and ponds. The trees looked like tiny toothpicks where recent logging occurred. The canopy cover was gone.

We passed over the North Branch of the Saranac River, which he told me was filled with brown trout and rainbows. We passed over an eagle nest atop a rocky outcrop. We passed over the West Branch of Ausable. We passed over potato fields spotted with huge spawns of pollen in the sky moving over the land.

It was the most amazing day for soaring like a bird. I asked what else needed to be done to create a more deep and vibrant ecology. The lynx and wolf were missing, Bryant told me. He pointed west and told me to look to the last ridges.

Soon we were there. I could see down, like a hawk, all the way into the deep flat St. Lawrence River Valley where the Adirondacks ended and the industrial agricultural world began. The valley was the "barrier," he said, the region that disrupted the flow of wildlife into the Adirondacks from northern forests. Bryant said, "Creating a viable corridor through the valley is key to repopulating the Adirondacks with more wolves and the lynx." I thought of the consequences of such a deep ecology, of having wolves in the Adirondacks, but also wondered if New Yorkers would go for that, having wolves in their wild lands. We flew over Mount Marcy, the highest peak in New York State. These were amazing mountains and absolutely gorgeous. They were certainly not the biggest, but they had something special. When we landed, I said good luck to Blinn. He told me that I should bring my family someday and he would take us all flying, and it seemed like a grand idea.

Bryant and I got back in the truck. He wanted to take me fishing at a lake he had found. I asked Bryant how he became interested in forests. With his hands on the wheel, we passed through the tiny gasoline-station towns along one of the back roads. He told me all of his life he had traveled the world and been exposed to forests in a most unique manner. As it turned out, his father posed as a forest industry executive traveling the globe to recruit agents to spy on the Russians in Africa and Europe. "I grew up in Africa and Asia and lived in the forests and so many wild lands I don't think you could resist the temptation."

"How'd you find out your dad was a CIA?"

"I was thirteen and going through my dad's stuff as thirteen-year-olds do, and I found about a dozen passports."

"I guess that's a pretty good tip off."

Bryant laughed. "Yeah, I'd say."

"Anyway, I was sworn to secrecy after that, but I guess it's okay now. It was a long time ago and the cold war is over."

Bryant began working on biodiversity issues in 1990. With

his background and ease at world travel, it was only natural that he should visit sites throughout the world, and he studied illegal logging operations for the World Resources Institute (WRI). In 1997, while at the WRI, Bryant began working with a team of top scientists to map out just how much of the world's forests had been cleared and how much was still intact "frontier forest."

"We found that half the planet's forests had been cleared and that most of the destruction occurred in the twentieth century. Today, only around twenty percent of ancients remain intact."

We hit a bumpy logging road. "Only three percent of the remaining intact forests are in what we would call temperate zones like what is here in the Adirondacks. When you see that we have only three percent of our temperate forest left intact on the planet, that makes you realize that all forests—even this one in our backyard—are critical. It is true that the Adirondacks do not have the ecological diversity of the rain forests, but, nonetheless, with the Adirondacks these are the biggest success stories east of the Mississippi and that is important to the planet. One hundred years ago, if we were going down this road, it would have looked like a moonscape—heavily logged with lots of spontaneous fires. But the state has picked up more and more land in its quest to protect its water supplies and so by now forty percent of Adirondack Pack is forest preserve and ten percent of the acreage consists of conservation easements.

"When the Nature Conservancy and New York State began working with Domtar Industries to obtain conservation easements and preserve some of the land as deep ecology, people naturally had strong emotions and concerns," he said. "They really worried over whether they would lose use of their lands. There are strong traditions in this area that are reflected, for example, in the many hunt clubs that dot the landscape. But, in the end, we worked on the ground with town hall meetings, and people began to see that land use could be sustained so that the old ways and things that they valued including their hunt clubs would remain."

Being on this ancient land, Dirk and I talked about a lot of things, including the people who used to live here. There is wisdom in this land that dates long before the white Europeans arrived. I see adopting the wisdom of the people of the Six Nations who traditionally, lived here to think seven generations ahead as a good antidote to those who see our future as a sprint to Armageddon—and that worried me. To me, when I think of God, I think of someone like my father who has handed me the keys to the car. I think that God expects me to leave that car in good shape. I think belief in God, if you are any of the major faiths, calls for green consciousness. Thus, what is happening now is part of America and the rest of the sane people of the planet recapturing their shared religious spirit.

We pulled into a grocery store. The building was gray and steeple roofed. We bought a couple of submarine-type sandwiches and some cold drinks.

Dirk and I drove a ways then got out and began walking. We were just hiking buddies now. But it was really hot. It was humid, and the forest really did a trick on my body. He talked about small towns in the area that were initially skeptical of the land deal. But, in the end, they were going to appreciate the deal because it meant jobs beyond just working at the local prison. He showed me a hunt club structure. I went up to it. It looked abandoned. It was just a big lodge in a clearing. Behind it was the wet forest. I looked inside. It was empty.

"People just enjoy being outdoors and shooting things," he said.

This is a great hunting region. The Iroquois hunted here, too, and lived in the valleys. The outdoors is a way of life here for people and everyone celebrates it uniquely. Families and friends have owned their hunt clubs for generations, and they just love to come out and walk in the forest. It was hard at first when we came here, and some people were suspicious of our motives. They thought we wanted to freeze everything and stop logging completely, and our vision was, in fact, very different and we had to get it across that taking a sustainable approach to their forest would ensure good jobs for years, so that small communities here could go beyond being so dependent on getting a correctional facility or go through booms and busts with families and friends uprooted. Today, there is a vital logging industry in the Adirondacks, but one that is based on sustainability. The hunt clubs remain. The good jobs only get better. I don't think this could have happened though without total cooperation between local residents, government, and, of course, industry. Domtar is an amazing wood products company, and their care of the land for so long has been exemplary. Now Lyme Timber will continue this management. Watersheds are protected. Moose and other animals once gone from this region are returning. Now it is going to be preserved, too, thanks to the land purchases. The hunt club participants are all for it now that they see it maintains the continuity of their heritage, since many of the clubs are handed down from generation to generation.

"No doubt, the hunting will get better," I said. I walked around the hunt club and looked into the forest. We walked into a forest of black spruce, tamarack, lichen, and blackflies.

He recalled walking along this road earlier during the times when there were community meetings and a man, who belonged to one of the hunt clubs that leased out thousands of acres, aimed his pickup at Bryant and tried to run him off the road. He didn't laugh telling the story. I didn't blame him. That was extreme.

The flies here were larger than in Topanga, and it was a lot more humid. It was flat, unlike my home in the Santa Monica Mountains, which was the opposite of flat and, in fact, never heard the word, as it has only up or down hills. I liked flat land. It was lithium to the soul.

We reached a clearing at the crossroads where two logging roads met. The forest hid everything at first, and then the deer emerged and one by one they stepped past.

We sat by a creek and ate sandwiches amidst the scratching of spruce needles, and under a flurry of viburnum and other berry shrubs, good food for the rare Spruce Grouse and its other deep ecology friends like the olive-sided flycatcher, black-backed woodpecker, rusty blackbird, boreal chickadee, gray jay, palm warbler, and Lincoln's sparrow.[5] Only about 175 were estimated to live statewide, and they needed deep forest, and the Adirondacks, in the whole United States, were one of the few regions where the birds continued to thrive. The birds needed boreal-type forests with only small openings. Otherwise they would become targets of hawks and other predatory birds, like eagles.

We got up and hiked and he showed me some moose prints. I wondered if we would see any bear or moose. The forest floor was soft and flat but it was hot, and soon I was more tired than I thought I would be hiking on flat land. There was water everywhere. The sun was shining through the canopy. He knew the way. I saw no trail.

We went hiking past another hunt club, and Dirk followed a trail I could not see. "I've been here before," he said. "I've never fished it though."

I had no idea if there was a trail, but he knew where he was going. It was just slightly uphill, but I was thirsty. I grabbed my drink and realized it was almost gone. There was water everywhere. But I didn't feel yet like lapping it up out of the earth—not yet. I was gone. But not that foregone. I'd hiked farther than this with less water. But this kind of humidity drew water from my skin into my clothing. The trail was muddy. He told me to expect that. I was okay with the mud. I had to go under a fallen tree. I went over a creek on a fallen tree. We were just hiking now and quiet, and the only sounds were things breaking on the forest floor and water rippling around my boots and falling from trees.

When we had hiked an hour, the pond came into view. I saw the dam at one end and realized this was a beaver pond, something you definitely had to respect. Beavers are superb water engineers. Once the beavers were almost all gone.

We sat at one end of the pond near the beaver dam. He handed over the pole. I casted my fishing line lazily and saw only minnows. "I'm not even sure what fish are in the lake," he said. I continued casting. Bryant wanted to walk more. He was always looking for great places to canoe and hike, and this was new. So I got up and walked along the edge of the pond and around the trees. It was hot, and we were out of water, and we didn't talk much, just took in being in this wild land. Down along the edge, I saw a mama catfish zealously guarding her young pups. She fended off the pulsating waves of water from my lure and made sure no other fishes came near her brood. You had to work at it, she was saying to me. You had to really want it with all your might.

If you cared about your children, didn't you care about their offspring? Counting yourself, that's three generations.

Since, besides looking ahead, we also look back, what about your parents? They make four. And most of us knew our grandparents, some our great grandparents. There we have six generations. It's not so tough to get to seven generations.

Most of us will see four, five, or more generations in our lifetime, if we are lucky.

It was just another day in paradise, doing what I loved, hiking, being with nature. I thought it was great. I guessed I always would.

Global warming is happening. We don't know for how long or all of its consequences. But we have seen disturbing signs.

Only a drunk could deny worldwide waters are rising. Everybody is telling us this from the front lines. Mammoth-source ivory fossil is more plentiful now in the Arctic, thanks to the thawing of the permafrost, than ivory from modern elephants in Africa and Asia.[6] On one Arctic island, where only ten thousand years ago mammoths roamed, natives make $25 to $50 a pound for the ancient mammoth tusks. The waters are rising. America has already almost lost New Orleans.

The Intergovernmental Panel on Climate Change, made up of twenty-five hundred of the world's leading scientists and economists, stated in 1995, "the balance of evidence . . . suggests that there is a discernible human influence on global climate."[7]

Ten years later in December 2005, Dr. R. K. Pachauri, chairman of the Intergovernmental Panel on Climate Change (IPCC) at the High Level Segment, told a Montreal audience, "The Earth's climate system has demonstrably changed on both global and regional scales since the pre-industrial era, and there is new and stronger evidence that most of the warming observed over the last 50 years is attributable to human activities."[8]

The increases in greenhouse gases are real. We ought to be taking these events seriously.

I'm a businessman. I run a publishing company. I have a family. I have kids. I love America. I bleed red, white, and blue, too.

But, as a businessman I want to know both the up and the down side of what we are doing. I figure things this way. If we act intelligently, if it is beyond reasonable doubt the effects on climate attributed to industrial activity are real, we will have staved off an ecological crisis.

If we don't get it right, even missing wildly, we will have fortified our defenses, improved our communities, and protected our children. We will have done good things and most likely the right thing, and we will have created an entirely new economy and many new markets to leave the Earth a better place to live for our children. We will have cut down on the immediate chemical toxicity problem. We will have reduced air pollution. These actions alone will have had a beneficial effect and saved or improved tens of millions of lives.

We will have made our nation strong. We will have lessened our need for foreign entanglements.

If we implement too many command and control regulations on business, however, we will have choked our freedom.

We're not going to get rid of our need for petroleum anytime soon, so let's quit that charade, too. The world is drunk on petroleum and wallowing in its addiction, forlorn, sightless, stumbling. Just this morning when I dropped my oldest son off at Topanga Elementary, I parked behind a big yellow school bus; it belched enormous diesel fumes. Big and long like a hot dog with mustard, it was a rumbling dinosaur of vast inefficiency not unlike what we saw in the Soviet Union before its fall. I don't believe you would want your children breathing the chemical petrochemical soup rising out of the dinosaur's tailpipes, but if your children are riding the bus to school, well, what do you think they are breathing? We can do better.

I know some people will think we are crazy. Someone who is sober will always be called crazy by the chemically dependent one for pointing out the obvious: that one has a dangerous addiction. We all know that drunks always try to make the sober person into the bad guy. But we still have to do the right thing.

The world is going to increase its consumption of fossil fuels in the next few decades; the rate of increase should be tempered. Coming up with carbon-neutral solutions will protect our future and address many key environmental issues such as the buildup of poisons in the environment and in the tissues of wildlife and human beings. Doing so will also help us to raise a generation of children who will be born with their full intellectual capacities, instead of being harmed during pregnancy and before conception, at the stages of life when so much chemical toxicity has such a sharp, cutting edge. If you are pro-life, you have to be green, too; otherwise you condone the use of toxic chemicals truly known to inflict subtle damage to the unborn. Each person in America who is prolife ought to join the mainstream environmental movement and join in on these chemical toxicity issues to show they really do put the unborn first. Some experts say these genetic assaults on IQ and behavior could start before conception due to chemical toxicity of the male sperm. So, get the picture? We can do a whole lot better.

Here's what we need to do now:

Communicate. Share your experience. Talk about how you have been awakened into being a better, more conscious person.

Inspire your friends. Do something crazy wonderful, and give a recycled gift to somebody special.[9]

Work on your ten steps daily. We're not going to be perfect, but if we keep in mind the powerful vision of being a green patiots and what it means to our personal health, our nation's security, and our children's future, we have the power to awake each morning with confidence and resolve that our personal actions are going to redeem our future as individuals, citizens, and as a nation.

Accept responsibility. I know in this live-for-today world, it is hard for us to think of much more than what the next ten minutes might hold, much less seven generations to come. You're going to need lots of help along the way, masters to keep your mind focused, mantras from which to gain strength, causes to care about, and people to love.

Learn from others.

Be sure to visit organizations like NRDC and Nature Conservancy, WWF, and others.

Leave a legacy. If you own open land, bequeath it to a preservation or conservation society like the Nature Conservancy or other organization dedicated to working to preserve planet Earth. If not a public bequest, create a covenant for all future owners.

Remake your world. Change your surroundings. Have icons of your new consciousness everywhere. Have green art and furniture.

Teach your children. I might sound like a recycling fanatic to the kids, but I know that recycling when they are young is something that helps sensitize them to environmental issues later when they are older. You do not have raise kids to be soldiers.

This is how you change the world.

Just think ahead. The carbon-neutral age is here. So let's get with the program, leave the spinning to Planet Blue, and do the right thing.

ONE
Chemical Nation

Center for American Progress

An excellent overview under Homeland Security

http://www.americanprogress.org/site/apps/s/custom.asp?c=biJRJ8OV
F&b=1573179

TWO
Be a Green Patriot

Organic Cotton Patriot T-Shirts

Besides organic cotton T-shirts with country flags, this site has cool T-shirts like "Fighting Filipinos World War II," "Fighting Terrorism Since 1492," "National Guard Dad," and many others, all made with organic cotton. These are great gifts for gung-ho organic Americans. Visit www.cafepress.com.

THREE
Put Good Food on Your Table

Community Sustainable Agriculture

Robyn Van En Center

www.csacenter.org

Home Delivery

Fresh Direct
New York area
www.freshdirect.com

Green Earth Organics
Toronto, Vancouver, Burnaby, Richmond, Canada
www.greenearthorganics.com

Healthy Home Foods
North Charleston, South Carolina
www.healthyhomefoods.com

Organic Express
California
www.organicexpress.com

Orlando Organics
Orlando, Florida
www.orlandoorganics.com

Pax Organica
Southern California
www.paxorganica.com

Pioneer Organics
Seattle
www.pioneerorganics.com

Small Potatoes Urban Deliver
Vancouver and Victoria, British Columbia
www.spud.ca

Westside Organics
San Francisco Bay area
www.westsideorganics.com

Natural Supermarkets

Whole Foods
More than 180 stores nationwide
www.wholefoods.com

Wild Oats
www.wildoats.com

Find Your Local Health Food Store

Health food stores are a great source of organic foods. Use our health food store locator service at www.freedompressonline.com and www.greenpatriot.us to find a health food store nearest you.

Carbon-Neutral Fast Food

Burgerville
Washington and Oregon
www.burgerville.com

Chipotle
Nationwide
www.chipotle.com

O'Naturals
Massachusetts and New Hampshire
www.onaturals.com

Sharky's Franchise Group LLC
Southern California
www.sharkys.com

Find an Organic Restaurant

Local Harvest
Use their national organic and natural restaurant locator service, or add your organic eatery to their database.
http://www.localharvest.org/restaurants/

Education

Anyone can grow some vegetables in a garden in a backyard or on a Chicago or Manhattan rooftop. Pick up a copy of Rodale's *Organic Gardening* magazine, or visit them online at www.rodale.com. Here are important written reports and documentaries:

Poisoned and Silenced: A Study of Pesticide Poisoning in the Plantations; Endosulfan Poisoning in Kasargod, Kerala, India; Report of a Fact Finding Mission, 2002
Pesticide Action Network Asia and the Pacific
P.O. Box 1170
10850 Penang, Malaysia
(604) 657 0271; fax (604) 657 7445
panap@panap.net
www.panap.net

Death in Small Doses: Cambodia's Pesticide Problems and Solutions
Environmental Justice Foundation.
5 St. Peter's Street
London N1 8JD
United Kingdom
(44-20) 7359 0440; fax (44-20) 7359 7123
info@ejfoundation.org
www.ejfoundation.org

Something in the Air, 2001
This video from Sylvie Dauphinais, director of the National Film Board of Canada, links high rates of childhood asthma with large-scale pesticide use on potato farms and golf courses on Prince Edward Island, Canada. Includes interviews with local activists, potato farmers, and families suffering from asthma. (Length: 24:50 minutes.) Available in French and English.
National Film Board of Canada
350 Fifth Ave, Suite 4820
New York, NY 10118
(212) 629-8890; fax (212) 629-8502
NewYork@onf.ca
www.nfb.ca

For prices in the United States, call (800) 542-2164; for prices in
Canada and elsewhere, call (800) 267-7710.

Playing with Poison, 2001

The video from John Ritchie, director of the Canadian Broadcasting Corporation's *The Nature of Things* and Force Four Entertainment, Inc., reports the findings of American anthropologist
Elizabeth Guillette from her studies of neurological effects of pesticides on children living at the Yaqui Valley, a large agricultural area
in Mexico. Examines the relevance of these and other pesticide exposures to children across North America. (Length: 46 minutes.)

$250; rental: $85; discounts available for individuals and activists.

Bullfrog Films
PO Box 149
Oley, Pennsylvania 19547
phone (800) 543-3764; fax (610) 370-1978
catalog@bullfrogfilms.com
www.bullfrogfilms.com.

FOUR
Put Good Products in Your Home

Cosmetics

Aubrey Organics
www.aubrey-organics.com

Avalon Organics
www.avalonorganics.com

Aveda
www.aveda.com

California Baby
www.californiababy.com

Dr. Hauschka
www.drhauschka.com

Eco Bella
www.ecobella.com

Lily Organics
www.lilyorganics.com

Logona
www.logona.com

Lotus Brands
www.lotusbrands.com

MyChelle
www.mychelle.com

Paul Penders
www.paulpenders.com

Terressentials
www.terresntials.com

Vermont Soapworks
www.vtsoap.com

Weleda
www.weleda.com

Household Cleaners

Ecos
www.ecos.com

Ecover
www.ecover.com

Lifekind
www.lifekind.com

Seventh Generation
www.seventhgeneration.com

Sun & Earth, Inc.
www.sunandearth.com

Trader Joe's
www.traderjoes.com.

What's in My Product?

Obtain major ingredient information about your household cleaning products from this federally administered Web site:
http://www.householdproducts.nlm.nih.gov .

Personal Care

Recycline
Recycled toothbrushes and razors.
www.recycline.com

Education

The Green Guide
An excellent guide to safe and healthy shopping (I am an advisory board member).
www.thegreenguide.com

Plenty
The well-reported and entertaining articles in this publication are helping to make green consciousness part of everybody's thinking.
www.plentymag.com

Leadership and Activism

Safe Cosmetic Campaign
Be sure to support their campaign to eliminate harmful ingredients from cosmetics and personal care products.
www.safecosmetics.org

FIVE
Plant a Tree

Flooring

Cork and Bamboo
www.sustainableflooring.com

Marmoleum
www.marmolelumstore.com

Recycled Wood Flooring

www.oldgrain.com
www.vitangelumber.com
www.trestlewood.com

Uncommon Goods
www.uncommongoods.com

Paper Companies

International Paper
www.ip.com

New Leaf Paper
www.newleafpaper.com

Pot Latch
www.potlatchcorp.com

Office Supplies

Greenline Paper Company
Premium recycled 9" x 12" white envelopes and many other
environmental papers of the highest quality
www.greenlinepaper.com

Office Depot
www.officedepot.com

Staples
www.staples.com

Treecycle Recycled Paper
Ultimate legal-style pads
www.treecycle.com

Sustainable Forestry Certification and Stewardship

Forest Stewardship Council
www.fsc.org.

Plant a Memory Tree

The National Arbor Day Foundation
www.arborday.org

Rain Forest Activism

Dogwood Alliance
www.dogwoodalliance.org

Eagle Law
Saving the rain forests of the Haida nation.
www.eaglelaw.org

Greenpeace
The group is working with other groups such as Rainforest Action
Network to save rain forests.
www.greenpeaceusa.org

The Paper Campaign
www.thepapercampaign.com/

Rainforest Action Network
Campaigns for the forests, their inhabitants, and the natural systems
that sustain life by transforming the global marketplace through
grassroots organizing, education, and nonviolent direct action.
www.ran.org

Rain Forest Herbal Medicine

New Chapter
www.new-chapter.com

Holistic Medicine Practices

Center for Holistic Urology
www.holisticurology.com

The Continuum Center for Health & Healing
http://www.healthandhealingny.org/highlights.asp

SIX
Be Kind to Animals

Sources of Natural Beef and Other Meats

Coleman Purely Natural
www.colemannatural.com

Dakota Beef LLC
www.dakotabeef.com

Laura's Lean Beef Company
www.laurasleanbeef.com

Adopt a Wildlife System

World Land Trust
www.worldlandtrust.org.

World Wildlife Fund
www.wwf.org

Natural Pet Food

Pet Promise
www.petpromise.com

Fair Trade and Organic Coffee

Audubon Coffee
www.auduboncoffeeclub.com.

Café Campesino
www.cafecampesino.com

Café Canopy
www.shade-coffee.com

Caffe Sanora
www.caffesanora.com

Dean's Beans
www.deansbeans.com

Equal Exchange
www.equalexchange.com

Grounds for Change
www.groundsforchange.com

Jim's Organic Coffee
www.jimsorganiccoffee.com

Peace Coffee
www.peacecoffee.com

Thanksgiving Coffee Company
www.thanksgivingcoffee.com

Wild Forest Coffee
www.wildforestcoffee.com

Natural Gardening

ARBICO

Excellent selection of a wide range of natural pest controls in all categories.
www.arbico-organics.com

Beneficial Insect Co.
Wide range of beneficial organisms and physical controls.
www.thebeneficialinsectco.com

Biotactics, Inc.
Beneficial mites.
www.benemite.com

SEVEN
Drive a Cool Car

Daimler-Chrysler
www.daimlerchrysler.com

Ford
www.ford.com

Honda
www.honda.com

Hyundai
www.hyundai.com

Toyota
www.toyota.com

Latest Auto Breakthroughs

Green Car Congress
www.greencarcongress.org

EIGHT
Stop Being Toxic

Pollution Records of Companies

www.scorecard.org/index.tcl

Ecologically Sensitive Shopping

Abundant Earth
www.abundantearth.com

Gaiam
www.gaiam.com

Greenfeet.com
www.greenfeet.com, (888) 562-8873.

Home Interiors

Eco by Design
www.ecobydesign.com

Recycled and Recyclable Trash Bags

www.seventhgeneration.com
www.websterindustries.com

Home Solar

Solar Living Center
www.realgoods.com

Uni-Solar
www.uni-solar.com

High Tech

Aeroseal
www.aeroseal.com

Affordable Internet Services Online
www.aiso.net

Computer TakeBack Campaign
www.computertakeback.org

Microplanet
www.microplanet.com

Home Renovation

Well Building
www.wellbuilding.com

Cabinets

Neil Kelly Company
www.neilkelly.com.

Poliform
www.poliform.com.

Appliances

Bosch
www.bosch.com

LG
www.lge.com

Maytag
www.maytag.com

Miele
www.miele.com

Mitsubishi
www.mitsubichielectric.com

Sun Frost
www.sunfrost.com

Vestfrost
www.vestfrost.com

Whirlpool
www.whirlpool.com

Recycling Appliances

Some companies recycle almost all the parts of your refrigerator or freezer, including the CFC-containing insulation foam. The two companies below—ARCA and JACO—received U.S. EPA Stratospheric Ozone Protection awards in 2004 for including proper CFC-containing foam disposal in their operations.

ARCA Inc.
www.arcainc.com

Earth 911
Visit Earth 911 for community-specific information on recycling and proper household hazardous waste disposal.
www.earth911.org

JACO Environmental
www.jacoinc.net

New Way of Thinking

Conscious Consumer
www.newdream.org/consumer

Renewables
www.thesustainablevillage.com

Energy Efficiency Ratings

Energy Star
www.energystar.gov.

Organic Clothing

American Apparel
www.americanapparel.net

Blue Canoe
www.bluecanoe.com

Chandler & Greene, Inc.
www.chandlergreene.com

Ecō-gănik
www.ecoganik.com
Inner Waves Organics Maui
www.innerwavesmaui.com

NatureUSA
www.natureusa.net

Of the Earth
soy-based clothes
www.oftheearth.com

Patagonia
www.patagonia.com

Stewart + Brown
www.stewartbrown.com

Fashion
Linda Loudermilk
www.lindaloudermilk.com

Organic Flowers
Organic Bouquet
www.organicboquet.com

Natural and Organic Mattresses and Bedding
Abundant Earth
www.abundantearth.com

A Happy Planet
www.ahappyplanet.com

A Natural Home
www.anaturalhome.com

Coyuchi
www.coyuchiorganic.com

Eco Bedroom
www.ecobedroom.com

Indika
www.indikahome.com

Lifekind
The only certified totally organic mattress manufacturer in the United States.
www.lifekind.com

Nirvana Safe Haven
www.nontoxic.com

Pure Slumber
www.pureslumber.com

Recycled Products

Crate and Barrel
www.cb2.com

Recycline
www.recycline.com

Lighting

Seagull Lighting
www.seagullighting.com

Low-heat Saunas

Sunlight Saunas
www.sunlightsaunas.com

www.saunaguy.com

NINE
Put Your Money Where Your Mouth Is

Banking

Chittenden
www.chittenden.com

ShoreBank
www.shorebankcorp.com

Investment Funds

Domini
www.dominifunds.com

Pax World Funds
www.paxworldfunds.com

Sierra Club
www.sierraclubfunds.com

New Consciousness

Business Roundtable
http://www.businessroundtable.org/index.aspx

David Suzuki Foundation
www.davidsuzuki.org

The Natural Step
www.naturalstep.com

Nike's Considered Eco Shoes
http://www.nike.com/nikebiz/nikeconsidered/index.jhtml

TEN
Think Seven Generations Ahead

Adirondack Park Agency
www.apa.state.ny.us

Domtar
www.domtar.com

Lyme Timber Company
www.lymetimber.com

Natural History Museum of the Adirondacks
www.wildcenter.org

THE GREEN 100 comprises companies that are unique and innovative and understand the imperative of being carbon-neutral. They are profitable and are significantly on their way to being good citizens.

Some, like GE, are enormous with global presence and documented unsavory environmental practices, but, for now, appear headed in the right direction, and with large and hugely influential companies that are so difficult to turn around this is important. Others are small and doing equally magnificent and important things when it comes to reducing greenhouse emissions and being good citizens.

I've put companies in the Green 100 whose categories range from appliances to personal care, high tech, home furnishings, manufacturing, printing, and more. It's an eclectic mix—and reflects my research. I hope it helps you to make informed shopping decisions.

Cleaning Products

AFM

The first and last name in the safest indoor paints, "whether you are an architect specifying materials for a fifty story building or a parent decorating a baby's room," the company says its "promise is the same: we strive to set the standard for the safest, most non-polluting products for your home, your health and the planet."

According to the company's Web site, in the early 1980s, "no one was thinking about indoor air pollution or chemical toxicity in household and building products." But AFM was working with environmental medicine physicians and their patients—people with allergies and chemical sensitivities—to formulate products that do not leave irritating chemical residues in the air after use. Today, they remain the leader in providing a complete range of chemically responsible building and maintenance products.

www.afmsafecoat.com

Seventh Generation

The best and most authentic household cleaning products in the United States come from Seventh Generation. This is a company that makes the LOHAS market real. Seventh Generation cleaning and paper products are widely available in supermarkets across the United States (as well as natural food supermarkets and health food stores).

www.seventhegeneration.com

Sun & Earth

Sun & Earth is also succeeding in the mainstream market for green non-petroleum-based cleaning products. "After many years of watching advertisements claiming that petrochemicals with mysterious names were the best way to clean house, we set out to prove that non-toxic cleaners can clean as well or better than the national brands," says the Web site for this Norristown, Pennsylvania, based company.[1] "We know people want products made with non-toxic ingredients but, don't want to sacrifice performance. After extensive research we developed cleaners made from coconut and orange oils that clean and shine beautifully." They also have a fresh citrus scent that people rave about.

www.sunandearth.com

Cosmetic and Personal Care Products

None of the companies test on animals or use animal ingredients.

Aubrey Organics

Aubrey Organics was the first cosmetic company in the United States to embrace natural cosmetics and in its practices has been carbon-neutral since its founding in 1967. Aubrey Hampton envisioned a green company in Aubrey Organics after leaving his work at Faberge where he was a formulator. Today, Aubrey is sourcing increasing numbers of individual ingredients from organic sources. Their commitment to nonpetrochemical formulations has been steadfast since their beginning. They've always been the safest cosmetics and personal care products available.

www.aubrey-organics.com

Avalon Organics

Avalon Organics' cosmetics are helping to make the organic concept part of the mainstream supermarket shopping experience. This makes them an important player for now. But, although the company was selected to be part of the Green 100, the Organic Consumers Association warned the company's use of floral waters was literally diluting the integrity of what it means to be organic. Part of the North Castle holding company whose partners include Roy Disney, Avalon Organics, nonetheless, has a chance to be a real leader if it does the right thing.

www.avalonorganics.com

Aveda

Not just a cosmetics company, in 2005, Aveda helped to raise over $1 million for their Earth Month conservation partners and sent 234,000 signatures to the White House and United Nations urging them to save threatened and endangered plants.

www.aveda.com

Lily Organics

An upstart organic cosmetics company, Lily Organics keeps it real and grows their own certified organic herbs for their cosmetic products on their certified organic farm in Henderson, Colorado—and their products are growing in popularity. Lily Morgan, the company founder, is a sixth-generation farmer, and she says Lily Organics sustains family farms in a profitable economic model that also curtails our dependency on oil.

www.lilyorganics.com

MyChelle Dermaceuticals

Myra Eby Michelle was a sales representative in the natural products industry who desired to raise the bar for everyone. She created a very environmentally conscious and natural line of dermaceuticals that combines science and technology with freedom from petrochemicals in favor of food-based, herbal, and other natural ingredients.

www.mychelleusa.com

Appliances and Electronics

Bosch

Not only does Bosch produce among the most energy efficient appliances for homes, many of us also know the Bosch name from the automotive industry.

Bosch is a leader in automotive hybrid technology. One of their big breakthroughs is to give hybrid drivers more control over when they go electric with the use of a new intuitive start/stop system that allows for drivers to increase fuel efficiency by 8 percent. Bosch expects the largest market growth in North America.[2]

However, another major breakthrough was the company's discontinued use of chlorinated hydrocarbons in 2005.[3]

www.bosch.com

GE

In your safe trip, where you are headed counts, and salvation is a real possibility. If so, Jeff Immelt has GE headed in the right direction when it comes to green salvation. GE's eco-imagination is a whole lot more than a catchy slogan. In many ways, if successful, GE's move to be a green company crystallizes the changeover in the world's industrial movement and financial centers. GE's foray into the green is going to be paying big dividends not only to GE shareholders but also to our environment. GE is a leader in energy efficiency technologies such as wind and nano-iodides. They need to be watched for both where they are going and how they handle their own history of environmental degradation. It wasn't okay.

www.ge.com

LG Electronics

LG Electronics says existing legal requirements are not always enough to secure the human health and the environment. If the impact on the environment and human health is not scientifically proven, but there is enough doubt that there might be an adverse effect, LG Electronics will follow the Precautionary Principle as referred to in the 1992 Rio Declaration (UN Earth Summit).[4] LG has already substituted PVC with a safer alternative and is planning to phase out the remaining use of PVC (mostly for power cables and adaptors) by the end of 2008. LG Electronics is also trying to replace brominated flame retardants with effective and less or completely nontoxic alternatives.

www.lge.com

Mitsubishi

Even before Japan's national Electrical Home Appliances Recycling Law passed in April 2001, Mitsubishi Electric had already established the Higashihama Recycle Center for consumers to return home electronics products. The company joined a consortium of other major Japanese electrical product manufacturers to establish and implement a network of fifteen recycling processing facilities throughout Japan.

Home appliances recycled in fiscal year 2002 included air conditioners, televisions, refrigerators, and washing machines. Personal computer products recycled included desktops, notebooks, CRT displays and LCDs.[5]

As stipulated in the company's 4th Environmental Plan, the entire group of Mitsubishi Electric companies should devote the utmost efforts to develop and introduce to the market Eco-Products and Hybrid Eco-Products that reduce negative environmental impact throughout the entire product life cycle. In its last report, the company stated that the ratio of Eco-Products was expected to rise to more than 70 percent by the end of fiscal year 2005.[6]

www.mitsubishi.com

Samsung

Samsung Electronics has devised a voluntary plan to lower emissions of greenhouse gases to 30 percent below their 2001 levels by 2010. In

2004, the company achieved an impressive 11 percent reduction from the 2001 level. The Cheonan Factory continued to decrease the amounts of gas and chemicals used in production operations.[7]

www.samsung.com

Sun Frost

A small company, Sun Frost has demonstrated that American appliances and solar can work together. This California-based company manufactures refrigerators and other appliances that are not only elegant but also so stunningly energy-efficient, they easily run on solar power or other low-output energy sources.[8]

www.sunfrost.com

Vestfrost

Vestfrost sets the standards for low-energy refrigerators and freezers, as well as for recycling products at the end of their useful lifespan.[9]

www.vestfrost.com

High-Tech

Affordable Internet Services Online

A Web site hosting company, Affordable Internet Services Online, Inc. is powered by the sun. They use "state-of-the-art solar panel arrays to power" their equipment. They have been in business since 1997 and also offer nationwide high-speed Internet access. According to the company's literature, "Power is generated using 120 solar panels located on the roof of our data center."

www.aiso.net

AMD

Texas-based microprocessor maker AMD recently pledged to power its entire Austin campus and operations with 100 percent renewable energy for the next ten years. This commitment made AMD the largest private federal EPA Green Power Partner in Texas and fifth largest private partner in the United States and twelfth largest overall partner in the nation, according to GreenBiz.com. In this case, the Austin Energy GreenChoice program, with which AMD is working, utilizes local wind power and landfill methane gas to provide carbon-neutral energy, improving air quality by lowering power plant emissions and reducing reliance on nonreplaceable fossil fuels. Turbines at three West Texas wind farms harness the wind to supply pollution-free energy. Two land-fills, one located just outside Austin and the other located near San Antonio, collect methane produced by decay to generate electricity. It fulfills every idea of what it is to stop being toxic.

www.amd.com

Intel

The World Economic Forum ranked Intel eighteenth among the 100 Most Sustainable Corporations in the world in 2004.[10] The company's progress since then has been consistent with improvements in reducing greenhouse gas emissions. In an unprecedented recycling initiative, Intel and eBay joined with leading technology companies, government agencies, and environmental groups to help pave the way for consumers and businesses to safely dispose of unwanted electronics. In September 2005, mailers went out to 3.2 million New York City households announcing the city's most ambitious personal computer, television, and cell phone recycling drive to date. Intel and Best Buy Co. both supported the drive, which ran on weekends in October.[11]

www.intel.com

Foods and Beverages

Amy's Kitchen

While you might never get childhood comfort foods like Swanson roast beef TV dinners completely out of your life, you just might have a chance with prepared foods from Amy's Kitchen. They make prepared food not only healthy but also absolutely tasty.

Their vegetarian dinners with plentiful organic ingredients are sold at health food stores and natural food markets as well, as supermarkets and club stores in the United States, Canada, and across the globe. Amy's Kitchen has created over eighty frozen meals, including pizzas, pocket sandwiches, pot pies, entrées, snacks, and whole meals, in a wide range of categories from Italian and Indian meals to Mexican and good old American vegetarian.

www.amyskitchen.com

Burgerville

Talk about fast food with convenience *and* conscience, not only does Burgerville purchase natural humanely raised beef for all its burgers, the chain is also powering all of its restaurants with nonpolluting wind power. In 2005, it committed to use renewable wind power produced in the Pacific Northwest to provide 100 percent of the electricity needs of all its Burgerville and Noodlin' restaurants in Northwest Oregon and Southwest Washington, as well as its local headquarters in Vancouver, Washington.

By utilizing wind power, the company will avoid adding 17.4 million pounds of carbon dioxide to the region annually. Eliminating this volume of the harmful greenhouse gas is the equivalent of taking approximately seventeen hundred cars off the road or reducing the number of miles driven in the region by 19 million.[12]

www.burgerville.com

Chipotle Mexican Grill

One of the biggest purchasers of all-natural meats in the United States with some 480 casual dining establishments, Chipotle, the Denver-based burrito restaurant, has tons of room to grow. Could the publicly traded chain formerly owned by McDonald's (who is a major shareholder) be the next McDonald's? With America's love affair with Latin foods, that's what some stock pickers say.

www.chipotle.com

Clif Bar

Founded in 1992 by Gary Erickson, the inspiration to create an energy bar occurred during a daylong, 175-mile bike ride with his buddy Jay. They had been gnawing on some other energy bars all day. Suddenly, despite his hunger, he couldn't take another bite. He thought, "I could make a better bar than this!" Today, Clif Bar, based in Berkeley, California, is thought to be valued at more than $60 million. They use organic ingredients in their delicious nutrition bars. In 2002, they redesigned their caddies (the cartons that hold our bars) to eliminate 90,000 pounds of shrink wrap per year. In 2003, they switched to a 100 percent (50 percent post-consumer) recycled paperboard for all caddies. Using recycled materials instead of virgin wood will save about 7,500 trees, conserve 3.3 million gallons of water, and avoid the production of 660,000 pounds of greenhouse gases each year, says the company's Web site. They offset office and bakery energy use with clean, renewable wind energy by purchasing green tags through Native Energy. They purchase only 100 percent postconsumer recycled paper for the office and use only unbleached, recycled paper and nontoxic inks for printing. All of their promotional T-shirts and tote bags are made of 100 percent certified organic cotton. Clif Bars shows how a relatively small company can make a big difference.[13]

www.clifbar.com

Coleman Purely Natural

Started in 1979, Coleman Purely Natural, based in Golden, Colorado, is the leading supplier today of natural and organic certified meat products. They've set the standards for what is natural and what is organic when it comes to beef, and Mel Coleman Jr. has traveled extensively across America to promote sustainable ranching, to build markets for America's family and small ranches, and to turn ranchers into America's grassland managers. Today, look for their growing brands, including Coleman Natural Meats, Petaluma Poultry, and Penn Valley Farms.

www.colemannatural.com

FreshDirect

Fresh Direct makes shopping for organic foods easy for New Yorkers with its easy online ordering system and delivery system. Their home delivery service keeps cars off the road, reducing greenhouse emissions. The company actively seeks to support local agriculture and has excellent certified organic offerings. If you live in Manhattan, I bet someone you know who is using Fresh Direct.

www.freshdirect.com

General Mills

Although not exclusively organic, General Mills has tremendous influence in the organic food industry with its Cascadian Farms and Muin Glen brands of certified organic foods.[14] Their marketing clout means that they have promoted and placed these brands into the hands of so many people who might otherwise never have discovered organic foods because they shop in the usual supermarket chains—ones that had not stocked much organic food before or had grouped it all in specialty organic sections.

Recently, General Mills has converted its nonorganic cereals to healthier whole grains. The company uses recycled materials for its boxes. Its next big step is to produce Cheerios with certified organic oats.

www.generalmills.com

Hain-Celestial

Hain Celestial Group, headquartered in Melville, New York, is a leading natural and organic beverage, snack, specialty food, and personal care products company in North America and Europe. Hain Celestial is a leader in almost all natural food categories—beverages, specialty teas, snacks, grocery, frozen foods—and the natural personal care category with national and international brands which include Celestial Seasonings, Terra Chips, Garden of Eatin', Health Valley, WestSoy, Earth's Best, Arrowhead Mills, Hain Pure Foods, Breadshop's, Casbah, Carb Fit, DeBoles, Nile Spice, Westbrae Natural, Rice Dream, Imagine, Soy Dream, Walnut Acres Certified Organic, Rosetto, Ethnic Gourmet, Yves Veggie Cuisine, The Good Dog, and in Europe, Lima, Biomarché, Natumi, and Milkfree. The company's principle specialty product lines include Hollywood cooking oils, Estee sugar-free products, Boston Better Snacks, and Alba Foods. The company's personal care product lines consist primarily of JASON pure, natural, and organic products, and Zia Natural Skincare. The Hain

Celestial Group common stock trades on the NASDAQ National Market under the symbol HAIN.[15]

www.hain-celestial.com

Horizon

Today, a supermarket leader and owned by Dean Foods, the Horizon brand includes milk, juices, yogurt, cheese, butter, sour cream, half and half and whipping cream, cream cheese, cottage cheese, smoothies, eggs, infant formula with iron, and eggnog.

Horizon Organic joined with Senator Hillary Rodham Clinton in 2006 in a show of support for New York farmers, announcing an initiative dedicated to helping more state farmers transition to organic, and processing more milk locally, to meet the ever-increasing demand for organic milk in New York and the region. Horizon Organic currently works with 119 certified organic dairy farmers in the state of New York, more than any other state in the country.[16] However, the same program is now being undertaken nationwide. This will help many smaller family dairies to stay in business.

www.horizonorganic.com

Laura's Lean Beef

Available at fresh meat counters in over forty-seven hundred grocery stores in forty-four states, Laura's Lean Beef, like other Green 100 food companies, has succeeded in putting a value-driven brand into major mainstream supermarkets throughout the country, creating greater consumer choice.

www.laurasleanbeef.com

O'Naturals

Begun in Massachusetts and New Hampshire and cofounded by Stonyfield Farm founder Gary Hirschberg and Mac McCabe, one-third to one-half the food at O'Naturals is certified organic or wild gathered— from salmon to poultry. To extend their green values, they say that franchising of the O'Naturals model is on the way.

www.onaturals.com

Organic Valley

As a producer of quality certified organic dairy and meat products, Organic Valley stands for quality and strongly supports sustainable and humane treatment of animals, particularly for its producers of not only beef but also hogs and dairy as well. The company stood up to retailing giant Wal-Mart and did not succumb to the giant's pressures to reduce pricing if it would have required them to dilute their product. Many people choose Organic Valley because of its outspoken commitment to small family farms—besides great taste.

www.organicvalley.com

Starbucks

Starbucks formed a partnership with Conservation International in 1998 to encourage environmentally sound coffee-growing practices and to improve farmer livelihoods.[17] The success of their first joint project in Chiapas, Mexico, is serving as a model for new and future projects. The company has pioneered use of postconsumer recycled content in hot beverage cups. It is offering more and more organically grown and fair trade coffees. Some 61 percent of its 1,544 stores that it operates have recycling programs, which indicates that the company is on the way to its goals but has a way to go in overcoming such hurdles as having shops within larger complexes that do not have optimal recycling practices.[18]

www.starbucks.com

Stonyfield

Stonyfield Farm, Inc., the New Hampshire–based manufacturer of natural and organic yogurts and ice cream, enjoys a strategic partnership with Groupe Danone (Danone), the France-based consumer products company known for its sales of bottled water, dairy products, and biscuits. Stonyfield is the largest organic yogurt producer in the world and the third largest yogurt brand in America. Over the last decade, Stonyfield has enjoyed the fastest compounded annual growth rate (24.3 percent) of any U.S. yogurt brand. The company has built a national reputation for its leadership in organics, natural nutrition, and corporate environmental responsibility and is the number one brand in the natural products segment.[19]

www.stonyfield.com

Trader Joe's

One of the critical influences today on organic food pricing, Trader Joe's, the privately held, ridiculously low-priced food chain that began in Southern California, is the biggest competition natural supermarket chains Whole Foods and Wild Oats face.

Trader Joe's always has the lowest pricing for certified organic foods. The Trader Joe's factor in the health food industry is widely discussed, and they are one reason why prices at natural food markets are becoming more competitive.

If you really want value for organic foods, wines, and beer, and in so many other categories, shop at Trader Joe's. New stores are opening up throughout the United States in Illinois, Missouri, New York, Virginia, and other regions.

www.traderjoes.com

Whole Foods

Founded in 1980 as one small store in Austin, Texas, Whole Foods Market® is now the world's leading retailer of natural and organic foods, with 181 stores in North America and the United Kingdom., according to its Web site. To date Whole Foods Market remains uniquely mission driven with a strong adherence to promotion of carbon-neutral living. They're ranked number fifteen in the Fortune 2006 100 Best Companies to Work for in America.

www.wholefoods.com

Wild Oats

Like Whole Foods, Wild Oats has enormous growth potential as a value-driven shopping experience; its stores include Wild Oats, Sun Harvest, Henry's, and Capers in Vancouver, Canada.

Wild Oats was one of the first to commit to "corn-tainers," the corn-based green containers for perishables from NatureWorks. The company encourages bulk food sales to avoiding wasting packaging. "Whether you need a pound of polenta or a pinch of nutmeg, buy as much or as little as you need. . . . Bulk foods are better for you and the environment because they eliminate packaging waste," says the company.

www.wildoats.com

Environmental Groups

Saving the environment is an important business with value. Without these groups and many others, our voices would be dim, indeed.

Greenpeace

Greenpeace has rallied millions of people to become environmentalists. Today, Greenpeace is regarded as having first alerted shoppers to the widespread hazards of PVC in ordinary consumer products.

www.greenpeace.org

Natural Resources Defense Council

The NRDC has worked in all areas of the environment from toxics by taking on Alar in the 1980s to promoting sustainable forestry and fisheries. Their top flight attorneys are in the thick of legal battles to protect our natural resources.

www.nrdc.org

Nature Conservancy

Nature Conservancy is critical to preserving deep ecological reserves throughout America and the world.

www.natureconservancy.org

Rainforest Action Network

This group is doing so much great work to empower consumers to influence the global investors in worldwide logging. Through consumer pressure RAN and Greenpeace organized, major banks such as Citigroup have negotiated new environmental standards for sustainability and investing.

www.ran.org

Sierra Club

Sierra Club deals with many local and national issues and has activist groups throughout the United States.

www.sierraclub.org

World Wildlife Fund

The WWF is instrumental in preserving critical wildlife habitat globally. Help them save elephants, orangutans, and other endangered species by adopting a portion or all of a wildlife corridor or preserve.

www.wwf.org

Home and Office Furniture

Lifekind Products

Lifekind is the single largest purchaser of organic cotton for mattresses and the only certified organic mattress manufacturer in the United States. Lifekind mattresses are also made with Naturally Safer® wool from American organic certified farmers. And what really distinguishes Lifekind is that they use an exclusive nonchemical sterilization process to sanitize the raw materials. While using absolutely no brominated fire retardants, all of the company's mattresses conform to all federal and state mattress laws for nonflammability.

www.lifekindproducts.com

Neil Kelly

Run by former U.S. Army Colonel Rick Fields, Neil Kelly is making it easy for consumers to furnish their homes with eco-furniture. "Neil Kelly has a responsibility to continuously improve our products and processes as we work toward the goal of becoming a sustainable company," says its Web site. "We understand that a healthy future for our children and grandchildren demands that we honor this pledge."

The Naturals Collection is drawing national interest and uses sustainably harvested woods, formaldehyde-free wheatboard case material, and low VOC finishes.

www.neilkelly.com

Recycline

You can now buy toothbrushes and razors made from 100 percent recycled materials, thanks to Recycline. By working with nearby Stonyfield Farms, Recycline turns yogurt packaging into toothbrushes, razors, and even Preserve Plateware and Cutlery that can be reused. The plates and cutlery can be recycled in communities with #5 plastics recycling, and the razors and toothbrushes returned to the company to be used again and again in an endless cycle of nontoxicity.

www.recycline.com

Lifestyle

Gaiam

Gaiam has tapped into the burgeoning LOHAS market with multimedia channels and today provides a complete carbon-neutral, natural lifestyle—sort of like the Martha Stewart of eco-lifestyles. Their eco-travel site is great.

The very vision behind Gaiam was that, given a choice, people would choose a lifestyle that was healthy and life enhancing, for themselves, their families, and the Earth.[20] Gaiam wanted to provide the products that would offer that choice.

Gaiam offers natural, eco-friendly or healthy versions with style, quality, and price comparable to conventional products. From organic cotton sheets to eco-friendly air fresheners, Gaiam offers options for a healthier lifestyle.

www.gaiam.com

Organic Bouquet

Organic Bouquet is the Internet's first eco-florist. Organic Bouquet was established in 2001 with the goal of establishing a national market for organically grown cut flowers.

The motivating factors behind this goal were to protect the environment and improve farm worker safety by eliminating millions of pounds of toxic pesticides from agricultural usage. Organic Bouquet has been successful in doing this by encouraging organic production for both small and large flower growers, and by creating awareness about the need for organic flowers among consumers and within the floral trade.

In 2004 Organic Bouquet broadened their product selection to include flowers grown under additional sustainable certification standards, including farming and harvesting methods such as biodynamic, green label, and wild crafted.

And if purchasing organic flowers for yourself or a loved one is not enough to get you smiling, this surely will: In 2006 Organic Bouquet partnered with Network for Good to create Flowers for Good.[21] Consumers can purchase Organic Bouquet arrangements, and send a donation to the charity of the consumer's choice; there are currently ten charities to choose from. Organic Bouquet is also available nationwide in natural food stores, including Whole Foods Markets.

www.organicbouquet.com

Clothing

Esperanza Threads

Esperanza Threads is a project of the Grassroots Coalition for Economic and Environmental Justice of Ohio. It is a democratically operated cooperative that employs low-income individuals for manufacturing organic cotton clothing in Bedford, Ohio. Their goal is to provide jobs and fair wages in our cooperative.

Esperanza Threads began in June 2000 as a part of The Grassroots Cooperative. In September 2001, they became an autonomous group. They are now a highly regarded organic clothing manufacturer that partners with faith-based communities and civic groups to work on the issues of fair wages, outreach to the unemployed and underemployed, and the need for reducing chemicals in our personal and global environment.

www.esperanzathreads.com

Maggie's

Since 1992, the makers of Maggie's organic clothing brand have found "a way to make a living doing what we love: providing comfy, basic, durable clothing and accessories, making them affordable, and all the while supporting our beliefs and values in integrity, social responsibility, humility, sustainability and fun," according to the company's Web site. Their name "says a lot about us, and our clothes, and how we want you to feel when you put them on; comfortable, soothed, warm and wonderful—clean. Not hyped, or sold, or like you had better hurry up and wear them before they go out of style. We want our clothes to be the ones you choose to put on time, after time . . . after time."

The company is dedicated to using raw materials that are grown organically and sustainably; processors that provide livable working conditions, and workers who have control of their lives; processing standards that assure quality with the minimum of "additives"; pricing and business policies that support partnership.

www.organicclothes.com

Nike

Next time you need some athletic shoes, buy Nike with confidence that this company shares your values and is moving toward implementing them in ever more meaningful ways. Since 1997, when they purchased 250,000 pounds of certified organic cotton for use in their fall 1998 products, they have steadily increased their reliance on organic cotton. The best estimates for 2003 show that more than 2.5 percent of the cotton the company used globally was organic, representing approximately 3 million pounds of organic cotton fiber and making Nike the largest retail user of organic cotton in the world, according to the Organic Exchange.

The organic cotton is blended throughout the product line, though this does not mean all of their cotton products contain organic. For example, their estimates for the 2004 retail year show that close to 30 percent of Nike apparel cotton materials contained some percentage of organic cotton fiber.

In 2004, the *Premier Organics* collections featured both *Nike Organics* products and apparel containing a blend of organic and conventional cotton. For spring and fall 2005, the White Label collections for men and women featured organic cotton.

Since fall 2002, they have increased the number of styles containing

100 percent certified organic cotton from six to ninety-eight, with the overall number of apparel units produced growing from ten thousand to just over 1 million.

"Our goal is to blend a minimum of 5 percent organic cotton into all of our cotton-containing materials by 2010, while steadily expanding our offering of 100 percent certified organic cotton products."

They currently source organic cotton fiber primarily in the United States, India, Turkey, and China.

Cotton is thought to be the most pesticide-drenched agricultural crop today. Collaboration between companies and members of the organic cotton supply chain is critical to growing the supply of organic cotton and creating a strong and self-sustaining market for organics. Nike works with the Organic Exchange and the Organic Trade Association to develop the organic cotton market.

www.nike.com

Patagonia

In 1996, Patagonia converted their entire sportswear line to 100 percent organically grown cotton. They decided never to go back to conventional cotton, regardless of the outcome. As part of their organic cotton program, hundreds at the company took tours of cotton fields where they could see the dangers of pesticide use and the benefits of organic farming. According to the company, "Many of us have since become activists on the issue and have shifted to buying organic foods and clothing for ourselves and our families."

www.patagonia.com

Timberland

With their obvious interest in the outdoors, it should not be surprising that environmental stewardship is particularly important to Timberland. "We realize that manufacturing our products and managing our business have an impact on the environment, and we're committed to doing something about it," says the company's Web site. "We collaborate with innovative organizations such as Clean Air–Cool Planet and the Organic Exchange to address our contribution to the climate change, reduce our use of harmful chemicals, and increase our use of more-sustainable natural resources."[22]

In the past few years, their emission reduction efforts represented a reduction of approximately ten of their greenhouse gas emissions. They now use water-based adhesives in place of solvent-based adhesives in more than 8 million pairs of shoes, and they have more than tripled their use of organic cotton to 167,000 pounds.[23]

www.timberland.com

Energy Efficiency

Energy Star

A government-business partnership that is funded with about $50 million per year, Energy Star has probably done more to reduce pollution and greenhouse emissions than anything else today. They make buying the most carbon-neutral appliances simple.

www.energystar.gov

MicroPlanet

Little things can produce big results. MicroPlanet is a great example of high tech meets environmentalism. One of the biggest wastes of energy today in the home is being supplied with more voltage than we actually need due to lack of feedback devices that alert energy providers with vital information. MicroPlanet's electronic voltage regulators precisely regulate voltage at the point of service delivery and return excess energy back to the grid to increase electrical service reliability and to reduce oil dependency, waste, and greenhouse gas emissions. These little devices should be in every home.

www.microplanet.com

Fashion

Global Exchange

Global Exchange is an international human rights organization dedicated to promoting environmental, political, and social justice. Global Exchange operates an online store and three brick and mortar stores: two in the California Bay Area and one in Portland, Oregon. These fair trade stores set a conscious example of working responsibly with world craft producers. They generate income for thousands of artisans and their families in over forty countries whose work is certified by the Fair Trade Federation, TransFair, and other certification groups. Global Exchange Fair Trade Stores feature products from around the world, with fair prices for consumers, and fair prices paid to producers.

Growing at an even faster pace is the Global Exchange Online Store, one of the highest rated stores among all of Yahoo!'s twenty thousand plus stores online.

www.globalexchange.org

Linda Loudermilk

If you think eco-fashion is about hippies and Luddites (who originally feared the coming of the power loom in nineteenth-century England) in scratchy hand-woven hemp tunics, think again. Linda Loudermilk is leading the eco-fashion revolution with her cutting-edge Luxury-Eco line. The line offers beautiful, luxurious options in fabrics made from sasawashi, bamboo, sea cell, soya, and other exotic self-sustaining plants.[24] Loudermilk is making it hip to make more than just a fashion statement with your clothing, and as celebrities continue to embrace her line, the eco-fashion/sustainable textiles trend is catching on.

www.lindaloudermilk.com

Finance and Banking

Bank of America

Bank of America, a major worldwide investment bank, adheres to the rain forest preservation guidelines it has worked on with the Rain Forest Action Network. As a result, they are one of two major financial institutions (along with Citigroup) to begin to strongly influence rain forest sustainability.

www.bankamerica.com

Chittenden

In 2003, the Community Investing Campaign, a project of the Social Investment Forum Foundation and Co-op America, singled out

Chittenden Bank's Socially Responsible Banking Program that supports entrepreneurial green projects.

Community development lending efforts include loans to support affordable housing, business and economic development, conservation and agriculture, downtown revitalization projects, and community building. As a socially responsible lending institution, Chittenden is in a position to influence projects that benefit our long-term sustainability.

www.chittenden.com.

Citigroup

Citigroup has established itself as leader in the environmental movement. It is a founding member of the Equator Principles, a set of voluntary guidelines to evaluate environmental and social risks related to financing development projects.

Most recently, Citigroup announced a commitment to reduce its greenhouse emissions on a global basis by 10 percent by the year 2011. And to cement this commitment, Citigroup joined the U.S. Environmental Protection Agency's Climate Leader Program. Citigroup is one of seventy-nine corporations in the voluntary program aimed at adopting aggressive goals and strategies for curbing greenhouse emissions at manufacturing and other facilities.

In the past, Citigroup has effectively met its commitments for improving energy efficiency, and reducing consumption. For example, their 2004 Citizenship Report shows CO_2 emissions as a reduction of 7 percent per employee.

www.citigroup.com

Dexia

Dexia came into being in 1996 as a result of a merger between Crédit Local of France and Crédit Communal of Belgium, forming one of the first cross-border mergers in the European banking sector.[25] Since its inception, Dexia has been committed to being *the* bank for sustainable development in Europe.[26] Dexia, however, is also building sustainable practices into its own operations on a very practical level to act as an example to other international investment banks.[27] There is a new focus on awareness raising, being played out in Italy, for example, through

Dexia Crediop which is in the process of obtaining ISO 14001 and Eco Management and Audit Scheme certification.

Waste management efforts are being ramped up; in France, office paper consumption for Dexia Credit Local decreased by a half-ton from 2003 to 2004, despite a larger number of employees. Management of premises is being looked at closely for energy efficiency. In addition, in Belgium a new heat pump and condensation boiler has allowed for a yearly reduction of CO_2 emissions of 220 tons. Finally, Dexia is making efforts to reduce energy consumption and emissions associated with transportation. This includes replacing business travel with video conferencing where possible, and a campaign to encourage and reward employee behavior that uses public transportation. In Brussels, 60 percent of employees use public transportation or nonpolluting methods of transportation.

www.dexia.com

ShoreBank

Since its inception in 1973, ShoreBank has been committed to making a difference. In fact, it was created to serve communities that were essentially being deliberately redlined by established financial institutions, and to demonstrate that a regulated bank could be instrumental in revitalizing these underrepresented communities.

For several decades, ShoreBank has been successful in these efforts. In 2000, with the thought that communities cannot achieve true prosperity without also attaining environmental well-being, ShoreBank made a new commitment to improve their own, as well as their customers', impact on the environment.

ShoreBank is off to a great start with this relatively new commitment. Over the past five years, more than $188 million has been lent for conservation improvements.

www.shorebank.com

Flooring

Eco Timber

Since 1992, EcoTimber has promoted forest conservation worldwide by selling sustainably harvested and reclaimed wood products. Their suppliers' forestry practices are certified by the prestigious Forest Stewardship Council and guarantee a perpetual yield of high-quality timber while maintaining or restoring healthy, self-regenerating forest ecosystems. They also offer wood that is reclaimed from old buildings and wood alternatives such as bamboo.

www.ecotimber.com

Forbo

If you are looking for a healthy petrochemical-free solution for floor coverings, look no further than Forbo, best known for their Marmoleum linoleum that has an excellent record of causing no adverse health issues. This is so during production, its useful life, and in disposal.

Marmoleum is a natural product made from linseed oil, woodflour, pine rosin, jute, and limestone and is available in a comprehensive range of design elements.[28] It is often the flooring of choice in medical facilities, and is recommended by health professionals for use in the homes of those suffering from respiratory disorders. It is also exceptionally easy to clean, and has natural antimicrobial properties, helping cut down on the breeding of microorganisms such as dust mites and allergy-causing bacteria. Considering the fact that floor coverings are often the most abundant source of toxins in the home, this is an exceptional record.

And to top it off, Forbo is just as committed to a healthy global environment as they are to a healthy indoor environment. And it's not just lip-service: In a life-cycle analysis used to quantify the potential environmental impacts of a product system over the life cycle (i.e., from the extraction of the raw materials to the disposal of the product at the end of its useful life), Marmoleum ranked first as a nature-friendly floor covering, together with pure, unlacquered wood.[29] Marmoleum also earned an honorable mention for its long lifespan.

www.forbo.com

Interface

In 1973 Interface Flooring created the first legitimate "free lay" carpet tile, a nonsewn textile created by directly adhering fibers to a patented backing system. It was extremely stable and dense, allowing it to be installed with a minimum of adhesive yet still perform extremely well. This was a step, perhaps unconsciously undertaken, in creating green carpeting, as it allowed for minimal waste in installation.

At Interface, the company continues to look for ways they can encourage sustainability through their product and beyond. The designers think through the entire life cycle, from manufacture to reclamation, and recycling. The goal is for all of their products to be sustainable. To make sustainability a reality in the long run, Interface has focused its green path on seven fronts including eliminating waste, benign emissions, renewable energy, closing the loop in recycling, resource efficient transportation, sensitizing shareholder, and redesigning commerce.

And to top it off, Interface has been recognized on several occasions, not just for their design, but also for their style.

www.interface.com

Furniture

Hermann Miller

In the early 1950s, D. J. DePree, founder of Hermann Miller, started the company on an environmentally aware and responsible path, declaring in a statement of corporate values that Hermann Miller "will be a good corporate neighbor by being a good steward of the environment."

DePree instated several policies that are in effect for today, including a mandate that all Hermann Miller buildings, including manufacturing sites, include windows so that the employees could benefit from natural light, and a commitment that 50 percent of any Hermann Miller corporate site will be set aside as "green space."

In 1995 under the leadership of Mike Volkema, Hermann Miller developed the Blueprint for Corporate Community, a declaration of corporate values clearly stating that Hermann Miller recognizes a responsibility to the environment, to others living in it, and to future generations.

Among Hermann Miller's most ambitious goals is an initiative called "Perfect Vision." Hermann Miller has designated the year 2020 as their deadline to achieve a range of sustainability targets, including zero landfill and zero hazardous waste generation.

www.hermannmiller.com

Ikea

You'll be happy to know that you don't have to break the bank, or your commitment to shopping green, to furnish your home. Ikea, the Swedish-based affordable furnishings superstore, has established itself as a leader in the green movement.

Ikea minimizes environmental impact by carefully selecting and developing lasting relationships with environmentally responsible suppliers (including a list of environmental qualifications).

To meet their long-term sustainability goals, Ikea has three cornerstone values:

Ikea is always looking for way to use fewer raw materials and create less waste and discharge; this is beneficial to the environment and reduces costs to shoppers.

Ikea also uses wood extensively in their products, as it is a recyclable, biodegradable, and renewable material. Ikea does not use any wood products derived from intact natural forests or forests with a clearly defined high conservation value. It is Ikea's long-term goal to source their wood only from well-managed forests that have been certified to meet their standards. To meet this goal, Ikea is currently involved in a variety of projects having to do with research and conservation of forests in several areas of the globe.

Ikea's final cornerstone is to train partners and engage them in environmental issues. This is played out in variety of ways, but, certainly, one of the biggest benefits is that is encourages other companies, and even other regions of the world, to adopt environmentally responsible principles.

www.ikea.com

Home Projects

Home Depot

As a major purchaser and a retail supplier, Home Depot is in a unique position to, as they say, "leverage their influence in the marketplace," on several fronts. And they are committed to doing so with their vendors, customers, associates, and communities, and in their business operations.

Home Depot issued its first wood-purchasing policy in 1999,

pledging to give preference to wood that has come from forests managed in a responsible way and to eliminate wood purchases from endangered regions of the world. As part of the fulfillment of that pledge, the company spent two years researching the origin of every wood product on its shelves—from lumber to brooms—and now knows, item by item, where their wood products are being made and from what forests or recycled products. Among their accomplishments since 1999, sales of Forest Stewardship Council–certified wood have gone from $16 million to $350 million. Home Depot is the largest retail seller of ecologically harvested wood in America today.

The company intends to go carbon-neutral. In their stores, Home Depot is committed to educating customers about healthier and more efficient choices for their homes, from carpeting to appliances. From 2003 to 2004, Home Depot had an increase of 35 percent in sales of Energy Star–certified appliances.

www.homedepot.com

Information and News

Co-op America

For years, Co-op America has been a lone voice in the wilderness of green anonymity putting together environmentally conscious consumers with environmentally conscious companies. Their Web site remains a great starting point for virgin green consumers to get their feet wet as they begin to submerge themselves in the total green consciousness experience.

Co-op America describes itself as "a nonprofit membership organization dedicated to harnessing the economic power of consumers, investors and businesses to promote social justice and environmental sustainability." So how are they doing it? Co-op America is working on several fronts to promote environmentally and socially responsible businesses and business practices.

First and foremost, it is a great resource for consumers and businesses looking for a green solution to just about any problem. Co-op America maintains a directory of green businesses called the National Green Pages, which is a great way to promote businesses that are doing the right thing. When the demand for green business is there, those businesses will prosper, and more businesses will follow suit to do the right thing.[30]

Co-op America also brings people and businesses together to take action against corporate irresponsibility. They do this by raising awareness so that people can make informed decisions about how to vote with their dollars and by organizing efforts to encourage changes in business practices, for example, people can send a letter encouraging ExxonMobil to start investing in renewable energy sources.[31] Co-op America even uses similar strategies for positive reinforcement, as with their letter to congratulate magazine publishers using environmentally preferable papers.[32]

www.coopamerica.org

Greenbiz.com

Information is critical to greening business. GreenBiz is the leading information resource on how to align environmental responsibility with business success. They provide valuable news and resources to large and small businesses through a combination of Web sites, workshops, daily news feeds, and e-newsletters. Their resources are free to all users.

www.greenbiz.com; see also www.climatebiz.com

Lawn and Garden

NaturaLawn

If you are making the effort to purchase organic foods to keep pesticides and chemical fertilizers out of kitchen, why not keep them out of your yard as well? NaturaLawn is making this possible. The fourth largest lawn care company in America, Naturalawn offers a natural organic-based system, including a natural organic-based fertilization program used together with an "Integrated Pest Management" program. This is a great alternative to traditional chemical fertilization programs with involving heavy use of pesticides.[33]

NaturaLawn offers lawn maintenance services, along with do-it-yourself natural lawn care products, so there are options for anyone who wants to reduce harmful chemicals on their lawn.

And NaturaLawn is helping to reduce your exposure to toxic fertilizers and pesticides outside your yard as well. In 2005 NaturaLawn was selected as a member of the EPA maintained Pesticide Environmental Stewardship Program (PESP), a voluntary program to reduce the risks associated with pesticide use.[34]

Not only has NaturaLawn made a formal agreement to support the goals of PESP, they will be working with other members of the Landscaping /Turf sector of PESP which focuses on residential and commercial properties, public spaces, and golf courses, to look at long-term solutions for reducing pesticide risks.

www.naturalawn.com

Manufacturing

Aloca

Alcoa is also actively increasing its supply of cost-effective renewable resources and actively supports the Green Power Market Development Group, a collaboration of thirteen leading corporations and the World Resources Institute dedicated to building corporate markets for green power.[35]

www.alcoa.com

NatureWorks/Cargill

Can one eat one's corn and wear it, too? Thanks to NatureWorks LLC, you can. You can even drink your morning coffee out of it. Changing the very nature of plastic, NatureWorks is using nontoxic polylactic acid, derived from natural plant carbon sugars that can be used in a broad range of applications, most often packaging, but also for textiles, fiberfill for bedding, and even for reusable plates and cups. This is a great because instead of using fossil fuels to create plastics as has been done in the past, NatureWorks is developing new applications and improving the technology for making plastics from renewable resources.

And as you might expect, Cargill's commitment to the environment spans beyond developing renewable plastics. Cargill is working steadily at meeting long-term goals of increasing energy efficiency and reducing waste. Cargill is also involved in Water Matters, an international partnership focusing on issues of water quality and sustainability. The company is a leader in ethanol fuel production and should rise in importance as American use of ethanol and other plant-derived fuels increases.

www.natureworks.com

www.cargill.com

Mutual Funds

Domini Social Investments

At Domini Social Investments, any company the fund invests in must meet a comprehensive set of social and environmental standards, ensuring Domini is investing in companies that are helping to create a "healthy and wealthy society with increased opportunities for everyone."[36]

Domini evaluates companies using environmental and social standards, as well as the Domini 400 Social Index, which uses four hundred U.S. corporations that meet a broad range of social standards to create a benchmark. A set of "exclusionary standards" was also looked at when creating the index. Companies receiving more than 2 percent of their revenues from military weapons, or receiving any revenues from the production of tobacco or alcohol, or any revenues from gambling products or services were eliminated, as were companies that own, operate, or design nuclear power.

Once a company has made the Index, Domini reserves the right to remove it if it violates any of their exclusionary standards or fails to meet their qualitative standards.[37]

www.domini.com

Green Century Funds

Green Century Funds is a family of environmentally responsible mutual funds founded by nonprofit environmental advocacy organizations and owned entirely by nonprofit advocacy groups. Green Century Funds uses a three-part strategy for green investing, including investing in companies that are committed to a greener future, avoiding companies that do not meet their environmental criteria and using shareholder advocacy to influence corporate behavior.[38]

And, as Green Century Funds is owned by nonprofit organizations, 100 percent of the net profits earned from fees for managing the funds belong to the nonprofit advocacy organization founders; this means that even the profits from management will be used to further environmental preservation and protection efforts including campaigning for clean air, clean water, and open space; filing lawsuits against companies that illegally pollute; and advocating for reduced use of toxic chemicals and reduced emissions of global warming gases.[39]

www.greencentury.com

Nutrition

Barlean's

Barlean's is the largest purchaser of organic flaxseed in America today, and with their fishery they provide Americans with key healthy nutrients, the omega-3 fatty acids, from wild salmon and organic flaxseed. These are good, healthy foods for all of us.

www.barleans.com

www.barleansfishery.com

Flora/Salus Haus

The American offshoot off Salus Haus, Flora, like the other nutrition companies to make the Green 100, takes pride in harvesting many of its own organic herbs from certified organic farms in Canada, the United States, and Chile. Their European headquarters have been recognized for their carbon-neutral practices.

Flora is dedicated to providing the best quality, chemical-free nutritional supplements. This means they consistently go above and beyond to make sure their ingredients are coming from the purest sources possible. Whenever possible, Flora uses organic ingredients in their formulations. Even the ingredients that are not certified organic are held to the highest standards. Flora only uses seeds and herbs from select farmers who do their own seed collecting, growing, harvesting, and drying. Flora also owns their own farmland for cultivating and testing a variety of certified organic herbs under the Washington State Department of Agriculture Organic Food Certification Program. These programs and guidelines provide the twofold benefit of environmentally sustainable farming and a superior product for the consumer.

Flora also chooses environmentally friendly recyclable glass to package their products, and uses ecologically sound, 100 percent biodegradable, starch-based packing peanuts for shipping. And all of their company trucks run on natural gas.

Flora also offers financial support to over thirty nonprofit organizations working to protect and preserve the environment.

Respect for nature is one of the founding principals of Salus Haus. It is because of this respect for nature and the life it provides us all that Salus Haus was the first health food company to receive certification from the European Community's "Eco Audit Directive." This directive is not easily attained and is only given to those companies that have made a decision to protect the environment, have implemented the necessary systems (as outlined by the European Community), and are willing to be independently audited at any time.

In the case of Salus Haus, the Eco Audit systems are so comprehensive, it not only takes into account major items, such as reduction of water consumption by 20 percent, but also smaller details such as dictating at what time of day, and under what weather conditions, lights are allowed to be on in the buildings. The Eco Audit is so encompassing, in fact, that all employees must sign papers stating that they will abide by the standards as set out by the Eco Audit system, as well as make every effort to apply the systems outside of work. At Salus Haua, the company philosophy of "in partnership with nature" is one in which every employee believes.

www.florahealth.com

www.salus.de

Gaia Herbs

American herbal medicine is an important source of international trade, and American-grown herbs are often prized for their vitality and health benefits. Gaia Herbs, with 250 certified organic acres in Brevard, North Carolina, has worked extensively with government grants to explore the health benefits of such heavyweight herbals as echinacea.

Their natural methods of cultivation and scientific insight into the active chemicals in such plants has led to a breakthrough in cultivation to make echinacea a potentially more useful cold and flu remedy.

Gaia has been committed to organic growing for over twenty years, and in this time has established itself as a leader in organic growing. Gaia is proud to be an Oregon Tilth certified grower. (Oregon Tilth is known for strict organic certification standards, and both the Gaia farm and processing facility are recertified each year.) Gaia established a small, ten-acre farm in Costa Rica in 2005; they are in the process of seeking organic certification.

Gaia's facilities were constructed from nontoxic building materials wherever possible, and follow architectural design principles of building in harmony with nature.

www.gaiaherbs.com

Garden of Life

Most well known for its top-selling Primal Defense and Perfect Food probiotic whole food supplements, "in a sense, Garden of Life began as a company committed to personal sustainability," CEO Greg Horn said in an interview. (Horn is also author of *Simple Sustainability*, published by The Freedom Press in 2006.)

"People who buy Garden of Life products have a real awareness of what they are putting into their bodies," he said.

Safety and prevention are two key concepts in health. However, "personal sustainability changes your world view and leads to a whole different set of evolving values. You begin to realize consuming organic milk and other organic foods is part of an expanding consciousness and awareness that your own actions have far-reaching implications. We are industry leaders and the people who come to Garden of Life so often are leaders too. Once people begin to see that their personal lives reflect larger values, they keep adding to their lifestyles in a positive manner. For example, eating organic foods can transform into a greater appreciation for sustainable fashion and organic cotton, and even sustainable shoes."

The company's first step into the public consciousness was one of survival and personal sustainability, and that will always be part of its core appeal. But, now, Horn says, "we're branching out to being committed to spending time and financial resources to improve our sustainability as an organization. We are not perfect. I do not want to set us up as being already there, but Garden of Life is definitely on a journey to long-term sustainability as a reflection of our own long-term corporate planning."

Garden of Life is now among the first companies of its size in the state of Florida to make a commitment to purchase 100 percent of the company's electricity for its West Palm Beach campus and other facilities from wind power certificates from 3 Phases Energy (www.3phases.com). It's important to further note that their purchase of pollution-free renewable energy is certified by the independent organization Green-E (www.green-e.org).

"This saves more than a million pounds of carbon dioxide from entering our atmosphere and prevents the burning of more than 300 tons of coal per year," said Horn.

Also, this spring look for more certified organic foods from Garden of Life, including certified organic honey, food bars, tea concentrates, and rain forest cacao.

Already a significant purchaser of certified organic wheat, rye, and other grasses grown in Utah and other states and countries, Garden of Life's rain forest cacao will be certified by the Fair Trade Federation (www.fairtradefederation.org) to have been harvested from an area in Ecuador in the Amazon "where there is a lot of poverty and potential for environmental degradation"—but also where there is now fair trade sustainable harvesting of this antioxidant- and polyphenols-rich rain forest treasure.

"All of our printing is being done on 100 percent post-consumer recycled paper, including our extensive catalogs, and with vegetable inks," adds Horn.

We think this marks real progress for Garden of Life as a maturing company, and that's one of the reason why we think they're the kind of company smart shoppers want to work with, too, to improve not only their health but also the health of their community.

www.gardenoflife.com

New Chapter

New Chapter's Zyflamend might just well be the most powerful and valued natural medicine in America today—one of those rare natural remedies that works like a cure for inflammatory conditions (see Chapter 5). Pioneering totally certified organic nutritional supplements that are made all the more potent with probiotic fermentation and now farming over two hundred certified organic acres to produce natural anti-inflammatory medicines, New Chapter, of Brattleboro, Vermont, is bringing the health benefits of rain forest herbs into Americans' lives. The health benefits to the nation, as more and more consumers turn to such natural medicines, cannot be underestimated; nor can the growth potential of the company.

Tom Newmark, president of New Chapter, points out, "Consumers want to be assured that they are purchasing products that are truly organic, but regulation is sorely needed if we plan to expand the organic movement."[40]

www.new-chapter.com

Pet Foods

Pet Promise

People care tremendously about their canine and feline friends and strive to provide them with the healthiest foods. Pet Promise helps to green your pet food, too. In keeping with its original purpose to help preserve family farms and rural communities, Pet Promise only obtains its meat from U.S. farmers and ranchers who are committed to eco-friendly, natural, and sustainable practices and who practice the humane treatment of animals. Their pasture-fed beef and free-range chicken come from certified natural producers, such as Coleman Natural Beef and Petaluma Poultry, and your purchase of their quality products helps support family farms that are committed to natural growing methods and a healthy environment that we all can share.

www.petpromise.com

Renewable Energy

BP

BP's stance on renewable energy sources and cleaner air is this: They are working toward a world powered by clean renewable energy, but they accept that hydrocarbons (i.e., coal, oil, and gas) are here to stay for the foreseeable future. So in the meantime, while developing cleaner renewable energy sources, BP will continue to reduce emissions from their energy products and help people use energy more efficiently.[41]

Currently, BP is looking to expand their solar energy market.[42] In 2004, the company announced plans to double its capacity from around 90 to 200 megawatts by 2006.

In 2004, the energy supplier opened a 4 megawatt solar farm (one of the largest in the world) in Germany that will supply enough energy to for 1,000 four-person households.

In California, BP is working with the Home Depot to promote their Solar Home Solutions package and make it widely available to consumers. BP expects its upcoming solar energy efforts to focus on providing "on-grid" installations in key markets, while continuing with "off-grid" projects in developing countries.

BP also sees a lot of potential in wind power. In 2004 BP's jointly owned 22.5 megawatt wind farm in the Netherlands completed its first full year of operation, providing enough power for 20,000 typical Dutch homes. BP is currently focusing their efforts on the development of wind farms at existing BP refineries and petrochemical plants; this has the additional benefit of curtailing the spread of industrialized land.

And as far as continued use of fossil fuels is concerned, BP is part of a major effort to find ways to reduce emissions and reduce consumption. For example, research at Princeton University, supported by BP and Ford, has produced several scenarios in transportation where, using existing technologies, emissions could be cut by as much as 3.5 billion tons of carbon dioxide annually. These scenarios include doubling the fuel economy of 2 million cars and creating conventional biofuels from crops and trees.

www.bp.com

Chevron

Chevron shares a concern about global climate change, and is taking action with a fourfold plan.[43] This plan includes reducing greenhouse-gas emissions and increasing energy efficiency; investing in research, development, and improved technologies; pursuing business opportunities in promising innovative energy technologies; and supporting flexible and economically sound policies that protect the environment.

Chevron has taken steps to reduce emissions by switching to cleaner energy sources in their own operations.

For example, Chevron switched to natural gas to generate electricity and steam in Kuwait's Wafra oil field and California's Kern River oil field, reducing CO_2 emissions by more than 1 million metric tons per year, and reducing air pollutants such as sulfur oxides and nitrogen oxides. At Chevron headquarters in San Ramon, California, a hydrogen fuel cell unit is the primary power source for the data center. Chevron has made a commitment to be more energy efficient in their own everyday operations, and new targets are set each year. Since 1992 Chevron's energy efficiency ahs increased by 24 percent.

And of course, Chevron is dedicated to helping other companies conserve as well.[44] Chevron Energy Solutions (CES), a subsidiary of Chevron, develops energy-efficient facility improvements for public institutions and businesses. Typically these improvements pay for themselves in energy savings, and they often include renewable power solutions, such as solar and fuel cell generation systems. In Richmond, California, improvements, including a solar electric system for the public library, are expected to save the city more than $9.5 million over the next twenty years. In West Sacramento, California, at the U.S. Postal Service's Processing and Distribution Center, CES installed the nation's largest nonmilitary federal solar power installation, among other energy efficient improvements. The improvements are expected to reduce the facility's power use by more than one-third and its annual electricity purchases by $615,000. CES will be upgrading dozens of other USPS mail facilities throughout Northern California under a major contract with the USPS.

www.chevron.com

GEOSOL

German-based Gesellschaft für Sonnenenergie, translated to the Society for Solar Energy, and most commonly known simply as GEOSOL, is a leader in solar power. The primary goal of GEOSOL is to change the energy industry by introducing and promoting renewable energy solutions. GEOSOL also functions as an intermediary between scientists, engineers, architects, the construction industry, industry authorities, and parliaments.

One of GEOSOL's most exciting accomplishments was to build the world's largest solar park, near Leipzig, Germany, which opened in 2004. GEOSOL initiated and developed the project, while Shell was the primary contractor.

www.geosol.de

Shell

A recent press release puts Royal Dutch Shell's investments in alternative energy at the equivalent of at least $1 billion, cementing Shell's place as a leader in the energy industry.[46] Shell is the world's largest marketer of biofuels, and a leading developer in the field. Biofuels are created using materials such as plant oil from crops, or even plant waste such as a straw, and they can be used either pure or blended with traditional fuels, with the potential for much lower CO_2 emissions than we see from traditional fuels.

Shell is currently partnered with Iogen of Canada to produce biofuels from plant waste. The fuel can be used in today's cars, cutting CO_2 life cycle emissions by 90 percent compared with conventional fuels. Shell recently announced a Memorandum of Understanding with Volkswagen and Iogen to explore the economic feasibility of producing cellulose ethanol in Germany. Shell Canada has been working with Iogen to develop a viable commercial framework for a facility in Canada.

Shell is also looking to grow its wind energy production capacity from its current 350 to 500 megawatts by 2007, including the first Dutch offshore project (in which Shell is a 50 percent partner), and an offshore project in the United Kingdom with the potential to produce 1,000 megawatts (Shell's share is one-third).

Shell is a leader in solar energy as well. In 2004, in partnership with GEOSOL, Shell opened the world's largest solar park in Leipzig, Germany.[47] The solar power station will produce energy for about 1,800 households, and save some 3,700 tons of CO_2 emissions annually. Shell is currently working on new solar technology such as CIS "thin film" which they believe will be more competitive in energy production than silicon-based technologies.

Of Shell's ventures in alternative energy, CEO Jeroen van der Veer says, "We aim to develop at least one alternative energy such as wind, hydrogen or advanced solar technology, into a substantial business. In addition, we continue our efforts to further expand our position as the largest marketer of biofuels."

www.shell.com

Uni-Solar

United Solar Ovonic, also known as Uni-Solar, is an industry leader in solar modules and system. They are working to make it simple for anyone to power a home or business with solar power. While solar power systems in the past had the potential to be somewhat of an eyesore on homes, Uni-Solar is offering options that are thin, lightweight, durable, easy to integrate into a roof, and produce more energy per hour than ever.[48] In addition to providing people with options for renewable energy, Uni-Solar is committed to producing products that minimize environmental impact throughout the life cycle (meaning not just during the product's energy producing life, but in production and disposal as well). Uni-Solar is also committed to continuously minimizing the environmental impacts of its operations.

www.uni-solar.com

Willie Nelson Biodiesel

"Put a B2O biodiesel blend in your tank and hit the road again with a clean burning, renewable fuel that is grown right here in America" says the Web site for Willie Nelson Biodiesel.[49] Part of the little answers that amount to one big answer to our dependency on Middle Eastern oil, Willie Nelson has lent his prestige and fame to helping American overcome its petroleum addiction.

The Biodiesel Venture GP, LLC partnership was established in December 2004. "The idea is to do something useful towards eliminating America's dependence on foreign oil, help put the American family farmer back to work, and clean up the environment we live in."[50]

Distribution Drive, distributor of Willie Nelson Biodiesel, is a wholly owned subsidiary of Earth Biofuels, Inc. Earth Biofuels is a publicly traded company under the ticker symbol EBOF.

On the top priority list for all biofuels, including those manufacturing and marketing biodiesel, is to eliminate the use of toxic methanol, a fossil fuel derivative, in processing and lowering nitric oxide emissions. These must be accomplished in short order to ensure that biofuels are totally carbon-neutral.

Retailers

Target

Take it from Target's own Web site, "what's good for the environment is good for everyone."[51] To live by this philosophy, Target is reducing waste and increasing energy efficiency and sustainability. Through recycling and reuse programs, Target has already cuts its waste by 70 percent. The ultimate goal is to be a "zero waste" company.[52] Additionally, Target sponsor's recycling programs in their communities. In 2004, twenty thousand pounds of rechargeable batteries were collected from customers and recycled. Target is reducing energy consumption by making their stores as energy efficient as possible, and by using renewable energy sources whenever it is feasible. Three of their Los Angeles stores even produce 20 percent of their own energy using rooftop solar panels (something good for LA with its still smoggy February days). Target also looks at sustainability and reuse when developing new properties, focusing on energy efficient sites, and assessing such issues as storm water run off. In 2004, one-third of Target's new store construction projects involved redevelopments, including environmentally impaired properties ("brownfields") or reuse of existing buildings.

Additionally, Target works closely with vendors to monitor compliance with Target's labor standards. These detailed standards include compliance with local laws, safe and healthy work environments, no use of forced or prison labor, limited work hours, fair wages, and no child labor.

www.target.com

Wal-Mart

Wal-Mart is making environmental leadership a priority as they continue to develop. Like many retailers, they are making efforts to reduce waste and increase energy efficiency, and, over the past several years, Wal-Mart has been working directly with suppliers to create better packaging designs that allow for less waste and for better shipping efficiency.[53] Wal-Mart entered into a major agreement with NatureWorks to begin using their sustainable PLA packaging for a variety of grocery items in their superstores and Sam's Clubs.[54]

Wal-Mart is taking steps in conservation with their experimental stores and trucks. In 2005, Wal-Mart launched its first two experimental stores: first in McKinney, Texas, then in Aurora, Colorado. Both stores experiment with materials, technology, and processes, which will reduce the amount of energy and natural resources needed to operate the store, reduce the amount of raw materials used in construction, and make use of renewable materials in the construction and maintenance. In what was labeled "The World's Largest Recycling Project," the Aurora store was built on a foundation made of recycled runway material from Denver's Stapleton Airport;[55] it will also obtain energy from vegetable oil from the store's deli, and the used motor oil from the tire center will be used to help heat the store. Their "2007-generation" experimental trucks rely on streamlined design and reduced weight to help increase fuel efficiency, while maintaining the capability to transport the same amount of goods. In a carbon-neutral move that also makes financial sense, Wal-Mart hopes to have cut its fuel consumption in half by 2015.

Wal-Mart is also committed to conservation efforts. Wal-Mart is working with the National Fish and Wildlife Foundation to conserve at least one parcel of priority wildlife habitat for every parcel developed in the United States over the next ten years.[56]

www.walmart.com

Printing

Greenerprinter.com

If you are looking for printing solutions that are green from start to finish, look no further than Greenerprinter.com, a company that is committed to making green printing an affordable option, without sacrificing quality or selection of products and services. Greenprinter.com uses soy inks and New Leaf Paper, which contains a high postconsumer recycled content; most varieties are whitened without chlorine or chlorine compounds. And you can receive an Environmental Benefits Statement with each print job, so you know specifically how much environmental benefit is derived from your choosing New Leaf paper.[57]

GreenerPrinter.com prides itself not only on green printing, but also green shipping as well. Greenprinter.com is certified as Climate Cool by the Climate Neutral Network as having a net-zero impact on the earth's climate. The climate impact of shipping finished print jobs is offset 100 percent through investments in WindBuilders and Green Tags.

www.greenerprinter.com

Quad/Graphics

The world's largest privately held commercial printer became the first corporation in the printing and publishing industry to join the Environmental Protection Agency's SmartWay Transport Partnership, a collaborative voluntary program to increase the environmental performance of freight shippers.[58]

Members of the partnership agree to utilize SmartWay-recommended techniques to increase the energy efficiency and energy security of our country. Consequently, SmartWay Partners significantly reduce air pollution while saving money for their operations.

The process to become "qualified" took Quad/Graphics nearly two years by first measuring the greenhouse gas emissions of its operations and then developing and implementing a plan to reduce those emissions even further. Measures taken by the printer included switching over to aerodynamic trucks, implementing anti-idling technology, and installing small diesel engines that heat and cool the cab of the truck so drivers do not have to keep the entire truck running while parked. The smaller engines consume just one pint of fuel per hour, which is one-eighth as much as the entire gallon used by an average truck engine.

Using an EPA formula, Quad/Graphics calculates it reduced carbon dioxide emissions by 9,614 tons via SmartWay-recommended techniques in 2004 alone. This is the equivalent of taking 1,888 passenger cars off the road for a year.

www.qg.com

RR Donnelley

RR Donnelley (RRD) offers a variety of printing service for businesses, including books, magazines, catalogs, and other large-scale print jobs. RRD recognizes that the printing industry is one with a great potential for negative environmental impacts, and is consistently taking measures to offset this potential damage.[59]

RRD has installed the best available air pollution control equipment at their global heat-set lithographic printing plants. Through improvements in solvent recovery systems, RRD has reduced total toluene emissions from their gravure printing operations by 77 million pounds since 1990. They have achieved 90 to 95 percent energy savings through the use of effective pollution control, which has also allowed for significant reduction in emissions of greenhouse gases. RRD is also engaged in the Air Permit Compliance Program, which requires substantial reporting, including mandatory self-reporting of noncompliance. Many of RRD's global locations have also received ISO 14001 certification to control the environmental impact of their operations.[60]

www.rrd.com

Transportation

BMW

Mobility is a socially desirable component of our culture and might even be stated as a basic need of humankind. However, for the development and well-being of society, not only is mobility essential, but also preservation of our environment. This conflict is exacerbated by the problem of the finite nature of fossil fuels and their pollution. BMW is facing up to these challenges.

BMW aims to make pioneering contributions to ensure "sustainable mobility" including "CleanEnergy," involving use of hydrogen obtained from renewable sources. To this end, BMW produced the world's first fleet of hydrogen-powered combustion engines (BMW 750hLs). BMW also embraces two additional concepts—"Design for Recycling" and "Life Cycle Assessment (LCA)" for the integration of environmental and recycling requirements.

Design for Recycling ensures that after its useful lifetime a BMW Group vehicle can be recycled simply and economically. To achieve this, recycling requirements are taken into account in the product development process. The result is that current BMW Group vehicles can be recycled economically and almost completely.

Life Cycle Assessment is more comprehensive. It evaluates the ecological impact of new component concepts and bodywork variants over their entire product life cycle. From the extraction of raw materials and the manufacturing process to vehicle utilization and recycling, all environmental impacts are analyzed. The aim is to identify, among the development alternatives, those offering the greatest potential for increasing environmental compatibility throughout the entire life cycle of the vehicle.

www.bmw.com

Ford

Ford is in tune with carbon-neutral production and Bill Ford Jr. is a CEO for his time. With a commitment to production of 250,000 or more hybrids by 2010 (which the company admits now in fall 2006 it is unlikely to meet) and plans in place for flex-fuel vehicles that can run on plant-based E85 ethanol, Ford is making major contributions to American national security.

www.ford.com

Honda

Honda has long been promoting "zero emission" concepts to reduce waste generated from, and environmental impacts caused by, its factories to the minimum and eventually to nothing. In July 2000, by reducing the generation of waste and promoting recycling, they achieved "zero landfill disposal" at all of their plants in Japan.

American Honda Motor Co., Inc. announced that the all-new Honda Civic earned *Motor Trend* magazine's prestigious 2006 Car of the Year award. The award extends to the entire Civic Sedan and Civic Coupe lineup, including the environmentally responsible Civic Hybrid and high-performance Civic Si models.

www.honda.com

Toyota

What can you say about this company that hasn't already been said when it comes to revolutionizing the driving experience? The EPA's 2006 Fuel Economy Guide places Toyota cars, trucks, SUVs, station wagons, and minivans in the top ten of more EPA vehicle categories than any other brand. Additionally, the sum of Toyota vehicles in the top ten of all EPA categories is greater than those of any other maker. Toyota and Scion vehicles hold the number one position in the midsize car, subcompact car, and small station wagon categories for gasoline-powered vehicles.[61]

Not only has Toyota captured the number one position in the U.S. carbon-neutral market, it is also conceptualizing incredible vehicles that boast superb drivability and performance. In 1800, Alessandro Volta arranged zinc and copper discs in a column and invented the battery. Some two hundred years later, Toyota has electrified automotive history with the first high-performance hybrid, named in his honor. The Volta's 408-horsepower Hybrid Synergy Drive (a 3.3-liter V6 with an electric motor for each axle) not only delivers 435 miles on a 13.7-gallon tank but also sports zero to sixty acceleration in a mere four seconds. I think Count Volta is smiling.

www.toyota.com

Travel

Virgin Airlines

With soaring gas prices, all of the airlines have to make adjustments wherever possible to improve fuel efficiency. So what makes Virgin stand out in this inherently emissions conscious category?

Virgin is the first airline to get serious about alternative fuel sources. In November 2005, Virgin Chairman Richard Branson revealed, "We are going to start building cellulosic ethanol plants (to make) fuel that is derived from the waste product of the plant."[62] Branson admits that they are still in the very early stages of development, but stated that he believes cellulosic ethanol will be the future of fuel, and over the next twenty to thirty years should replace traditional fuels.

As for what we can expect in the next few years, of the 700 million gallons of fuel used each years by Virgin's four airlines, Branson says, "I hope that over the next five to six years we can replace some or all of that" with plant-based ethanol.[63]

www.virgin-atlantic.com

Waste and Environmental Management

Waste Management, North America's largest waste and environmental management company in the United States, has shown some consciousness (though, as one of their customers, I think they have a lot further to go in terms of educating on recycling and making the process more friendly to their customers. On the other hand, I see glimmers of hope.) In April 2003, BMW hosted a press conference in Greenville, South Carolina, to celebrate a methane gas-to-energy project created by BMW, Waste Management, and Ameresco Energy Services.[64] The project produces both electricity and hot water and will supply 25 percent of the plant's energy. The methane, conveyed by the 9.5-mile Ameresco pipeline to the plant, fuels four turbines that power generators to create electricity for heating and air conditioning and for heating water for manufacturing needs.

The project, providing enough energy to heat fifteen thousand homes a year, offers a consistent source of fuel and helps stabilize the plant's power costs. The plant, with more than forty-six hundred employees, produces BMW Z4 roadsters and X5 sports activity vehicles. As a result of this project, BMW is one of the largest private holders of greenhouse gas emissions reduction credits in the United States.

Other significant and progressive moves that the company has made follow.

In January 2003, Waste Management announced the formation of a new recycling organization, Recycle America Alliance (RAA). The goal of the Alliance is to optimize the capacity and improve the profitability of the company's recycling line of business by combining assets and operations with a number of other key domestic recycling processors and marketers. The first partner in the Alliance is Milwaukee, Wisconsin–based The Peltz Group, the country's largest privately held recycler that handles more than 2 million tons of recyclable fiber annually.[65]

Under the agreement, Waste Management will combine the majority of its recycling processing assets with The Peltz Group's assets to form a new company that will provide recycling, materials to brokerage services, container processing and trading, a service that allows customers to stabilize the price of their commodities. Waste Management will own approximately 90 percent of Recycle America Alliance and will be consolidating the company financially. The Peltz Group will own the remaining interest of the new company, which will operate as a consolidated subsidiary of Waste Management and will be directed by a management team made up of former officers and managers of both companies.

In January 2003, Waste Management, along with fourteen other companies, joined the Chicago Climate Exchange as a founding member. The CCX is a nongovernmental entity established to develop a voluntary marketplace for reducing and trading greenhouse gas emissions.[66]

Wood Products

Bowater

One of the world's largest paper suppliers, Bowater has taken a leadership role by signing a solemn covenant with the Southern forest protection group Dogwood Alliance to engage in certified sustainable harvesting and the elimination of purchases made from privately managed monoculture forests that eliminate biological diversity. Bowater is one of the nation's largest purchasers of recycled tires and newspapers, which it uses for energy and as a major paper source.

www.bowater.com

Centex

Centex, one of the leading home builders in the United States, is also a leader in land conservation efforts. The Centex Homes Land Legacy

Fund, managed by the highly respected Conservation Fund, helps to finance land and water preservation projects across the United States.

Additionally, Centex is committed to using responsible wood suppliers who are certified through one of Centex's three accepted certification programs. Since 2000, the number of certified producers Centex works with has jumped from 28 percent to 80 percent. This not only demonstrates their commitment to responsible forestry in certified forests, but also a commitment to eliminate the use of wood from endangered forests.

In an effort to save Indonesia's rain forests, Centex eliminated purchases of Indonesian lauan as flooring under layer since the tropical hardwood is often derived through illegal forestry practices.

www.centex.com

Domtar

Although a forest products company, Domtar truly strives to leave as small a footprint as possible on the forests they are managing. The company is highly regarded within the industry and by environmentalists who recognize that the company is serious about its responsibilities, shown most clearly by Forest Stewardship Council certification of some eighty-four thousand acres of forest lands in the Adirondacks. Domtar uses recycled fibers wherever possible. However, because most of their products require virgin fibers, Domtar works with the Forest Stewardship Council to develop extensive guidelines for the forests they manage. The company holds its suppliers accountable as well.

Domtar also obtained ISO 14001 environmental certification for its forestry management practices in over 18 million acres of directly managed forest land. ISO 14001 is the internationally recognized standard for Environmental Management Systems and demonstrates that companies are meeting, or striving to meet, exemplary standards of environmental and, in this case, forest, stewardship. The ultimate goal is for Domtar to have all suppliers certified to Forest Stewardship Council or equivalent certification standards. The company gives preference to Forest Stewardship Council–certified suppliers.

www.domtar.com

Forest Stewardship Council

Thanks to the FSC, forests throughout the world are being managed to provide long-term value and to retain asset value, as well as to promote biological diversity and act as carbon sinks. Be wary of other so-called certifying groups, some of which are more lax and funded by the industry itself.

www.fsc.org

International paper

International Paper is among the charter members of the U.S. Environmental Protection Agency's National Environmental Performance Track program. This program is for facilities that are really going above and beyond in terms of doing what is right for the communities in which they are located and for the environment as a whole. When you are a paper company and whole towns and communities depend on your longevity, the ripple effect of good deeds or not so good deeds can actually morph into a locally occurring tidal wave. The EPA program recognizes facilities that consistently exceed regulatory requirements, work closely with their communities, and excel in protecting the environment and public health. As Dan Fiorino, director of National Environmental Performance Track puts it, "Performance Track status is reserved for those who are truly committed to environmental improvement and public outreach."

As you might expect, International Paper is committed to sustainable forestry in the forests they manage, and they use their status as the world's largest paper and forest products company to proactively encourage sustainability wherever possible. They are also partnered with the National Recycling Coalition to protect Canada's boreal forests and the southern forests of the United States.

www.internationalpaper.com

Lyme Timber Company

Lyme Timber is unique in that it is a forest land investor as opposed to a pure timber investor. In 1976 it was organized to invest in timberland and rural real estate for its own account and in partnership with other investors.

An important part of Lyme's forest-land investment strategy is to seek out properties with high conservation values, often in partnership with nonprofit conservation organizations or government agencies. Lyme's goal, when purchasing land, is not to simply purchase potentially profitable land for logging, but to invest in forest-land tracts with compelling qualities and values not fully recognized by others.

Lyme Timer follows the nine principles of sustainability set out by the Northern Forest Lands Council, including:[67]

- Maintenance of soil productivity
- Conservation of water quality, wetlands, and riparian zones
- Maintenance or creation of a healthy balance of forest age classes
- Continuous flow of timber, pulpwood, and other forest products
- Improvement of the overall quality of the timber resource as a foundation for more value-added opportunities
- Maintenance of scenic quality by limiting adverse aesthetic impacts of forest harvesting, particularly in high-elevation areas and vistas
- Conservation and enhancement of habitats that support a full range of native flora and fauna
- Protection of unique or fragile areas
- Continuation of opportunities for traditional recreation
  www.lymetimber.com

Endnotes

Preface

1. Nieves, E. "Antiwar Sentiment Galvanizes Thousands. Groups See Numbers Rise as They Reach Out to Supporters Via Internet, E-Mail." *Washington Post*, January 19, 2003:A16.

2. The editorial committee for Working Assets includes the following people: Peter Drekmeier, an environmental activist for fifteen years and cofounder of Bay Area Action who has worked on Earth Day 1990 and 2000, as well as statewide initiatives and local campaigns; Josh Karliner, founder and former executive director of CorpWatch and author of two books on globalization and the environment who is currently writing a third on climate change; China Brotsky, coauthor of the 1991 report *War in the Gulf: An Environmental Perspective* and vice president of Special Projects at Tides and on the board of Global Greengrants Fund and CorpWatch; Gar Smith, former editor of the award-winning *Earth Island Journal* and currently editor of weekly online ecozine *The Edge*; and Gopal Dayeneni, an antiwar and environmental activist and former oil campaigner for Project Underground. Other groups with prominent steering committee members include People and the Planet, Ecology Center, Tides Foundation, Rainforest Action Network, Friends of the Earth, Greenpeace, Student Environmental Action Coalition, Global Exchange, People for Livable and Affordable Neighborhoods, Plutonium Free Future, CorpWatch, Tri-Valley CAREs, Bay Area Nuclear Waste Coalition, Greenbelt Alliance,

Sierra Club, International Rivers Network, Environment California, Plight of the Redwoods Campaign, Environmental Working Group, and Environmental Law Foundation. Environmentalists Against War, from Berkeley, California, is another prime example.

ONE
Chemical Nation

1. "The Terrorist Threat to Ports." Office of the Attorney General. Office of Counter-Terrorism. Intelligence Report, Iddur 05-005, May 11, 2005.

2. In documents dated May 11, 2005, and labeled for OFFICIAL USE ONLY "The Terrorist Threat to Ports." Office of the Attorney General. Office of Counter-Terrorism. Intelligence Report, Iddur 05-005, May 11, 2005.

3. Bayonne with its large Italian and Irish populations: www.city data.com. "Bayonne, New Jersey." Viewed September 24, 2005 at: http://www.city-data.com/city/Bayonne-New-Jersey.html.

4. Jersey City with a higher percentage of African Americans: www.citydata.com. "Jersey City, New Jersey." Viewed September 24, 2005, at: http://www.city-data.com/city/Jersey-City-New-Jersey.html.

5. Elizabeth (largely hispanic): www.citydata.com. "Elizabeth, New Jersey." Viewed September 24, 2005, at: http://www.city-data.com/city/Elizabeth-New-Jersey.html.

6. Newark (more than half African American): www.citydata.com. "Newark, New Jersey." Viewed September 24, 2005, at: http://www.city data.com/city/Newark-New-Jersey.html.

7. "Chemical Time Bombs." *New York Times*, May 10, 2005. See the excellent series of articles and editorials from the *New York Times* at nytimes.com/insecurenation.

8. "An Insecure Nation; Our Unnecessary Insecurity." *New York Times*, Late Edition, Final, February 20, 2005:8.

9. Kilian, M. "Risk Seen at Chemical Plants." *Chicago Tribune*, July 14, 2005:16.

10. Malone, J. "Study: Refineries put Millions of People at Risk. 50 Sites, Including 12 in Texas, Use Toxic Acid; They're Called 'Sitting

Ducks' for Terrorism." *Austin American-Statesman*, August 5, 2005. Viewed at: http://www.statesman.com/news/content/news/stories/08/5refineries.html#.

11. "Agenda. Securing Our Chemical Plants." www.corzine. senate.gov." Viewed September 24, 2005, at: http://corzine.senate.gov/priorities/chem_sec.html.

12. Fortunately, in the event of an attack: "Senate Unanimously Passes Corzine Resolution on Plant Security." *Newsday*, July 14, 2005, 12:42 PM EDT. Viewed September 24, 2005, at: http://corzine.senate.gov/clippings/chemsec_newsday.pdf.

TWO
Be a Green Patriot

1. John Paige, a member of the Pentagon police force. Interview with Paige, September 18, 2005, at the Pentagon entrance. Thank you, John, for a great talk, and good luck with the Mobile DJ.

2. Schwartz, P. and Randall, D. "An Abrupt Climate Change Scenario and Its Implications for United States National Security." Emeryville, Calif.: Global Business Network, October 2003: 22 pp. Obtained at www.gbn.com.

3. Townsend, M. and Harris, P. "Now the Pentagon Tells Bush: Climate Change Will Destroy Us." *The Observer*, February 22, 2004. Viewed September 25, 2005, at: http://observer.guardian.co.uk/international/story/0,6903,1153513,00.html.

4. Stipp, D. "Climate Collapse. The Pentagon's Weather Nightmare. The Climate Could Change Radically, and Fast. That Would Be the Mother of All National Security Issues." *Fortune*, January 26, 2004.

5. Andrew Marshall Townsend, M. and Harris, P. "Now the Pentagon tells Bush: Climate Change Will Destroy Us." *The Observer*, February 22, 2004. Viewed September 25, 2005, at: http://observer.guardian.co.uk/international/story/0,6903,1153513,00.html.

6. McGray, D. "The Marshall Plan." *Wired*, February 2003 (11.20). Viewed at: http://www.wired.com/wired/archive/11.02/marshall.html.

7. "Two very simple events triggered the report" Interview with Peter Schwartz by phone, April 6, 2005.

8. Stipp, D. "Climate Collapse. The Pentagon's Weather Nightmare. The Climate Could Change Radically, and Fast. That Would Be the Mother of All National Security Issues." *Fortune*, January 26, 2004.

9. Adams, J. et al. "Sudden Climate Transitions during the Quaternary." *Progress in Physical Geography*, 1999;23(1):1–36. Viewed at: http://www.ingentaconnect.com/content/arn/pipg/1999/00000023/000 00001/art00001.

10. Taylor, K.C. et al. "The 'Flickering Switch' of Late Pleistocene Climate Change." *Nature*, 1993;361:432–36.

11. "A Chilling Possibility." Science@NASA, March 5, 2004. Viewed at: http://science.nasa.gov/headlines/y2004/05mar_arctic.htm.

12. Gagosian, R. B. "Abrupt Climate Change: Should We Be Worried?" Prepared for a panel on abrupt climate change at the World Economic Forum, Davos, Switzerland, January 27, 2003.

13. Friedman, T. L. "The Geo-Green Alternative." *New York Times*, January 30, 2005.

14. Friedman, T. L. Interview on Imus in the Morning. MSNBC, January 31, 2005.

15. Haass, R. "The World on His Desk: A Briefing for the Weary Winner from the Man in Charge of Policy and Planning at the State Department in 2001–03." *The Economist*, November 4, 2004.

16. Sachs, J. D. "Ecology and Political Upheaval." *Scientific American*, July 2006:37.

THREE
Put Good Food on Your Table

1. Luna, C. "Driver Is Shot from Pickup Truck." *Los Angeles Times*, April 25, 2005, B1, B7.

2. Wright, M. A. Interview with director of sustainable transportation at Ford. LOHAS, 2005.

3. Koenig, B. "Moody's Rates GM, Ford Stock Junk." *Detroit Free Press*, August 25, 2005. Viewed at: http://www.freep.com/money/autonews/moodys25e_20050825.htm.

4. Presented as Carl O. Sauer Memorial Lecture, Alumni House, University of California, Berkeley, April 30, 1986. Professor Parsons

became Professor Emeritus at the university two months after this lecture, which is here slightly revised from the original.

5. *Gasping for Air*. The Women's Foundation of California, p. 3. Viewed at: http://www.womensfoundca.org/atf/cf/{F4E8B0D2-94CD-4B29-B9F4-FEE4BA76EAE1}/cv.pdf.

6. *Gasping for Air*. The Women's Foundation of California, p. 1. Viewed at: http://www.womensfoundca.org/atf/cf/{F4E8B0D2-94CD-4B29-B9F4-FEE4BA76EAE1}/cv.pdf.

7. *California's Central Valley*, NPR series profiles the state's "backstage" rural breadbasket, November 11–14, 2002. Part Two: "The Problem with Pesticides." Viewed at: http://www.npr.org/programs/atc/features/2002/nov/central_valley/.

8. Kegley, S. et al. *Hooked on Poison: Pesticide Use in California 1991–1998*. San Francisco, Calif.: Pesticide Action Network and Californians for Pesticide Reform, 2002; cited in Funders Agricultural Working Group (2001), p. 6. Available online at www.panna.org/campaign/docsWorkers/CPRreport.pdf>.

9. Presented as Carl O. Sauer Memorial Lecture, Alumni House, University of California, Berkeley, April 30, 1986. Professor Parsons became Professor Emeritus at the university two months after this lecture, which is here slightly revised from the original.

10. *Gasping for Air*. The Women's Foundation of California, p. 1. Viewed at: http://www.womensfoundca.org/atf/cf/{F4E8B0D2-94CD-4B29-B9F4-FEE4BA76EAE1}/cv.pdf.

11. "Farm Subsidy Database." Environmental Working Group. Viewed June 29, 2005, at: http://www.ewg.org/farm/top_recips.php?fips=06000&progcode=total.

12. According to the Environmental Working Group: Most taxpayers have probably never heard of an obscure USDA corporate subsidy program for cotton, called "Step 2." First established in the 1990 Farm Bill, "Step 2" cost $2.16 billion over the past nine years, and provided a handful of corporations more than $80 million apiece. The program is also at the center of a major international debate over the adverse impacts of U.S. subsidies on agriculture and poverty in developing countries. The "Step 2" program takes money from taxpayers and gives it to American companies that export or mill (i.e., process into fabric or yarn)

cotton, so that they will buy cotton grown right here in the United States. The financial encouragement is necessary because U.S. cotton is considerably more expensive than cotton grown elsewhere around the world. Why is it more expensive? Because of other subsidies taxpayers provide—to American cotton farmers. Those subsidies, which totaled $14.1 billion between 1995 and 2003, artificially push the price of U.S. cotton above world market levels, reducing the international competitiveness of U.S. cotton farmers and their crop.

Without "Step 2" subsidies, its proponents argue, cotton exporters would not be able to sell overpriced, subsidized American cotton overseas. They would be priced out of the international market, a major problem, considering that over 30 percent of U.S. cotton is exported. "Step 2" payments allow American cotton exporters to sell cotton at a competitive price because American taxpayers subsidize the transactions.

Similarly, "Step 2" payments to cotton millers make it possible for them to buy cotton grown here, instead of importing foreign cotton that costs less—often substantially less—because its price is not inflated by farmer subsidies. The reason, again, is that American taxpayers make up the difference.

An EWG review of data obtained from the USDA under the Freedom of Information Act (FOIA) shows that a total of $2.16 billion in "Step 2" payments were made to 311 cotton exporters and millers between 1995 and 2003. The payments ranged from $151,480,436 reported for the Allenberg Cotton Company of Cordova Tennessee, to $126 reported paid to Hogan & Associates, Inc., of Humboldt, Tennessee. Most "Step 2" payments were highly concentrated among only fourteen firms (4 percent), each of which collected at least $50 million and together accounted for half the total payments, or $1.2 billion. The top four firms collected more than $100 million each from taxpayers over this period, a total of $530 million, or 25 percent of total program payments.

13. Buttonwillow Land & Cattle Co. "Farm Subsidy Database." Environmental Working Group. Viewed June 29, 2005, at: http://www.ewg.org/farm/top_recips.php?fips=06000&progcode=total.

14. Coye, M. and Goldman, L. R. "Summary of Environmental Data: McFarland Childhood Cancer Cluster Investigation," Environmental

Epidemiology and Toxicology Program, California Department of Health Services, 1991. Filename: 10-Coye-1991-Summary.rtf. Viewed July 29, 2005, at: http://www.ehib.org/cma/papers/10_Coye_1991_McFarland.pdf.

15. Warren, J. "Mysterious Cancer Clusters Leave Anxiety in 3 Towns." *Los Angeles*, July 12, 1992:1.

16. Coye, M. and Goldman, L.R. "Summary of Environmental Data: McFarland Childhood Cancer Cluster Investigation," Environmental Epidemiology and Toxicology Program, California Department of Health Services, 1991. Filename: 10-Coye-1991-Summary.rtf. Viewed July 29, 2005, at: http://www.ehib.org/cma/papers/10_Coye_1991_McFarland.pdf.

17. Interview with McFarland Public Works Office, April 22, 2005.

18. M. Anway et al. "Epigenetic Transgenerational Actions of Endocrine Disruptors and Male Fertility," *Science* 308 (June 3, 2005):1466–69.

19. Tonga McCormick, E. and Reynolds, H. "Too Young to Die." *San Francisco Chronicle*, October 3, 2004.

20. "Summary of Results from the California Pesticide Illness Surveillance Program—2002." California Environmental Protection Agency, Department of Pesticide Regulation Worker Health and Safety Branch, 1001 I Street, Sacramento, California 95814, February 26, 2004. Viewed June 29, 2005 at: http://www.cdpr.ca.gov/docs/whs/pdf/hs1851.pdf.

21. Arax, M. and Polakovic, G. "A Bumper Crop of Bad Air in San Joaquin Valley." *Los Angeles Times*, December 8, 2002, A1. Viewed at: www.sactaqc.org/Resources/Literature/AirQuality/AQ_SJ_120802.html.

22. Grossi, M. "For Sixth Year, Valley Leads Nation in Clean Air Violations. 104 Eight-Hour Days Far Ahead of LA, Houston." *Fresno Bee*, November 6, 2004. Viewed at the *Modesto Bee* site July 22, 2005, at: http://www.modbee.com/local/story/9383520p-10291544c.html.

23. News report. KGET 970, Kern County, California, May 23, 2005.

24. "Pesticide (POISON) Mist Forces Evacuations." Associated Press, November 15, 1999. Viewed July 22, 2005, at: http://www.safe2use.com/ca-ipm/0099-11-17.html.

25. German, E. "A Toxic Nightmare: The Dunsmuir Metam Sodium Spill Revisited. *Sonoma County Free Press*, July 1997. Viewed at: http://www.sonomacountyfreepress.com/reaction/a_toxic_nightmare.html.

26. Steinbeck, J. *The Grapes of Wrath*. Garden City, N.Y.: Sun Dial Press, 1941:345–46.

27. Wilkes, J. A. "CBRNE-Lung-Damaging Agents, Chloropicrin." EMedicine, December 13, 2005. Viewed at: http://www.emedicine.com/EMERG/topic907.htm.

28. "Organic Diet Makes Rats Healthier." University of Tyne Upon Newcastle. Press Release. Sciencedaily.com, March 29, 2005. Viewed at: http://www.sciencedaily.com/releases/2005/03/050328182123.htm.

29. Brandt, K. "Re: Organic Diet." E-mail, April 15, 2005.

30. Ettel, H. "Reich Orders EPA to Reinstate Scientist. Extends Jurisdiction of Environmental Whistleblower Laws to EPA Employees." National Whistleblower Center, February 10, 1994. Viewed at: http://www.fluoridealert.org/health/cancer/ntp/marcus3.html.

31. Herbert, H. J. "EPA Ordered to Reinstate Whistleblower." Associated Press, December 8, 1992. Viewed at: http://www.fluoridealert.org/health/cancer/ntp/marcus1.html.

32. FDA Total Diet Study "Food and Drug Administration Total Diet Study. Summary of Residues Found Ordered by Food and Market Baskets 91-3-01-4. U.S. Food and Drug Administration, June 2003. Viewed at: http://www.cfsan.fda.gov/~acrobat/TDS1byfd.pdf.

33. This is in addition to the petrochemicals benzene, carbaryl, chlorpyrifos, diazinon, endosulfan, toluene and trichloroethylene, styrene, and propargite. See "Food and Drug Administration Total Diet Study." Ibid.

34. Malins, D.C. et al. "The Etiology and Prediction of Breast Cancer." *Cancer* 75(2) (1995):503–17.

35. "Potentially Cancer-Causing Damage Common in Breast." PR Newswire, January 8, 1995.

36. Lyman, F. "New Reasons for Eating Organic? Study Finds Pesticide-Free Diet May Be Beneficial for Children." MSNBC. Your Environment, November 4, 2003. Viewed at: http://msnbc.msn.com/id/3076638/.

37. *Environmental Health Perspectives* Curl, C. L., Fenske, R. A., and Elgethun, K. "Organophosphorus Pesticide Exposure of Urban and Suburban Preschool Children with Organic and Conventional Diets." *Environmental Health Perspectives* 111 (2003):377–82.

38. Lawrence, F. "Food Study Reveals Hidden £9bn Costs of Transport."

The Guardian, July 15, 2005, online edition. Viewed July 15, 2005, at: http://www.guardian.co.uk/waste/story/0,12188,1528964,00.html.

39. Fulmer, M. "Lure of the Aisles: Ronald Burkle Has Made Billions in Supermarket Deals. Now He Hopes to Turn Around Two Struggling Chains." *Los Angeles Times*, April 11, 2005.

FOUR
Put Good Products in Your Home

1. "President Bush Delivers State of the Union Address." United States Capitol, Washington, D.C. The White House. Viewed at: http://www.whitehouse.gov/news/releases/2006/01/20060131-10.html.

2. Goffman, E. "God Humanity, and Nature: Comparative Religious Views of the Environment." Viewed at: http://www.csa.com/discoveryguides/envrel/review.php.

3. Polyethylene pellets are used "PVC v. PE Pellets in Beanie Babies." About Beanies.com. Accessed June 2, 2005, at: http://www.aboutbeanies.com/articles/print.cgi?file=pvc.html.

4. Viewed at: http://www.vinylinfo.org/pressmaterials/factsheets/benefits_safety.html.

5. Chiazze, L. et al. "Mortality Among Employees of PVC Fabricators." *Journal of Occupational Medicine* 19(9) (September 1977): 623–28.

6. Maltoni, C. et al. "Carcinogenicity Bioassays of Vinyl Chloride Monomer: A Model of Risk Assessment on an Experimental Basis." *Environmental Health Perspectives* 41 (1981):3–30.

7. Feron, V. J. et al. "Life-Span Oral Toxicity Study of Vinyl Chloride in Rats." *Food Cosmetics Toxicology*. 19 (1981):317–33.

8. Infante, P. F. and Pesák, J. "A Historical Perspective of Some Occupationally Related Diseases of Women." *Journal of Occupational Medicine* 36(8) (1994):826–31.

9. "PVC v. PE Pellets in Beanie Babies." About Beanies.com. Accessed June 2, 2005, at: http://www.aboutbeanies.com/articles/print.cgi?file=pvc.html.

10. Davidson, S. "Putting the Squeeze on Petroleum: Chemists Make Plastics from Oranges." Cornell News Service. Viewed at: http://www.news.cornell.edu/Chronicle/05/1.20.05/plastics-oranges.html.

11. This list includes Calgon Hawaiian Ginger Body Mist, Calgon Turquoise Seas Body Lotion, Charlie Cologne Spray, Escape by Calvin Klein, Eternity by Calvin Klein, Fire & Ice Cologne Spray, Freedom, Jovan White Musk, Lancome Paris Tresor, Liz Claiborne Eau De Toilette Spray, Oscar Parfums de Coeur White Tahitian Ginger Fantasy, Poison by Christian Dior, Red Door, The Healing Garden Pure Joy Body Treatment, White Diamonds Elizabeth Taylor, and Wind Song Extraordinary Cologne by Prince Matchabelli.

12. See for example: http://www.nottoopretty.org/goodbad.htm.

13. See for example: http://www.nottoopretty.org/goodbad.htm.

14. According to its Web site, the Campaign for Safe Cosmetics is a coalition of public health, educational, faith, labor, women's, environmental, and consumer groups. Their goal is to protect the health of consumers and workers by requiring the health and beauty industry to phase out the use of chemicals linked to cancer, birth defects, and other health problems and replace them with safer alternatives. Accessed June 3, 2005, at: http://www.safecosmetics.org/about/.

15. "The Rules Governing Cosmetic Products in the European Union." European Commission. Enterprise Directorate-General, 1999. Accessed June 3, 2005, at: http://pharmacos.eudra.org/F3/cosmetic/pdf/vol_1en.pdf.

16. Consumer Product Safety Commission. "CPSC Releases Study on Phthalates in Teethers, Rattles and Other Children's Products." December 2, 1998. Release # 99-031.

17. Latini, G. et al. "In Utero Exposure to Di-(2-ethylhexyl)-phthalate and Human Pregnancy Duration." Environmental Health Perspectives, 111(14) (2003):1783–1785

18. "Quick Facts. Preterm Birth Overview." March of Dimes. Accessed June 3, 2005, at: http://www.marchofdimes.com/peristats/tlanding.aspx?reg=99&lev=0&top=3&slev=1.

19. Boggan, S. "Is my baby a boy? Is it a girl? No one could tell me." the London Times, July 26, 2005. Viewed at: http://timesonline.co.uk/printFriendly/0,,1-100-1707787,00.html

20. Chepesiuk, R. "Synthetic Chemicals In Household Products Damaging the Human Species?" StraightGoods.com 8-13-1. Accessed at: http://www.rense.com/general12/species.htm.

21. Sugiura-Ogasawara, M. "Exposure to Bisphenol A Is Associated with Recurrent Miscarriage." *Human Reproduction*. Advance Access published online on June 9, 2005. Viewed June 13, 2005 at: http://humrep.oxfordjournals.org/cgi/content/abstract/deh888v1?maxtoshow=&HITS=10&hits=10&RESULTFORMAT=1&author1=Sugiura-Ogasawara&andorexacttitle=and&andorexacttitleabs=and&andorexactfulltext=and&searchid=1118655515408_685&stored_search=&FIRSTINDEX=0&sortspec=relevance&fdate=6/1/2004&journalcode=humrep.

22. "Bisphenol-A linked to recurrent miscarriages." *Food Production Daily*, June 13, 2005. Viewed at: http://www.foodproductiondaily.com/news/news-ng.asp?n=60610-new-study-links.

23. Anonymous. "Occupational Exposure to Synthetic Estrogens—Puerto Rico." *Morbidity and Mortality Weekly Report*, Centers for Disease Control 26(13) (1977):101.

24. Schell, O. *Modern Meat*. New York: Random House, 1985: 281–96.

25. Colón, I. et al. "Identification of Phthalate Esters in the Serum of Young Puerto Rican Girls with Premature Breast Development." *Environmental Health Perspectives* 108(9) (2000):895–900.

26. Cosmetic Ingredient Review. *1996 CIR Compendium*. Washington, D.C.: Cosmetic Ingredient Review, 1996:42.

27. "Bioassay of 1,4-Dioxane for Possible Carcinogenicity (CAS No. 123-91-1)." National Toxicology Program, TR-80.

28. *Report on Carcinogens*, 11th ed. U.S. Department of Health and Human Services, Public Health Service, National Toxicology Program. Viewed at: http://ntp.niehs.nih.gov/ntp/roc/eleventh/profiles/s080diox.pdf.

29. *Sixth Annual Report on Carcinogens, 1991. Summary*. U.S. Department of Health and Human Services, Public Health Service. National Institute of Environmental Health Sciences, Research Triangle Park, North Carolina, 1991:192–95.

30. Black, R. E. et al. "Occurrence of 1,4-Dioxane in Cosmetic Raw Materials and Finished Cosmetic Products." *Journal of the Association of Official Analytical Chemists*.

31. Spath, D. P. "1,4-Dioxane Action Level." March 24, 1998. Memorandum from Spath who is chief of the Division of Drinking Water and Environmental Management Department of Health Services, 601 North

7th Street, Sacramento, California 95814 to George Alexeeff, Deputy Director for Scientific Affairs, Office of Environmental Health Hazard Assessment. Accessed June 6, 2005, at: http://www.oehha.ca.gov/water/pals/pdf/PAL14DIOXAN.pdf.

32. "Toxicology and Carcinogenesis Studies of Coconut Oil Acid Diethanolamine Condensate (CAS NO. 68603-42-9) in F344/N Rats and B6C3F1 Mice (Dermal Studies)." National Toxicology Program, TR-479.

33. "Toxicology and Carcinogenesis Studies of Lauric Acid Diethanolamine Condensate (CAS NO. 120-40-1) in F344/N Rats and B6C3F1 Mice (Dermal Studies)." National Toxicology Program, TR-480.

34. The discovery of the estrogenicity of the parabens serves to strengthen the case that cosmetics can have a profound impact on human health. Recent reports raise disturbing questions about the safety of preservatives called parabens (namely, methyl-, ethyl-, propyl-, and butylparaben), which are listed on labels and have been identified as xenoestrogens.

Researchers who've studied the estrogenicity of the parabens conclude that, "Given their use in a wide range of commercially available topical preparations, it is suggested that the safety in use of these chemicals should be reassessed."

Leave-on products such as facial makeup and skin lotions are of greatest concern because of the long exposure time and opportunity for migration via the skin into the bloodstream. In addition, all products used by women of childbearing age and on young children should also be cause for concern.

In this case, our concern is the recently discovered inadvertent estrogenicity of the parabens. The estrogenic effects of certain synthetic chemicals, and their subsequent effects on the endocrine system of humans and wildlife, has been extensively documented—especially in relation to women's risk of breast cancer and reproductive abnormalities in young boys exposed to such chemicals either prior to puberty or as fetuses, which may increase risk for undescended testicles, testicular cancer, sperm abnormalities, and prostate disorders.

The Paraben Paradox

For many years, parabens were considered among those preservatives with low systemic toxicity, primarily causing allergic reactions. However, as we have become aware that some synthetic chemicals mimic the female hormone estrogen, our understanding of the toxic effects of both synthetic and natural substances has changed.

Now, researchers from the Department of Biology & Biochemistry, Brunel University, Uxbridge, Middlesex, have found that alkyl hydroxy benzoate preservatives (namely methyl-, ethyl-, propyl-, and butyl-paraben) are weakly estrogenic. In an estrogen receptor-binding assay, butylparaben was able to compete with the female hormone estradiol for binding to the rat estrogen receptor with an affinity approximately five orders of magnitude lower than that of diethylstilbestrol (a highly carcinogenic synthetic estrogen), and between one and two orders of magnitude less than nonylphenol (an estrogenic synthetic industrial chemical).

Although it is reassuring to note that when administered orally, the parabens were inactive, and subcutaneous administration of butylparaben produced a positive estrogenic response on uterine tissues. Although approximately one hundred thousand times less potent than 17 beta-estradiol, greater exposure to the parabens may compensate for their lower potency.

The researchers conclude that "given their use in a wide range of commercially available topical preparations, it is suggested that the safety in use of these chemicals should be reassessed."

Effects on Developing Fetuses

Parabens are p-hydroxybenzoic acid ester compounds widely used as preservatives in foods, cosmetics, toiletries, and pharmaceuticals. These compounds exert a weak estrogenic activity as determined by *in vitro* estrogen receptor and *in vivo* uterotrophic assays. Their use in cosmetics is particularly troubling because their absorption into the bloodstream bypasses the gastrointestinal tract where they might be broken down. In other words, cosmetic products likely deliver one of the most potent dosages.

In the July 2002 issue of the *Archives of Toxicology*, Dr. S. Oishi of the Department of Toxicology, Tokyo Metropolitan Research Laboratory of

Public Health, Japan, reported that exposure of newborn male mammals to *butyl*paraben "adversely affects the secretion of testosterone and the function of the male reproductive system."

"In this paper, we have shown that butylparaben had an adverse effect on the male mouse reproductive system and that it damaged the late steps of spermatogenesis in the testis," the researcher reports. "A dose-dependent decrease of both round and elongated spermatid counts in stages VII–VIII seminiferous tubules was observed, and the elongated spermatid counts were significantly lower in all of the treated groups. . . . The serum testosterone concentration decreased in a dose-dependent fashion and was significant at 1.00%. These data demonstrated that butylparaben can exert an adverse effect on the male reproductive system *at doses that are well below those of the accepted daily intake (ADI) in Japan.*"

A few months later in the December issue of *Food and Chemical Toxicology*, the researcher reported that closely related *propyl*paraben "adversely affects the hormonal secretion and the male reproductive functions." The cauda epididymal sperm reserves and concentrations decreased in a dose-dependent manner and the difference was significant at higher doses. "Daily sperm production and its efficiency in the testis of all groups receiving propylparaben significantly decreased. The serum testosterone concentration decreased in a dose-dependent manner and the decrease was significant in the group that received the highest dose. *The exposure level at which this effect was observed is the same as the upper-limit acceptable daily intake (10 mg/kg body weight/day) of parabens in the European Community and Japan.*"

Earlier, Dr. Oishi reported that sperm counts among animals receiving the highest doses of specific parabens were 58.2 percent of control values. "The daily sperm production (DSP) in the testis was also significantly lower in all treated groups when compared to controls. Serum testosterone concentration was lowered dose-dependently and was significant at 0.1% or more." Once again, we are reminded the daily intake of butylparaben that caused these disruptions "is similar to the lower level of acceptable daily intake (ADI) for parabens in the European Community (EC) and in Japan. The results of the present experiments show for the first time that exposure of a postweaning mammal to butylparaben had an adverse effect on the secretion of testosterone and in the functions of the male reproductive system."

These results are confirmed and extended by additional experimental research independent of the work of Dr. Oishi and reported on in the March 2002 issue of the *Journal of Veterinary Medical Science*.

Not only were live birth and postnatal survival rates decreased among newborns whose mothers were exposed to parabens during pregnancy, but also "the weights of testes, seminal vesicles and prostate glands were significantly decreased," report researchers at the Department of Veterinary Public Health, College of Veterinary Medicine and School of Agricultural Biotechnology, Seoul National University, Suwon, Korea. The Korean researchers further state, "The sperm count and the sperm motile activity in the epididymis were significantly decreased at doses of 100 and 200 mg/kg of BP (i.e., butylparaben). In accordance with the sperm count in the epididymis, the number of round spermatids and elongated spermatids in the seminiferous tubule (stage VII) were significantly decreased by BP. . . . Taken together, these results indicated that maternal exposure of BP might have adverse effects on the . . . male offspring."

35. 1992 Toxics Release Inventory. Public Data Release. Office of Pollution Prevention and Toxics (7408), U.S. Environmental Protection Agency, Washington, D.C.

36. "CBC MARKETPLACE: Household Cleaners: If You Can't Pronounce It, Should You Use It?" Reporter: Wendy Mesley; Producer: Gaelyne Leslie; Researcher: Louisa Jaslow. Viewed at: http://www.cbc.ca/consumers/market/files/home/cleaners/index2.html.

37. fresh round of studies Ibid.

38. Till, C. et al. "Prenatal Exposure to Organic Solvents and Child Neurobehavioral Performance." *Neurotoxicology and Teratology* 23(3) (2001):235–45.

39. Lazlo-Baker, D. et al. "Child Neurodevelopmental Outcome and Maternal Occupational Exposure to Solvents." *Archives of Pediatric & Adolescent Medicine.* 158 (2004):956–61.

40. Shaffer, D. "Former 3M Chemical Is Widespread." *Star Tribune*, August 15, 2004.

41. Heilprin, J. "EPA Seeks Teflon Penalties against DuPont." Associated Press, December 6, 2004. Viewed at: http://www.enn.com/today.html?id=538

42. Olsen, G. W., Burlew, M. M., Burris, J. M., and Mandel, J. H.

A cross-sectional analysis of serum perfluorooctanesulfonate (PFOS) and perfluorooctanoate (PFOA) in relation to clinical chemistry, thyroid hormone, hematology and urinalysis results from male and female employee participants of the 2000 Antwerp and Decatur fluorochemical medical surveillance program. Final report. 3M Medical Department, 2001a.

43. Olsen, G. W., Burlew, M. M., Burris, J. M., and Mandel, J. H. A longitudinal analysis of serum perfluorooctanesulfonate (PFOS) and perfluorooctanoate (PFOA) in relation to lipid and hepatic clinical chemistry test results from male employee participants of the 1994/95, 1997, and 2000 fluorochemical medical surveillance program. Cited at: http://www.ewg.org/issues/pfcs/20041216/index.php.

44. Alexander, B. Mortality study of workers employed at the 3M Cottage Grove Facility. Final Report. Division of Environmental and Occupational Health, School of Public Health, University of Minnesota. AR 226-1136. Washington, D.C.: U.S. Environmental Protection Agency, 2001.

45. Eilperin, J. "Teflon Chemical's Potential Risk Cited." *Washington Post*, January 13, 2005.

46. Dauncey, G. "Earth Future: Ten Steps to Reduce Your Carbon Emissions. U.S. Version." Viewed June 9, 2005, at: http://www.earthfuture.com/tenstep/us.asp.

47. "About Us." Seventh Generation. Viewed at: http://www.seventhgeneration.com/site/pp.asp?c=coIHKTMHF&b=83249.

48. According to the company's Web site "Over 15 Years of Making a Difference. How Sevbenth Generation Came to Be . . ." Seventh Generation. Viewed at: http://www.seventhgeneration.com/site/pp.asp?c=coIHK-TMHF&b=90086.

49. Cortese, A. "Business; They Care about the World (and They Shop, Too)." *New York Times*, July 20, 2003.

50. Nachman-Hunt, N. "The Hunt for the Aging 78 Million-Pound Elephant." *LOHAS Journal* (spring 2003):26–31.

51. "Future Looks Bright for Green Commercial Cleaner Companies." *Nutrition Business Journal* (September 2004):10–11.

52. "Natural Cleaning Products Arise Later on the Healthy Lifestyles Learning Curve." *National Business Journal* (September 2004):8–9.

53. "About Us." Sun & Earth. Viewed at: http://www.sunandearth. com/aboutus.html.

54. "Future Looks Bright for Green Commercial Cleaner Companies." *Nutrition Business Journal* (September 2004):10–11.

55. "The Story of Uruku." Aveda. Viewed at: http://aveda.aveda. com/protect/we/default.asp#.

56. "Poisoned Cosmetics, Not too Pretty. American Products." Not Too Pretty. Viewed at: http://www.nottoopretty.org/goodbad.htm.

FIVE
Plant a Tree

1. Brophy, J. M. "Cardiovascular Risk Associated with Celecoxib." *New England Journal of Medicine* 352(25) (2005):2648–50; author reply 2648–50.

2. "Costa Rica Country Brief." The World Bank. Viewed at: http://web.worldbank.org/WBSITE/EXTERNAL/COUNTRIES/LA CEXT/COSTARICAEXTN/0,,menuPK:295422~pagePK:141132~piP K:141107~theSitePK:295413,00.html.

3. Welcome to Whole Foods Market. Whole Foods. Viewed at: http://www.wholefoodsmarket.com/company/index.html.

4. Oregon Tilth, an internationally recognized organic certification organization that ensures growers comply with organic standards, ensured the company's organic certification and that absolutely no pesticides or herbicides were being used.

5. Matsuyama, M., et al. "Expression of lipoxygenase in human prostate cancer and growth reduction by its inhibitors. *Internation Journal of Oncolology*, 24(4) (2004):821–27.

6. Ghosh, J. and Myers, C. E. "Arachidonic Acid Stimulates Prostate Cancer Cell Growth: Critical Role of 5-lipoxygenase." *Biochemical and Biophysical Research Communications*, 235(2) (1997):418–23.

7. Nie, D. et al. "Role of Eicosanoids in Prostate Cancer Progression." *Cancer and Metastasis Review.* 20(3–4) (2001):195–206.

8. In the February 2001 issue of *Cancer*, which is published by the highly regarded American Cancer Society, researchers tell us that they have "verified 5-LO up-regulation in malignant tissue that was not

present in benign tissue." Furthermore, these researchers add, levels of 5-HETE were found to be 2.2 fold greater in malignant prostate tumor tissue compared with benign tissue. "This study suggests that . . . selective 5-LO inhibitors in particular may be useful for prevention or therapy in patients with prostate carcinoma." See Gupta, S. et al. "Lipoxygenase-5 Is Overexpressed in Prostate Adenocarcinoma." *Cancer* 91(4) (2001):737–43.

The evidence becomes even more compelling. At the University of Virginia School of Medicine, Charlottesville, researchers note that "when the formation of 5-HETE is blocked, human prostate cancer cells enter apoptosis [programmed cell death] in less than one hour and are dead within two hours." However, "exogenous 5-HETE can rescue these cancer cells. These findings indicate that 5-HETE is a potent survival factor for human prostate cancer cells."

In another report from these same University of Virginia researchers, they assert that inhibition of 5-LO "triggers massive apoptosis in human prostate cancer cells." See Ghosh, J. and Myers, C. E. "Inhibition of Arachidonate 5-lipoxygenase Triggers Massive Apoptosis in Human Prostate Cancer Cells." *Proc Natl Acad Sci* 95(22) (1998):13182–87.

Some medical experts also now believe that benign prostatic hyperplasia (enlarged prostate) is linked with excess inflammatory mediators, such as 5-LO as well. So by inhibiting the 5-LO cascade, we also can reduce symptoms of BPH and risk for occurrence. See Myers, C. E. and Ghosh, J. "Lipxoygenase Inhibition in Prostate Cancer." *European Urology*, 35(5–6) (1999):395–98.

9. Gupta, S. et al. "Lipoxygenase-5 Is Overexpressed in Prostate Adenocarcinoma." *Cancer* 91(4) (2001):737–43.

10. Ghosh, J. and Myers, C. E. "Inhibition of Arachidonate 5-lipoxygenase Triggers Massive Apoptosis in Human Prostate Cancer Cells." *Proceedings of the National Academy of Sciences*, 95(22) (1998):13182–87.

11. *Cancer Letters* 172(2) (2001):111–18.

12. *Carcinogenesis* 24(9) (2003):1515–24.

13. Katz, A. *Dr. Katz's Guide to Prostate Health*. Los Angeles, Calif.: Freedom Press, 2006.

14. "Who We Are." Viewed at: http://www.bluelinxco.com/whoWeAre/main.asp.

15. "Investigation Finds 'IMD' In Indonesia: JP Morgan Chase and BlueLinx Linked to Illegal Logging of Endangered Forests and Resulting Humanitarian Crisis." Rainforest Action Network, February 24, 2005. Viewed at: http://www.enn.com/aff.html?id=434.

16. "Who We Are." Viewed at: http://www.bluelinxco.com/whoWeAre/main.asp.

17. An investigation in 2005 . . . ties JP Morgan Chase. On September 2, 2004, BlueLinx filed paperwork with the Securities and Exchange Commission for an initial public offering of common stock raising approximately $120 million. The required registration statement declared that BlueLinx has "a substantial amount of debt." An attached amendment submitted November 26, 2004, documented a credit agreement dated October 26, 2004, as Exhibit 10.18 listing JP Morgan Chase Bank as a documentation agent and a leading lender for a $165 million loan.

18. International Paper (IP), for example, recently completed two projects that illustrate how environmentally conscious projects benefit not only the company's own bottom line but also public health and local communities. At its mill in Courtland, Alabama, where IP makes the famous Hammermill brand of bond papers and Influence-coated web stock (for magazine and other types of industrial printing), steam was being released from time to time on a normal basis and within the air emissions permit. With natural gas prices rising, however, the mill decided to capture that steam (actually called waste heat) and reuse it in the process for heating water or drying paper. In so doing, the mill saves money, prices of products remain stable, and the reduced air emissions are equivalent to taking 12,800 SUVs off of our highways on an annual basis. Meantime, at IP's Bucksport, Maine, based mill, where the papermaker manufactures Liberty brand lightweight coated grades, company officials worked with EPA and Maine agencies on a project to reduce water use, solid waste generation, and air emissions. Instead of tackling one area or one compound, the group attacked all areas with a single solution. The installation of a new power-generating turbine resulted in lower natural gas consumption (favoring mill costs) and 70 percent reduced air emissions.

19. "Investigation Finds 'IMD' In Indonesia: JP Morgan Chase and BlueLinx Linked to Illegal Logging of Endangered Forests and

Resulting Humanitarian Crisis." Rainforest Action Network, February 24, 2005. Viewed at: http://www.enn.com/aff.html?id=434.

20. Barbara Tinley "Barbara V. Tinsley, Secretary/General Counsel at BlueLinx Holdings, Incorporated." Forbes.com. Viewed at: http://72.14.203.104/search?q=cache:-KZROHcIuUAJ:forbesbest.com/finance/mktguideapps/personinfo/FromPersonIdPersonTearsheet.jhtml%3FpassedPersonId%3D342344+,+Barbara+Tinsley,+bluelinx+general+counsel+compensation&hl=en.

21. "BlueLinx Holdings Inc. (BXC)." Salary.com. Viewed at: http://swz.salary.com/execcomp/layouthtmls/excl_companyreport_C10 02924_summary.html.

22. Olson, B. "RE: Bluelinx response from RAN." E-mail, September 29, 2005.

23. "[Indonesian] Timber Companies Go Bankrupt." *Jakarta Post*, May 14, 2005.

24. Report from the Forest Stewardship Council Cited in: "Lumber and Paper Giants to Announce Ban of Indonesian Wood and Pulp." Rainforest Action Network, May 15, 2003. Viewed at: http://www.ran.org/ran_campaigns/old_growth/indonesia/. Available for download at: http://www.walhi.or.id/. The Indonesian Forum for Environment (WALHI—Friends of the Earth Indonesia) is the largest forum of nongovernment and community-based organizations in Indonesia. It is represented in twenty-five provinces and has over 438 member organizations (as of June 2004). It stands for social transformation, people's sovereignty, and sustainability of life and livelihoods. WALHI works to defend Indonesia's natural world and local communities from injustice carried out in the name of economic development.

25. *"Illegal" Logging and Global Wood Markets: The Competitive Aspects on the U.S. Wood Products Industry*. Prepared for the American Forest & Paper Association by Seneca Creek Associates, LLC, 17203 Lightfoot Lane, Poolesville, Maryland 20837. Viewed at: http://www.afandpa.org/Content/NavigationMenu/About_AFandPA/Public_Calendar_and_Industry_Events/Events_Calendar/AFPAIlle galLoggingSummaryFINAL.pdf.

26. Bendeich, M. "Malaysia Seeks Crisis Talks over Choking Haze." August 11, 2005. Released at 02:26:17 GMT.

27. "Investigation Finds 'IMD' in Indonesia: JP Morgan Chase and BlueLinx Linked to Illegal Logging of Endangered Forests and Resulting Humanitarian Crisis." Ewire, February 24, 2005. Viewed at: http://www.ewire.com/display.cfm/Wire_ID/2491.

28. "A Leader in Global Financial Services." www.JPMorgan Chase.com. Viewed September 6, 2005, at: http://www.jpmorgan chase.com/cm/cs?pagename=Chase/Href&urlname=jpmc.

29. "Wood Purchasing Policy." Viewed at: http://www.homedepot.com/HDUS/EN_US/corporate/corp_respon/wood_purchasing_policy.shtml.

30. "Wood Purchasing Policy." Corporate Responsibility. The Home Depot. Viewed at: http://www.homedepot.com/HDUS/EN_US/corporate/corp_respon/wood_purchasing_policy.shtml.

31. See, for example: Staples Recycled Copy Paper. Accessed May 25, 2005, at: http://www.staples.com/Catalog/Browse/Sku.asp?PageType=1& Sku=492072.

32. "Recycled Copy Paper. Federal Standards and Testing." Minnesota Office of Environmental Assistance. (In the 2005 legislative session, the Office of Environmental Assistance and the Minnesota Pollution Control Agency became a new, combined department, "working to help Minnesotans protect their environment through assistance, training, permitting, compliance and outreach. By coordinating these approaches the new department will be able to work more effectively at protecting, conserving and improving our resources.") Viewed at: http://www.moea.state.mn.us/lc/purchasing/copypaper.cfm and http://www.moea.state.mn.us/about/index.cfm.

33. Ibid.

34. "Environmental Initiatives Overview." www.bowater.com. Accessed May 26, 2005, at: http://www.bowater.com/env_recycle.html.

35. Ashley, L. "#5 Coated Stock." Personal communication from Laura Ashley, senior marketing analyst for the Bowater Coated & Specialty Papers Division, via e-mail, May 17, 2005.

36. "Forest Watch. Photo Gallery." Dogwood Alliance. Viewed at: http://www.dogwoodalliance.org/site/fw_photo.asp.

37. World Wildlife Fund–US. "World Wildlife Fund Applauds Potlatch Corporation for Commitment to Responsible Forestry." May 4, 2005, Washington, D.C.

38. The specific products that carry the FSC certification include Synergy White 100PCW and Natural 100PCW. They are elemental chlorine free, and available as 24 lb Writing; 50, 70, 80 and 100 lb Text; 80 lb Cover and 110 lb Cover Double-Thick, in standard cut-size or folio sizes.

39. "About FedEx. Packaging and Recycling." Accessed at: http://www.fedex.com/us/about/responsibility/environment/recycling.html

40. See, for example: the company's information about their white paper towels. Viewed at: http://www.seventhgeneration.com/site/apps/nl/content.asp?c=coIHKTMHF&b=88674&ct=97125.

41. "The Latest Buzz on Recycling: Starbucks to Make Cups from Recycled Materials." *Nontoxic Times*, January 2005. Viewed at: http://www.seventhgeneration.com/site/pp.asp?c=coIHKTMHF&b=294329.

42. "America's Great Brands Applaud." Testimonials. Accessed May 25, 2005, at: http://www.rpa100.com/testimonials.html.

43. "Commitment." Viewed at:3http://www.generalmills.com/corporate/commitment/hse.aspx.

44. Pimm, S. L. and Jenkins, C. "Sutaining the Variety of Life." *Scientific American* (September 2005):66–73.

45. "Swingers and Gliders, Creepers and Crawlers." *Kids Discover Rain Forests*, p. 8. Viewed at: http://kidsdiscover.com/exploreFR.htm.

46. only 750 species Ibid.

47. Bryant, D. "The Last Frontier Forests: Ecosystems and Economics on the Edge." World Resources Institutes, 1997.

48. "About the Nature Conservancy." The Nature Conservancy. Viewed at: http://nature.org/aboutus/.

49. "Facts about Rainforests." The Nature Conservancy. Viewed at: http://nature.org/rainforests/explore/facts.html.

50. Cox, P. M. et al. "Acceleration of Global Warming Due to Carbon-Cycle Feedbacks in a Coupled Climate Model." *Nature* (2000);408.

51. See also Schimel, D. et al. in *Climate Change 1995: The Science of Climate Change*, edited by Houghton, J. T. et al. Cambridge, Mass.: Cambridge University Press, 1995:65–131.

SIX
Be Kind to Animals

1. Gordon, G. and Joiner-Bey, H. *The Omega-3 Miracle*. Los Angeles: Freedom Press, 2004.

2. Hites, R.A., et al. "Global Assessment of Organic Contaminants in Farmed Salmon." *Science* 303(5655) (2004):226–29.

3. Avril, T. "Study Finds Farm-Raised Salmon Laden with Cancer-Causing Chemicals." *Philadelphia Inquirer*, January 9, 2004.

4. Foran, J. et al. "Risk-Based Consumption Advice for Farmed Atlantic and Wild Pacific Salmon Contaminated with Dioxins and Dioxin-like Compounds." *Environmental Health Perspectives* 113(5) (2005):552–56.

5. Dr. Tom Saldeen Gordon, G. and Joiner-Bey, H. *The Omega-3 Miracle*. Los Angeles: Freedom Press, 2004.

6. "Effects of Global Warming on Trout and Salmon in U.S. Streams." Defenders of Wildlife and Natural Resources Defense Council, May 2002, 46 pp. Viewed at: http://www.defenders.org/public ations/fishreport.pdf.

7. "Spring Ritual Honors Tribe's Historic Reliance on Fish for Sustenance." *Canku Ota*, June 5, 2004, Issue 114. Viewed at: http://www.turtletrack.org/Issues04/Co06052004/CO_06052004_First_Salmo n.htm.

8. Russo, K. "The Lummi Indian Tribe and Life with the Salmon." Sustainable Communities Network Case Studies. Viewed at: http://www.sustainable.org/casestudies/washington/WA_af_lummi.html.

9. "Chum Salmon." Alaska Department of Fish & Game. Viewed at: http://www.adfg.state.ak.us/pubs/notebook/fish/chum.php.

10. Glueck, G. "The Line between Species Shifts, and a Show Explores the Move." *New York Times*, August 26, 2005:B25.

11. "Cancer Chemotherapy. A Chemical Needle in a Haystack." *Pharmaceutical Archives*. Viewed at: http://www.chemheritage.org/Educ ationalServices/pharm/chemo/readings/ages.htm.

12. Dao, T. L. "The Role of Ovarian Hormones in Initiating the Induction of Mammary Cancer in Rats by Polynuclear Hydrocarbons." *Cancer Research* 22(1962):973–981.

13. Yang, N. C. et al. "Polynuclear Aromatic Hydrocarbons, Steroids and Carcinogenesis." *Science* 134 (1961):386–87.

14. Burlington, H. and Lindeman, V. F. "Effect on Testes and Secondary Sex Characteristics of White Leghorn Cockerels." *Proceedings of the Society for Experimental Biology and Medicine* 74 (1950):48–51.

15. Fisher, A. L. et al. "Estrogenic Action of Some DDT Analogues." *Procedings of the Society for Experimental Biology and Medicine* 81 (1952):439–41.

16. Bulger, W. H. and Kupfer, D. "Estrogenic Activity of Pesticides and Other Xenobiotics on the Uterus and Male Reproductive Tract." In *Endocrine Toxicology*, edited by J. A. Thomas, K. S. Korach, and J. A. McLachlan. New York: Raven Press, 1985:1–33.

17. Scribner, J. D. and Mottet, N. K. "DT(?) Acceleration of Mammary Gland Tumors Induced in the Male Sprague-Dawley Rat by 2-acetamidophenanthrene." *Carcinogenesis* 2 (1981):1235–39.

18. Schmidt, C .W. "Poisoning Young Minds." *Environmental Health Perspectives*107(6) (1999). Viewed June 26, 2005, at: http://www.schmidtwriting.com/articles/clients/ehp/poisoning.html.

19. Fein, G. et al. "Prenatal Exposure to Polychlorinated Biphenyls: Effects on Birth Size and Gestational Age." *J Pediatr* 105(2) (1984):315–20.

20. Jacobson, J. L. and Jacobson, S. W. "Intellectual Impairment in Children Exposed to Polychlorinated Biphenyls in Utero." *New England Journal of Medicine* 335(11) (1996):783–89.

21. Fein, Greta, et al. *Intrauterine Exposure of Humans to PCBS; Newborn Effects.* Duluth, Minnesota: U.S. Environmental Protection Agency, Environmental Research Laboratory, 1984; available for $13.95 from National Technical Information Service (NTIS), Springfield, Virginia 22161; phone (703) 487-4600. Ask for publication No. PB8418-888-7.

22. Raloff, J. "Food for Thought." *Science News Online*, September 14, 1996. Viewed June 26, 2005, at: http://www.sciencenews.org/pages/sn_arch/9_14_96/food.htm.

23. Eskenazi, B. "*In Utero* Exposure to Dichlorodiphenyltrichloroethane (DDT) and Dichlorodiphenyldichloroethylene (DDE) and Neurodevelopment among Young Mexican American Children." *Pediatrics* 118(1) (July 2006):233–41.

24. Cone, M. "DDT Study Finds New Hazard to Young Children."

Los Angeles Times, July 5, 2006. Viewed at: http://www.latimes.com/news/local/la-me-ddt5jul05,1,6223584.story.

25. Daly, H. B. "The Evaluation of Behavioral Changes Produced by Consumption of Environmentally Contaminated Fish." In *The Vulnerable Brain and Environmental Risks*, edited by Robert L. Isaacson and Karl F. Jensen. New York: Plenum Press, 1992:151–71. See also Daly, H .B. "Reward Reductions Found More Aversive by Rats Fed Contaminated Salmon." *Neurotoxicology and Teratology*13 (1991):449–53.

26. Cone, M. "Sewage Altering fish, Study Reports." *Los Angeles Times*, November 14, 2005. Viewed at: http://www.latimes.com/news/local/la-me-fish14nov14,1,1354342.story.

27. Vreugdenhil, H. J. I. et al. "Effects of Perinatal Exposure to PCBs and Dioxins on Play Behavior in Dutch Children at School Age." *Environmental Health Perspectives* 110 (2002):A593–A598.

28. An analysis of the study is on the Our Stolen Future Web site; Viewed June 26, 2005, at: http://www.ourstolenfuture.org/New Science/behavior/2002/2002-09vreugdenhiletal.htm.

29. Colborn, T. Interview. July 13, 2005.

30. Cone, M. "Hermaphrodite Frogs Linked to Pesticide Use. Study Finds More Sex Organ Abnormalities in 1950s, When Chemicals Were More Widespread." *Los Angeles Times*, March 2, 2005.

31. United States Geological Survey (USGS). *Distribution of Selected Herbicides and Nitrate in the Missippie River and Its Major Tributaries, April through June 1991*. USGS Water Resources Investigations Report 91-4163, 1991, as cited in NRDC, 1993: 20.

32. Hecker, M. et al. "Effects of Atrazine on CYP19 Gene Expression and Aromatase Activity in Testes and on Plasma Sex Steroid Concentrations of Male African Clawed Frogs (*Xenopus laevis*)." *Toxicological Sciences* 86(2) (2005):273–80. Viewed at: http://toxsci.oxfordjournals.org/cgi/content/abstract/86/2/273.

33. EXTOXNET. Extension Toxicology Network Pesticide Information Profiles, June 1996. A Pesticide Information Project of Cooperative Extension Offices of Cornell University, Oregon State University, the University of Idaho, and the University of California at Davis and the Institute for Environmental Toxicology, Michigan State University. Major support and funding was provided by the USDA/Extension Service/

National Agricultural Pesticide Impact Assessment Program. EXTOXNET primary files maintained and archived at Oregon State University. Accessed May 29, 2005, at: http://extoxnet.orst.edu/pips/atrazine.htm.

34. *Sixth Annual Report on Carcinogens. Summary 1991*. Research Triangle Park, N.C.: National Institute of Environmental Health Sciences: 150.

35. Pintér, G. et al. "Long-Term Carcinogenicity Bioassay of the Herbicide Atrazine in F344 Rats."

36. International Agency for Research on Cancer, Volume 53. "Occupational Exposures in Insecticide Application, and Some Pesticides: Atrazine." (1991):441–66.

37. Donna, A. et al. "Ovarian Mesothelial Tumors and Herbicides: A Case-Control Study." *Carcinogensis* 5(7) (1984):941–42.

38. Donna, A. et al. "Triazine Herbicides and Ovarian Epithelian Neoplasms." *Scand J. Work Environ Health* 15 (1989):47–53.

39. Hopenhayn-Rich, C. et al. "Regional Assessment of Atrazine Exposure and Incidence of Breast and Ovarian Cancers in Kentucky." *Archives of Environmental Contamination and Toxicology*, 42(1) (2002):127–36.

40. Cone, M. "Polar Bears Face New Toxic Threat: Flame Retardants." *Los Angeles Times*, January 9, 2006. Viewed at: http://www.latimes.com/news/local/la-me-polarbears9jan09,0,4066814.story?coll=la-home-headlines.

41. *Revkin, A. C. "Big Arctic Perils Seen in Warming." New York Times, October 30, 2004: A1.*

42. *Revkin, A. C. "Big Arctic Perils Seen in Warming." New York Times, October 30, 2004: A1.*

43. Wary of the use of hormones and other animal drugs Department of Animal Science, Texas A&M University. *The EEC Ban against Growth Promoting Hormones: A Scientific Review*, January 1989.

44. Murphy, D. "Three Extraordinary Men Offer Prism That Refracts Industry's Future." October 18, 2002. Viewed at: http://www.foodwatch.ca/press/media/20021018.htm.

45. I made a Freedom of Information Act request to the FDA to obtain files detailing levels of hormones in beef from implanted animals. These confidential Food and Drug Administration documents reveal:

The implant REVALOR, containing both trenbolone acetate (a synthetic form of testosterone) and estradiol, is used to increase the rate of weight gain in steers in feed lots. It causes significantly greater gains in weight in the uterus and ovaries "due to the hormonal action of the test materials." It also markedly stimulated division of breast cells. Synovex-S, estradiol and progestin, is also used for growth promotion in steers. Synovex-S increases estradiol concentrations in muscle by twelvefold; in liver by sixfold; in kidney by ninefold; and in fat by twenty-three-fold. When cattle are slaughtered shortly following implantation, levels are even higher. With multiple implants, they are higher still; with intramuscular implants, yet even higher. Synovex-H, estradiol and testosterone, is used for growth promotion in cows. Estradiol concentrations after implantation were sixfold higher in muscle; fifteenfold in liver; eightfold in kidney; and more than sixfold in fat. Melengestrol acetate, a potent progestin that stimulates estrogen production, is fed to cows in feed lots. It induces rapidly invasive breast cancers in experimental animals. Marked estrogenic influences were found in cattle, including increased size of ovarian follicles. At typical levels, for 180 days, concentrations up to nearly thirty-two parts per billion were found in fat, twelve parts per billion in muscle, and fourteen parts per billion in liver. RALGRO, the fungal toxin zeranol, is converted in the body into the carcinogenic zeralenone. It induces liver and pituitary tumors in male rodents; increased uterine weight, a clear-cut estrogenic effect; and enlargement of ovarian follicles. The FDA concluded that these "significant effects [can be] attributed to its hormonal activity." Under normal use, residues as high as .13 ppb are found in muscle and .3 ppb in fat. For organ cuts, levels range up to eight parts per billion in liver and two parts per billion in kidney. These are extraordinarily high concentrations that, combined with its greater hormonal activity, present risks thousands of times greater than pseudoestrogenic pesticides and industrial chemicals. Yet, zeranol is used without any withholding time for most cattle right up until slaughter.

More than two decades ago and during a time when DES was being implanted in cattle meant for market, Roy Hertz, then director of endocrinology of the NCI and a world authority on hormonal cancer, warned of the carcinogenic risks of estrogenic feed additives, particularly for hormonally sensitive tissues such as breast tissue, because they could increase normal body hormonal levels and disturb delicately poised hormonal balances. In 1977 Dr. Hertz responded to the cattle industry's trivializing women's exposure to hormonal animal drugs:

> The average woman will have on any given day in her total plasma volume approximately 20 micrograms equivalent of estrogen activity. We know also, from the standpoint of cancer, that if we cut that level of estrogen in half, by ovariectomy, in a third of the cases we can get a regression of a preexisting breast cancer. We also know that if we add back that amount of estrogen to a woman with breast cancer who has previously been ovariectomized, we can exacerbate her disease. . . . So that gives you an order of magnitude of the kind of trace substance we're involved with. This business of thousands of tons of beef is a *reductio ad absurdum* which has no pertinence to the physiological problem before us. . . .
>
> We're talking about the addition to an important food item of a substance at a level of concentration which is of the same order of magnitude as that which has profound physiological effects in the human body normally, in the human body affected by breast cancer.

46. Doc and Connie Hatfield Associated Press. "Mad Cow Boosts Natural Beef Sales. Vegetable-Fed, No-Hormone Beef One of Fastest-Growing Sector." October 13, 2005. Viewed at: http://72.14.203.104/search?q=cache:G3JM_1lmTm8J:www.cnn.com/2005/HEALTH/diet.fitness/10/13/natural.meat.ap/+coleman+natural+beef&hl=en.

47. Murphy, D. "Three Extraordinary Men Offer Prism That Refracts Industry's Future." October 18, 2002. Viewed June 19, 2005 at: http://www.foodwatch.ca/press/media/20021018.htm.

48. Lowengart, R.A. et al. "Childhood Leukemia and Parents' Occupational and Home Exposures." *Journal of the National Cancer Institute*, 79(1 (1987)):39–46.

49. Hayes, H. M. et al. "Case-Control Study of Canine Malignant Lymphoma: Positive Association with Dog Owner's Use of 2,4-dichlorophenoxyacetic Acid Herbicides." *Journal of the National Cancer Institute*, 83(17) (1991):1226–31.

50. Maria Rodale Fraser, L. "Coffee That's Great to the Last Drop." *Organic Style* (March 2005):45–49.

SIX
Drive a Cool Car

1. "Invasion of the Green Machines." *U.S. News & World Report*, May 9, 2005:49–54.

2. "Moneyline. Wednesday Markets. Briefly." *USA Today*, August 25, 2005, 1B.

3. Durbin D.-A. "Ford Unveils Second Hybrid." *Daily News*, July 12, 2005, Business Section, 1.

4. Hoffman, B. G. "The Gods Must Love Mercury. Ford Brand Survives Another Near-Death." *Detroit News*, November 27, 2005. Viewed at: http://www.detnews.com/apps/pbcs.dll/article?AID=/20051127/AUTO 01/511270326/1148.

5. Vanderwerp, D. "Ford Escape Hybrid 4WD." *Car & Driver*. Viewed at: http://www.caranddriver.com/article.asp?section_id=3&article_id=8777.

6. Ibid.

7. "Sales Numbers and Forecasts for Hybrid Vehicles." Hybridcars.com. Viewed July1, 2005, at: http://www.hybridcars.com/sales -numbers.html.

8. Wald, M .L. "Hybrid Cars Burning Gas in the Drive for Power." *New York Times*, July 18, 2005. Viewed at: http://www.nytimes.com/ 2005/07/17/automobiles/17hybrid.html?.

9. Vanderwerp, D. "Ford Escape Hybrid 4WD." *Car and Driver*. Viewed at: http://www.caranddriver.com/article.asp?section_id=3& article_id=8777.

10. Ihlwan, M. "Hyundai Goes Hybrid." *BusinessWeek*, January 5, 2006. Viewed at: http://www.businessweek.com/autos/content/jan2006/ bw20060105_695165.htm?campaign_id=search.

11. "GM, Ford in Ethanol Deals." Bloomberg News (from the *Los Angeles Times*), February 9, 2006. Viewed at: http://www.latimes.com/ business/la-fi-ethanol9feb09,1,1294630.story.

12. "Investor Pressure Drives Ford Motor Co. to Prepare Climate Risk Report." GreenBiz.com, April 1, 2005. Viewed July 1, 2005, at: http://www.greenbiz.com/news/news_third.cfm?NewsID=27887&CFI D=833829&CFTOKEN=20221791.

13. Michael Tamor "Global Warming." Hybridcars.com. Viewed July 1, 2005, at: http://www.hybridcars.com/global-warming.html.

14. Ibid.

15. "Investor Pressure Drives Ford Motor Co. to Prepare Climate Risk Report." GreenBiz.com, April 1, 2005. Viewed July 23, 2005, at: http://www.greenbiz.com/news/news_third.cfm?NewsID=27887&CFI D=833829&CFTOKEN=20221791.

16. "Global Warming." Hybridcars.com. Viewed July 1, 2005, at: http://www.hybridcars.com/global-warming.html.

17. "Investor Pressure Drives Ford Motor Co. to Prepare Climate Risk Report." GreenBiz.com, April 1, 2005. Viewed July 23, 2005, at: http://www.greenbiz.com/news/news_third.cfm?NewsID=27887&CFI D=833829&CFTOKEN=20221791.

18. "A Responsible Energy Plan for America." Natural Resources Defense Council. Viewed at: http://www.nrdc.org/air/energy/rep/rep.pdf.

19. Newman, R. J. "Invasion of the Green Machines." *U.S. News & World Report*, May 9, 2005, 49–54.

20. Ibid.

21. "GM's Hybrid Propulsion System for Transit Buses." Viewed at: http://www.gm.com/company/gmability/adv_tech/300_hybrids/index_bus.html.

22. "GM's Hybrid Propulsion System for Transit Buses." Viewed at: http://www.gm.com/company/gmability/adv_tech/300_hybrids/index_bus.html.

23. *Dangerous Addiction: Ending America's Oil Dependence*, January 2002. Natural Resources Defense Council and the Union of Concerned Scientists. Viewed at: http://www.nrdc.org/air/transportation oilinx.asp.

24. "Reducing U.S. Oil Dependence. A Real Energy Security Policy." Natural Resources Defense Council. Viewed at: http://www.nrdc.org/air/energy/fensec.asp.

25. Tom LaSorda "Chrysler Group CEO Reiterates Focus on Diesel and Biofuels." Green Car Congress, January 23, 2006. Viewed at: http://www.greencarcongress.com/2006/01/chrysler_group_.html#more.

26. Maynard, M. "Ford Plans Shift in Focus Away from Hybrids." *New York Times*, June 30, 2005, C1–C2.

27. Juhae Lee, M. "Green Cars." *Green Guide* (July/August 2005):109.

28. Carey, J. "Giving Hybrids a Real Jolt. A Plug-in Gas-Electric Vehicle May Be Key in Saving Fuel and Cutting Pollution." *Business Week*, April 11, 2005. Viewed at: http://www.businessweek.com/maga zine/content/05_15/b3928103.htm.

29. Ibid.

30. Caruso, D. B. "NY Hails Hybrid Cabs." Associated Press. Viewed July 31, 2005, at: http://www.ecomall.com/greenshopping/hybridcabs.htm.

31. "TLC Approves Hybrid-Electric Models for Hack-Up as Medallion Taxicabs." Viewed at: http://www.nyc.gov/html/tlc/html/home/home.shtml.

EIGHT
Stop Being Toxic

1. "Sustainable Hotel Siting, Design, and Construction." The International Tourism Partnership. Viewed at: http://www.international-tourismpartnership.org/sustainable.htm.

2. "Chemical Profile: Alachlor." Scorecard—The Pollution Information Site. Viewed at: http://www.scorecard.org/chemical-profiles/summary.tcl?edf_substance_id=15972-60-8.

3. "Pesticide Contamination of Nebraska Tap Water, 1996–1997." *Tough to Swallow: How Pesticide Companies Profit from Poisoning America's Tap Water*. Environmental Working Group, Washington, D.C., August 12, 1997. Viewed at: http://www.ewg.org/reports/toughtoswallow/NE.html.

4. "Acetochlor—Identification, Toxicity, Use, Water Pollution Potential, Ecological Toxicity and Regulatory Information." PAN Pesticides Database—Chemicals. Pesticide Action Network North America. Viewed at: http://www.pesticideinfo.org/Detail_Chemical.jsp?Rec_Id=PC34114.

5. "Water Quality Report—2004." Metropolitan Utilities District. Viewed at: http://www.mudomaha.com/water/04report.html.

6. "Special Report. America's Largest Private Companies . . . #1 Cargill." *Forbes*, November 11, 2005. Reifman, S. and Wong, S. N.,eds. Viewed at: http://www.forbes.com/lists/2005/21/5ZUZ.html.

7. "About Us." Viewed at: http://www.cargill.com/about/index.htm.

8. "Lewis and Clark Campsites: August 3 and 4, 1804." Nebraska

State Historical Society. Viewed August 31, 2005, at: http://www.nebraskahistory.org/publish/markers/texts/lewis_and_clark_a3-4.htm.

9. Sheftel, V. O. "Harmful Substances in Plastics." Viewed at: http://www.mindfully.org/Plastic/Harmful-Substances-Plastics-Sheftel.htm.

10. "Green Success. Presidential Awards Honor Chemists for Developing Cleaner and Economically Viable Technologies." *Science & Technology* 83(26) (June 27, 2005):40–43.

11. genius of green chemistry Ibid.

12. "What Is Green Chemistry?" U.S. Environmental Protection Agency. Viewed July 31, 2005, at: http://www.epa.gov/greenchemistry/whats_gc.htmlIewed.

13. "Metathesis." Viewed at: http://www.wordreference.com/definition/metathesis.

14. On October 5, 2005, green chemists Associated Press. "Trio Wins Nobel Prize for 'Green Chemistry.' Frenchman, 2 Americans Develop Environmentally Friendly Methods." MSNBC. Updated: 12:08 P.M. ET October 5, 2005. Viewed at: http://msnbc.msn.com/id/9595718/.

15. "Metathesis—A Change-Your-Partners Dance." The Royal Swedish Academy of Sciences, October 5, 2005. Viewed at: http://nobelprize.org/chemistry/laureates/2005/press.html.

16. "Cargill to Build Biodiesel Plant at Its Iowa Falls Facility." Cargill.com. New Release, June 8, 2005. Viewed July 9, 2005 at: http://www.cargill.com/news/news_releases/050608_biodiesel.htm#TopOfPage.

17. "Case Study: Telluride Bluegrass Festival Debuts Compostable Serviceware—NatureWorks PLA." Viewed at: http://www.natureworksllc.com/corporate/news_retail_casestudy.asp?id=4.

18. "Case Study: Compostable Cups Help Brewery Stand Out from Crowd." Viewed at: http://www.natureworksllc.com/corporate/news_retail_casestudy.asp?id=6.

19. Ingeo Web site Viewed at: http://www.ingeofibers.com/ingeo/home.asp.

20. "PANNA Corporate Profile: Dow Chemical Company." Pesticide Action Network North America, April 2004. Viewed at: http://www.panna.org/campaigns/caia/corpProfilesDow.dv.html.

21. Brubaker, H. "Wal-Mart Goes More Eco-Friendly." *Philadelphia*

Inquirer, October 20, 2005. Viewed at: http://www.philly.com/mld/inquirer/business/12948647.htm.

22. Simon, S. "To Replace Oil, U.S. Experts See Amber Waves of Plastic. American Crops Could Be Used in Place of Many Products' Petroleum Base, Some Scientists Say." *Los Angeles Times*, June 26, 2005. Viewed July 31, 2005 at: http://www.latimes.com/news/printedition/lana-grain26jun26,1,6073251.story.

23. Herrick, T. "One Word of Advice: Now It's Corn. Plastics Manufactured from the Plant Grow More Appealing Amid Soaring Oil Prices." *Wall Street Journal*, October 12, 2004, B1.

24. Lingle, R. "Biota's High-Water Mark in Sustainable Packaging." *Packaging World*, January 2005, 62.

25. Lingle, R. "Biota's High-Water Mark in Sustainable Packaging." *Packaging World*, January 2005. Viewed at: http://www.packworld.com/cds_search.html?rec_id=18654.

26. Herrick, T. "One Word of Advice: Now It's Corn. Plastics Manufactured from the Plant Grow More Appealing Amid Soaring Oil Prices." *Wall Street Journal*, October 12, 2004, B1.

27. "Natural Living Ingeo Fiber Bed." Viewed at: http://www.lnt.com/product/index.jsp?productId=1763833. "Novafoam Ultimate Mattress Topper." Viewed at: http://www.lnt.com/searchHandler/index.jsp?searchId=5425706202&keywords=mattress+topper.

28. Viewed at: http://www.target.com/gp/detail.html/sr=2-1/qid=1133124527/ref=sr_2_1/601-0828544-1896944?%5Fencoding=UTF8&asin=B00028MSGE. Viewed at: http://www.target.com/gp/detail.html/ref=br_1_2/601-0828544-1896944?%5Fencoding=UTF8&frombrowse=1&asin=B00006AALJ.

29. Brubaker, H. "Wal-Mart Goes More Eco-Friendly." *Philadelphia Inquirer*, October 20, 2005. Viewed at: http://www.philly.com/mld/inquirer/business/12948647.htm.

30. A Megajourle (Mg) is a unit of energy equal to one million joules or 0.278 kWh.

31. MacDonald, E. "Plastic Fantastic. Kaathleen Bader Wants to Save the World from Polluting Oil Plastics with Her Healthy Corn Polymers." *Forbes*, March 28, 2005:, 108–11.

32. "Plastic Bottles Equivalents, Ingredients Only." Cited in:

MacDonald. E. "Plastic Fantastic. Kaathleen Bader Wants to Save the World from Polluting Oil Plastics with Her Healthy Corn Polymers." *Forbes*, March 28, 2005, 108–11.

33. Lovins, A. B. "More Profit with Less Carbon." *Scientific American* (September 2005):74–83.

34. Ibid.

35. "Oildale, California." Viewed at: http://www.city-data.com/city/Oildale-California.html.

36. "NPL Site Narrative for Chevron Chemical Co. (Ortho Division). Chevron Chemical Co. (Ortho Division), Orlando, Florida. Federal Register Notice, *May 31, 1994*." U.S. Environmental Protection Agency. Viewed at: http://www.epa.gov/cgi-bin/epaprintonly.cgi.

37. Georgi, S. "SolarMine—An Energy Saving Project U.S. Oil." *Batteries Digest*, May 2004: 98-1-98-11.

38. Campbell Daiglish and Catherine Oberg "Solar Success Stories. Searching for the Right Solar Energy System." Uni-Solar. Viewed at: http://www.uni-solar.com/interior.asp?id=73.

39. "Solar Showcase: Coca-Cola Bottling's Green Bulding." Viewed at: http://www.uni-solar.com/uploadedFiles/0.4.1_los_angeles_ca.pdf.

40. Real Goods Schaeffer, J. Personal e-mail, December 7, 2005.

41. Lifsher, M. "Governor's Solar Plan Is Generating Opposition." *Los Angeles Times*, June 27, 2005, C1.

42. "Albany County Invests in Alternative Energy Source for Hockey Facility." AlbanyCounty.com. Viewed September 5, 2005, at: http://www.albanycounty.com/departments/executive/news.asp?id=765.

43. Dixon, C. "Shortages Stifle a Boom Time for the Solar Industry." *New York Times*, August 5, 2005. Viewed at: http://www.nytimes.com/2005/08/05/national/05solar.html?.

44. "German Solar Market and Technology." German Solar Industry Association. Visited August 30, 2005, at: http://www.bsi-solar.de/english/solar_market/index.asp.

45. "Judge Announces Settlement to End PG&E Bankruptcy. California Public Utilities Commission Staff, PG&E Reach Agreement." California Public Utilities Commission, June 19, 2003. Viewed at: http://www.cpuc.ca.gov/PUBLISHED/NEWS_RELEASE/27310.htm.

46. Murtagh, H. "Grease to Generate Power." *Daily Journal*, January

22, 2005. Viewed at: http://www.smdailyjournal.com/article_preview.php?id=48915&eddate=09/22/2005.

47. "From Grills to the Grid: City of Millbrae and Chevron Energy Solutions Create a Novel Way to Generate Electricity." Chevron Energy Solutions, Newsroom. Viewed at: http://www.chevronenergy.com/news_room/default.asp?pr=pr_20050921.asp.

48. See the Humboldt County Web site, accessed at <http://www.co.humboldt.ca.us/portal/about.asp.>

49. "Administration Slashes Funding for Energy Efficiency Climate Protection, While Censoring Environment Report." American Council for an Energy-Efficient Economy, June 23 2003. Viewed at: http://www.aceee.org/press/0306climate.htm.

50. "What Is Energy Star?" Viewed at: http://www.energystar.gov/index.cfm?c=about.ab_index.

51. Suozzzo, M. "Energy-Efficient Office Equipment." CoopAmerica. Viewed September 2, 2005, at: http://64.233.167.104/search?q=cache:6w2RZwgQsnAJ:www.coopamerica.org/business/Beefficient.HTM+A+typical+small+business,+with+10+computers,+10+monitors,+one+printer,+one+fax+machine,+and+one+medium-volume+copier,+can+use+power-managed+equipment+and+save+more+than+3,500+kilowatt-hours+&hl=en.

52. "Environment. Eco-Products. Daily Life." Mitsubishi Electric. Viewed at: http://global.mitsubishielectric.com/company/environ/pepdl_b.html.

53. "An Overview of the EU Eco-label Scheme." Viewed October 15, 2005, at http://europa.eu.int/comm/environment/ecolabel/index_en.htm.

54. Taking Energy Star even further is the EU's Community Eco-label with its green flower motif. When shopping in the EU, look for products bearing this label. These products must be recycled as far as possible, and such products neither deplete the ozone layer nor add to the greenhouse effect. As with Energy Star, appliances such as refrigerators and freezers must be energy efficient.

55. McRandle, P. W. "Cutting Costs in a Fuel-Scarce World." *The Green Guide* (September–October 2005). Viewed October 15, 2005, at: http://www.thegreenguide.com/doc.mhtml?i=110&s=fuel.

56. "Environmental Release Report. Maytag Appliances. Amana

Refrigeration Products." Scorecard: The Pollution Information Site. Viewed at: http://www.scorecard.org/env-releases/facility.tcl?tri_id= 52204MNRFRFIRST#major_chemical_releases.

57. Daggett, J. "Query from Freedom Press." E-mail. December 8, 2005.

58. "Environmental Release Report. Whirlpool Corp." Scorecard: The Pollution Information Site. Viewed October 27, 2005, at: http://www.scorecard.org/env-releases/facility.tcl?tri_id=72903WHRLP6400J#major_chemical_releases.

59. E-mail response, December 3, 2005, from Jody Lau, Manager, Global Communications, Whirlpool, Administrative Center, Benton Harbor, Michigan 49022.

60. "Environmental Release Report. Robert Bosch Corp." Scorecard: The Pollution Information Site. Viewed October 27, 2005, at: http://www.scorecard.org/env-releases/facility.tcl?tri_id=29621RBRTBHWY81#major_chemical_releases>.

61. Viewed at: http://www.scorecard.org/env-releases/cap/facility.tcl?facility_id=17031-0191#air_rankings>.

62. "Environmental Release Report. Robert Bosch Corp." Scorecard: The Pollution Information Site. Viewed October 27, 2005, at: http://www.scorecard.org/env-releases/search.tcl?facility=Robert+bosch

63. Ibid

64. Ibid.

65. Ibid.

66. Ibid.

67. "Energy Star." Miele. Viewed at: http://www.miele.com/usa/energy/energy-star.asp?bhcp=1.

68. "Environmental Release Report. Samsung Austin Semicon-ductor." Scorecard: The Pollution Information Site. Viewed at: http://www.scorecard.org/env-releases/facility.tcl?tri_id=78754SMSNG12100#major_chemical_releases.

69. "The Greening of Products. Development of Alternatives to Hazardous Substances." Samsung. Viewed at: http://www.samsung.com/AboutSAMSUNG/ELECTRONICSGLOBAL/SocialCommitment/Greport/02_management/echo_02_04.htm.

70. "Environmental Release Report. Hewlett-Packard." Scorecard: The

Pollution Information Site. Viewed at: http://www.scorecard.org/env-releases/facility.tcl?tri_id=83714HWLTT11311#major_chemical_releases.

71. "Climate. Things You Can Do for Free." Rocky Mountain Institute. Viewed October 15, 2005, at: http://www.rmi.org/sitepages/pid346.php.

NINE
Put Your Money Where Your Mouth Is

1. "Folklore Tribute to Disney's Paul Bunyan." Viewed October 22, 2005, at: http://www.angelfire.com/music3/EB/Logo.html.

2. "Estimated Canadian Population." Statistics Canada. Viewed at: http://www.statcan.ca/english/edu/clock/population.htm.

3. "Regenerative Thermal Oxidizer." Anguil Environmental Systems. Viewed at: http://www.anguil.com/prregthe.php.

4. "Environmental Release Report: Quebecor World Buffalo, Inc." Scorecard.org. Viewed at: http://www.scorecard.org/env-releases/facility.tcl?tri_id=14043RCTGRTCIND#major_chemical_releases.

5. "Air Pollution Control Board Enforcment Action Order by Consent Issued to Quebecor World San Jose, Inc. Permit No. 50880." Quebecor World San Jose, Inc. Permit No. 50880. Virginia Department of Environmental Quality, 2002 (not further dated). Viewed at: http://www.deq.virginia.gov/enforcement/finalorders/quebecor.pdf.

6. "The Nature of Things." The Museum of Broadcast Communications, viewed October 22, 2005, at: http://www.museum.tv/archives/etv/N/htmlN/natureofthi/natureofthi.htm.

7. "Nature of Things." Viewed at: http://www.tv.com/nature-of-things/show/31359/summary.html.

8. "David Suzuki." *Wikipedia*. Viewed October 22, 2005, at: http://en.wikipedia.org/wiki/David_Suzuki.

9. Federico, M. J. and Liu, A. H. *Pediatric Clinics of North America* 50(3) (2003):655–75, vii.

10. McKitrick, R. "Smog Deaths: 0. Air Pollution Poses a Serious Health Risk to Toronto Residents, Right? Wrong, Said a New Study That Should Change the Way to Look at the Issue." *Financial Post*,

February 5, 2004. Viewed at: http://www.uoguelph.ca/~rmckitri/research/smogdeaths.pdf.

11. Cotter, J. "Canada Needs Plan to Secure Natural Gas for Industry, Consumers: Report." www.moneycanoe.ca., October 5, 2005;18:50:00. Viewed at: http://72.14.203.104/search?q=cache:ZTn6t EorU34J:money.canoe.ca/News/Other/2005/10/05/1249948-cp.html+ canada+running+out+of+natural+gas&hl=en.

12. Martin, P. "Complete Text of the Speech from the Throne (October 5, 2004)." Office of the Prime Minister. Viewed October 22, 2005, at: http://pm.gc.ca/eng/sft-ddt.asp.

13. Marks, M. "Debunking the False Dichotomy." Speech to the Dallas Sierra Club, October 8, 2003, by Martha Marks, President of REP America. Viewed at: http://www.rep.org/opinions/speeches/29.html.

14. "Study Disproves 'Jobs vs. Environment' Myth. States Ranked on Economic & Environmental Health." Institute for Southern Studies, November 16, 2000. Viewed Environmental Justice Resource Center, August 27, 2005, at: http://www.ejrc.cau.edu/nov162000report.htm.

15. This is all entirely detailed in: Diamond, J. *Collapse*. New York: Viking, 2004:442.

16. "Are You Being Served?" *The Economist*, April 23, 2005, 76–78.

17. Daly, H. "Economics in a Full World." *Scientific American* (September 2005). Viewed at: http://www.sciam.com/article.cfm?chanID= sa006&colID=1&articleID=000455EA-FE0B-1304-B72683414B7F0000.

18. "The Forestry Insurance Product." ForestRe. Viewed at: http://www.forestre.com/product.htm.

19. "Are You Being Served?" the *Economist*, April 23, 2005, 76–78.

20. Brigid Barnett cited in: Tavia, G. "Wild Weather Brings Change of Attitude for Insurers. As the Hurricane Season in the U.S. Has Shown, the Threat Posed by Climate Change Cannot Be Dismissed, Officials Say." the *Globe and Mail*, October 11, 2005: B19. Viewed at: http://www.theglobeandmail.com/servlet/ArticleNews/TPStory/LAC/2 0051011/RINSURER11/TPBusiness/MoneyMarkets.

21. Lynas, M. *High Tide*. New York: Picador, 2003; see, for example, the chapter, "Feeling the Heat."

22. Penson, S. "ANALYSIS—Europe Greenhouse Gas Trade Hots Up as Prices Soar." Reuters, July 13, 2005.

23. Balfour, F., Cohn, L., and Lakshman, N. "In Asia, a Hot Market for Carbon. The Market for Carbon Credits Is Cutting Pollution in Developing Countries." *BusinessWeek*, December 12, 2005. Viewed at: http://www.businessweek.com/magazine/content/05_50/b3963409.htm.

24. Scott, L. "Our CEO on the Environment." Walmartstores.com. Viewed at: http://walmartstores.com/GlobalWMStoresWeb/navigate.do?catg=442.

25. "Green Gazelles Project Report." A Project of the Center for Small Business and the Environment, May 2004. Viewed September 15, 2005, at: http://www.greengazelles.org/GREEN_GAZELLES_REPORT_May_20 04.doc.

26. "Many Companies Are Dramatically Reducing . . ." David Suzuki Foundation. "Climate Change. Solutions. Green Leaders." Viewed October 22, 2005, at: http://www.davidsuzuki.org/Climate_Change/Solutions/Green_Leaders.asp.

27. Chad Holliday TBA

28. "World Wildlife Fund Recognizes IBM for Its Leadership on Climate Change." IBM, October 4, 2005. Viewed at: http://www.ibm.com/ibm/environment/news/wwf_climatesavers_2005.shtml.

29. "Solutions: Green Leaders." David Suzuki Foundation. Viewed October 24, 2005, at: http://www.davidsuzuki.org/Climate_Change/Solutions/Green_Leaders.asp.

30. "Insight from Vice President Footwear Design John Hoke the Conversation, Nike Considered." Viewed at: http://www.nike.com/nikebiz/nikeconsidered/conversation.jhtml.

31. "GE Misdeeds." Viewed at: http://www.cleanupge.org/gemisdeeds.html.

32. Bradley, R. "Green Things to Life." *Plenty* (October/November 2005):54–59.

33. Bylinsky, G. "How GE Captures New Energy Markets. Hydrogen, Biofuels, Solar, Nukes—GE Has Staked Big R&D Bets on Every Energy Future." *Forbes*, December 12, 2005, T178[B]-T178[H].

34. "Is There a Green Movement in the Air? More Companies Are Adopting Eco-friendly Strategies to Help a Planet under Siege." Special Advertising Section. *Forbes*, December 12, 2005, S1–S10.

35. "Environment, Technology & The Economy." Business Roundtable.

Viewed at: http://www.businessroundtable.org/TaskForces/TaskForce/document.aspx?qs=6605BF159FF49514481138A77BE7A7A19BB6487BA6F36.

36. "Is There a Green Movement in the Air? More Companies Are Adopting Eco-friendly Strategies to Help a Planet under Siege." Special Advertising Section. *Forbes*, December 12, 2005, S1–S10.

37. "Fighting Global Warming, One Poorly Illuminated Candy Bar at a Time." Green Life. Viewed at: http://www.thegreenlife.org/greenwasherseptember2004.html.

38. Dr. Karl-Henrik Robèrt "History." The Natural Step. Viewed at: http://www.naturalstep.org/about/history.php.

39. Spence, M. "Building Sustainable Cities. Scandinavia's 'Eco-Municipalities' Show the Way." *E Magazine* (September–October 2005):20–23.

40. Hollender, J. and Fenichell, S. *What Matters Most*. New York, NY: Basic Books, 2004:100–101.

41. Montague, P. "#771—Subsidizing the Destruction of Commons." *Rachels Environment & Health News*, June 12, 2003, page 38.

42. Milne, J. E. "Green Taxes: How Government Can Use Taxes for Environmental Protection." Vermont Businesses for Social Responsibility. Viewed September 10, 2005, at: http://www.vbsr.org/greentax.htm

43. "Businesses Soaking Up Sun's Power." October 23, 2003. *Grist-Magazine.com*.

44. "Is There a Green Movement in the Air? More Companies Are Adopting Eco-friendly Strategies to Help a Planet under Siege." Special Advertising Section. *Forbes*, December 12, 2005, S1–S10.

45. Polyak, I. "Do Blue Chips Belong in a Social Purist's Portfolio?" *New York Times*, May 1, 2005, 8.

46. *GreenMoney Journal GreenMoney Journal* 14(3) (spring 2006):58. Viewed at: http://www.greenmoneyjournal.com/article.mpl?newsletterid=23&articleid=241.

47. Warner, M. "What Is Organic? Powerful Players Want a Say." *New York Times*, November 1, 2005. Viewed at: http://www.nytimes.com/2005/11/01/business/01organic.html?ex=1131685200&en=ec81ecc28b01b0ec&ei=5070.

48. Aurura's farm Ibid.

49. "USDA Dismisses Complaint against Aurora Organic Dairy. Government Agency Emphasizes Official Rule Making Is Method to Resolve Differences." Aurora Organic Dairy. Viewed at: http://www.auroraorganic.com/aodweb/site/news/press_4.pdf.

50. Steinman, D. and Epstein, S. *The Safe Shopper's Bible*. Garden City, N.Y.: John Wiley & Sons, 1995.

51. Rayne Oakes, S. "How Fashion Got Its Soul Back. The Rise of Eco-fashion." *Yogi Times*, Los Angeles (September 2005):38–43.

TEN
Think Seven Generations Ahead

1. Tang Soo Do. Our art is a variation of tang soo do (art of the knife hand) known as Tony Do Khan Tang Soo Do, which Grand Master Tony Montgomery created to modernize this ancient offshoot of Chinese kung fu (flowing hands). In our variation, we also emphasize boxing skills, grappling, and judo, thanks to Montgomery's experience as a top professional boxer and his top student sensei Benny Castaneda's grappling skills.

2. "Governor Pataki Announces Agreement to Protect More than 104,000 Acres of Land in Adirondack Forest." New York State Department of Environmental Conservation. Environment DEC Newsletter, January 2005. Viewed August 6, 2005, at: http://www.dec.state.ny.us/Web site/environmentdec/2005a/landagreement010405.html.

3. "Wildlife of the Adirondack Park." New York State Adirondack Park Agency. Viewed at: http://www.apa.state.ny.us/About_Park/wildlife.htm.

4. "Wildlife of the Adirondack Park." New York State Adirondack Park Agency. Viewed at: http://www.apa.state.ny.us/About_Park/wildlife.htm.

5. Aprill, D. "Rare Birds. Are Spruce Grouse and Other Adirondack Boreal Species Losing Ground?" *Adirondack Life Annual Guide 2004*. See www.adirondacklife.com.

6. Myers, S. L. et al. "The Big Melt. Old Ways of Life Are Fading as the Arctic Thaws." *New York Times*, October 20, 2005. Viewed October 20, 2005, at: http://www.nytimes.com/2005/10/20/science/earth/20arctic.ready.html.

7. The Intergovernmental Panel on Climate Change Intergovernmental

Panel on Climate Change. *IPCC Second Assessment—Climate Change 1995*. World Meteorological Association and the United Nations Environment Program, 1995.

8. Pachauri, R. K. Address at 11th Conference of the Parties to the United Nations Framework Convention on Climate Change and 1st Conference of the Parties serving as Meeting of the Parties to the Kyoto Protocol, Montreal, Canada, December 7, 2005. Viewed at: http://www.ipcc.ch/press/sp-07122005.htm.

9. I was thinking particularly of English Retreads, for example, the company that rescues fossil fuel–manufactured truck and tractor rubber inner tubes from landfills and gives them life beyond sixty thousand miles, hand crafting the rubber into absolutely stylish and earth-friendly handbags, totes, purses, book bags, and backpacks. How carbon-neutral is that? Visit www.englishretreads.com.

Green 100

1. "About Us." Sun & Earth. Viewed at: http://www.sunandearth.com/aboutus.html.

2. "Micro Hybrid with Start/Stop Function Ready for Production in 2006." Bosch.com, Environment. Current News and Further Issues. Press Release, December 7, 2005. Bosch Web site. Viewed at: http://www.bosch-umwelt.de/up/en/html/index_449.htm.

3. "Environmental Objectives for 2004 Achieved." Bosch.com, Environment. Current News and Further Issues. Press Release, September 22, 2005. Viewed at: http://www.bosch-umwelt.de/up/en/html/index_402.htm.

4. "Hazardous Substances Management." LGE Environment. Viewed at: http://www.lge.com/about/environment/html/Hazardous_Substances_Management.jsp/.

5. "Recycling, Collection and Processing of Reusable Materials." Mitsubishi. Viewed at: http://global.mitsubishielectric.com/company/environ/index.html.

6. "Eco-Products. Daily Life." Mitsubishi Electric. Viewed at: http://global.mitsubishielectric.com/company/environ/index.html.

7. "The Greening of Processes. Global Warming Prevention." Samsung. Viewed at: http://www.samsung.com/AboutSAMSUNG/ELECTRONICS GLOBAL/SocialCommitment/Greport/02_management/process_01.htm.

8. "Refrigerators and Freezers." Sun Frost. Viewed at: http://www.sunfrost.com/refrigerators_main.html.

9. Brooks, N. "Freeze." *The Ethical Consumer* (February/March 2000). Viewed at: http://www.ethicalconsumer.org/magazine/buyers/fridges/fridges.htm.

10. "Survey Ranks 20 U.S. Companies in the World's Top 100; Intel Among World's Best in Sustainability." Intel. Viewed at: http://www.intel.com/intel/other/ehs/highlights/sustainability.htm.

11. "Intel, Best Buy Help New York City Run Citywide Electronics Recycling Drive." Viewed at: http://www.intel.com/intel/finance/corp_social_resp.htm#greener.

12. "The Holland Inc. Standardizes on 100 Percent Wind Power." Burgerville.com. Viewed at: http://www.burgerville.com/bv.html.

13. "Green Business Practices." Clif Bar viewed at: http://www.clifbar.com/ourstory/document.cfm?location=environment&web subsection=recycled.

14. "Our brands." Viewed at: http://www.generalmills.com/corporate/brands/view_all_brands.aspx.

15. "Welcome to Hain-Celestial.com!" Viewed at: http://www.hain-celestial.com/.

16. "Horizon Organic Joins with Senator Clinton to Announce Company's New Statewide Initiative to Help More New York Farmers Transition to Organic," January 27, 2006. Viewed at: http://www.horizonorganic.com/aboutus/press/2006_1_27.html.

17. "Environmental Activities from Bean to Cup." Viewed at: http://www.starbucks.com/aboutus/beantocup.asp.

18. "Recycling." Viewed at: http://www.starbucks.com/aboutus/recycling.asp.

19. "Stonyfield Farm & Groupe Danone Partnership Summary." Viewed at: http://www.stonyfield.com/AboutUs/StonyfieldDanone.cfm.

20. Viewed at: http://www.gaiam.com/retail/gai_shophome.asp.

21. Viewed at: http://www.flowersforgood.com/i_175/FFG-About Us.html.

22. "Message from Our CEO." Viewed at: http://www.timberland.com/timberlandserve/content.jsp?pageName=timberlandserve_inform.

23. "Our Commitment to the Environment." Timeberland. Viewed

at: http://www.timberland.com/timberlandserve/content.jsp?pageName=
timberlandserve_inform_environmental.

24. Viewed at: http://www.lindaloudermilk.com/home.html.

25. Viewed at: http://www.dexia.com/e/discover/profile.php.

26. Viewed at: http://www.dexia.com/e/discover/sustainable_
strategy.php.

27. "Dexia Sustainable Development Report 2004." Viewed at:
http://www.dexia.com/e/discover/sustainable_strategy.php.

28. "Maroleum." Viewed at: http://www.forbo-flooring.com/framework/
DesktopDefault.aspx?menu_id=29&old_menu_id=29&ssm=1.

29. "Taking Care of the Environment . . ." The Marmoleum Store.
Viewed at: http://www.themarmoleumstore.com/framework/Desktop
Default.aspx?menu_id=269.

30. Viewed at: http://www.coopamerica.org/greenbusiness/sealof
approval.cfm.

31. Viewed at: http://www.coopamerica.org/takeaction/exxon/.

32. Viewed at: http://www.coopamerica.org/takeaction/ecomags/.

33. Viewed at: http://www.naturlawn.com/about_organic_lawn_
care.html.

34. Viewed at: http://www.naturlawn.com/pressreleases/releases/
ipr01.05.htm.

35. "What We Believe about Climate Change." Viewed at: http://www.
alcoa.com/global/en/environment/climate_change/climate_overview.asp.

36. Viewed at: http://www.domini.com/Social-Screening/index.htm.

37. "Domini Standards—Why We Buy." Viewed at: http://
www.domini.com/Social-Screening/index.htm.

38. Viewed at: http://www.greencentury.com/greeninvesting/.

39. Viewed at: http://www.greencentury.com/about/.

40. Viewed at: http://www.newchapter.info/media/press_releases/
2005_05_05.html.

41. Viewed at: http://www.bp.com/sectiongenericarticle.do?category
Id=9002320&contentId=3072059.

42. Viewed at: http://www.bp.com/sectiongenericarticle.do?category
Id=9002323&contentId=3072081.

43. Viewed at: http://www.chevron.com/social_responsibility/
environment//.

44. Viewed at: http://www.chevron.com/social_responsibility/energy_conservation/.

45. Viewed at: http://www.uni-solar.com/interior.asp?id=33.

46. Viewed at: http://www.shell.com/home/Framework?siteId=investoren&FC2=/investor-en/html/iwgen/news_and_library/press_releases/2006/zzz_lhn.html&FC3=/investoren/html/iwgen/news_and_library/press_releases/2006/ren_announcement_02022006.html.

47. Viewed at: http://www.greenatworkmag.com/magazine/newslines/04winter.html#a09.

48. Put a biodiesel blend Viewed at: http://www.wnbiodiesel.com/.

49. The idea is to do something useful. Viewed at: http://www.wnbiodiesel.com/company.html.

50. Viewed at: http://sites.target.com/site/en/corporate/page.jsp?contentId=PRD03-001086.

51. Viewed at: http://sites.target.com/site/en/corporate/page.jsp?contentId=PRD03-001095.

52. Viewed at: http://walmartstores.com/GlobalWMStoresWeb/navigate.do?catg=352.

53. Viewed at: http://www.walmartfacts.com/keytopics/environment.aspx#a1408

54. Viewed at: http://www.walmartfacts.com/newsdesk/article.aspx?id=1485#more.

55. Viewed at: http://walmartstores.com/GlobalWMStoresWeb/navigate.do?catg=443.

56. Viewed at: http://www.greenerprinter.com/grp/jsp/about.jsp.

57. The world's largest privately held "Commercial Printer Joins EPA's Smartway Transport Program." Greenbiz.com, February 2, 2006. Viewed at: http://www.greenbiz.com/news/news_third.cfm?NewsID=30289.

58. Viewed at: http://www.rrdonnelly.com/wwwRRD/AboutUs/EHS/EnvironmentalAccomplishments.asp.

59. Viewed at: http://www.rrdonnelly.com/wwwRRD/AboutUs/EHS/EnvironmentalManagementSystems.asp.

60. "Toyota Environnmental Updates." December 2005, 35th issue. Viewed at: http://www.toyota.com/about/environment/news/index.html.

Acknowledgments

THERE ARE SO many people I have to thank for making this story possible that I could not possibly list them all without leaving off somebody. Everybody has been so extremely kind and helpful that the smartest thing to do is to list names in alphabetical order.

I wish to thank: David and Barbara Barlean and family; Jade Beutler; Jodey Brown; Ross Browne; Carey Buckles; Gerard "Ged" Caddick; Sidney J. Caspersen; Mark Chimsky; William Clark; Theo Colborn; David Cue; James Davis; Devra Lee Davis; Teresa DeAnda; Anita Diggs; Samuel S. Epstein; Thomas Frantz; Michael Freund; Jim Fulton; Cassandra Glickman; Al Gore; Gene Haplea; Thomas Greither; Brian Hall; Aubrey Hampton; Paul Hawken; Kim Henderson; Michael Hollander; Jeffrey Hollender; Joanna Hurley; Susan Hussey-Hampton; Doug Kaufmann; Jeanne Kirkaldy; Terry Lemerond; Herb Lewis; Donald Malins; Marshall Miller; Tom Newmark; Hermann Ng; John Oakes; Brant Olson; John Paige; Scot Quaranda; Diane Sable; Paul Schulick; Juan Manuel Rodriguez; Mary Rosenberg; John Schaeffer; Stephen G. Serrao; Sandra Steingraber; David Suzuki; Jim Turner; Paul West; and Mary Ann Wright; and, of course, my family—thank you for putting up with me.

Index